A Guide to Web Development Using Macromedia® Dreamweaver® MX

with Fireworks® MX and Flash™ MX

Elaine Malfas
Beth Brown
Jan Marrelli

Copyright 2003
by

First Edition

ISBN 1-58003-029-7 (softcover)
ISBN 1-58003-030-0 (hardcover)

All rights reserved. No part of this work covered by the copyright may be reproduced or used in any form or by any means — graphic, electronic, or mechanical, including photocopying, recording, taping, or information storage and retrieval systems — without the written permission of the publisher, with the exception of programs, which may be entered, stored, and executed in a computer system, but not reprinted for publication or resold in any other form.

Printed in the United States of America

All orders including educational, Canadian, foreign, FPO, and APO may be placed by contacting:

> Lawrenceville Press, Inc.
> P.O. Box 704
> Pennington, NJ 08534-0704
> (609) 737-1148
> (609) 737-8564 fax

This text is available in softcover and hardcover editions.

20 19 18 17 16 15 14 13 12 11 10 9 8 7 6 5 4 3 2 1

The text is written and published by Lawrenceville Press, Inc. and is in no way connected with Macromedia® Inc. or the Microsoft® Corporation.

Macromedia®, Macromedia® Dreamweaver®, Macromedia® Fireworks®, and Macromedia® Flash™ are either registered trademarks or trademarks of Macromedia Inc. in the United States and/or other countries. Screen Shots reprinted with permission from Macromedia® Inc.

Microsoft®, Microsoft® Internet Explorer, Microsoft® Notepad and Microsoft® Outlook Express are either registered trademarks or trademarks of the Microsoft Corporation in the United States and/or other countries. Screen Shots and Icons reprinted with permission from Microsoft® Corporation.

ExamView is a registered trademark of FSCreations, Inc.

Names of all other products mentioned herein are used for identification purposes only and may be trademarks of their respective owners.

Preface

We believe the best way to introduce students to Web development is with an applications course that meets two primary expectations. First, students should be taught general design concepts and the process of developing a Web site from sketches to publishing. Second, students need to gain considerable "hands on" computer experience using Web development tools such as Macromedia Dreamweaver, Fireworks, and Flash. An introductory course for Web development should include an explanation of networks, the Internet and intranets, and copyright issues. Learning basic HTML and the vocabulary of the World Wide Web is also important. Students can achieve these expectations with this text. The text is designed to strengthen problem-solving skills, which can be applied to a wide range of related topics, and is written to be used either in a one or two term course by students with little or no previous computer experience.

A Guide to Web Development Using Macromedia Dreamweaver MX

Our applications texts have established Lawrenceville Press as a leader in the field of educational textbook publishing, with more than two million students having been introduced to computing using our "hands-on" approach. With this text, we have made significant improvements to our approach based on the many comments we received, a survey of instructors, and our own classroom experiences.

This text presents material for Dreamweaver, Fireworks, Flash, Internet Explorer, Outlook Express, and Notepad. The text is written to be appropriate for students at a variety of levels. Chapters introduce all aspects of Web site development, including Web page layout, typography, color, editing, and graphics. Other chapters introduce the Internet and the World Wide Web, publishing a Web site, and cascading style sheets.

A Guide to Web Development Using Macromedia Dreamweaver MX is available in hardcover and softcover editions. The softcover edition has a sewn lay-flat binding, which keeps the text open at any page and gives the book additional strength.

Design and Features

Format Each chapter contains numerous examples and screen captures to help students visualize new concepts. Menus are displayed in the margins for easy reference.

Expectations An outline of the significant topics that will be covered is presented at the beginning of each chapter.

Sidebars Additional topics that complement the text are introduced in manila boxes in the margin.

Hands-on Practices Concepts are presented, discussed, and then followed by a "hands-on" practice that requires the student to test newly learned skills using the computer. The practices also serve as excellent reference guides to review commands. Answers to all the practices are included in the *Teacher's Resource Package*.

Chapter Summaries Each chapter concludes with a summary that briefly discusses the concepts covered in the chapter.

Vocabulary Sections At the end of each chapter is a list of new terms and definitions and a list of Dreamweaver commands and buttons.

Review Questions Numerous review questions are keyed to each section of a chapter, providing immediate reinforcement of new concepts. Answers to all review questions are included in the *Teacher's Resource Package*.

Exercises Each chapter includes a set of exercises of varying difficulty, making it appropriate for students with a wide range of abilities. Answers to all exercises are included in the *Teacher's Resource Package*.

Networks, Internet Explorer, and Outlook Express Before learning to use Dreamweaver, Chapters 1 and 2 introduce students to a brief history of the Internet, how networks function, an introduction to Internet Explorer and Outlook Express, and the vocabulary needed to understand concepts presented in later chapters.

HTML and CSS An introduction to HTML is presented before students are introduced to Dreamweaver. CSS style sheets are presented after students are familiar with HTML and creating Web pages.

Copyright Concerns The issues related to copyright, copyright protection, and the use of copyrighted materials are discussed throughout the text.

Web-Related Careers It is hoped that many students will become interested in IT and Web-related careers based upon their experience in this course. Chapter 2 includes information on different careers related to IT and the educational requirements needed to pursue them.

Appendices Appendix A lists HTML tags. Appendix B discusses ActionScript. Appendix C discusses digital camera files. Appendix D discusses collaboration for Web site development using templates.

Teacher's Resource Package

When used with this text, the Lawrenceville Press *Teacher's Resource Package* provides all the additional material required to offer students an excellent introductory computer applications course. These materials place a strong emphasis on developing the student's problem-solving skills. The Package contains the following features that correspond to each of the chapters in the text:

- **Assignments**   Suggested reading and problem assignments.
- **Teaching Notes**   Helpful information that we and our reviewers have learned from classroom experience.
- **Discussion Topics**   Additional material that supplements the text and can be used in leading classroom discussions.
- **Worksheets**   Problems that supplement the exercises in the text by providing additional reinforcement of concepts.
- **Review Question answers**   Printed answers for the review questions presented in the text.

A Resource CD, included with the Package, contains the following:

- **Supplements**   A Web site that presents material from the text.
- **Data files**   All files the student needs to complete the practices and exercises in the text, as well as the files needed to complete the worksheets and **Exam**View® questions included in the Package.
- **Exam**View® **Test Generator**   Question banks and **Exam**View® software are included so that multiple tests and assessment materials can be created for each chapter.
- **Answer files**   Answers to the practices, exercises, worksheets, and **Exam**View® questions.

Student data diskettes that contain the files needed to complete the practices and exercises can easily be made by following the directions in the Teacher's Resource Package Introduction.

As an added feature, the Package is contained in a 3-ring binder. This not only enables pages to be removed for duplication, but also allows the instructor to keep notes in the Package.

Acknowledgments

We thank Nanette Hert of Saint Andrew's School for reviewing the text. She has also contributed exercises, produced answer files, and assisted with other aspects of producing such a comprehensive text.

Special thanks to Dana Fritzinger, Doug Mattocks, and Barbara Ferguson of Unity School for their support. Thanks also to the following Unity School students for their candid evaluation of this text:

Nicholas Benavides	Jakob Gittelmacher	Jonathon Goldberg
Jake Hoffman	John Husak	Joey Kinderman
Artie Lang	Michael Lewin	Alex Muzii
Calvin O'Brien	Alexandra Pachter	Tony Saker
Marisa Vinas	Hunter Workman	Andrew Zinman

Credit is due to Douglas Powers and Elaine Malfas for the underwater photography used in the SCUBA Web site. Photographs of Greece and of various cacti used in the GREECE and CACTUS Web sites courtesy of Elaine Malfas.

We value the expertise of John Olivari and Jeanne Morris at Courier Book Companies, Inc., who supervised the printing of this text.

The success of this and all of our texts is due to the efforts of Heidi Crane, Vice President of Marketing at Lawrenceville Press. Joseph Dupree and Christina Albanesius run our Customer Relations Department and handle the thousands of orders we receive in a friendly and efficient manner. Richard Guarascio and Michael Porter are responsible for the excellent service Lawrenceville Press offers in the shipping of orders.

About the Authors

Beth A. Brown, a Computer Science graduate of Florida Atlantic University, is director of development at Lawrenceville Press where she has coauthored a number of applications and programming texts and their accompanying Teacher's Resource Packages. She has taught computer applications and programming at the high school level.

Elaine Malfas is a graduate of Hartwick College and earned her M.S. degree in Technical Communication from Rensselaer Polytechnic Institute. Ms. Malfas has coauthored several computer texts and their accompanying Teacher's Resource Packages. She has taught computer applications and desktop publishing at the high school level.

Jan Marrelli has a Bachelor of Science in Business Administration from Lake Superior State University and a Bachelor of Education from the University of Western Ontario. She has been a Business Coordinator and taught computer applications and programming for the Algoma District School Board as well as participating in curriculum development and assessment projects for the Ontario Ministry of Education.

Table of Contents

The data files used in this text can be downloaded from

www.lpdatafiles.com

Also available for downloading are separate chapters that describe different operating systems and a chapter for reinforcing keyboarding skills.

Chapter 1 – Introducing Networks and the Internet

1.1	Networks	1–1
1.2	Transmission Media	1–3
1.3	Network Protocols	1–4
1.4	Using a Network	1–4
1.5	The Internet	1–4
1.6	Accessing the Internet	1–5
1.7	Telecommunications	1–5
1.8	Internet Services	1–5
1.9	Intranet and Extranet	1–7
1.10	Internet Privacy Issues	1–7
1.11	Internet Use Agreements	1–8
1.12	The Social and Ethical Implications of Computers	1–8
1.13	Protecting Computer Software and Data	1–9
1.14	The Ethical Responsibilities of the Web Developer	1–10
1.15	Where can you go from here?	1–10
	Chapter Summary	1–11
	Vocabulary	1–12
	Review Questions	1–14
	Exercises	1–16

Chapter 2 – Introducing the World Wide Web and Internet Explorer

2.1	What is the World Wide Web?	2–1
2.2	What is on the Web?	2–2
2.3	Web Browsers	2–5
2.4	URLs	2–6
2.5	Using Internet Explorer	2–6
2.6	Surfing	2–8
	Practice 1	2–8
2.7	The History List	2–9
	Practice 2	2–9
2.8	The Favorites List	2–10
	Practice 3	2–11
2.9	Print Preview and Printing a Web Page	2–12
	Practice 4	2–14
2.10	Searching the Web	2–14
	Practice 5	2–15
2.11	Searching by Category	2–15
	Practice 6	2–16
2.12	Advanced Search Techniques	2–17
	Practice 7	2–18
2.13	Evaluating Web Sites	2–18

2.14	Citing Web Pages	2–19		HTML Tags	3–19
	Practice 8	2–19		Notepad Commands	3–20
2.15	What is E–mail?	2–19		Internet Explorer Commands and Buttons	3–20
2.16	Using Outlook Express	2–20			
2.17	E–mail Etiquette	2–22		Review Questions	3–21
2.18	IT Careers	2–22		Exercises	3–22
2.19	IT Companies	2–24			
2.20	Pursuing an IT Career	2–24			
	Chapter Summary	2–25			
	Vocabulary	2–27			

Chapter 4 – Introducing Dreamweaver

	Internet Explorer Commands and Buttons	2–28
	Outlook Express Commands and Buttons	2–28
	Review Questions	2–29
	Exercises	2–31

4.1	Dreamweaver MX	4–1
4.2	Defining a Web Site using Dreamweaver	4–2
	Practice 1	4–2
4.3	Saving and Naming a Web Page Document	4–5
4.4	Creating the Home Page	4–6
4.5	Changing the Page Title	4–6
4.6	Web Page Document Views	4–6
	Practice 2	4–7
4.7	Using a Table to Arrange Content	4–8
4.8	Creating a Table	4–10
4.9	Changing Cell Width and Height	4–11
4.10	Adding and Deleting Rows and Columns in a Table	4–11
	Practice 3	4–12
4.11	Adding Text Content to a Table	4–13
4.12	Checking Spelling	4–14
	Practice 4	4–15
4.13	Printing a Web Page Document	4–16
4.14	Closing a Web Page Document and Quitting Dreamweaver	4–17
4.15	Editing a Web Site	4–17
	Practice 5	4–18
4.16	Opening a Web Page Document	4–19
4.17	Creating a New Web Page Document	4–19
	Practice 6	4–20
4.18	Text Hyperlinks	4–22
	Practice 7	4–23
	Chapter Summary	4–24
	Vocabulary	4–26
	Dreamweaver Commands and Buttons	4–27
	Review Questions	4–29
	Exercises	4–30

Chapter 3 – Introducing HTML

3.1	What is HTML?	3–1
3.2	Creating an HTML Document	3–2
3.3	Using Notepad	3–3
	Practice 1	3–4
3.4	Viewing HTML Documents in a Web Browser	3–5
	Practice 2	3–6
3.5	Refreshing the Web Browser Display	3–6
	Practice 3	3–7
3.6	Creating Paragraphs	3–7
3.7	Paragraph Alignment	3–9
	Practice 4	3–10
3.8	Creating Headings	3–11
	Practice 5	3–12
3.9	Adding Horizontal Rules	3–12
3.10	Adding Color	3–13
3.11	Using Comments	3–13
	Practice 6	3–13
3.12	Hyperlinks	3–14
	Practice 7	3–15
3.13	The Source Command	3–16
	Practice 8	3–17
3.14	Where can you go from here?	3–17
	Chapter Summary	3–17
	Vocabulary	3–19

Chapter 5 – Web Site Development

5.1	Web Site Development	5–1
5.2	Defining the Purpose and Target Audience	5–2
	Practice 1	5–3
5.3	Determining the Web Pages and Navigation Structure	5–3
5.4	Determining the Content	5–4
	Practice 2	5–5
5.5	Defining Navigation Bars	5–5
5.6	The Web Page Layout	5–7
	Practice 3	5–7
5.7	Concepts of Design	5–8
5.8	Design Concepts: Appropriateness	5–8
5.9	Design Concepts: Placement	5–9
5.10	Design Concepts: Consistency	5–10
5.11	Design Concepts: Usability	5–10
	Practice 4	5–11
5.12	Organizing Files and Folders	5–12
	Practice 5	5–13
5.13	Maintaining Consistency in a Web Site	5–15
5.14	Merging and Splitting Cells	5–15
	Practice 6	5–17
5.15	Creating Library Items	5–19
5.16	Editing Library Items	5–20
5.17	Inserting a Date	5–20
5.18	E-mail Hyperlinks	5–20
5.19	Copyright Information	5–21
	Practice 7	5–21
	Chapter Summary	5–23
	Vocabulary	5–26
	Dreamweaver Commands and Buttons	5–27
	Review Questions	5–28
	Exercises	5–30

Chapter 6 – Images in Dreamweaver and Fireworks

6.1	Graphic File Formats for Web Pages	6–1
6.2	Alternative Text	6–2
6.3	Graphic Hyperlinks	6–3
	Practice 1	6–3
6.4	What is an Image Map?	6–5
6.5	Creating an Image Map	6–6
	Practice 2	6–7
6.6	Using a Spacer GIF	6–8
	Practice 3	6–9
6.7	Aligning an Image	6–11
6.8	Resizing an Image	6–11
	Practice 4	6–12
6.9	Introducing Fireworks MX	6–13
6.10	Drawing Objects in Fireworks	6–15
6.11	Adding Text in Fireworks	6–16
6.12	Aligning Objects in Fireworks	6–18
6.13	Modifying the Canvas	6–18
6.14	Optimizing and Exporting a Fireworks Document	6–18
	Practice 5	6–21
6.15	Creating a Button Symbol in Fireworks	6–24
6.16	Button Symbol Rollover Behavior	6–26
	Practice 6	6–27
6.17	Exporting HTML and Images from Fireworks	6–30
6.18	Using an Exported HTML Document in Dreamweaver	6–32
6.19	Changing Behaviors in Dreamweaver	6–32
	Practice 7	6–33
6.20	Cropping Images in Fireworks	6–36
6.21	Editing an Image in Fireworks from Dreamweaver	6–37
	Practice 8	6–37
	Chapter Summary	6–38
	Vocabulary	6–40
	Dreamweaver Commands and Buttons	6–41
	Fireworks Commands and Buttons	6–42
	Review Questions	6–43
	Exercises	6–45

Chapter 7 – Typography, Style Sheets, and Color

7.1	Typography	7–1
7.2	Design Considerations: Text	7–2
7.3	Paragraph Alignment	7–3
7.4	Design Considerations: Paragraphs	7–4
7.5	What is a Style Sheet?	7–4
7.6	Linking to a CSS Style Sheet	7–5
7.7	Creating and Applying a CSS Rule	7–6
7.8	Creating and Applying a CSS Class	7–7
7.9	Inserting Tags	7–8
	Practice 1	7–8
7.10	Working with CSS Styles	7–11
7.11	Strong and Emphasized Text	7–11
	Practice 2	7–12
7.12	Formatting Headings	7–12
	Practice 3	7–13
7.13	Using Blockquotes	7–15
	Practice 4	7–15
7.14	Using Lists	7–16
	Practice 5	7–17
7.15	Using Color in a Web Site	7–18
7.16	Changing Background Color	7–19
7.17	Changing Text Color	7–20
	Practice 6	7–20
7.18	Hyperlinks to Named Anchors	7–21
7.19	Changing Hyperlink Colors	7–22
	Practice 7	7–23
7.20	Using Content from Other Sources	7–24
	Practice 8	7–25
	Chapter Summary	7–25
	Vocabulary	7–27
	Dreamweaver Commands and Buttons	7–28
	Review Questions	7–29
	Exercises	7–30

Chapter 8 – Introducing Flash

8.1	What is Flash?	8–1
8.2	Creating Flash Buttons in Dreamweaver	8–2
8.3	Arranging Flash Buttons in a Web Page Document	8–3
	Practice 1	8–4
8.4	Using Movie Files	8–6
	Practice 2	8–6
8.5	Creating Flash Text in Dreamweaver	8–7
	Practice 3	8–9
8.6	What is Animation?	8–10
8.7	Introducing Flash MX	8–10
8.8	The Flash Tools Panel	8–11
8.9	Creating a Flash Movie	8–12
8.10	Frame-by-Frame Animation	8–13
8.11	Editing Techniques	8–14
	Practice 4	8–15
8.12	Exporting a Flash Document	8–17
8.13	Organizing and Using Flash Movie Files in Dreamweaver	8–18
	Practice 5	8–19
8.14	Shape Tweening	8–20
	Practice 6	8–21
8.15	Creating Symbols to Optimize a Flash Movie	8–22
8.16	Motion Tweening	8–24
	Practice 7	8–25
8.17	Using Layers	8–28
8.18	Animating Text	8–29
	Practice 8	8–31
8.19	Importing Sound Files	8–32
	Practice 9	8–33
8.20	Importing Video	8–34
	Practice 10	8–36
	Chapter Summary	8–37
	Vocabulary	8–39
	Dreamweaver Commands and Buttons	8–40
	Flash Commands and Buttons	8–41
	Review Questions	8–42
	Exercises	8–44

Chapter 9 – Web Site Categories and Types

9.1	Web Site Categories	9–1
9.2	Personal Web Sites	9–1
9.3	The Electronic Portfolio	9–2
9.4	Electronic Portfolio Design Considerations	9–2
9.5	The Informational Web Site	9–3
9.6	The Corporate Presence Web Site	9–4
9.7	The Dreamweaver Site Map	9–5
	Practice 1	9–7
9.8	Creating a FAQ Page	9–8
9.9	External Hyperlinks	9–8
9.10	Displaying a Linked Web Page in a New Window	9–9
	Practice 2	9–9
9.11	Using Tables to Display Tabular Data	9–10
	Practice 3	9–11
9.12	A Site Map Web Page	9–12
	Practice 4	9–12
9.13	The Jump Menu Form Object	9–13
	Practice 5	9–14
9.14	Dynamic Database-Driven Web Applications	9–15
9.15	What is a Form?	9–16
9.16	Creating a Form	9–17
	Practice 6	9–18
9.17	The Check Box And Radio Button Form Objects	9–19
9.18	The List/Menu Form Object	9–21
	Practice 7	9–22
	Chapter Summary	9–25
	Vocabulary	9–27
	Dreamweaver Commands and Buttons	9–28
	Review Questions	9–29
	Exercises	9–30

Chapter 10 – Publishing and Promoting a Web Site

10.1	Publishing a Web Site	10–1
10.2	Checking Spelling and Grammar	10–2
10.3	Checking the Download Time	10–2
	Practice 1	10–3
10.4	Target Browsers	10–3
10.5	Previewing in a Target Browser	10–4
	Practice 2	10–5
10.6	Testing the HTML for Target Browser Compatibility	10–5
10.7	Testing for Broken Links and Missing Links	10–6
10.8	Checking for HTML Problems	10–7
	Practice 3	10–8
10.9	What is a Web Host?	10–8
10.10	Publishing to a Web Server	10–9
10.11	Publishing to a Local/Network Server	10–10
10.12	Maintaining a Web Site	10–12
10.13	Promoting a Web Site	10–13
	Practice 4	10–14
10.14	Measuring Success	10–15
	Chapter Summary	10–15
	Vocabulary	10–17
	Dreamweaver Commands and Buttons	10–18
	Review Questions	10–19
	Exercise	10–20

Appendix A – HTML

Appendix B – Banner Ads and ActionScript

B.1	Banner Ads	B–1
B.2	Ad Templates in Flash	B–1
B.3	Creating a Banner Ad	B–3
B.4	Adding a Banner Ad Content	B–4
B.5	Creating a Button Symbol	B–4
B.6	Adding ActionScript	B–5
B.7	Completing and Testing the Banner Ad	B–7
B.8	Other Types of Web Ads	B–7

Appendix C – Digital Cameras

C.1   Digital Camera File Formats C–1
C.2   Maintaining Image Quality
        in JPG Files C–1
C.3   Digital Camera Image Resolution C–2
C.4   Changing Image Size and Resolution
        in Fireworks C–2

Appendix D – Templates

D.1   Templates D–1
D.2   Using the Templates Category D–2
D.3   Adding Editable Regions to a
        Template D–2
D.4   Creating a Web Page Document
        from a Template D–3

Chapter 1
Introducing Networks and the Internet

Chapter 1 Expectations

After completing this chapter you will be able to:
1. Explain what a network is and describe the benefits of using a network.
2. Define network architecture.
3. Identify the differences in network topologies.
4. Distinguish between different types of transmission media.
5. Understand network protocols.
6. Apply netiquette rules when using a network.
7. Summarize how the Internet works and explain how to access the Internet.
8. Identify various Internet services.
9. Distinguish between an intranet and extranet.
10. Describe cookie files and Web bugs.
11. Analyze Internet privacy issues.
12. Understand the need for an Internet Use Agreement.

This chapter introduces computer networks, the Internet, and Internet services. Internet privacy issues are also discussed.

1.1 Networks

A *network* is a combination of software and hardware that allows computers to exchange data and share software and devices, such as printers. Networks are widely used by businesses, universities, and other organizations because a network:

- allows users to reliably share and exchange data
- can reduce costs by sharing devices such as printers
- can be set up to allow users access to only specific files
- simplifies the process of creating backup copies of files
- allows users to communicate with e-mail

Networks are classified by their size, architecture, and topology. A common size classifications is *LAN* (Local-Area Network), which is a network used to connect devices within a small area such as a building or a campus. A *WAN* (Wide-Area Network) is used to connect devices over large geographical distances. A WAN can be one widespread network or it can be a number of LANs linked together.

The computers and other devices in a LAN each contain a circuit board called a *network interface card*:

MAN and HAN

A MAN (Metropolitan Area Network) and a HAN (Home Area Network) are network technologies classified by the size of a network. A MAN is a high-speed network that can span a distance of up to 75 km. A HAN is used to connect personal devices within the home.

network interface card

Pronunciation

LAN, WAN, MAN, and HAN all rhyme with Jan.

network interface card

A cable plugs into the network interface card to connect one device to another to form the LAN.

Introducing Networks and the Internet   1 – 1

operating system

Along with the physical, or hardware, aspects of setting up a network, there is also the software aspect. An *operating system* is software that allows the user to communicate with the computer. The operating system installed must be capable of supporting networking functions, such as security access features and support for multiple users. Operating systems capable of network functions are Windows and Mac OS X Server software.

network architecture

client/server

peer-to-peer

Network architecture refers to the structure of a network, which determines how network resources are handled. Two common models are client/server and peer-to-peer. A *client/server* network consists of a group of computers, called *clients*, connected to a server. A *server* is a powerful computer used to manage network functions such as communications and data sharing. A *peer-to-peer* network does not have a server. Each computer on the network is considered equal in terms of responsibilities and resource sharing.

topology

node

Physical *topology* refers to the arrangement of the nodes on a network. A *node* is a location on the network capable of processing information, such as a computer or a printer. There are three common physical topologies:

bus topology

bus

- The *bus topology* is a physical LAN topology that uses a single central cable, called the *bus* or backbone to attach each node directly:

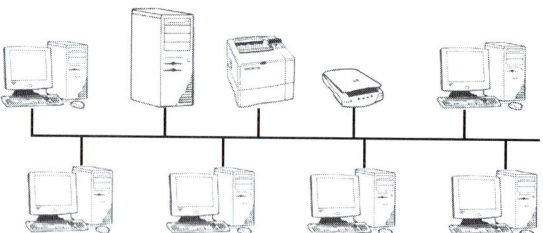

LAN using a bus topology

star topology, hub

- In a *star topology*, each node is attached to a *hub*, which is a device that joins communication lines at a central location on the network:

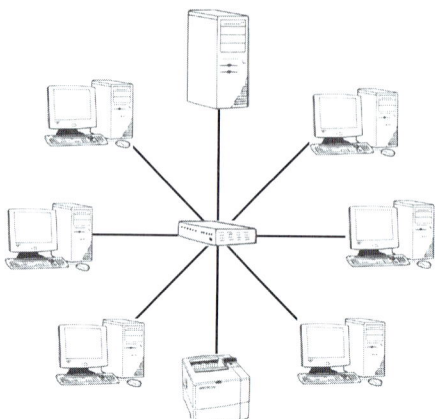

LAN using a star topology

1 – 2   *A Guide to Web Development Using Macromedia Dreamweaver MX*

ring topology

- In a *ring topology*, each node is connected to form a closed loop. A LAN with a ring topology can usually cover a greater distance than a bus or star topology:

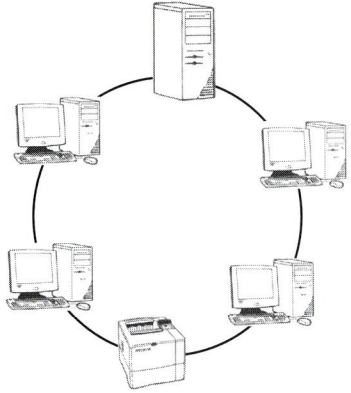

LAN using a ring topology

logical topology

Another type of topology is *logical topology*, which refers to the way data is passed between the nodes on a network. A LAN's logical topology is not always the same as its physical topology.

1.2 Transmission Media

Transmission media is what joins the nodes on a network to enable communication. The amount of data and the speed at which the data can travel over the transmission media is called its *bandwidth* and is measured in *bps* (bits per second). Each type of transmission media has different length or range restrictions, data transmission rates, costs, and installation requirements:

bandwidth

- *Twisted-pair wiring* consists of pairs of insulated strands of copper twisted around each other to form a cable. Twisted-pair wiring is the least expensive transmission media. Older telephone systems use twisted-pair wiring.

- *Coaxial cable* is made up of a central copper wire, a layer of insulation, a braided metal shield, and an outer shield. Coaxial cable provides a greater bandwidth than twisted-pair cable, but is more expensive. It is widely used in networks and is the type of cabling used for cable television.

- *Fiber optic cable* is composed of a bundle of thin strands of glass or plastic fibers that transmits data modulated onto light waves. Fiber optic cable has a greater bandwidth than twisted-pair and coaxial cable, but it is expensive. Traditional phone lines are continually being replaced with fiber optic cable.

- *Wireless networks* use high frequency radio waves or infrared signals instead of cables to transmit data. WLANs (Wireless Local-Area Networks) are becoming more common as the cost decreases and performance improves.

Bit

A bit (BInary digiT) is the smallest unit of information that can be represented on a computer. A single bit is one of two values: 0 or 1.

Baseband and Broadband Technology

Most LANs use baseband technology which means the transmission media carries one signal at a time. Broadband technology allows for data transmission of more than one signal at a time and is found in WANs.

Introducing Networks and the Internet

Bob Metcalfe
1946 –

Bob Metcalfe developed the theory of Ethernet technology while working at Xerox Corporation. Ethernet was developed in cooperation with the Digital Equipment Corporation and the Intel Corporation.

1.3 Network Protocols

Computer companies have developed standards, or *protocols*, for Local Area Networks. One widely used protocol is Ethernet. Ethernet was developed by Bob Metcalfe in 1976. It quickly became a leading LAN protocol and significantly contributed to the growth of LANs in the late 1970s and 1980s. Networking equipment, such as network interface cards, are designed around the Ethernet standards.

Ethernet uses a bus or star topology and connects the network devices by twisted-pair wiring, coaxial cable, or fiber optic cable. In its original form, Ethernet operated at a bandwidth of 10 Mbps (Megabits per second). Newer versions of Ethernet include Fast Ethernet which operates at 100 Mbps and Gigabit Ethernet which operates at 1 Gbps (Gigabit per second).

Other LAN protocols include IBM's Token Ring network, Apple Computer's AppleTalk, and Datapoint Corporation's ARCnet.

1.4 Using a Network

Network users are given a user name and password to log on to a network. Users are also assigned a level of access to maintain security.

netiquette Network users should follow a certain etiquette referred to as *netiquette*:

- Do not attempt to access the account of another user without authorization.

- Do not share your password, and change it periodically.

- Use appropriate subject matter and language, and be considerate of other people's beliefs and opinions. This is especially important when posting messages that will be sent to every user on the network.

History of the Internet

The history of the Internet can be traced to an early network known as ARPANET.

ARPANET was created in the late 1960s by the Department of Defense's ARPA (Advanced Research Projects Agency.) ARPANET initally connected computers at the University of California Los Angeles and the Stanford Research Institute.

The Internet evolved from ARPANET and the theory of open architecture networking, meaning internetworking different networks regardless of what type of network technology they used.

1.5 The Internet

The largest and most widely accessed network is the *Internet*, a worldwide network of computers that is not controlled by any one organization. The Internet has had an undeniable impact on modern society because it allows users world-wide to communicate in a matter of seconds.

The Internet is actually numerous networks all linked together through routers. *Routers* are devices that can connect different network technologies together. Networks connected to routers use *TCP/IP* (Transmission Control Protocol/Internet Protocol) software to communicate.

Computers on the Internet are either servers or clients. A *client* computer is sent information from a server computer. The client/server structure of the Internet is called *interactive* because the information accessed is a result of selections made by the user. For example, a computer with just minimal software for accessing the Internet is a client. The client user selecting options from the Internet is receiving the information from a server, a computer with additional software and files that is also connected to the Internet.

1.6 Accessing the Internet

ISP
online information service

Many organizations link their networks to the Internet. Individuals can get access to the Internet through telecommunications and an Internet service provider or an online information service. An *ISP* (Internet Service Provider) offers access to the Internet for a fee. An *online information service*, such as AOL, offers access to the Internet as well as other services for a fee.

ISPs and online information services typically charge a fee that is usually a flat, monthly rate, but is sometimes based on access time. They also provide the necessary software, a username, password, and dial-up number for a conventional modem.

1.7 Telecommunications

Telecommunications is the transmitting and receiving of data. Data can be in various forms including voice and video. Telecommunications requires a modem or adapter and a line or cable. The speed of data transmission is measured in *Kbps* (thousands of bits per second) or *Mbps* (millions of bits per second). Numerous telecommunications options are available, which vary in speed and cost:

> **Conventional Modem**
>
> A conventional modem converts a computer's binary data into tones that can be transmitted over phone lines. To receive data, a modem converts the tones from the phone line into binary data. This process involves what is called signal modulation and demodulation, hence the name modem.

- A *conventional modem* uses standard telephone lines to convert analog signals to digital data. A conventional modem is a 56 Kbps modem, which transmits data at 28.8 Kbps and 36.6 Kbps, and receives data at 56 Kbps. Home computers sometimes use a conventional modem.

- A *DSL* (Digital Subscriber Line) *modem* uses standard telephone lines with data transmission up to 640 Kbps. Data receipt is from 1.5 Mbps to 9 Mbps. ADSL (Asymmetric DSL) is the most common form used.

- A *cable modem* transmits data through a coaxial cable television network. Data transmission is from 2 Mbps to 10 Mbps and data receipt is from 10 Mbps to 36 Mbps.

- *Leased/Dedicated lines* are being used by many businesses and schools for Internet access. They allow for a permanent connection to the Internet that is always active. The cost of a leased line is usually a fixed monthly fee. A T-1 carrier is a type of leased line that transmits data at 1.544 Mbps.

- *ISDN* (Integrated Services Digital Network) is a digital telephone network provided by a local phone company. ISDN is capable of transmitting and receiving data at up to 64 Kbps. ISDN requires the use of an ISDN terminal adapter instead of a modem.

1.8 Internet Services

Web

The most widely used Internet service is the World Wide Web (WWW), also called the Web. The *Web* can be used to search and access information available on the Internet. A Web browser application such as Microsoft Internet Explorer provides a graphical interface to present

Web site information in the form of a Web site. Each *Web site* consists of a series of related Web pages. The Web page below is a part of the CNN Web site:

e-mail Another widely used Internet service is *e-mail* or *electronic mail*, which allows an individual with an e-mail account to send messages to another person with an e-mail account. E-mail can be received in a matter of seconds, even if the recipient is located half way around the world. E-mail is discussed further in Chapter 2.

IRC A very popular service provided through the Internet and online information service providers is called *Internet Relay Chat* (IRC) or just *chat*. IRC was developed in 1988 by Jarkko Oikarinen. Chatting is communicating with someone else who is also online by typing messages back and forth to each other. After one person writes something the other person receives the message and replies. Although there may be a short delay while the person responds, chatting is considered to be a *real-time* event. *Real time* means that data reflects an event as it occurs.

BBS A *bulletin board service*, sometimes referred to as a *BBS*, allows a user to participate in a discussion group. There are thousands of bulletin board services with topics ranging from accounting to zoology. Businesses often maintain a bulletin board service for their employees only. Other bulletin board services allow any network user to join.

network news *Network news* is a popular BBS available on the Internet. This system
newsgroup uses the term *newsgroup* to refer to an individual bulletin board, and
article *article* refers to the message posted to the newsgroup. Subscribers of a newsgroup can check for new articles and post (send) articles regarding
USENET the topic of discussion. *USENET* refers to the collection of all the servers that offer network news.

listserv Internet users can also join a listserv. A *listserv* is a discussion group
LISTSERV that uses e-mail to send messages. *LISTSERV* is a program that maintains
mailing list the *mailing list*, a list of the e-mail addresses of the users who subscribe to the listserv. When a subscriber posts a message to a listserv, every subscriber receives a copy of the message.

HTTP   *HTTP* (Hypertext Transfer Protocol) is used for handling the transmission of pages between a Web server and a Web browser.

FTP   *FTP* (File Transfer Protocol) is used to rapidly transfer (upload and download) files from one computer to another over the Internet. FTP is also discussed in Chapter 2.

Telnet   *Telnet* is a program that is used on networks such as the Internet to allow users to remotely log on to a server on the network. The server can then be controlled from the remote computer. Telnet is commonly used to control Web servers.

gopher   *Gopher* was one of the first widespread Internet browsing services. It is a text-based environment that is used to locate information on the Internet.

1.9 Intranet and Extranet

intranet   An *intranet* is a network that is used by a single organization, such as a corporation or school, and is only accessible by authorized users. The purpose of an intranet is to share information, just like the Internet, but an intranet is able to use a firewall to lock out unauthorized users. A **firewall**   *firewall* is a network security system that prevents unauthorized network access.

extranet   An *extranet* extends an intranet by providing various levels of accessibility to authorized members of the public. For example, a corporation may extend their intranet to provide access to specific information, such as their ordering system to registered customers.

1.10 Internet Privacy Issues

The growth of the Internet has caused additional concerns about personal privacy. Searching for information on the Internet is not as anonymous as it might seem.

online profiling   The collection of online data about consumers is a marketing technique known as *online profiling*. When a commercial Web site is visited on the Internet, information about the user may be collected using various methods such as cookies or Web bugs.

cookies   A *cookie* is a text file created by the server computer when a user enters information into a Web site. The cookie file is then stored on the user's computer and accessed each time the user visits that Web site. Cookies are often created when online purchases are made. Although cookies can only store information that the user has selected or entered, their use has raised concerns over privacy issues.

Web bugs   *Web bugs* are tiny, transparent graphics located on Web pages and are used to collect data about the Web page user. Usually the monitoring is done by an outside advertising company. The information a Web bug collects includes the IP address of the computer, the URL being visited, the time the Web page was viewed, the type of browser being used, and the cookie file.

Introducing Networks and the Internet

privacy policy

Before providing a company with personal information through a Web site, check the site's privacy policy. A *privacy policy* is a legally binding document that explains how any personal information will be used.

The Internet has also opened up access to many files that were previously inaccessible. To protect both the privacy of an individual and the accuracy of data stored about individuals, several laws have been passed:

- The **Electronic Communications Privacy Act of 1986** (ECPA) makes it a crime to access electronic data without authorization. It also prohibits unauthorized release of such data.

- The **Electronic Freedom of Information Act of 1996** (E-FOIA) requires federal government agencies to make certain agency information available for public inspection and is designed to improve public access to agency records by making more information available online.

- The **Children's Online Privacy Protection Act of 1998** (COPPA) requires commercial Web sites that collect personal information from children under the age of 13 to obtain parental consent.

- The **Safety and Freedom through Encryption Act of 1999** (SAFE) gives Americans the freedom to use any type of encryption to protect their confidential information.

> **Encryption**
>
> Encryption is the process of translating data into a code that is not readable without the key to the code. Encryption prevents unauthorized access to data. Data that is encrypted is referred to as cipher text.

1.11 Internet Use Agreements

Concerns about Internet content, unproductive use, and copyright have prompted many schools and businesses to develop an Internet Use Agreement or Acceptable Use Policy. Internet Use Agreements typically contain rules similar to:

- Use appropriate language.
- Do not reveal personal address or phone numbers.
- Do not access, upload, download, or distribute inappropriate materials.
- Do not access another user's account.
- Use of the network for private business is prohibited.
- Only administrator installed software may be used on the computers. Adding, deleting, or modifying installed software is not permitted.

1.12 The Social and Ethical Implications of Computers

information age

The society in which we live has been so profoundly affected by computers that historians refer to the present time as the *information age*. This is due to the computer's ability to store and manipulate large amounts of information (data). As an information society, we must consider both the social and ethical implications of our dependence on computers. By ethical questions we mean asking what are the morally right and wrong ways to use computers.

Probably the most serious problem associated with computers is the possibility of invading our privacy. Because computers can store vast amounts of data we must decide what information is proper to store, what is improper, and who should have access to the information. Every time you use a credit card, make a phone call, withdraw money, reserve a flight, or register at school a computer records the transaction. These records can be used to learn a great deal about you—where you have been, when you were there, and how much money was spent. Should this information be available to everyone?

Computers are also used to store information about your credit rating, which determines your ability to borrow money. If you want to buy a car and finance it at a bank, the bank first checks your credit records on a computer to determine if you have a good credit rating. If you purchase the car and then apply for automobile insurance, another computer will check to determine if you have traffic violations. How do you know if the information being used is accurate? Laws such as those listed below have been passed to help ensure that the right to privacy is not infringed by the improper use of data stored in computer files:

- The **Fair Credit Reporting Act of 1970** gives individuals the right to see information collected about them for use by credit, insurance, and employment agencies. If a person is denied credit they are allowed to see the files used to make the credit determination. If any of the information is incorrect, the person has the right to have it changed. The act also restricts who may access credit files to only those with a court order or the written permission of the individual whose credit is being checked.

- The **Privacy Act of 1974** restricts the way in which personal data can be used by federal agencies. Individuals must be permitted access to information stored about them and may correct any information that is incorrect. Agencies must insure both the security and confidentiality of any sensitive information. Although this law applies only to federal agencies, many states have adopted similar laws.

- The **Financial Privacy Act of 1978** requires that a government authority have a subpoena, summons, or search warrant to access an individual's financial records. When such records are released, the financial institution must notify the individual of who has had access to them.

1.13 Protecting Computer Software and Data

piracy

Because computer software can be copied electronically, it is easy to duplicate. Such duplication is usually illegal because the company producing the software is not paid for the copy. This has become an increasingly serious problem as the number of illegal software copies distributed through *piracy* has grown. Developing, testing, marketing, and supporting software is an expensive process. If the software developer is then denied rightful compensation, the future development of all software is jeopardized.

Introducing Networks and the Internet — 1–9

Persons found guilty of using illegally copied software can be fined, and their reputation damaged. Therefore, when using software it is important to use only legally acquired copies, and to not make illegal copies for others.

cracker, hacker

Newspapers have carried numerous reports of *crackers*, or *hackers*, gaining access to large computer databases to perform acts of vandalism. These acts are usually illegal and can cause very serious and expensive damage. The Electronic Communications Privacy Act of 1986 specifically makes it a federal offense to access electronic data without authorization.

virus

One illegal and especially harmful act is distributing a virus. A *virus* is a series of instructions buried into a computer file that causes the computer to destroy data when given a certain signal. For example, a virus might check the computer's clock and then destroy data when a certain time is reached. A virus is easily duplicated when the file is copied, which spreads it other computers, hence the name virus. Computer viruses have become so widespread that anti-virus programs are typically installed on computers to detect and erase viruses before they can spread or damage data.

The willful destruction of computer data is no different than any other vandalization of property. Since the damage is done electronically the result is often not as obvious as destroying physical property, but the consequences are much the same. It is estimated that computer crimes cost the nation billions of dollars each year.

1.14 The Ethical Responsibilities of the Web Developer

dynamic pages

Web sites often contain *dynamic pages* that link to databases to provide the user real-time information. It is extremely difficult, if not impossible, for a Web developer to guarantee that data is always valid. A cause for concern is the increased reliance by computer users on the data presented. This places a strong ethical burden on the Web developers to ensure, as best they can, the reliability of the data.

As capable as computers have proven to be, we must be cautious when allowing them to replace human beings in areas where judgement is crucial. As intelligent beings, we can often detect that something out of the ordinary has occurred which has not been previously anticipated and then take appropriate actions. Computers will only do what they have been programmed to do, even if it is to perform a dangerous act.

1.15 Where can you go from here?

This chapter introduced Internet services including the World Wide Web and e-mail. The next chapter introduces the Web browser Microsoft Internet Explorer, which is used to view Web pages. It also introduces the e-mail software Microsoft Outlook Express.

Chapter Summary

A network is a combination of software and hardware that allows computers to exchange data and to share software and devices, such as printers. Hardware requirements include a network interface card, and software requirements include an operating system to allow the user to communicate with the computer.

Networks are classified by their size, architecture, topology, and protocol. Common network size classifications are LAN and WAN. Two common network architecture models are client/server and peer-to-peer. Topology refers to the physical arrangement of the nodes on a network. Three common physical topologies are the bus, star, and ring topology. One widely used protocol is Ethernet.

Transmission media is what joins the nodes on a network to enable communication. The amount of data and the speed at which it can travel over the transmission media is called its bandwidth and is measured in bps. Types of transmission media include twisted-pair wiring, coaxial cable, fiber optic cable, and wireless networks.

Telecommunications is the transmitting and receiving of data. Telecommunication options include a conventional modem, a DSL modem, a cable modem, leased/dedicated lines, and ISDN. Access to the Internet also requires the use of an ISP or an online information service.

The largest and most widely accessed network is the Internet. The most widely used Internet service is the World Wide Web (WWW), also called the Web. Another widely used Internet service is e-mail. Other Internet services include IRC, BBS, network news, listserv, HTTP, FTP, Telnet, and gopher.

An intranet is a network that is used by a single organization and is only accessible by authorized users. A firewall is a network security system that prevents unauthorized network access. An extranet extends an intranet by providing various levels of accessibility to authorized members of the public.

The growth of the Internet has caused concerns about personal privacy. Online profiling, cookies, and Web bugs are all areas of concern. Before providing personal information through a Web site, check the site's privacy policy. To protect an individual's privacy, several laws have been passed.

Concerns about Internet content, unproductive use, and copyright have prompted many schools and businesses to develop an Internet Use Agreement. Network users should use netiquette.

Historians refer to our present time as the information age. The potential for the use of cimputers to invade our right to privacy has prompted legislation to protect individuals. Priacy is the illegal act of duplicating software without permission. A virus is a computer file that erases data and can cause considerable damage.

Web developers should ensure, as best they can, the reliability of the data they provide in dynamic Web pages.

Vocabulary

Article A message posted to a newsgroup.

Bandwidth The amount of data and the speed at which the data can travel over the transmission media.

BBS (bulletin board service) A network service that allows a user to participate in a discussion group.

bps Bits per second.

Bus A central network cable.

Bus topology A physical LAN topology that uses a single central cable to attach each node directly.

Cable modem A modem that transmits data through a coaxial cable television network.

Chat *See* IRC.

Client A computer that is sent information from a server computer.

Client/server network A type of network that consists of a group of computers, called clients connected to a server computer.

Coaxial cable Cable made up of a central copper wire, a layer of insulation, a braided metal shield, and an outer shield.

Conventional modem A modem that uses standard telephone lines to convert analog signals to digital data.

Cookie Text file created by the server computer when a user enters information into a Web site.

Cracker Person who enters a computer system without authorization.

Dedicated line *See* Leased line.

DSL (Digital Subscriber Line) modem A modem that uses standard telephone phone lines. ADSL is the most common form used.

Dynamic pages Web pages that link to databases to provide the user real-time information.

Ethernet A widely used protocol for LANs that uses a bus or star topology and connects the network devices by twisted-pair wiring, coaxial cable, or fiber optic cable.

E-mail (electronic mail) An Internet service that allows an individual with an e-mail account to send messages to another person with an e-mail account.

Extranet An extended intranet that provides various levels of access to authorized members of the public.

Fiber optic cable Cable that is composed of a bundle of thin strands of glass or plastic fibers that transmits data modulated onto light waves.

Firewall A network security system that prevents unauthorized network access.

FTP (File Transfer Protocol) Used to rapidly upload and download files from one computer to another over the Internet.

Gopher One of the first widespread Internet browsing services.

Hacker *See* Cracker.

HTTP (Hypertext Transfer Protocol) Used for handling the transmission of pages between a Web server and a Web browser.

Hub A communication device that joins communication lines at a central location on the network.

Information age Present time characterized by increasing dependence on the computer's ability to store and manipulate large amounts of information.

Interactive Information accessed as a result of selections made.

Internet The largest and most widely accessed network.

Intranet A network that is used by a single organization and only accessible by authorized users.

IRC (Internet Relay Chat) An Internet and online information service that allows users to communicate with someone online by typing messages back and forth.

ISDN (Integrated Services Digital Network) A digital telephone network provided by a local telephone company.

ISP (Internet Service Provider) A company that offers access to the Internet for a fee.

Kbps Thousands of bits per second.

Leased line A telecommunication option used for a permanent connection to the Internet that is always active.

Listserv A discussion group that uses e-mail to send messages.

Local Area Network (LAN) A network used to connect devices within a small area.

Logical topology Refers to the way in which data is passed between the nodes on a network.

Mailing list A list of e-mail addresses of the users who subscribe to a listserv.

Mbps Millions of bits per second.

Netiquette The etiquette that should be followed when using a network.

Network A combination of software and hardware that allows computers to exchange data and to share software and devices, such as printers.

Network architecture The structure of a network.

Network interface card A circuit board that goes into the a computer or other device in a LAN.

Network news A BBS available on the Internet.

Newsgroup An individual bulletin board.

Node A location on the network capable of processing information, such as a computer or a printer.

Online profiling A marketing technique that collects online data about consumers.

Online information service A company that offers access to the Internet as well as other services for a fee.

Operating system Software that allows the user to communicate with the computer.

Peer-to-peer network A type of network that does not have a server.

Piracy Illegally copying or distributing software.

Privacy policy A legally binding document that explains how any personal information will be used.

Protocol A standard.

Real time Data that reflects an event as it occurs.

Ring topology A physical LAN topology where each node is connected to form a closed loop.

Router A device that connects different network technologies.

Server A computer used to manage network functions such as communication and data sharing.

Star topology A physical LAN topology where each node is attached to a hub.

TCP/IP (Transmission Control Protocol/Internet Protocol) software Software used by networks connected to routers to communicate.

Telecommunications The transmitting and receiving of data.

Telnet A program that is used on networks such as the Internet to allow users to remotely log on to a server on the network.

Topology The physical or logical arrangement of the nodes on a network.

Transmission media The media that joins the nodes on a network to enable communication.

Twisted-pair wiring Wiring that consists of pairs of insulated strands of copper twisted around each other to form a cable.

USENET The collection of servers that offer network news.

Virus Series of instructions buried into a computer file that causes the computer to destroy data when given a certain signal.

Web *See* World Wide Web.

Web bug A tiny, transparent graphic located on a Web page used to collect data about the Web page user.

Web site A series of related Web pages.

Wide Area Network (WAN) A network used to connect computers over large geographical distances.

Wireless network A type of network that does not require the use of cables.

World Wide Web (WWW) The most widely used Internet service.

Review Questions

Sections 1.1 — 1.4

1. What is a network?

2. List four benefits of using a network.

3. a) What are the two common size classifications for networks?
   b) What size classification is used to connect devices over large geographical distances?

4. a) What is an operating system?
   b) List two networking functions.

5. a) What does network architecture refer to?
   b) List two common network architecture models.

6. a) What does physical topology refer to?
   b) What is a node?
   c) Which topology uses a hub?
   d) Which topology connects each node to form a closed loop?
   e) What is the difference between physical and logical topolgy.

7. a) What is transmission media?
   b) What is bandwidth?
   c) Describe four types of transmission media.

8. a) What is a protocol?
   b) What is a widely used protocol for Local Area Networks?
   c) List two other LAN protocols besides the one used in part (b).

9. List three netiquette rules.

Sections 1.5 — 1.15

10. What is the largest and most widely accessed network?

11. What is a router?

12. a) How does a client interact on the Internet?
    b) Why is the client/server structure called interactive?

13. a) How can an individual get access to the Internet?
    b) List an example of an online information service.

14. a) What is telecommunications?
    b) List three telecommunications options.

15. a) If a business needed constant access to the Internet, what type of connection line would be a good choice? Why?
    b) What does a cable modem use instead of analog phone lines?

16. What is the most widely used Internet service?

17. a) What is e-mail?
    b) List one benefit of e-mail over standard mail.

18. a) What is chatting?
    b) What is meant by real time?
    c) Why is chatting considered a real-time event.

19. What does a bulletin board service allow a user to participate in?

20. a) What is a listserv?
    b) What is HTTP used for?
    c) What is FTP used for?

21. Gopher locates information on the Internet using what type of environment?

22. a) What is an intranet?
    b) What is an extranet?

23. What is online profiling?

24. What is a cookie?

25. a) What is a Web bug?
    b) Who usually monitors the information collected by Web bugs?

26. What is a privacy policy?

27. Name and briefly describe one law that helps protect the privacy of an individual.

28. a) List three reasons why many schools have developed an Internet Use Agreement.
    b) List an example of a rule that typically appears on an Internet Use Agreement.

29. What is meant by the information age?

30. a) How do you believe society is benefitting from the information age?
    b) What are some of the negative aspects of the information age?

31. How can computers be used to invade your privacy?

32. What can you do if you are turned down for credit at a bank and believe that the data used to deny credit is inaccurate?

33. a) What is necessary for a federal government authority to access an individual's financial records?
    b) What must the financial institution do after the records are accessed?

34. a) What is computer piracy?
    b) What is a computer cracker?
    c) What is a computer virus?

35. a) What ethical responsibilities does a Web developer have when creating dynamic Web pages?
    b) Can a Web developer guarantee that data presented is valid? Why or why not?

Exercises

The exercises in this chapter require written information. If a word processor is used, be sure to use an appropriate header, footer, and file name.

Exercise 1

Expand on the information presented in this chapter by researching one of the following topics:
- Network Protocols
- Operating Systems
- The History of the Internet

a) Use the Internet, magazines, and books to find at least three sources of information.

b) Write a two page report that summarizes your research.

c) On a separate sheet, titled References, cite each source.

Exercise 2

In this exercise you will research your classroom computer network by answering a series of questions.

a) Is your computer network a LAN or a WAN?

b) List one device that is shared on the network.

c) Locate the cable that plugs into the network interface card on your workstation.

d) What type of physical topology is used?

e) What type of transmission media is used?

f) What network protocol is used?

g) What operating system is used?

h) What telecommunication option is used?

i) Does the school have an intranet?

j) List four rules on the school's Internet Use Agreement.

Exercise 3

In this exercise you will research and compare the advantages and cost of obtaining Internet access through three different telecommunication options.

    a) Use the Internet and newspapers to find ISP advertisements.

    b) Summarize the cost and compare the advantages of the three different telecommunication options.

    c) Write a one paragraph conclusion that explains what telecommunication option would be the best choice.

Exercise 4

In this exercise you will further research privacy issues to find real-life examples of how this issue has impacted individuals.

    a) Use the Internet, magazines, and books to find at least three sources of information.

    b) Write a two-page report that summarizes your research.

    c) On a separate sheet, titled References, cite each source.

Exercise 5

In this exercise you will research another social or ethical issue associated with computer use, such as identify theft, piracy, or viruses, to find real-life examples of how these issues have impacted companies or individuals.

    a) Use the Internet, magazines, and books to find at least three sources of information.

    b) Write a two-page report that summarizes your research.

    c) On a separate sheet, titled References, cite each source.

Chapter 2
Introducing the World Wide Web and Internet Explorer

Chapter 2 Expectations

After completing this chapter you will be able to:

1. Define terminology associated with the World Wide Web.
2. Describe several categories of Web sites and the purpose of each.
3. Explain what a banner ad is and why Web sites host them.
4. Recognize an HTML document and explain how a Web browser interprets HTML.
5. Describe each part of a URL.
6. Demonstrate the basic features and functions of Internet Explorer.
7. Use the History list and Favorites list in Internet Explorer.
8. Use the print preview function and print a Web page.
9. Use search engines and subject trees.
10. Apply advanced search techniques.
11. Evaluate and cite Web pages.
12. Describe how copyright applies to material on the Internet.
13. Demonstrate the basic features and functions of Outlook Express and apply e-mail etiquette.
14. Discuss IT careers.

This chapter introduces the World Wide Web, Internet Explorer, and Outlook Express.

2.1 What is the World Wide Web?

The *World Wide Web* is the total collection of Web pages that are stored on Web servers located all over the world. Schools, companies, and other organizations often have their own Web server. Web servers are also *Web hosts* provided by Web hosting companies or *Web hosts*. Web authors post their Web sites to a Web server and the site becomes part of the World *posting* Wide Web. *Posting* is the process of copying Web site files to a Web server.

Web sites contain pages with information on a wide variety of topics. For example, the CNN page provides news about current events:

Tim Berners-Lee
1955 –

Tim Berners-Lee is credited with creating the World Wide Web in 1991 while working at CERN, the European Laboratory for Particle Physics in Geneva, Switzerland.

Berners-Lee now heads a non-profit group, the W3C (World Wide Web Consortium), which sets technical standards for the Web.

A Web page has similar features to a page you might see in a printed book or magazine, such as formatted text and colorful pictures. A Web page's purpose is the same as any printed material, which is to communicate with the reader. What makes a Web page so different from

Introducing the World Wide Web and Internet Explorer   2 – 1

hyperlink printed materials is that it can contain hyperlinks. A *hyperlink* or *link* is text or graphics on a Web page that can be clicked to display another portion of that same page or another Web page.

Web site, home page A series of related Web pages that are connected by hyperlinks make up a *Web site*. The main page is designated as the *home page* and is the starting point of the Web site. The home page usually contains links to the rest of the pages of the Web site.

2.2 What is on the Web?

The Web offers access to a multitude of information and most Web sites fall into one of the following categories: personal, commercial, informational, media, and portal.

personal Web site *Personal Web sites* are created by individuals for the purpose of displaying information about themselves. A personal Web site might contain pages about the individual's hobbies, pets, family members, or links to their favorite Web sites:

Internet Safety

A personal Web site should not contain any identifying information such as a home address, telephone number, or age.

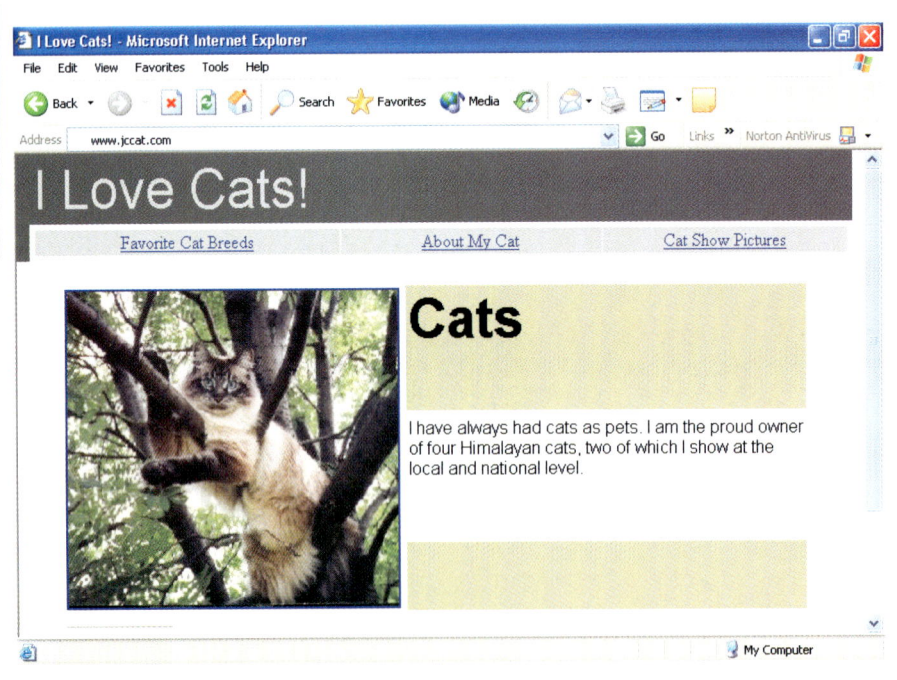

---

personal Web site

commercial Web site *Commercial Web sites* include *corporate presence Web sites*, which are created by companies and organizations for the purpose of displaying information about their products or services. It also includes *e-commerce Web sites*, which are created by businesses for the purpose of selling their products or services to consumers online:

---

dot-com

A dot-com refers to a company that does business primarily on the Web.

---

2 – 2   *A Guide to Web Development Using Macromedia Dreamweaver MX*

Amazon.com

Amazon.com is a well known e-commerce Web site. Founded by Jeff Bezos in 1994, Amazon.com Inc. is an Internet retailer of books, music, toys, electronics, software, and other products.

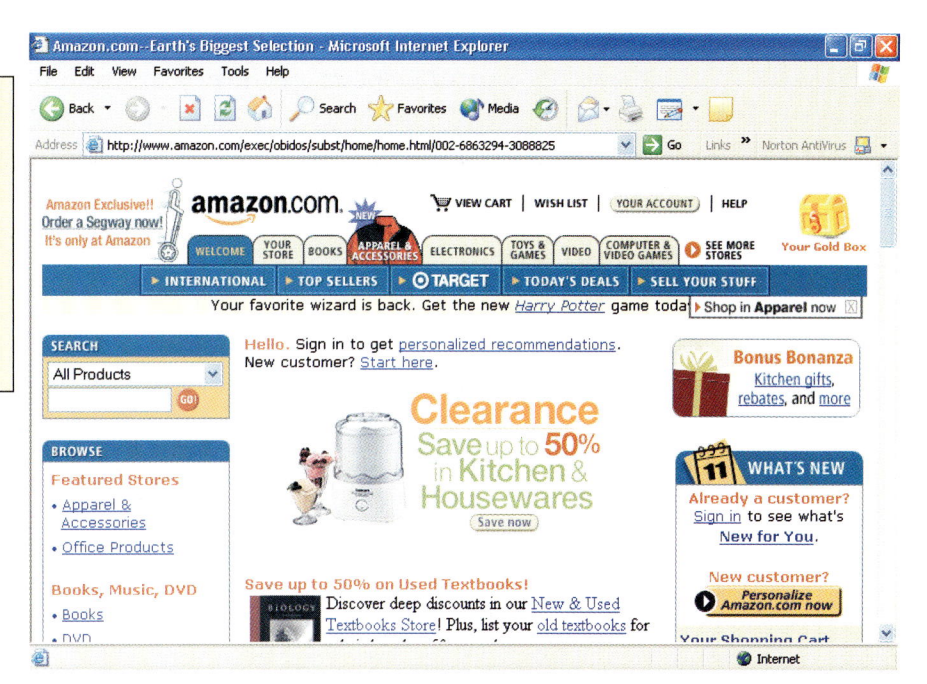

e-commerce Web site

informational Web site — Informational Web sites are created for the purpose of displaying factual information about a particular topic

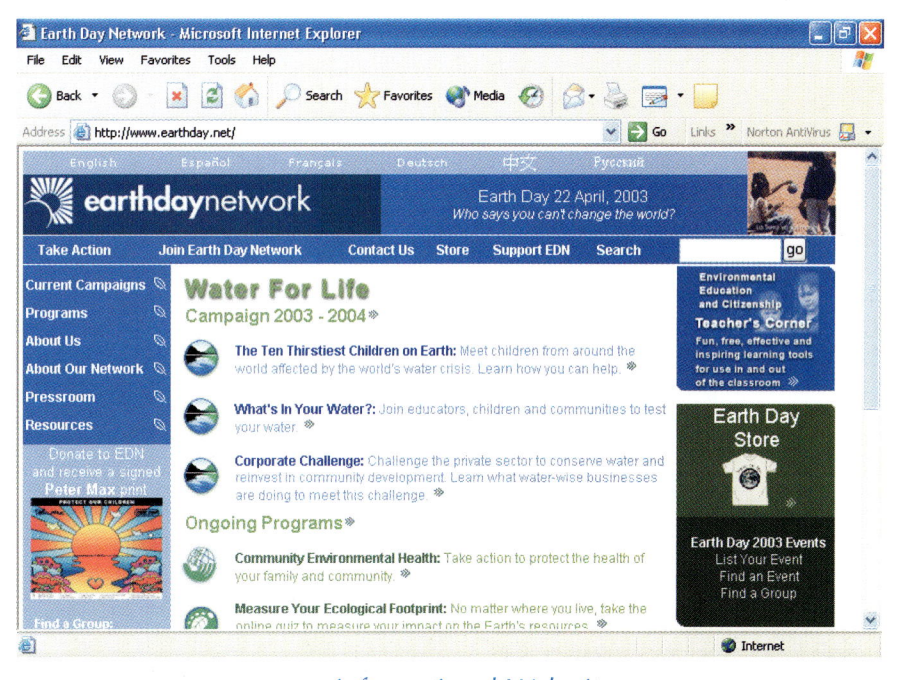

informational Web site

Informational Web sites are often created by educational institutions, governments, and organizations.

Blog

Blog is short for Weblog and is a type of Web site where users can post entries in a journal format.

Introducing the World Wide Web and Internet Explorer 2 – 3

media Web site   *Media Web sites* are online newspaper and periodicals that are created by companies for the purpose of informing readers about current events and issues:

> **Growth of the Internet**
>
> It is estimated that there will be between 700 and 900 million Internet users worldwide in 2004.

media Web site

portal Web site   *Portal Web sites* are created by businesses for the purpose of creating a starting point for people to enter the Web. Portals contain hyperlinks to a wide range of topics, such as sport scores and top news stories, and most portals include access to a search engine:

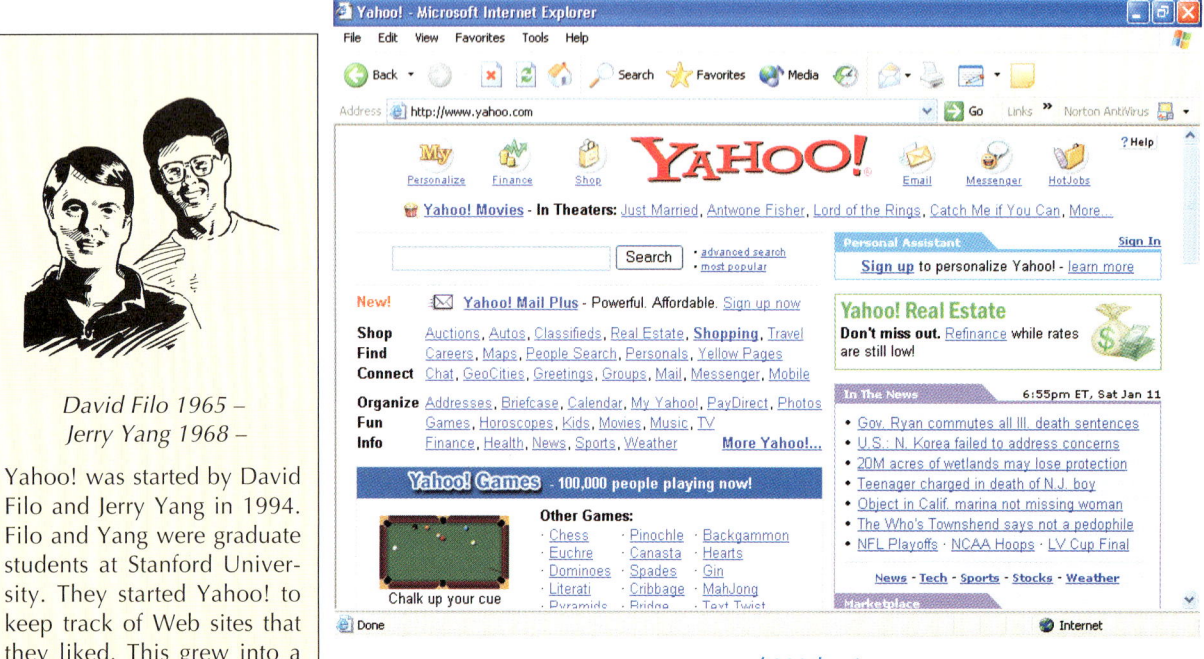

> *David Filo 1965 –*
> *Jerry Yang 1968 –*
>
> Yahoo! was started by David Filo and Jerry Yang in 1994. Filo and Yang were graduate students at Stanford University. They started Yahoo! to keep track of Web sites that they liked. This grew into a database that could be accessed by other Internet users. Millions of Internet users each day use Yahoo! to find information on the Web.

portal Web site

    The categories discussed are very general and not all Web sites fall under exactly one category.

2 – 4   *A Guide to Web Development Using Macromedia Dreamweaver MX*

Web Ads

Banner ads have been the most common form of Web advertising. However, new Web ad technology includes interstitial, Hyperstitial, or SUPERSTITIAL[tm].

An interstitial ad appears in a separate browser window while a Web page loads. Hyperstitial ads also play while a Web page loads, but are often presented in a full-screen, commercial-like format. A SUPERSTITIAL ad uses a technology created by Unicast to display animated, interactive ads that occur after the user interacts with a site, such as clicking a mouse.

HTML

HTML is discussed further in Chapter 3.

Marc Andreesen
1971 –

Mosaic was the first point-and-click graphic Web browser capable of displaying inline images. It was developed in 1993.

One of the developers, Marc Andreesen, founded Mosaic Communications Corporation, which later became Netscape Communications. Netscape Navigator remains a popular Web browser.

While the Internet and Web were originally developed to help the academic and scientific communities, the Web is being used more and more for advertising and e-commerce. It is common to find advertisements, called *banner ads*, on Web sites:

A banner ad is designed to entice a user to click it, which in turn displays the advertiser's page. Most Web sites host banner ads for a fee.

2.3 Web Browsers

A Web page is a document created with *HyperText Markup Language* (HTML) and possibly other code, and published to a Web server. An HTML document defines the content and layout of a Web page with tags that are surrounded by angle brackets (<>). The following HTML document contains five different tags:

```
<html>

<head>
<title>Example HTML Document</title>
</head>

<body>
<p>This is an example HTML document.</p>
</body>

</html>
```

This HTML document contains <html>, <head>, <title>, <body>, and <p> tags

A *Web browser* interprets an HTML document to display a Web page. Popular Web browsers are Internet Explorer and Netscape Navigator. When the HTML document shown above is interpreted by Internet Explorer it is displayed as:

This is an example HTML document.

Note the text enclosed by the <title> tags of the HTML document is displayed on the title bar of the browser window. The text enclosed by the <body> tags is displayed as the Web page content.

HTML documents are interpreted similarly regardless of the browser, but each browser has its own features and capabilities that can account for differences in the way a Web page is displayed.

Introducing the World Wide Web and Internet Explorer

2.4 URLs

Domain Names

A domain name can give clues about the organization that posted the Web page. For example, in the URL www.palmbeachpost.com, palmbeachpost represents the Palm Beach Post newspaper, and com is a top level domain that indicates a commercial organization. Other top level domains and their meaning include:

edu	educational institution
gov	government agency
mil	military facility
net	network organization
org	organization (nonprofit)
ca	Canadian site
uk	United Kingdom site

Every Web page has a URL (Uniform Resource Locator) associated with it. A *URL* is an address that is interpreted by a Web browser to identify the location of a page on the Web. For example, consider the URL for the Earth Day Network:

   http://www.earthday.net

The first part of the URL, *http*, is the Web protocol used to handle requests and the transmission of pages between a Web server and a Web browser. The two forward slashes (//) following the colon separate the protocol from the domain name, in this case www.earthday.net. A *domain name* is used to identify a particular Web page and is made up of a sequence of parts, or subnames, separated by a period. The subnames are called *labels* and may represent a server or organization. The suffix of a domain name is called the *top-level domain* and identifies the type of Web site. In this case .net indicates the site is a network organization.

A URL that contains a slash followed by a document name after the top level domain, such as www.earthday.net/about, indicates a Web page that is part of the Web site, but not the home page.

2.5 Using Internet Explorer

starting Internet Explorer

A Web browser is needed to view Web pages. In this text, the Internet Explorer Web browser is discussed. Internet Explorer is started by selecting Start → All Programs → Internet Explorer, which displays a browser window:

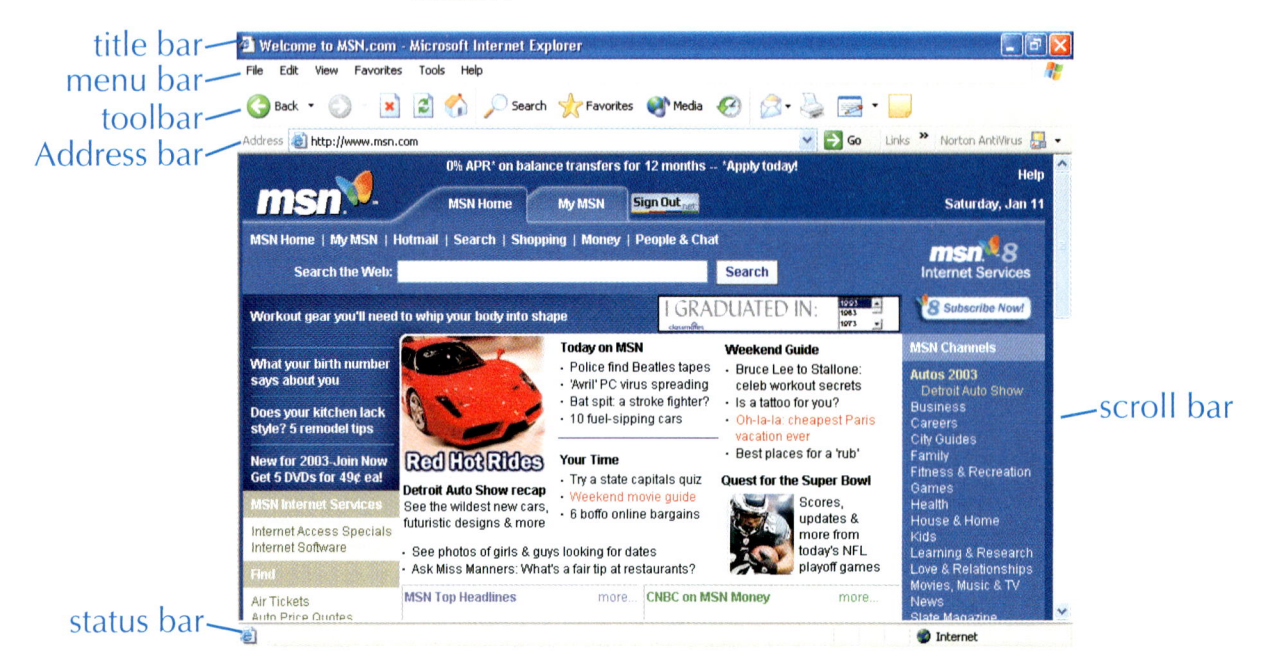

> **Home Page**
>
> The Web page that appears every time Internet Explorer is started is called the home page. The home page that appears can be changed by selecting **Tools → Internet Options** and then specifying a URL in the Home page Address box.

- The **title bar** displays the title of the displayed Web page, in this case Welcome to MSN.com.
- The **menu bar** contains the names of drop-down menus, which contain commands.
- The **toolbar** contains buttons that represent different actions.

    Back button Displays the previously displayed Web page.

    Forward button Displays the next Web page from the previously selected pages.

    Stop button Turns red when a Web page is loading. Can be clicked to stop the transmission of a Web page.

    Refresh button Updates the displayed Web page. Used to update the information on a page that changes frequently (e.g. stock prices) or when graphics do not load properly.

    Home button Displays a preselected Web page, which is the Web page that is displayed when Internet Explorer is first started.

    Search button Displays a pane used to locate Web pages that contain particular information.

    Favorites button Displays a pane with the Favorites list, which can be used to quickly view Web pages frequently accessed.

    History button Displays a pane with the URLs of Web sites that have been visited in the previous days and weeks.

    Print button Prints the currently displayed Web page.

- The **Address bar** displays the URL for displayed Web page. The Address bar is also used to display a Web page by typing the URL and pressing the Enter key.
- The **scroll bar** is dragged to bring unseen parts of the document into view.
- The **status bar** displays the progress of a loading Web page.

accessing a Web page

Typing a URL in the Address bar and then pressing Enter or clicking the Go button (Go) opens that Web page. Note that with Internet Explorer and most other browsers, it is not usually necessary to type the http:// of a URL because the browser will automatically add it. For example, the URL of the CNN home page is http://www.cnn.com, but it is only necessary to type www.cnn.com in the Address bar.

As the Web page opens, the status bar displays messages on the progress of opening the Web page, such as Web site found... or Opening page.... When the transmission is complete, the Stop button is dimmed and the status bar displays Done. If a transmission or transfer is taking too long, clicking the Stop button ends the attempted transmission. Another URL can then be entered.

Internet Explorer is quit by selecting **File → Close**, which closes the Internet Explorer window and removes the application from the computer's memory.

Introducing the World Wide Web and Internet Explorer   2 – 7

2.6 Surfing

Surfing means to browse Web pages looking for information on topics of interest. Hyperlinks are used for surfing and can be in the form of text or graphics. Text hyperlinks are typically blue and underlined, and a previously visited link is purple. As the mouse pointer is moved across a hyperlink, it changes to a hand shape (👆). Hyperlinks display a different part of a Web page, another page in the Web site, or a page in a different Web site.

The Web page below contains many hyperlinks:

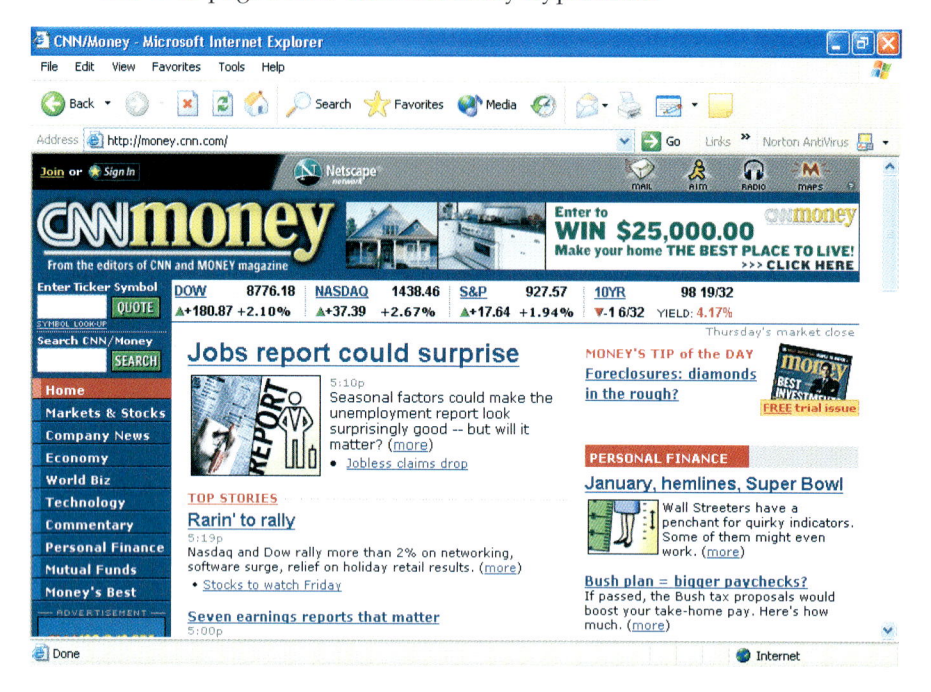

> **Surfing the Net**
>
> The phrase "surfing the net" was coined in 1992 when a librarian named Jean Armour Polly used a mouse pad with a picture of a surfer on it.

Practice 1

In this practice you will surf. This practice assumes you have Internet Explorer and access to the Internet.

① START INTERNET EXPLORER

Select Start → All Programs → Internet Explorer. Internet Explorer is started. Note that it may take a few seconds for the preselected home page to load.

② GO TO THE MSNBC HOME PAGE

a. In the Address bar, replace the existing URL with www.msnbc.com, the URL for the MSNBC home page.

b. Press Enter. The Web page is opened. Note the messages on the status bar as the Web page is loading.

c. Use the scroll bar if necessary to scroll through the home page.

③ VIEW MSNBC STORIES

a. Click a hyperlink that interests you.

b. Continue to surf MSNBC Web pages. Realize that a hyperlink may display a Web page at a site other than MSNBC. You can easily return to the MSNBC site by clicking the Back button (⬅ Back ▾) on the toolbar.

④ **QUIT INTERNET EXPLORER**

Select File → Close. Internet Explorer is closed.

2.7 The History List

The *History list* is a list of the pages that have been visited in the last 20 days. Clicking the History button ( ) on the toolbar displays the History pane on the left side of the Internet Explorer window:

History list viewed By Date

Sizing and Closing a Pane

A pane in a window may need to be sized in order to view the information in the pane. A pane is sized by pointing to a pane border to display a double-headed arrow and then dragging the mouse pointer.

A pane, such as the History pane or Favorites pane will be displayed in the left side of the window until closed. Clicking the Close button (x) in the pane closes the pane and the Web page in the right pane is expanded to fill the space.

The View button in the History pane can be used to specify how the History list is displayed. When viewing the History list By Site, clicking one of the sites in the list displays a sublist of that Web site's pages that were accessed. Clicking a page displays that page in the right pane. When viewing the History list By Date, clicking a category displays the URLs for the Web sites accessed for that category. Viewing the History list By Most Visited or By Order Visited Today displays the most viewed pages and the pages accessed that day, respectively.

Practice 2

In this practice you will view two Web pages and then return to selected pages using the History list.

① **START INTERNET EXPLORER**

② **GO TO THE CNN HOME PAGE**

  a. In the Address bar, replace the existing URL with www.cnn.com, the URL for the CNN home page.

  b. Press Enter. The Web page is opened. Use the scroll bar if necessary to scroll through the CNN home page.

Introducing the World Wide Web and Internet Explorer   2 – 9

③ GO TO THE FLORIDA ATLANTIC UNIVERSITY HOME PAGE

a. In the Address bar, replace the existing URL with www.fau.edu, the URL for the Florida Atlantic University home page.

b. Press Enter. The Web page is opened. Use the scroll bar if necessary to scroll through the Florida Atlantic University home page.

④ USE THE HISTORY LIST TO ACCESS WEB PAGES

a. On the toolbar, click the History button ( ). The History pane is displayed on the left side of the window.

b. In the History pane, click the View button and then select By Order Visited Today.

c. Click CNN.com. The CNN home page is displayed.

d. In the History pane, click the View button and then select By Date. Note a folder is displayed for sites visited today.

e. Click the Today folder.

f. Click the fau folder. The Internet Explorer link to the Florida Atlantic University home page is displayed. Click the link. The Florida Atlantic University home page is displayed.

2.8 The Favorites List

The *Favorites list* is used to maintain a list of Web pages. Clicking the Favorites button (Favorites) on the toolbar displays the Favorites pane in the left side of the window:

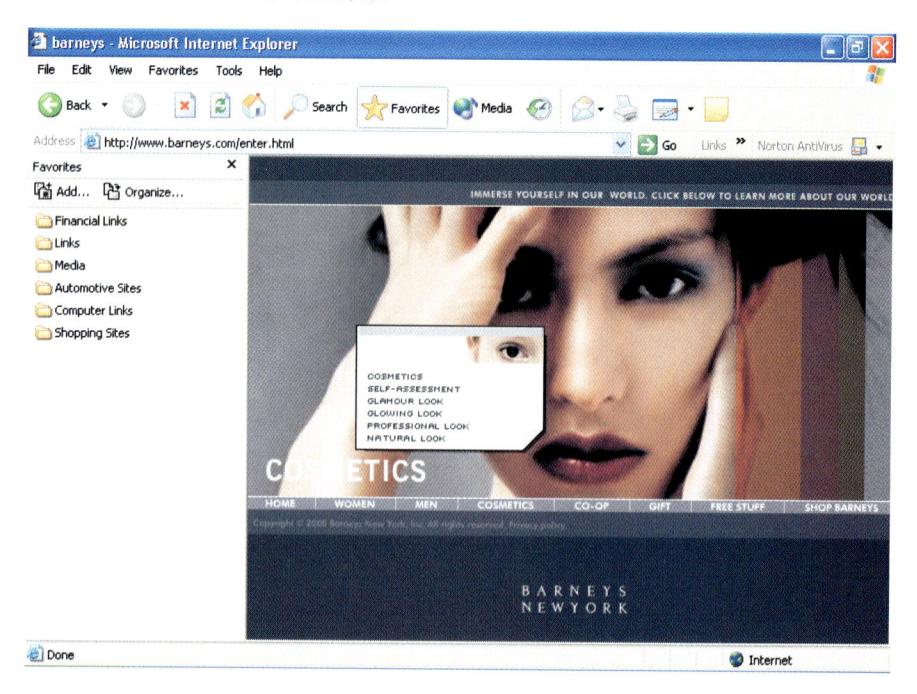

Selecting any of the Web pages in the list will access that page and display it in the pane in the right side of the window. A Favorites list can be organized using folders, as shown above and on the next page. Clicking a folder displays the Web pages stored in that folder.

The currently displayed Web page can be added to the Favorites list by clicking the Add button (Add...) in the Favorites pane, which displays a dialog box:

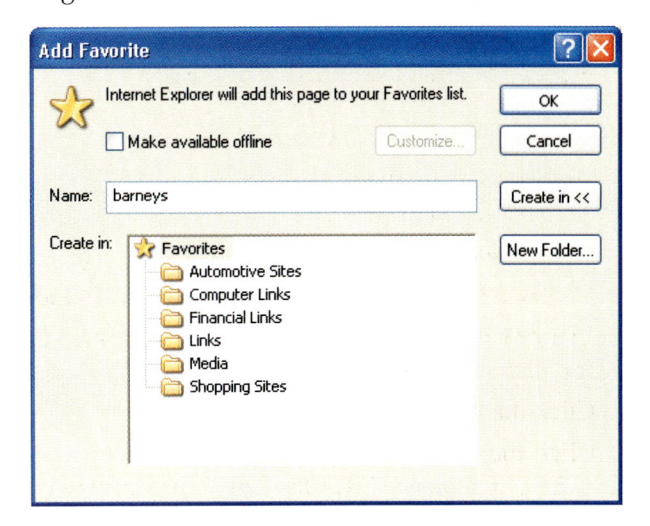

Add Favorite

Internet Explorer will add this page to your Favorites list.

☐ Make available offline

Name: barneys

Create in: Favorites
- Automotive Sites
- Computer Links
- Financial Links
- Links
- Media
- Shopping Sites

[OK] [Cancel] [Create in <<] [New Folder...]

> **Folders**
>
> Folders are used to organize related files. More information about folders can be found by downloading the appropriate operating system chapter at www.lpdatafiles.com.

Clicking a folder in the Create in list and then selecting OK adds the page title to the list in that folder. Clicking New Folder displays a dialog box for creating a new folder in the Favorites list.

The Organize button (Organize...) in the Favorites pane is used to display a dialog box where folders can be created and renamed, moved, or deleted. The URLs can also be moved, renamed, or deleted. Commands from the Favorites menu can also be used to view and organize the Favorites list.

Practice 3

In this practice you will access a Web page and add it to the Favorites list. Start Internet Explorer if it is not already displayed.

① GO TO THE GAP HOME PAGE

  a. In the Address bar, replace the existing URL with www.gap.com, the URL for the Gap home page.

  b. Press Enter. The Web page is opened. Use the scroll bar if necessary to scroll through the Gap's home page.

② ADD A WEB PAGE TO THE FAVORITES LIST

  a. On the toolbar, click the Favorites button (Favorites). The Favorites pane is displayed in the left side of the window.

  b. In the Favorites pane, click the Add button (Add...). A dialog box is displayed.

   1. Select the New Folder button. Another dialog box is displayed.

      a. In the Folder name box, type Shopping Sites.

      b. Select OK. The dialog box is removed.

   2. Select OK. The dialog box is removed and the current page is added to the Shopping Sites folder in the Favorites list.

Introducing the World Wide Web and Internet Explorer   2 – 11

③ **GO TO ANOTHER WEB PAGE**

    a. In the Address bar, replace the existing URL with www.roots.com, the URL for the Roots home page.

    b. Press Enter. The Web page is opened. Use the scroll bar if necessary to scroll through the Roots home page.

④ **RETURN TO A FAVORITE WEB PAGE**

    a. In the Favorites pane, click the Shopping Sites folder to display the page you added.

    b. Click the link for Gap Online. The selected page is displayed in the right pane.

⑤ **DELETE A FOLDER FROM THE FAVORITES LIST**

In the Favorites pane, click the Organize button (Organize...). A dialog box is displayed.

    1. Click the Shopping Sites folder to select it.

    2. Click the Delete button. A warning is displayed. Select Yes to delete the folder and its contents.

    3. Select Close. The dialog box is removed.

⑥ **CLOSE THE FAVORITES PANE**

2.9 Print Preview and Printing a Web Page

Long Web pages may require several sheets of paper for a printout. Selecting File → Print Preview displays the Web page as it will appear when printed, indicating the number of pages, as in the Earth Day Network home page print preview:

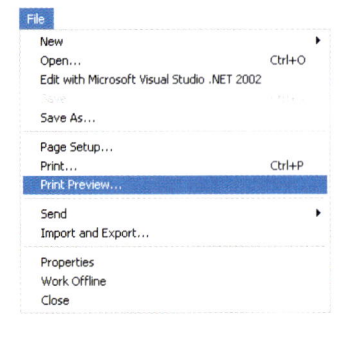

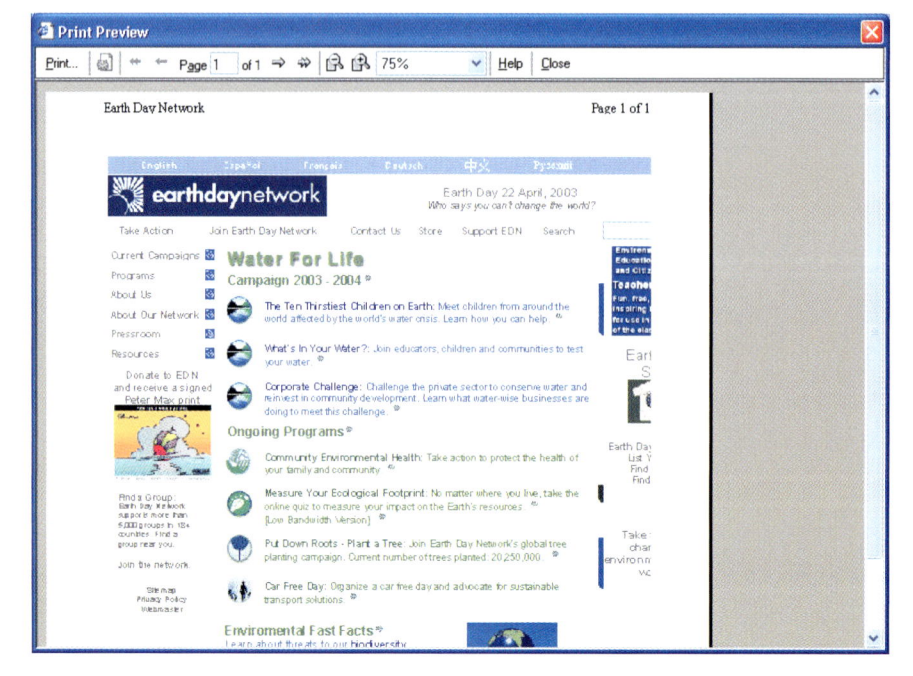

A Guide to Web Development Using Macromedia Dreamweaver MX

Buttons in the print preview window can be used to change the displayed page:

→ **Next page button** Displays the next page of a multipage document. The next page can also be displayed using the vertical scroll bar.

← **Previous page button** Displays the previous page of a multipage document. The previous page can also be displayed using the vertical scroll bar.

⇉ **Last page button** Skips to the last page.

⇇ **First page button** Skips to the first page.

Zoom In button Enlarges the preview so that details can be seen.

Zoom Out button Reduces the preview size.

Close **Close button** Closes the Print Preview window.

Print... **Print button** Displays the Print dialog box similar to:

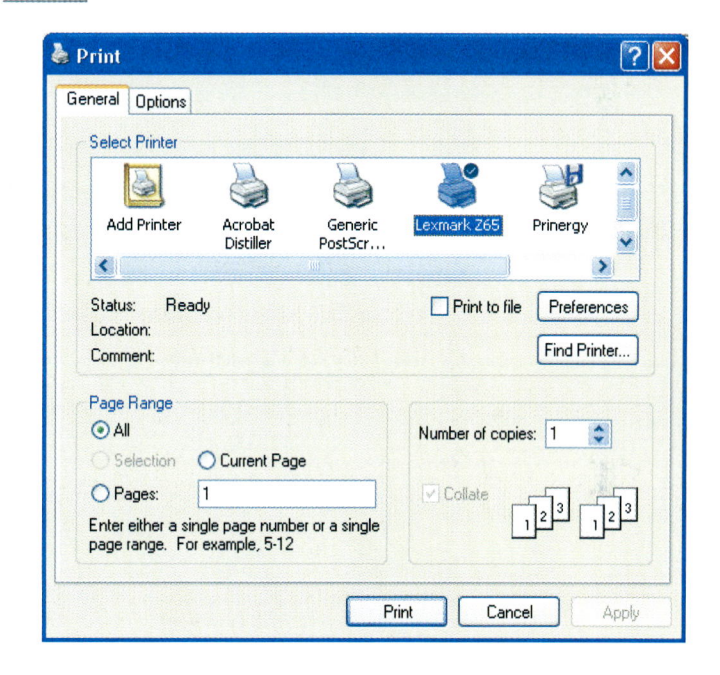

The Pages box is used to print specific pages. The Number of copies box is used to select or type a number corresponding to the number of copies to be printed. Selecting Print begins printing.

Selecting File → Print also displays the Print dialog box. The Print button (🖨) on the toolbar can also be used to print the displayed Web page using the default print settings.

Introducing the World Wide Web and Internet Explorer   2 – 13

Practice 4

In this practice you will use the print preview and then print a Web page. Start Internet Explorer if it is not already displayed.

① **GO TO THE EARTH DAY NETWORK HOME PAGE**

In the Address bar, replace the existing URL with www.earthday.net, the URL for the Earth Day Network home page. Press Enter.

② **PRINT PREVIEW AND THEN PRINT THE EARTH DAY NETWORK HOME PAGE**

   a. Select File → Print Preview. The Print Preview window is displayed.
   b. Click the Zoom In button ( ) twice to enlarge the preview.
   c. Click the Zoom Out button ( ) twice to reduce the preview.
   d. Click the Next Page button (→) to preview page 2.
   e. Click the Previous Page button (←) to preview page 1.
   f. Click the Print button (Print...). A dialog box is displayed.
      1. Select Print to accept the default print settings. The Web page is printed.

2.10 Searching the Web

A *search engine* is a program that searches a database of Web pages for keywords and then lists hyperlinks to pages that contain those keywords. Commonly used search engines include:

Yahoo! (www.yahoo.com)
Northern Light (www.northernlight.com)
HotBot (www.hotbot.com)
Excite (www.excite.com)
Snap.com (www.snap.com)
Ask Jeeves (www.ask.com)
Go Network (www.go.com)
Google (www.google.com)
Overture (www.overture.com)
Lycos (www.lycos.com)
WebCrawler (www.webcrawler.com)
FAST Search (www.alltheweb.com)
About.com (www.about.com)
AltaVista (www.altavista.com)
Looksmart (www.looksmart.com)

Search Engines

A search engine usually works by sending out an agent, such as spider. A *spider* is an application that gathers a list of available Web page documents and stores this list in a database that users can search by keywords. Refer to Chapter 10 for more information about keywords.

search criteria

match

A search engine can be queried to display specific Web pages. *Search criteria* can include single words or phrases that are then used by the engine to determine a match. A *match* is a Web page that contains the search criteria. For example, to locate information about the Leaning Tower of Pisa, the search criteria Leaning Tower of Pisa could be entered. The search engine will then display hyperlinks to pages in its database that contain information about the Leaning Tower of Pisa. The search criteria could also be the words Pisa or tower, but the more specific the search criteria, the better the chance the information will be found.

Practice 5

In this practice you will search the Web using a search engine. Start Internet Explorer if it is not already displayed.

① **GO TO THE YAHOO! SEARCH ENGINE**

In the Address bar, replace the existing URL with www.yahoo.com, the URL for Yahoo!'s home page, and then press Enter. The Yahoo! home page is displayed.

② **TYPE SEARCH CRITERIA**

a. In the Search text box, type stonehenge

b. Click Search to start the search. After a few moments a list of Web site hyperlinks are displayed. How many matches are there?

c. Scroll down to display the results of the search, then click one of the hyperlinks that interests you to go to its Web page. A new page is transmitted and displayed.

③ **SELECT OTHER WEB PAGES LOCATED IN THE SEARCH**

a. On the toolbar, click the Back button (Back). The Web site hyperlinks are again displayed. Click a different Web page hyperlink.

b. Continue this process to access additional pages.

2.11 Searching by Category

subject tree, Web directory

Some search engines provide a *subject tree*, or *Web directory*, which is a list of sites separated into categories. The term subject tree is used because many of the categories "branch" off into subcategories. These subcategories allow the user to narrow down the subject and display a list of appropriate hyperlinks, which are at the lowest level of the tree. One search engine that uses a subject tree is Google:

Introducing the World Wide Web and Internet Explorer

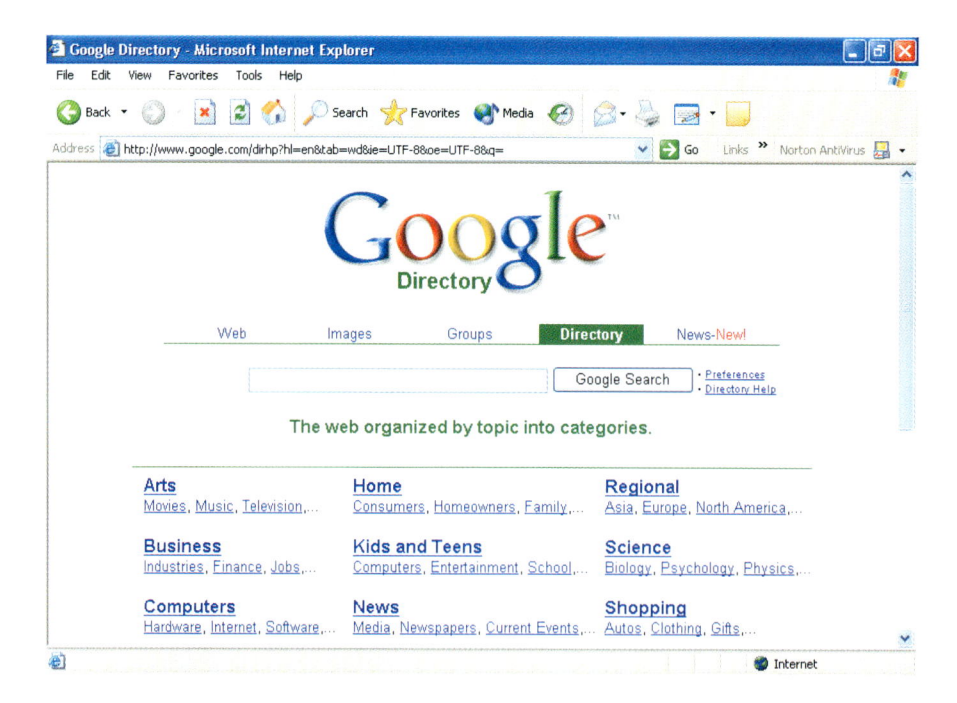

Clicking a category link produces a large list of subcategories. As selections are made, the list is narrowed until Google finally displays a list of appropriate sites including descriptions and hyperlinks to the sites. Note that for any subject tree, a staff of editors has determined which sites to include, a list that is far from all inclusive.

Practice 6

In this practice you will search the Web using Google's subject tree. Start Internet Explorer if it is not already displayed.

① **GO TO THE GOOGLE SEARCH ENGINE**

   a. In the Address bar, replace the existing URL with www.google.com, the URL for Google's home page, and then press Enter. The Google home page is displayed.

   b. Click the Directory link. The Google Directory page is displayed.

② **FIND A SOFTWARE RETAILER USING A SUBJECT TREE**

   a. Scroll down if necessary and click the Computers link in the list of Google Directory categories. Links to Computers subcategories are displayed.

   b. Scroll down if necessary and click the Shopping link.

   c. In the Computer Shopping subcategories list, click the Software Retailers link. A list of hyperlinks to appropriate sites is displayed.

   d. Click on one of the hyperlinks. The corresponding home page is displayed.

2.12 Advanced Search Techniques

Most searches yield far too many matches to be useful. Limiting the number of matches to a reasonable number can usually be accomplished by using Boolean logic in the search criteria. For example, entering hawaii as the criteria using the AltaVista search engine returns more than 4,500,000 matches, but the criteria hawaii +museums reduces the results to around 61,000 matches.

+ plus sign

Separating words with a space finds Web pages that contain all the words in the criteria. The + (plus sign) can also be used in search criteria to limit a search to only Web pages that contain all of the specified words. For example, a search for florida +hotel or florida hotel returns only links to pages containing both words. More than one + can be used to refine a search, for example the criteria florida +hotel +pool returns only links to pages containing all three words. AND can be used in place of + in most search engines.

AND

OR

OR can be used in most search engines to find Web pages that contain any one of the words in the criteria. For example, the criteria florida OR hotel returns links to pages containing either of the words. This is useful to search for a word that has more than one possible spelling, for example color OR colour.

– minus sign

The – (minus sign) is used to exclude unwanted Web pages. For example, the search for shakespeare –play returns hyperlinks to pages containing the word shakespeare, but eliminates pages that also contain the word play. NOT can be used in place of – in most search engines. For example, the criteria florida NOT hotel returns only hyperlinks to pages containing the word florida, but eliminates pages that also contain the word hotel.

NOT

Boolean Logic

A search can be more precise by applying Boolean logic in search criteria. Boolean logic uses three logical operators:

AND locates pages that include both words

OR locates pages that include one word or the other

NOT locates pages that include the first word, but not the second word

A boolean expression always evaluates to TRUE or FALSE with pages that match the search condition evaluating to TRUE.

The +, –, and space can be combined to produce more precise criteria. For example:

horse +buggy –carriage

tuna salmon –salad

recipe chicken –soup

university +connecticut –yale

Phrases can be used as search criteria by surrounding several words with quotation marks. For example, a search for "to be or not to be" or "rock and roll" will only return Web pages that contain the entire phrase.

Not all search engines make use of plus signs, spaces, minus signs, and quotation marks as described in this section. Before using a search engine, read that search engine's help pages to determine how to best structure the criteria.

Introducing the World Wide Web and Internet Explorer

Practice 7

In this practice you will search the Web using advanced search techniques. Start Internet Explorer if it is not already displayed.

① GO TO THE YAHOO! SEARCH ENGINE

In the Address bar, replace the existing URL with www.yahoo.com, the URL for Yahoo!'s home page, and then press Enter. The Yahoo! home page is displayed.

② ENTER AND REFINE THE SEARCH CRITERIA

a. Perform a search using the criteria shakespeare. Scroll to Web Matches to check the number of matches.

b. Refine the criteria to shakespeare +"Globe Theatre" and see how many Web page matches there are. Note the Next Search box is at the bottom of the page.

c. Refine the criteria to shakespeare +"Globe Theatre" +reconstruction and see how many Web page matches there are.

d. Further refine the criteria to shakespeare +"Globe Theatre" +reconstruction –usa and see how many Web page matches there are.

e. Click a few of the hyperlinks to determine if their Web pages include the type of information that is being searched for.

2.13 Evaluating Web Sites

Information found at a Web site, like most information, should be evaluated for accuracy. Anyone can post a Web site on the Web. There are no rules as to the accuracy or reliability of the information. This means that you must discriminate, read carefully, and check sources.

A few topics to think about and questions to answer when evaluating a source are:

- **Up-to-date.** On what date was the Web page last updated? Is the information current?

- **Bias.** Is the information incorrect or incomplete in order to give a particular or slanted view of a topic?

- **Validity.** Is the information truthful and trustworthy? What is the primary source of the information? Information posted by NASA or Yale University is more likely to be valid than information posted by a high school student who cites no sources.

- **Author.** Does the author present his or her credentials? A well established authority in the field you are researching is probably a trustworthy source.

copyright

A *copyright* protects a piece of work (artwork, documents, etc.) from reproduction without permission from the work's author. This includes material in an electronic format, such as information found on the Internet. Therefore it is necessary to cite sources. Material found on the Internet may be protected by copyright laws even if a copyright notice is not displayed.

2.14 Citing Web Pages

The primary purpose of a citation is to give credit to the original author and allow the reader to locate the cited information. A widely accepted form for citation is published by the Modern Language Association (MLA) in its publication *MLA Handbook for Writers of Research Papers, Fourth Edition*. A citation for material located at a Web site should start with the author's name, and include either an underlined title of the site or a plain description of the Web page. The citation should also include the name of any organization associated with the site, the date it was accessed, and the URL surrounded by the angle brackets (<>):

MLA

Author's Last Name, First Name MI. <u>Site Title</u>. Access date. Organization name. <URL>.

For example:

Rawlings, Julie. <u>Cellular Biology Online</u>. 23 Dec. 2004. Ivy University. <http://www.lpdatafiles.com>.

Citing Online Sources

Information used to support research must be cited. This includes online sources of information such as e-mail, graphics, sounds, video clips, and newsgroups. The MLA's Web site (www.mla.org) contains information on how to cite many types of online sources.

Practice 8

In this practice you will cite a Web page. Start Internet Explorer if it is not already displayed.

① SEARCH FOR INFORMATION

Use one of the search engines listed in Section 2.10 to search for Web pages about the Egyptian Step Pyramid of Djoser.

② EVALUATE WEB SITES

Browse the links to find a Web page that contains reliable information.

③ CITE THE WEB PAGE

Use the information on the Web page to write an example citation.

2.15 What is E-mail?

E-mail means electronic mail and is the sending and receiving of messages and computer files over a communications network such as a LAN or the Internet.

An e-mail address is required in order to send and receive e-mail messages. E-mail addresses are provided when you sign up with an ISP or an online service. A typical e-mail address is similar to:

christina@lpdatafiles.com

user name — host or domain name — top-level domain

Introducing the World Wide Web and Internet Explorer

Ray Tomlinson
1941 –

Ray Tomlinson created the first e-mail application in 1971. His use of the @ sign in an e-mail address to connect the user name with the domain name has become standard.

E-mail software is also required for sending and receiving e-mail messages. Examples of e-mail software include Outlook Express and Eudora. Free e-mail accounts, known as browser-based e-mail, are also available through numerous sites such as Yahoo! and Hotmail. These accounts require only a Web browser such as Internet Explorer.

2.16   Using Outlook Express

Outlook Express is the e-mail messaging software discussed in this text. Outlook Express is accessible from Internet Explorer by using the Mail button ( ) on the toolbar. Clicking Read Mail in the Mail button starts Outlook Express, and displays the Inbox window:

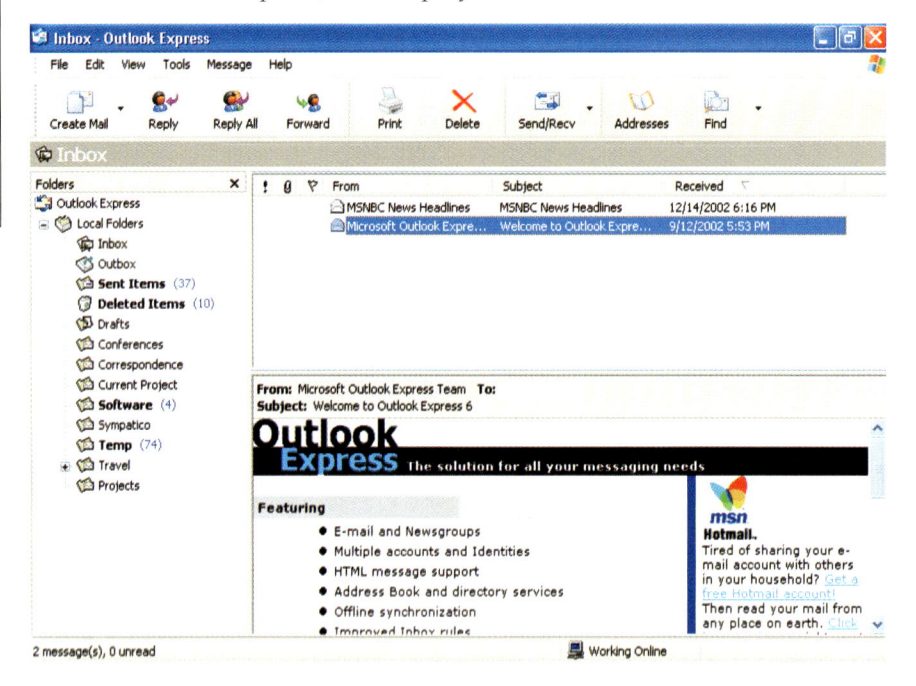

The Inbox window contains three panes. The pane on the left is the Folders list where e-mail messages are stored. The top pane lists the messages in the selected folder, and the bottom pane displays the selected message.

Clicking the Create Mail button ( ) on the toolbar displays a New Message window where an e-mail message can be composed:

A Guide to Web Development Using Macromedia Dreamweaver MX

Agents and Daemons

Agents and daemons are programs that work in the background to perform a task. System agent and mailer-daemon programs move e-mail between hosts on a network.

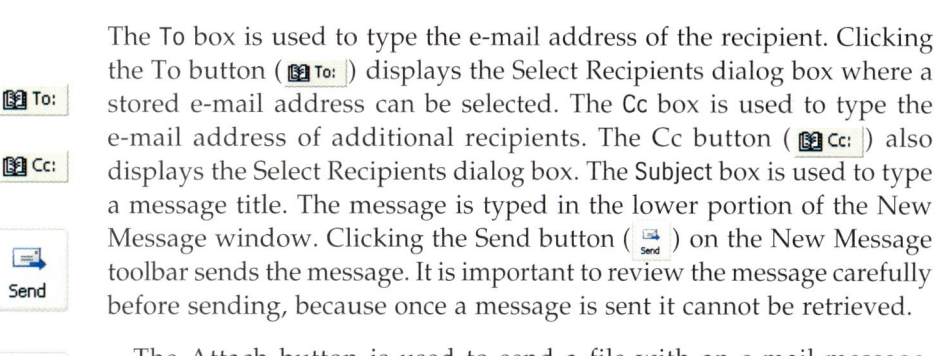

The To box is used to type the e-mail address of the recipient. Clicking the To button ( ) displays the Select Recipients dialog box where a stored e-mail address can be selected. The Cc box is used to type the e-mail address of additional recipients. The Cc button ( ) also displays the Select Recipients dialog box. The Subject box is used to type a message title. The message is typed in the lower portion of the New Message window. Clicking the Send button ( ) on the New Message toolbar sends the message. It is important to review the message carefully before sending, because once a message is sent it cannot be retrieved.

The Attach button is used to send a file with an e-mail message. Clicking the Attach button ( ) displays the Insert Attachment dialog box:

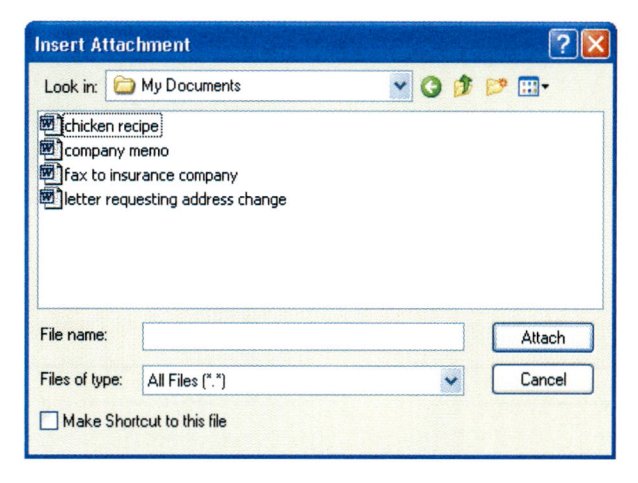

The Look in list and contents box below it are used to navigate to the file to be attached. Clicking the file name in the contents box and then selecting Attach attaches a copy of the file to the e-mail message.

When an e-mail message is sent, it resides in an electronic mailbox on a mail server until it is retrieved. The Send and Receive All button ( ) on the toolbar is clicked to receive messages from the e-mail server and place them in the Inbox folder.

Introducing the World Wide Web and Internet Explorer 2 – 21

> **POP3**
>
> The way sent messages are received varies from system to system. POP3 (Post Office Protocol 3) is the most common protocol used to retrieve messages from an e-mail server.

Other commonly used features in Outlook Express include:

Reply button   Displays an e-mail message window that includes the original message and the sender's e-mail address in the To box. The Reply button should be used to respond to an e-mail message so that the recipient can refer to the original message.

Forward button   Sends a selected e-mail message to another e-mail address. A forwarded message includes the original e-mail message and the original sender's e-mail address. Additional information can be added above the original message.

Print button   Prints the displayed e-mail message.

Delete button   Places the selected e-mail message in the Deleted Items folder. The e-mail can be permanently deleted by right-clicking the Deleted Items folder in the Folders list and selecting Empty 'Deleted Items' Folder and clicking Yes.

Address Book button   Display the address book for editing purposes.

Find button   Searches for specific messages.

quitting Outlook Express

Outlook Express is quit by selecting File → Exit, which closes the Outlook Express window and removes the application from the computer's memory.

2.17   E-mail Etiquette

E-mail is not private and should be thought of the same way as sending a postcard where others may read the message. E-mail goes through several mail servers before it reaches the designated desktop, making it easily accessible for others to read. Therefore, professional courtesy should be used when sending electronic messages:

- Send messages through your account only.
- Use appropriate subject matter and language.
- Be considerate of other people's beliefs and opinions.

> **Viruses**
>
> Computer viruses have varying effects, such as displaying annoying messages, causing programs to run incorrectly, and erasing the contents of the hard drive. Antivirus software should be installed and updated frequently to help avoid viruses.
>
> Antivirus software will detect many types of viruses by scanning incoming e-mail messages before they are opened. If a virus is detected, the software will display a warning and try to remove the virus.

When receiving e-mail, it is important to take precautions to avoid computer viruses. A virus can come from a familiar e-mail address because many viruses target address books. Messages from unfamiliar individuals or companies require extra precautions. Just opening an infected e-mail could spread the virus to your computer. Computer viruses are also in the form of e-mail attachments. Always save an attached file and virus check the file before opening it.

2.18   IT Careers

The growth of the Web has created many new job opportunities in the IT (information technology) field. *IT* encompasses all aspects of computer-related technology.

education

Education requirements for IT careers vary widely. However, a formal education, such as an undergraduate degree in computer science, engineering, or business, is often required. A graduate degree may also be required in highly specialized fields. Some careers require a specialized certification course in an area such as networking. Other skills that are required in this industry are teamwork, problem-solving skills, oral and written communication, up-to-date technical knowledge, and computer experience.

Web careers

IT careers include Web careers, a job market that is continually expanding and changing. Web career job titles, duties, and education and experience requirements vary from company to company. Typically the larger the company, the more specialized the job will be. For example, in a large company, a Web developer may just implement a Web site. Whereas, in a small company the Web developer may design, implement, and maintain the Web site.

> **Information Architect**
>
> An information architect is a person who creates a vision of what a Web site will look like and defines how it will work. Their job involves all aspects of planning the site, and may include helping with the implementation.

Web professionals often specialize in areas of expertise such as information architecture, programming, graphics, animations, or marketing, to name just a few. Job experience and specialized training are usually required to gain expertise in a particular area.

Typical Web career titles and job descriptions include:

Web developer

Web developers design, build, and program Web sites. They determine the Web site strategy, which includes the hardware to be used and the design and navigation of the site. They also design tools, such as reports and databases, to measure the success of the Web site.

Web developers require programming and technical skills. Often the development is divided into back-end development and front-end development. Back-end development involves designing the hardware and database infrastructure, such as where orders are fulfilled. Front-end development involves the navigation and design of the Web site.

Web designer

Web designers create the Web page layouts and graphics for Web sites. The work a Web designer does usually determines whether users will stay at a Web site. Their job involves presenting Web pages so they are interesting and accessible.

A Web designer requires knowledge of HTML, Web implementation software such as Dreamweaver and Flash, and graphic editing software such as Fireworks, PhotoShop, or Illustrator. Since technology changes rapidly, Web designers must keep up-to-date on new technologies, techniques, and design standards.

Webmaster

Webmaster responsibilities can include designing and creating Web pages and maintaining the site. A Webmaster is also responsible for answering e-mail about the Web site. A Webmaster possesses extensive Internet knowledge, programming skills, and design experience.

Web author

Web authors create textual content for Web pages. A Web author has good writing skills and carefully considers the text as it will be presented on the Web.

Introducing the World Wide Web and Internet Explorer

2.19 IT Companies

Most large companies have an IT department. Careers in these departments include the Web careers discussed in Section 2.18 as well as:

intranet analyst
- *Intranet analysts* set up and maintain an intranet for a company or organization. This involves managing company intranet projects, technical support, and creating reports. This job requires technical knowledge of networks, network security features, computers, and software as well as personal communication skills.

network administrator
- A *network administrator* is responsible for a company's network. Duties could include installing the network hardware and software, as well as maintaining the network so it runs properly. LAN manager is another term for network administrator.

There are also many small to large companies that strictly provide IT services. These companies include:

ISP
- *ISPs* (Internet Service Providers) provide access to the Internet. Employees have a wide range of technical knowledge about networks, computers, and software since clients will have a variety of equipment. Personal communication skills are also necessary for sales and technical support.

Web host
- *Web hosts* provide space on a server where users can post their Web pages. Employees have technical knowledge of networks, computers, and the World Wide Web. Personal communication skills are also necessary for sales and technical support.

2.20 Pursuing an IT Career

The growth of the Web has resulted in colleges and universities changing their program offerings to better prepare students for careers in IT. Some degree options that are offered at a variety of schools include:

- Media, Information, and Technoculture
- Computer Arts
- Computer Engineering
- Computer Animation
- Information Technologies Support Services
- International Telecommunications Systems and Service
- Internet Commerce and Technology
- Electronic Media, Arts, and Communication

When selecting a college or university program, factors such as cost, length of program, program location, and course content should be examined. It is always a good idea to visit the school campus before deciding on a program.

A program that sounds interesting at a college or university should be matched to the job market. Employment opportunity ads should be examined to determine the demand for the specific job, job locations, salary range, and educational requirements.

Many colleges and universities are requiring students to submit an electronic portfolio as part of the admissions process. An example electronic portfolio is created using Dreamweaver in Chapter 9.

It is a good idea to keep an updated list of any acquired computer skills and knowledge in order to update a portfolio, create a resume, or complete a job application. Working through this text will help develop valuable computer skills that could help with a future job including:

- data entry skills
- knowledge of HTML
- Web site design and development using Dreamweaver

Chapter Summary

The World Wide Web is the total collection of Web pages that are stored on Web servers located all over the world. A series of related Web pages that are connected by hyperlinks make up a Web site. The main page is designated as the home page.

Most Web sites fall into one of the following categories: personal, commercial, informational, media, and portal. Web sites often host banner ads for a fee.

A Web page is a document created with Hypertext Markup Language (HTML). A Web browser interprets the HTML to display a Web page. A URL is an address that is interpreted by a Web browser to identify the location of a page on the Web.

A Web browser is needed to view Web pages. Surfing means to browse Web pages using hyperlinks, which can be in the form of text or graphics.

In Internet Explorer, the History list is a list of the pages that have been visited in the last 20 days and the Favorites list is used to maintain a list of important Web pages. Long Web pages may require several sheets of paper for a printout. Selecting File → Print Preview displays the Web page as it will appear when printed, indicating the number of pages.

A search engine is a program that searches a database of Web pages for keywords and then lists hyperlinks to pages that contain those keywords. Search criteria is entered, which is used by the search engine to determine a match. Limiting the number of matches to a reasonable number can be accomplished using Boolean logic in the search criteria. Some search engines also provide a subject tree, or Web directory.

Information found at a Web site should be evaluated for accuracy. A copyright protects a piece of work (such as artwork or documents) from reproduction without permission from the work's author. This includes material in an electronic format.

Introducing the World Wide Web and Internet Explorer　　2 – 25

There are guidelines for citing electronic material on the Internet. The primary purpose of a citation is to give credit to the original author and allow the reader to locate the cited information.

E-mail is the sending and receiving of messages and computer files over a communications network such as a LAN or the Internet. E-mail software is required for online communications. E-mail is not private and should be thought of the same way as sending a postcard where others may read the message. Professional courtesy should be used when sending electronic messages. Many computer viruses have been associated with e-mail attachments.

The growth of the World Wide Web has created many new job opportunities in the IT field. IT stands for information technology and encompasses all aspects of computer-related technology.

Web careers include Web developer, Web designer, Webmaster, and Web author. Many companies have IT departments with positions for intranet professionals and network administrators. Other companies, such such as ISPs and Web hosts, specialize in IT services. Positions at these companies require a wide range of technical knowledge about networks, computers, and software. Careers in sales and technical support are also available.

The growth of the Web has resulted in colleges and universities changing their program offerings to better prepare students for careers in Web authoring or IT. Consider factors such as cost, length of program, program location, and course content when selecting a college or university program. Keep an updated list of your computer skills and knowledge to include in portfolios, resumes, or job applications.

Vocabulary

Banner ad One type of advertisement on Web sites.

Commercial Web site A business-related Web site such as corporate presence or e-commerce.

Copyright Protects a piece of work from reproduction without permission from the work's author.

Corporate Presence Web site A Web site created by companies and organizations for the purpose of displaying information about their products or services.

E-commerce Web site A Web site created by businesses for the purposes of selling their products or services to consumers online.

E-mail (electronic mail) The sending and receiving of messages and computer files over a communications network such as a LAN or the Internet.

Favorites list A list of Web pages that have been added to the Internet Explorer Favorites list.

History list A list of the Web pages that have been visited in the last 20 days in Internet Explorer.

Home page The main page of a Web site.

Hyperlink Text or graphics on a Web page that can be clicked to display another portion of that same page or another Web page.

Hypertext Markup Language (HTML) The markup language used to create Web pages.

Informational Web site A Web site created by educational institutions, governments, and organizations for the purpose of displaying information about a particular topic.

Intranet analyst Sets up and maintains intranets for companies or organizations.

IT (Information Technology) A term that encompasses all aspects of computer-related technology.

Link *See* Hyperlink.

Match A Web page that contains the search criteria.

Media Web site Online newspaper and periodicals that are created by companies for the purpose of informing readers about current events and issues.

Minus sign (–) Used in search criteria to exclude unwanted Web pages.

Network administrator Responsible for a company's network. Also called LAN Manager.

Personal Web site A Web site created by an individual for the purpose of displaying information about themselves.

Plus sign (+) Used in search criteria to limit a search to only those Web pages containing two or more specified words.

Portal Web site A Web site created by businesses for the purpose of creating a starting point for people to enter the Web.

Post The process of copying Web site files to a Web server.

Search criteria Single words or phrases that are used by the search engine to match Web pages.

Search engine A program that searches a database of Web pages for keywords and then lists hyperlinks to pages that contain those keywords.

Spaces Used to separate words in search criteria to find pages that contain any of the criteria words.

Subject tree A list of sites separated into categories.

Surfing Browse Web pages looking for information on topics of interest to the user.

URL An address that is interpreted by a Web browser to identify the location of a page on the Web.

Web author Writes content for Web pages.

Web browser Interprets an HTML document to display a Web page.

Web designer Creates the Web page layouts and graphics for Web sites.

Web developer Designs, builds, and programs Web sites.

Web directory *See* Subject tree.

Web host A company that provides a Web server for Web authors to post their Web sites to.

Webmaster Designs and creates Web pages, creates graphics for the site, and maintains the site.

Web site A series of related Web pages that are connected by hyperlinks.

World Wide Web (WWW) The total collection of Web pages that are stored on Web servers located all over the world.

Internet Explorer Commands and Buttons

Back button Displays the previously selected Web page. Found on the toolbar.

Close command Used to quit Internet Explorer. Found in the File menu.

Favorites button Displays a pane with the Favorites list, which can be used to quickly view Web pages frequently accessed. Found on the toolbar.

Forward button Displays the next Web page from the previously selected pages. Found on the toolbar.

Go button Opens the Web page that has the URL that was typed in the Address bar. Found on the Address bar.

History button Displays a pane with the URLs of Web sites that have been visited in the previous days and weeks. Found on the toolbar.

Home button Displays a preselected Web page, which is the Web page that is displayed when Internet Explorer is first started. Found on the toolbar.

Internet Explorer command Starts Internet Explorer. Found in the Programs submenu in the Start menu on the Windows Taskbar.

Mail button Displays a submenu of Outlook Express commands. Found on the toolbar.

Print command Prints the currently displayed Web page. Found in the File menu. The Print button on the toolbar can be used instead of the command.

Print Preview command Displays the Web page as it will appear when printed. Found in the File menu.

Refresh button Updates the displayed Web page. Found on the toolbar.

Search button Displays a pane used to locate Web pages that contain particular information. Found on the toolbar.

Stop button Turns red when Internet Explorer is loading a Web page. Can be used to stop the transmission of a Web page. Found on the toolbar.

Outlook Express Commands and Buttons

Address Book button Displays the address book. Found on the toolbar.

Attach button Displays a dialog box that is used to send a file with an e-mail message. Found on the New Message toolbar.

Cc button Displays the address book that is used to select e-mail addresses for additional recipients. Found in the New Message window.

Create Mail button Displays a New Message window that is used to compose an e-mail message. Found on the toolbar.

Delete button Places the selected e-mail message in the Deleted Items folder. Found on the toolbar.

Exit command Closes the Outlook Express window and removes the application from the computer's memory. Found in the File menu.

Find button Searches for specific messages. Found on the toolbar.

Forward button Sends a selected e-mail message to another e-mail address. Found on the toolbar.

Print button Prints the selected e-mail message. Found on the toolbar.

Reply button Displays an e-mail message window that includes the original message and the sender's e-mail address in the To box. The Reply button should be used to respond to an e-mail message. Found on the toolbar.

Send/Receive button Receives messages from the e-mail server. Found on the toolbar.

To button Displays the address book that is used to select an e-mail address. Found in the New Message window.

Review Questions

Sections 2.1 — 2.9

1. a) What is the World Wide Web?
   b) What does a Web host provide?
   c) What does it mean to post a Web site?

2. a) What is a hyperlink?
   b) What is a Web site?

3. a) List five categories of Web sites.
   b) What is the purpose of a personal Web site?
   c) List two types of Web sites that are categorized as commercial Web sites?
   d) What is the purpose of a portal Web site?

4. Why do Web sites host banner ads?

5. What language is used to create Web pages?

6. a) What is displayed when a Web browser interprets an HTML document?
   b) What could account for differences in the way a Web page is displayed?

7. a) What is a URL?
   b) Label and describe each part of the URL http://www.cnn.com.

8. What is needed to view Web pages?

9. In Internet Explorer, where is a URL typed?

10. List the step required to quit Internet Explorer.

11. What term is used to describe browsing Web pages?

12. a) What is the History list?
    b) List three ways that the History list can be viewed.

13. a) What is the Favorites list used for?
    b) List the steps required to add a page to the Favorites list.
    c) What is the Organize button used for in the Favorites pane?

14. a) List the steps required to print only page 5 of a 10-page document.
    b) What settings are used if a document is printed using the Print button on the toolbar?

Sections 2.10 — 2.14

15. a) What is a search engine?
    b) List two commonly used search engines.
    c) What is search criteria?
    d) What is a match?

16. What is the purpose of a subject tree?

17. Write search criteria to locate Web pages that contain the following information:
    a) restaurants in Los Angeles
    b) art museums in Boston
    c) auto repair jobs in Montreal, Canada
    d) mosquitoes and bees, but not ants
    e) the English author Jane Austen
    f) the phrase *to each his own*
    g) George Washington and John Adams, but not Thomas Jefferson
    h) travel to Ireland, but not Dublin

18. Why is it difficult to determine if information on the Web is accurate?

19. How can you attempt to determine the accuracy of information on a Web page?

20. What does a copyright protect?

21. a) Why is it necessary to cite sources?
    b) On August 2, 2003 you accessed Tara Perez's Ivy University master's degree thesis titled *Bird Watching in South Florida's Soccer Fields* on a Web page at http://www.tarap.ufl.edu. Write a citation for a research paper that quotes Tara's thesis.

Sections 2.15 — 2.20

22. a) What two things are required to send and receive e-mail messages?
    b) Write an example of a typical e-mail address and label the parts of the address.

23. What is the Reply button in Outlook Express used for?

24. a) Sending an e-mail message should be thought of the same as sending a postcard. Explain this statement.
    b) Why is it important to save and virus check an attachment file before opening it?

25. List four Web careers.

26. a) What are the responsibilities of a Web developer?
    b) What skills are required for Web designers?

27. a) What do ISPs provide?
    b) Which career includes setting up and maintaining an intranet for a company or organization?

28. What duties could be included for a network administrator?

29. List two degree options that are offered at some colleges and universities.

30. Why is it a good idea to keep an updated list of any acquired computer skills and knowledge?

Exercises

Note that the exercises below require written information. If a word processor is used, be sure to use an appropriate header, footer, and file name.

Exercise 1

You are interested in finding a job in San Francisco, California and are skilled in television production, including editing, camera work, etc. A full-time position with a local TV or cable access channel would be ideal.

a) Conduct a search on the Internet using at least two search engines to find two possible positions.

b) Write a brief description of each of the positions that you found.

c) Once you have found the position of your choice, you need information on making the move to San Francisco. First, you will want to rent an apartment and cannot afford more than $1,200 a month. Conduct a search on the Internet to come up with brief descriptions of three apartments in San Francisco that rent for $1,200 or less.

d) Add a paragraph that describes all three apartments, including number of bedrooms and bathrooms and rent per month.

Exercise 2

Your English instructor has assigned a report on the American authors Kurt Vonnegut, Jr. and Ernest Hemingway. Keep in mind that knowledge of information like the titles of their books might help in your search. Because people maintain Web pages as homages to their favorite authors, but are not obligated to check their facts for accuracy, it is a good idea to double check the information you find with more than one Web page.

a) Conduct a search on the Internet using at least two search engines to find biographical data on each author.

b) Write a paragraph of biographical information for each author.

c) On a separate sheet titled References, cite each source.

Introducing the World Wide Web and Internet Explorer

Exercise 3

You have decided to purchase an automobile that costs $15,000 or less. A used car will probably give you the best value.

   a) Conduct a search on the Internet using at least two search engines to find four used cars in your price range.

   b) List each car's specifications and price.

   c) Select one of the four cars for purchase and explain your choice in a paragraph.

   d) You will need automobile insurance for your used car. Search the Internet and find two insurance companies that offer automobile insurance.

   e) List the contact information for two insurance companies.

Exercise 4

A good friend has just injured her elbow playing tennis and would like you to find out as much as you can about her injury.

   a) Conduct a search on the Internet using at least two search engines to find four Web pages that have information about tennis elbow injuries.

   b) Write a one-paragraph description of the injury.

   c) In a second paragraph, write about possible treatments for the injury.

   d) On a separate sheet titled References, cite each source.

Exercise 5

You and a friend have decided to take a trip to New Zealand. Before you go you should find out about airfare, hotels, climate, travel documents, and restaurants. Information about New Zealand's museums and tourist attractions would also be helpful in planning your trip.

   a) Conduct a search on the Internet using at least two search engines to find six Web pages that have information about New Zealand.

   b) Write a one-paragraph description of the country.

   c) In a second paragraph, write about the places that you might visit.

   d) On a separate sheet titled References, cite each source.

Exercise 6

Your history instructor has assigned a research paper on the building of the pyramids in Egypt.

a) Conduct a search on the Internet using at least two search engines to find six Web pages that have information about the pyramids in Egypt.

b) Write a detailed description of the pyramids.

c) On a separate sheet titled References, cite each source.

Exercise 7

You have decided to change careers and become a marine biologist.

a) Conduct a search on the Internet using at least two search engines to find six graduate degree programs in marine biology.

b) List each programs' location (college name), the degree (M.S., Ph.D., etc.), and the number of credits required to finish a degree.

Exercise 8 (advanced)

Each of the following people has made a major contribution to the world of art or music. Select one of the six artists listed below and then find a minimum of five Web pages that provide information about the artist, including pictures of his or her works. Using the information you find, write a two-page report. On a separate sheet titled References, cite each source.

- Mary Cassatt
- Georgia O'Keeffe
- Maxfield Parrish
- Frederic Remington
- Pablo Picasso
- Annie Leibovitz

Exercise 9 (advanced)

Select one of the six topics listed below and then find a minimum of five Web pages that provide information on your topic. Using the information you find, write a two-page report. On a separate sheet titled References, cite each source.

- hurricanes
- the ocean floor
- earthquakes
- tornadoes
- the ozone layer
- solar energy

Introducing the World Wide Web and Internet Explorer

Exercise 10 (advanced)

Select one of the topics listed below and then find a minimum of five Web pages that provide information on your topic. Using the information you find, write a two-page report. On a separate sheet titled References, cite each source.

- fuzzy logic
- artificial intelligence
- speech recognition software
- virtual reality
- neural networks
- computer viruses
- nonotechnology

Chapter 3
Introducing HTML

Chapter 3 Expectations

After completing this chapter you will be able to:
1. Identify the parts of an HTML document.
2. Create an HTML document using Notepad.
3. View HTML documents in a Web browser.
4. Refresh the Web browser display.
5. Distinguish between the break tag and the paragraph tag.
6. Use attributes in tags.
7. Create headings and horizontal rules.
8. Change the background and text color of an HTML document.
9. Use comments to clarify HTML for a reader.
10. Create hyperlinks to different HTML documents.
11. View the HTML associated with a document that is displayed in a browser.

This chapter introduces HTML. Using Notepad and viewing an HTML document in a browser are also discussed.

3.1 What is HTML?

HTML (HyperText Markup Language) is a set of special codes, called *tags*, that are used to "mark up" plain text so that a browser application, such as Internet Explorer, knows how to display the text in a browser window. Text that has been marked up with HTML is called an *HTML document*, as in the document:

```
<html>

<head>
<title>An example HTML document</title>
</head>

<body>
<p>Hello world!</p>
</body>

</html>
```

An HTML document

> **HTML Documents vs Web Pages**
>
> HTML documents can be opened by a Web browser application, and may be on a local computer or intranet. Web pages are documents that are marked up with HTML and possibly contain other code to provide additional features. Web pages are copied to a Web server and are available on the Internet.

Text in this document has been marked up with <title> and </title> to display An example HTML document in the title bar of the browser window. The text Hello world! is marked to be displayed as a paragraph (<p> and </p>) in the body of the browser window (<body> and </body>).

element

A tag is comprised of an *element* inside angle brackets (<>). For example, <title> is called the title tag, where title is the element. Tags affect the text they surround, and are usually paired to indicate the start and end of an instruction. A slash (/) before the element indicates the end of an instruction, such as </body>. A tag should not have any spaces between the opening bracket and the element or slash.

attribute

Tags may also contain attributes. An *attribute* is placed in the start tag and set to a value that modifies the element. For example, setting the bgcolor attribute changes the color of the browser window:

bgcolor

```
<body bgcolor = "Purple">
```

The bgcolor attribute is discussed in more detail in Section 3.10.

3.2 Creating an HTML Document

HTML documents are plain text files and can be created using any text editor such as Notepad or by using a word processor.

In general, the structure of an HTML document should be similar to:

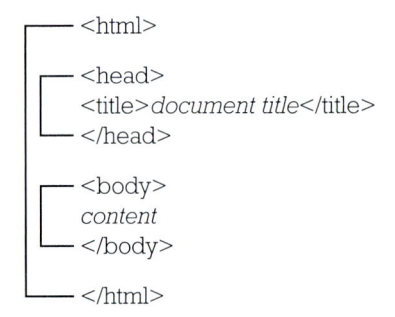

```
<html>
    <head>
    <title>document title</title>
    </head>

    <body>
    content
    </body>

<html>
```

document tags   The html, head, title, and body tags are called *document tags*:

- The html tag tells the browser that the file contains HyperText Markup Language.

- The head tag defines the section that contains information about the document, including its title. This section will not be displayed as part of the document content.

- The title tag marks the document title. The title section must be within the head section. The document title should be descriptive and meaningful because it is displayed in the title bar of the browser's window and is also used when the user adds the document to the browser's Favorites list.

- The body tag defines the body section, which contains the document's content. All content must be enclosed in the appropriate tags. For example, in Section 3.1, the content is marked as a paragraph. Paragraph tags are discussed in more detail in Section 3.6.

document style   The document tags appear on separate lines, except for the title tags, and blank lines are used to separate sections of HTML. This helps make the document easier to understand and edit. Note that HTML is not case sensitive, so tags may be uppercase or lowercase. This text uses lowercase tags to be consistent with the format used by Dreamweaver.

free-form   HTML documents are *free-form*, which means that spaces and blank lines generally have no effect on how the document is interpreted. Therefore, the document:

```
<html><head><title>An example HTML document</title>
</head>
<body>    <p>Hello world!</p></body></html>
```

Poorly structured HTML document

displays exactly the same as the HTML document in Section 3.1. However, editing a poorly structured document can be time-consuming and error-prone.

3.3 Using Notepad

Notepad is a text editor that comes with the Windows operating system and is well suited for creating and editing plain text files, such as HTML documents.

starting Notepad

Notepad is started by selecting Start → All Programs → Accessories → Notepad, which displays a new, blank document in the Notepad window.

saving a document

A document is saved by selecting File → Save. The Save As dialog box is displayed the first time a document is saved:

> **The Word Wrap Command**
>
> Selecting Format → Word Wrap in Notepad wraps text as it is typed in the window, which makes long paragraphs of text easier to read.

The Save in list and the contents box below it are used to navigate to the location where the file is to be saved. The Text Documents (*.txt) option should be selected in the Save as type list. A descriptive file name is typed in the File name box and selecting Save creates a file with the typed name that contains the HTML document.

naming a file

A file must be given a *file name* to identify it. File names can be up to 255 characters long and can contain letters, the underscore character (_), and numbers. File names cannot contain colons (:), asterisks (*), question marks (?), and some other special characters. Any letters in HTML document file names should be lowercase, and there should not be any spaces. The underscore character should be used to separate words in a file name. The .htm extension needs to be added to HTML document file names so that a browser recognizes the file as an HTML document. An example of a valid file name is hello_world.htm. A descriptive file name is important because it makes the HTML document easily identifiable.

.htm

printing a document

A document is printed by selecting File → Print. Notepad automatically prints a centered header containing the file name and a centered footer containing the page number.

Introducing HTML

3 – 3

creating a new document

> **Opening HTML Documents**
>
> An HTML document can also be viewed in a browser by locating the document in the My Computer window and then double-clicking the document to open it.

A new document is created by selecting File → New. An existing document is opened by selecting File → Open, which displays a dialog box. The Files of type must be changed to All Files to display the HTML document file name in the contents box. The appropriate file name is then clicked and then Open selected to open the document.

When Notepad is no longer needed, it should be quit properly. Notepad is quit by selecting File → Exit. Attempting to quit without saving changes to a document displays the message:

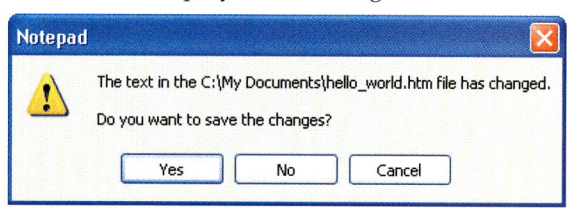

Selecting Yes saves the modified document to the file and quits Notepad. Selecting No exits Notepad without saving the document. Selecting Cancel reverses the Exit command and leaves Notepad running.

Practice 1

In this practice you will create, save, and print an HTML document using Notepad. This practice assumes that you have Notepad.

① START NOTEPAD

Select Start → All Programs → Accessories → Notepad. Notepad is started and a new, blank document is displayed.

② CREATE AN HTML DOCUMENT

Type the following HTML document exactly as shown. Be sure to include a blank line between sections, as indicated, and replace Student Name with your name:

```
<html>

<head>
<title>First HTML Document</title>
</head>

<body>
<p>My name is Student Name. Hello world!</p>
</body>

</html>
```

③ SAVE THE HTML DOCUMENT

a. Select File → Save. A dialog box is displayed.
   1. Use the Save in list to select the appropriate location for the file to be saved.
   2. In the Save as type list, select Text Documents (*.txt) if it is not already selected.
   3. In the File name box, replace the existing text with: first_document.htm
   4. Select Save. The document is saved in the selected location with the name first_document.htm.

④ *PRINT THE HTML DOCUMENT AND QUIT NOTEPAD*

    a. Select File → Print. Note the printout automatically displays the file name centered at the top of the page and the Page 1 centered at the bottom of the page.

    b. Select File → Exit to quit Notepad.

3.4 Viewing HTML Documents in a Web Browser

A Web browser is used to view HTML documents that have been published to a Web server. HTML documents on a personal computer can also be opened and viewed in a browser. In Internet Explorer, selecting File → Open displays the Open dialog box:

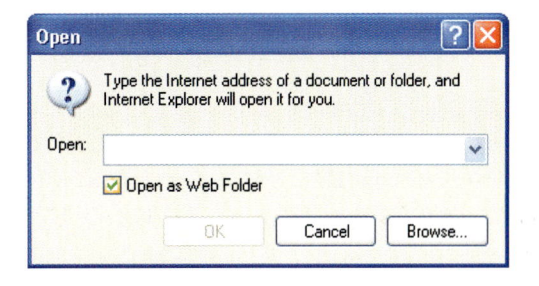

The complete location and file name, including the .htm extension, must be typed in the Open box. If the complete location or file name is not known, selecting Browse displays a dialog box that can be used to find this location:

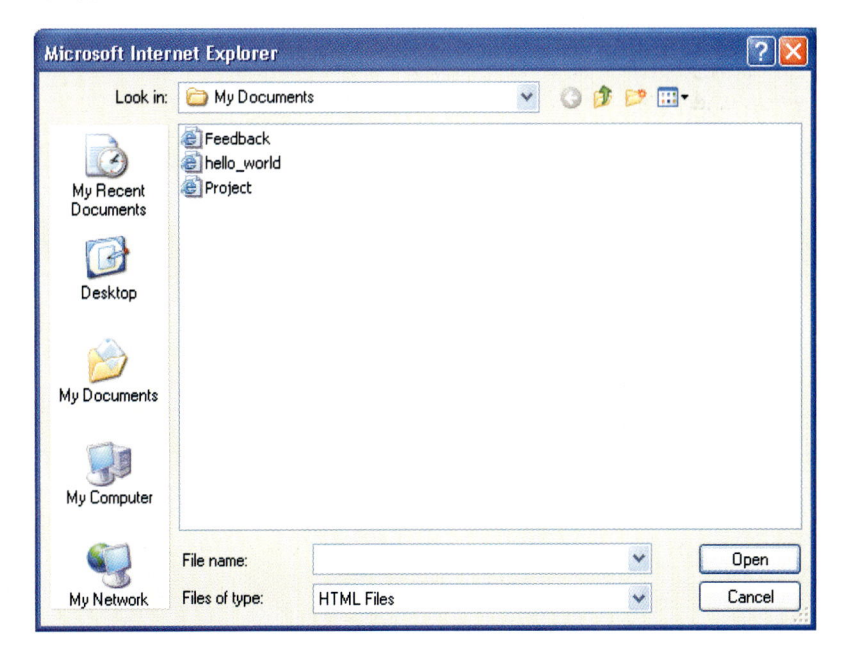

The Look in list displays a location name, with the location contents displayed in the box below. Double-clicking a folder in the contents box places that folder name in the Look in list and displays its contents in the box below. When the contents box displays the appropriate file name,

Introducing HTML   **3 – 5**

> **Netscape**
>
> In Netscape 7, an HTML document is opened by selecting File → Open Source.

clicking that file name and then selecting Open places the file name with its complete path in the Open dialog box. Selecting OK in the Open dialog box displays the HTML document in the browser window:

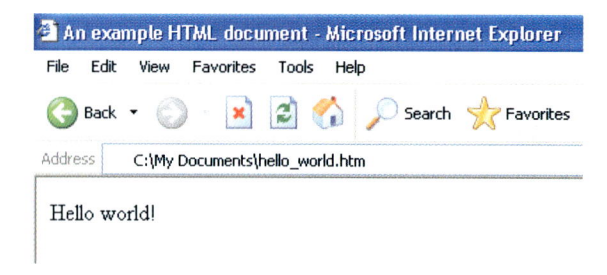

An HTML document opened and viewed in a Web browser

Practice 2

In this practice you will view an HTML document in Internet Explorer.

① **START INTERNET EXPLORER**

② **OPEN FIRST_DOCUMENT.HTM IN INTERNET EXPLORER**
   a. Select File → Open. A dialog box is displayed.
      1. Select Browse. A dialog box is displayed.
         a. Use the Look in list and the contents box below it to display the file name first_document.htm.
         b. In the contents box, click: first_document.htm
         c. Select Open. The dialog box is removed and the location and file name are placed in the Open box.
      2. Select OK. The tags are interpreted and the HTML document appears in the browser. Note the document title in the title bar.

3.5 Refreshing the Web Browser Display

When developing an HTML document, frequent viewing in a browser is usually necessary. This is easily done by having both Notepad and Internet Explorer running at the same time. The Windows taskbar can then be used to quickly switch between the applications.

In Internet Explorer, the Refresh button ( ) is used to check the HTML file for changes and then update the document in the browser window. Any changes to the HTML document in Notepad must be saved before refreshing the browser. For example, if the HTML document is modified in Notepad to include additional content, the HTML document needs to be saved, and then in Internet Explorer, the Refresh button needs to be clicked to update the page to include the additional content.

> **Multitasking**
>
> Multitasking is an operating system feature that allows more than one application to run at a time. For example, both Notepad and Internet Explorer can run simultaneously.

Practice 3

In this practice you will edit an HTML document and refresh the view. Open first_document.htm in Internet Explorer if it is not already displayed.

① START NOTEPAD

Start Notepad. Note that now there are two buttons on the Windows taskbar, one for Internet Explorer and one for Notepad.

② MODIFY FIRST_DOCUMENT.HTM

a. Select File → Open. A dialog box is displayed.
   1. In the Files of type box, select All Files.
   2. Use the Look in box and the contents box below it to display the file name first_document.htm.
   3. Select the Open button, a copy of first_document.htm is transferred to the computer's memory and the document is displayed in Notepad.

b. Place the insertion point to the right of the ! in world! and type a space followed by This is my first HTML document.

c. Save the modified file.

③ SWITCH TO INTERNET EXPLORER AND REFRESH THE VIEW

a. On the taskbar, click the Internet Explorer button. The first_document.htm document is displayed without the additional content.

b. On the toolbar, click the Refresh button ( ). Internet Explorer updates the document.

④ CHANGE THE title

a. On the taskbar, click the Notepad button. Notepad is displayed.

b. Replace the document title text, First HTML Document, with the text Example HTML Document.

c. Save the modified file.

d. Quit Notepad. Internet Explorer is displayed.

⑤ REFRESH THE VIEW

On the toolbar, click the Refresh button ( ). The updated document title text is now displayed in the title bar.

3.6 Creating Paragraphs

<p>

The body section of an HTML document includes the content and tags that format the content, such as the paragraph tag. Text enclosed by <p> and </p> is a paragraph. Lines of paragraph text are automatically wrapped by the browser, and a blank line is added after each paragraph. For example, the document on the next page contains two paragraphs:

Introducing HTML 3 – 7

```
<html>

<head>
<title>Images</title>
</head>

<body>
<p>Images can come from a variety of sources including clip art, draw programs, scanners, and digital cameras.</p>
<p>There are many different image formats. Three formats are GIF (Graphics Interchange Format), JPG (Joint Photographic Experts Group), and PNG (Portable Network Graphic).</p>
</body>

</html>
```

When viewed in a browser, the HTML document will look similar to:

[Browser screenshot showing the rendered page: "Images can come from a variety of sources including clip art, draw programs, scanners, and digital cameras. There are many different image formats. Three formats are GIF (Graphics Interchange Format), JPG (Joint Photographic Experts Group), and PNG (Portable Network Graphic)."]

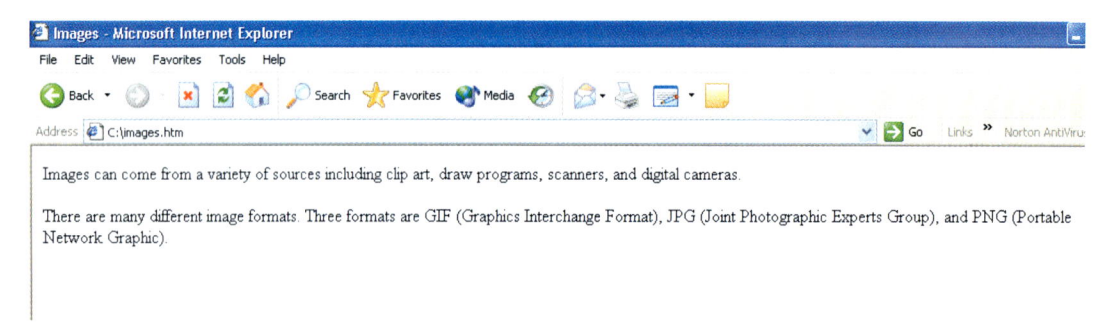

Any multiple spaces in the text between the paragraph tags are changed to a single space.

\<br\>   To move a line of text within a paragraph to the next line, a break tag <br> can be used. For example, the body section of the HTML document above could be modified to include line breaks:

```
<body>
<p>Images can come from a variety of sources including clip art, draw programs, scanners, and digital cameras.</p>
<p>There are many different image formats. Three formats are:<br>
GIF (Graphics Interchange Format)<br>
JPG (Joint Photographic Experts Group)<br>
PNG (Portable Network Graphics)</p>
</body>
```

Note that the break tag is one of the few HTML tags that does not need to be paired. When viewed in a browser, the HTML document will look similar to:

Images can come from a variety of sources including clip art, draw programs, scanners, and digital cameras.

There are many different image formats. Three formats are:
GIF (Graphics Interchange Format)
JPG (Joint Photographic Experts Group)
PNG (Portable Network Graphics)

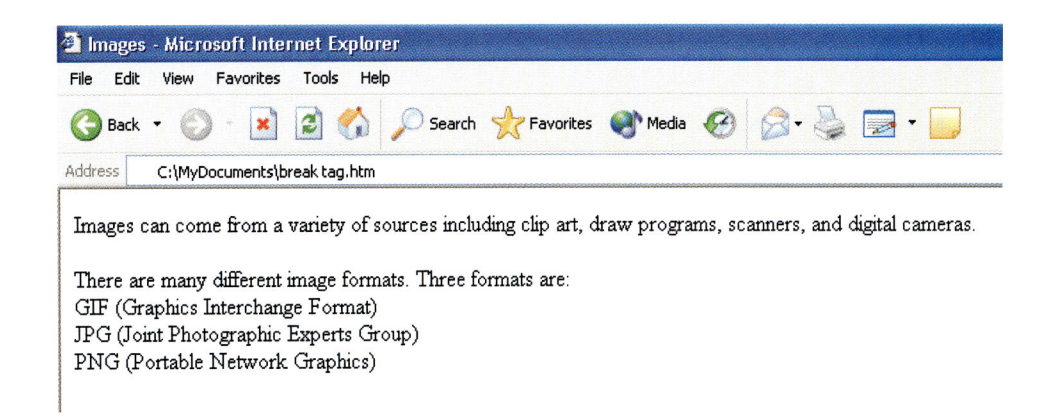

3.7 Paragraph Alignment

alignment   The *alignment* of text in a paragraph refers to its position relative to the sides of the document: left, centered, right, and justified. For example:

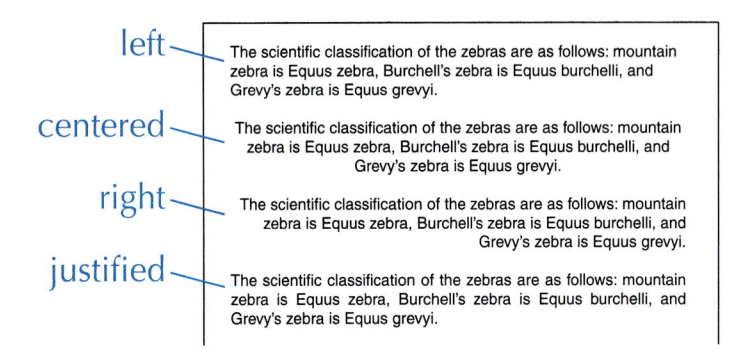

- left — The scientific classification of the zebras are as follows: mountain zebra is Equus zebra, Burchell's zebra is Equus burchelli, and Grevy's zebra is Equus grevyi.
- centered — The scientific classification of the zebras are as follows: mountain zebra is Equus zebra, Burchell's zebra is Equus burchelli, and Grevy's zebra is Equus grevyi.
- right — The scientific classification of the zebras are as follows: mountain zebra is Equus zebra, Burchell's zebra is Equus burchelli, and Grevy's zebra is Equus grevyi.
- justified — The scientific classification of the zebras are as follows: mountain zebra is Equus zebra, Burchell's zebra is Equus burchelli, and Grevy's zebra is Equus grevyi.

align   The paragraph tag left aligns text by default. The alignment of a paragraph can be modified by setting the align attribute. For example, setting the align attribute to "center" displays the text centered in the browser window:

```
<p align="center">This paragraph will be centered.</p>
```

Other align attribute settings include:

```
<p align="right">This paragraph will be right aligned.</p>
<p align="justify">This paragraph will be justified.</p>
```

Introducing HTML

Practice 4

In this practice you will create an HTML document that contains break and paragraph tags.

① START NOTEPAD

② CREATE A NEW HTML DOCUMENT

Type the following HTML document exactly as shown, replacing Student Name with your name:

```
<html>

<head>
<title>Computer Viruses</title>
</head>

<body>
<p align="center">Computer Viruses</p>
<p>A computer virus is a program that is loaded onto the computer
without the user's knowledge. Computer viruses have varying
effects, such as:<br>
displaying annoying messages<br>
causing programs to run incorrectly<br>
erasing the contents of the hard drive</p>
<p>In order to protect against viruses:<br>
install an antivirus program</p>
<p>Report by: Student Name</p>
</body>

</html>
```

③ SAVE THE DOCUMENT

Save the document in the appropriate folder with the name: student_report.htm

④ VIEW STUDENT_REPORT.HTM

Open student_report.htm in a browser. Note the formatting of the text.

⑤ PRINT THE HTML DOCUMENT

a. Switch back to Notepad.
b. If necessary, make corrections to the HTML document and then check it in the browser.
c. Print a copy of the HTML document.
d. Quit Notepad.

3.8 Creating Headings

<h1> through <h6>

Heading tags are used to emphasize text. There are six levels of headings, which are numbered 1 through 6 and represented with tags <h1> through <h6>. The HTML document below includes all six heading tags:

```
<html>

<head>
<title>Heading Formats</title>
</head>

<body>
<h1>Heading 1</h1>
<h2>Heading 2</h2>
<h3>Heading 3</h3>
<h4>Heading 4</h4>
<h5>Heading 5</h5>
<h6>Heading 6</h6>
</body>

</html>
```

Each heading level has specific formatting associated with it, which includes font size, bold text, and space above and below the heading. Heading 1 has the largest font size and is used to represent the most important information. Heading 6 has the smallest font size. For example, the above HTML document viewed in a browser will look similar to:

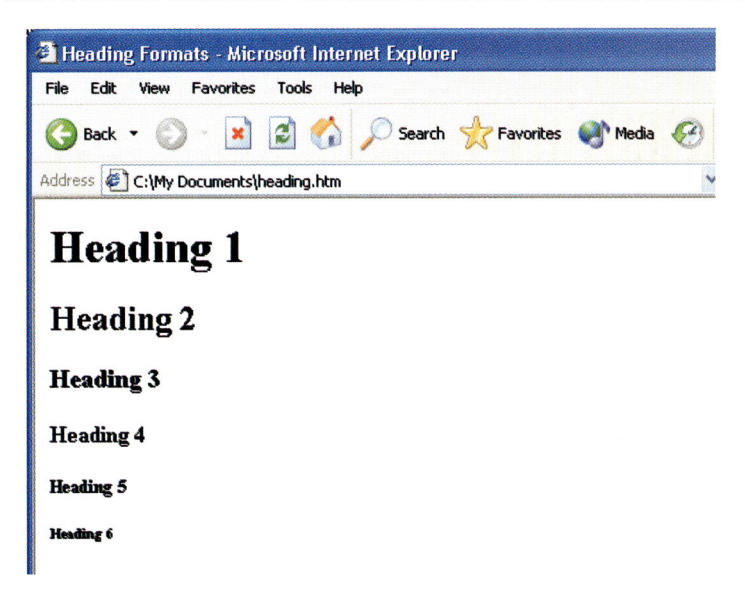

Note that only one heading level can be displayed on a line. The formatting associated with the heading tags varies between browsers and is dependent on the preferences set by the user.

Practice 5

In this practice you will create an HTML document that contains heading tags.

① **START NOTEPAD**

② **CREATE AN HTML DOCUMENT**

Type the following HTML document exactly as shown, replacing Student Name with your name:

```
<html>

<head>
<title>Heading Formats</title>
</head>

<body>
<p>Student Name</p>
<h1>Heading 1</h1>
<h2>Heading 2</h2>
<h3>Heading 3</h3>
<h4>Heading 4</h4>
<h5>Heading 5</h5>
<h6>Heading 6</h6>
</body>

</html>
```

③ **SAVE THE HTML DOCUMENT**

Save the document in the appropriate folder with the name: headings.htm

④ **VIEW HEADINGS.HTM**

Open headings.htm in a browser. Note the formatting of the heading text.

⑤ **PRINT THE HTML DOCUMENT**

a. Switch back to Notepad.
b. If necessary, make corrections to the HTML document and then check it in the browser.
c. Print a copy of the headings HTML document.

3.9 Adding Horizontal Rules

The <hr> tag places a horizontal *rule* (line) across the width of the browser window. This feature is used to divide the text in the browser window into sections for easier reading. The width, align, and size attributes of the <hr> tag can be used to modify the features of the rule:

    <hr width="50%" align="left" size="4">

This tag includes attributes that display a rule across half of the browser window (50%), left aligned, and with a thickness of 4 pixels:

Pixel

A pixel (picture element) is a single point in a graphic and the smallest unit that hardware and software use when creating graphics and text. A graphic is typically made up of thousands of pixels displayed closely together.

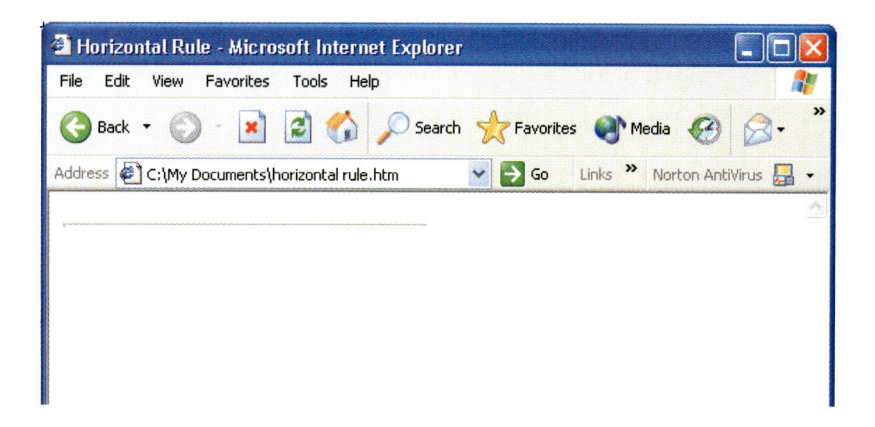

The default alignment is centered for a horizontal rule and the default size is 100%. The horizontal rule tag does not need to be paired.

3.10 Adding Color

The <body> tag can include bgcolor and text attributes. These attributes modify the document's background color and the text color:

```
<body bgcolor="Black" text="Silver">
```

This tag's attributes sets the document's background color to black and the text color to silver. The attribute values can be a hexadecimal value or a color constant. For example, the background color could be set to black using the color constant "Black" or the hexadecimal value "#000000". A list of color constants and corresponding hexadecimal values can be found in Appendix A.

> **Hexadecimal**
>
> Hexadecimal is a base-16 numbering system that consists of the numbers 0 through 9 and the letters A through F.

3.11 Using Comments

<!--comment-->

Comments are text used to explain and clarify HTML to the reader of an HTML document. They do not appear in a browser window. Comments start with an angle bracket, followed by an exclamation mark and two hyphens. At the end of the comment are two more hyphens and an ending bracket. For example the comment below describes the horizontal rule tag that follows:

```
<!--draws a centered horizontal line across 75% of the screen-->
<hr width="75%">
```

Practice 6

In this practice you will modify an HTML document to include a comment, color, and a horizontal rule.

① **START NOTEPAD**

② **OPEN STUDENT_REPORT.HTM**

Introducing HTML 3 – 13

③ **ADD A COMMENT AND A HORIZONTAL RULE**
   a. Place the insertion point to the right of the </p> tag that appears after "Computer Viruses". Press the Enter key.
   b. Type:
   ```
   <!--Horizontal rule will have a thickness of 4 pixels-->
   <hr size="4">
   ```

④ **ADD COLOR**
   Modify the body element to include attributes:
   ```
   <body bgcolor="Black" text="Silver">
   ```

⑤ **SAVE THE MODIFIED DOCUMENT**

⑥ **VIEW STUDENT_REPORT.HTM**
   Open student_report.htm in a browser. Note the rule, background color, and text color. Also note that the comment is not displayed.

⑦ **PRINT THE HTML DOCUMENT**
   a. Switch back to Notepad.
   b. If necessary, make corrections to the HTML document and then check it in the browser.
   c. From Notepad, print a copy of the student_report HTML document.

3.12 Hyperlinks

A *hyperlink*, also called a *link*, is text displayed in a browser window that can be clicked to display a different HTML document in the browser window. Hyperlinks are typically displayed as blue, underlined words in the browser window. Countless documents can all be linked, allowing the user to go from topic to topic, or browse HTML documents.

The anchor tag (<a>) is used in an HTML document to mark text that is a link. The href attribute is set in the tag to the name of the linked document:

```
<html>

<head>
<title>Images</title>
</head>

<body>
<p>Images can come from a variety of sources
including <a href="digicam.htm">digital cameras</a></p>
</body>

</html>
```

An HTML document that contains a digital cameras hyperlink

Ted Nelson
1937 –

Ted Nelson coined the term hypertext in 1965 based on his vision of a document management system where all stored documents would be accessible by a link.

> **Hypertext vs. Hyperlink**
>
> A hypertext system is a type of database where objects can be linked.
>
> A hyperlink is an element in an electronic document that is clicked to display a related document. Hyperlinks are what make a hypertext system, such as the Web, work.

The text digital cameras is called the *hyperlink label*. This text will be displayed as blue, underlined in the browser window. When viewed in a browser, the HTML document with a hyperlink will look similar to:

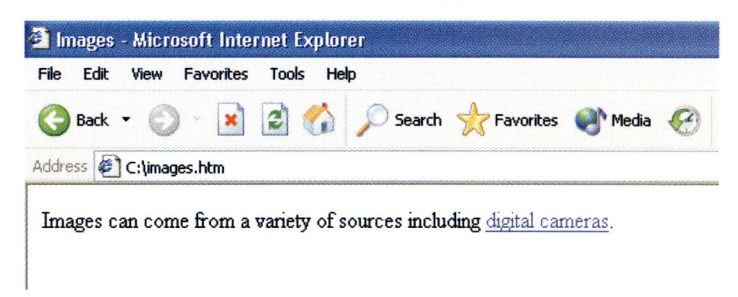

[Browser screenshot: Images - Microsoft Internet Explorer, Address C:\images.htm, showing text "Images can come from a variety of sources including digital cameras."]

Clicking digital cameras displays the digicam.htm document.

Practice 7

In this practice you will create a new HTML document and add a hyperlink to an existing HTML document.

① **START NOTEPAD**

② **CREATE AN HTML DOCUMENT**

Type the following HTML document exactly as shown, replacing Student Name with your name:

```
<html>

<head>
<title>Antivirus Program</title>
</head>

<body>
<p align="center">Checking for Viruses</p>
<p>A computer can be checked for viruses using an antivirus program. An antivirus program is a utility that scans a hard disk for viruses. If a virus is located, it will be removed by the antivirus program.</p>
<p>Report by: Student Name</p>
</body>

</html>
```

③ **SAVE THE DOCUMENT AND PRINT A COPY**

    a. Save the document in the same folder as student_report.htm and name it: antivirus.htm

    b. Print a copy of the document.

④ **OPEN STUDENT_REPORT.HTM IN NOTEPAD**

Introducing HTML   3 – 15

⑤ ADD A HYPERLINK TO ANOTHER DOCUMENT

a. Place the insertion point right after the text install an, which is near the bottom of the body of the content.

b. Type the tag:

   <a href="antivirus.htm">

c. Place the insertion point to the right of the text "antivirus program" and to the left of </p> and then add the tag </a>

Check — The line should look like: install an <a href="antivirus.htm">antivirus program</a></p>

⑥ SAVE THE MODIFIED HTML DOCUMENT

⑦ VIEW STUDENT_REPORT.HTM AND TEST THE LINK

a. Open student_report.htm in a browser. Note the text antivirus program is displayed as a blue, underlined hyperlink.

b. Click antivirus program. The antivirus.htm document is displayed in the browser.

⑧ PRINT THE HTML DOCUMENT

a. Switch back to Notepad.

b. If necessary, make corrections to the HTML document and then check it in the browser.

c. From Notepad, print a copy of the student_report HTML document.

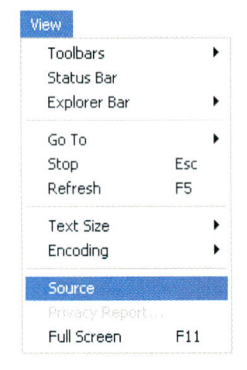

3.13   The Source Command

When viewing a document in a browser, the HTML associated with the document can be viewed in a separate window. In Internet Explorer, selecting View → Source displays a window with the HTML associated with the document in the browser:

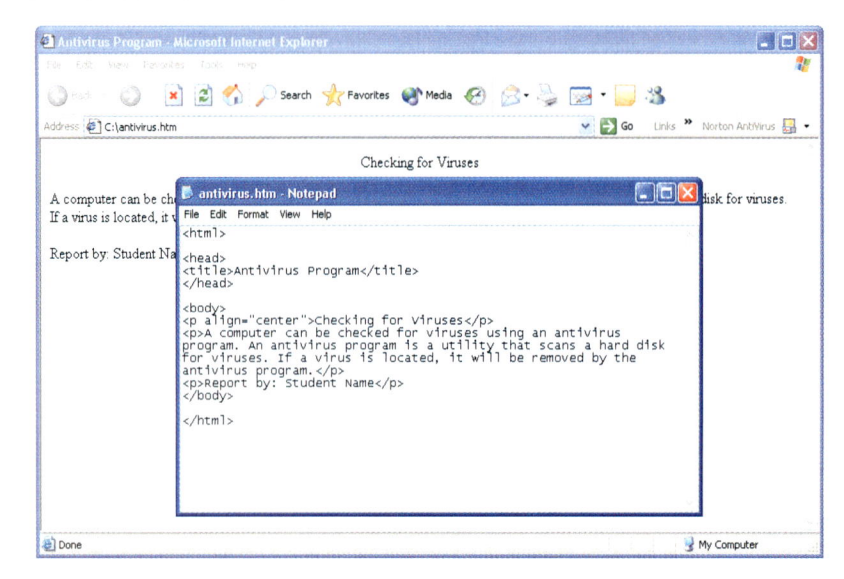

Examining the HTML of a document is one useful way to learn more about HTML. The Source command can be used with any HTML document in a browser, including documents published to the Web.

copyright   The HTML associated with a document is the designer's intellectual property and is protected by copyright. This applies even if a copyright notation (©) is not included on the document.

Practice 8

In this practice you will view the HTML of a document that has been published to a Web server.

① **START INTERNET EXPLORER**

② **GO TO THE LP_HELLO_WORLD HOME PAGE**

    a. In the Address bar, replace the existing URL with www.lpdatafiles.com/dmx/lp_hello_world and press Enter. The LP Hello World document is displayed.

    b. Select View → Source. A new window is displayed with the HTML for the LP Hello World home page.

    c. Scroll to view the different tags used to create the HTML document. Locate all of the document tags.

    d. Locate the title tag and write down the document title.

    e. Close the source window.

③ **QUIT INTERNET EXPLORER**

3.14 Where can you go from here?

This chapter has introduced the basics of HTML. You can now create, edit, format, and display HTML documents. There are many other HTML tags listed in Appendix A.

Chapter Summary

HTML (HyperText Markup Language) is a set of special codes, called tags, that are used to "mark up" plain text so that a browser application, such as Internet Explorer, knows how to display the text in a browser window. Text that has been marked up with HTML is called an HTML document.

A tag is comprised of an element inside angle brackets (<>). Tags affect the text they surround, and are usually paired to indicate the start and end of an instruction. A slash (/) before the element indicates the end of an instruction, such as </body>. The HTML, head, title, and body tags are called document tags. Other tags introduced in this chapter include the paragraph tag, <p>, the break tag, <br>, the heading tags, <h1> through <h6>, the horizontal rule tag, <hr>, and the anchor tag, <a>. Tags may also contain attributes.

HTML documents are plain text files and can be created using any text editor such as Notepad or a word processor. Notepad is started by selecting Start → All Programs → Accessories → Notepad, which displays a new, blank document. An existing HTML document is opened by selecting File → Open and changing the Files of type to All Files (*.*). A document is saved as an HTML document by selecting File → Save and typing a descriptive file name with the extension .htm.

An HTML document can be opened in Internet Explorer by selecting File → Open. Both Notepad and Internet Explorer can be running at the same time when developing an HTML document, and the Windows taskbar is used to switch between the applications. In Internet Explorer, the Refresh button is used to check the HTML document for changes and update the displayed page.

A document is printed by selecting File → Print. Notepad automatically prints the file name in a centered header and the page number in a centered footer. Notepad is quit properly by selecting File → Exit.

The body tag can include bgcolor and text attributes. Comments explain and clarify an HTML document for a reader but do not appear in a browser window.

A hyperlink, also called a link, is text displayed in a browser window that can be clicked to display a different HTML document in the browser window.

The HTML associated with the document in a browser window can be viewed in Internet Explorer by selecting View → Source.

HTML documents that are posted to the Internet are the designer's intellectual property and are protected by copyright. This applies even if a copyright notation (©) is not included on the page.

Vocabulary

Alignment Position of text in a paragraph relative to the sides of the page: left, right, centered, and justified.

Attribute Used to modify the features of an element in an HTML tag.

Comment Text used to explain and clarify HTML for a reader.

Document tags The html, head, title, and body tags.

Element The part of an HTML tag placed inside angle brackets (<>). For example, <title> is called the title tag, where title is the element.

File name Descriptive name used to identify a file.

Free-form Spaces and blank lines generally have no effect on how the document is interpreted. The format of an HTML document.

HTML (HyperText Markup Language) A set of tags that are used to "mark up" plain text so that a browser application knows how to display the text.

HTML document Text that has been marked up with HTML.

Hyperlink Text that can be clicked to display another HTML document. Also called a link.

Link See hyperlink.

Rule A line in a browser window for dividing content.

Tag Comprised of an element inside angle brackets that is used to "mark up" plain text so that a browser application knows how to display the text.

HTML Tags

`<a>` The anchor tag. Used in an HTML document to link text to another HTML document. Attributes include href.

`<body>` The body tag. Used in an HTML document to indicate the content of the document. Attributes include bgcolor and text.

`<br>` The break tag. Used in an HTML document to move a line of text within a paragraph to the next line.

`<!--comment-->` A comment tag. Used in an HTML document to explain and clarify HTML to the reader.

`<h1>` through `<h6>` The heading tags. Used in an HTML document to emphasize text.

`<head>` The head tag. Used in an HTML document to indicate information about the document, including its title.

`<hr>` The horizontal rule tag. Used in an HTML document to indicate a line is to be displayed in the browser window. Attributes include width, align, and size.

`<html>` The HTML tag. Used in an HTML document to indicate that the file contains HTML.

`<p>` The paragraph tag. Used in an HTML document to format the content. Attributes include align.

`<title>` The title tag. Used in an HTML document to indicate the document title to be displayed in the title bar of the browser window. Must be in the head section of an HTML document.

Notepad Commands

Exit command   Quits Notepad. Found in the File menu.

New command   Creates a new document. Found in the File menu.

Notepad command   Starts Notepad. Found in the Accessories menu in the All Programs menu in the Start menu.

Open command   Displays a dialog box that is used to open an existing document. Found in the File menu.

Print command   Prints a copy of the document. Found in the File menu.

Save command   Displays a dialog box that is used to copy the document to a file. Found in the File menu.

Internet Explorer Commands and Buttons

Open command   Displays a dialog box that is used to open an HTML document. Found in the File menu.

Refresh button   Used to check the HTML file for changes and then update the page.

Source command   Displays the HTML of the current document. Found in the View menu.

Review Questions

Sections 3.1 — 3.5

1. a) What is HTML?
   b) What is an HTML document?

2. What is the element in the tag <html>?

3. What does a slash (/) before the element indicate?

4. What does an attribute modify?

5. What type of files are HTML documents?

6. a) Draw the structure of an HTML document.
   b) List the four document tags.

7. Are HTML tags case sensitive?

8. a) What is meant by a document being free-form?
   b) Why is it important to have properly structured HTML?

9. What is Notepad?

10. Why is it necessary to add the .htm extension to the file name when saving an HTML document in Notepad?

11. What does Notepad automatically add to a printed document?

12. List the steps required to open an HTML document in Notepad.

13. What will happen if you attempt to quit Notepad without saving changes?

14. List the steps required to open and view an HTML document in a Web browser.

15. How can you switch quickly between open applications?

16. What button is used in Internet Explorer to update the document in the browser window?

Sections 3.6 — 3.13

17. a) Which tag is used to enclose a paragraph of text?
    b) What happens to any multiple spaces in the text between paragraph tags when a document is viewed in a browser?

18. What tag is used to move a line of text within a paragraph to the next line?

19. a) What does the alignment of text in a paragraph refer to?
    b) Write an HTML tag that would change a paragraph's alignment to centered.

20. a) What are heading tags used for?
    b) Which tag is used to represent heading level 3?
    c) Which heading tag is often used to represent the most important information?

21. a) What does the <hr> tag add to a Web page?
    b) Which attributes can be used to modify the <hr> tag?

22. a) What attribute is used in the <body> tag to modify the document's background color?
    b) What attribute is used in the <body> tag to modify the document's text color?

23. a) What are comments used for in an HTML document?
    b) Write a comment that describes the tag <hr width="25%" align="right">

24. a) What is a hyperlink?
    b) Write a tag to link the text cats to an HTML document named pets.htm.

25. a) List the step required to display the HTML associated with a current document in Internet Explorer.
    b) List one reason for examining the HTML of a Web page?

26. Is HTML protected by copyright?

Exercises

Exercise 1

Most schools have their own Web site. Find out what the URL is for your school's Web site and use Internet Explorer to complete the following steps:

a) Go to your school's Web site.

b) Locate and write down the title of the Web page.

c) Add this site to your Favorites list. Write down the text that is added to your Favorites list. Does it match the title?

d) View the HTML. Locate and write down an example of information that is displayed using a tag discussed in this chapter.

Exercise 2

Using Internet Explorer complete the following steps:

a) Go to the Web site with the URL www.nasa.gov.

b) Locate and write down the title of the Web page.

c) View the HTML. Locate the <html> and </html> tags that indicate the start and end of an HTML document.

Exercise 3

Using Internet Explorer, complete the following steps:

a) Go to the Web site with the URL www.pbs.org.

b) Locate and write down the title of the Web site.

c) View the HTML. Locate the title in the HTML and write down the HTML necessary to display the title including the tags.

d) Locate the start and end of the head section.

Exercise 4 ———————————————————————— personal.htm

Create an HTML document that displays your school and graduation year by completing the following steps:

a) Using Notepad, create an HTML document that includes:

- the title School Information
- an appropriate background and text color
- your name in Heading 1 format

- your school name in Heading 2 format
- your graduation year in Heading 3 format

b) Save the HTML document naming it personal.htm and print a copy.

c) View the document in a Web browser and print a copy.

Exercise 5 — tourist_attractions.htm

Create an HTML document that lists tourist attractions for a particular city by completing the following steps:

a) Research tourist attractions in a particular city by using the Internet, magazines, and books.

b) Using Notepad, create an HTML document that includes:
- a comment with your name
- the title Tourist Attractions
- an appropriate background and text color
- the city name and state name in Heading 1 format
- Tourist Attractions in Heading 2 format
- a horizontal rule across the width of the page
- at least five tourist attractions, each displayed on a separate line, in Heading 4 format

c) Save the HTML document naming it tourist_attractions.htm and print a copy.

d) View the document in a Web browser and print a copy.

Exercise 6 — school_sports.htm

Create an HTML document that lists the sports offered at your school by completing the following steps:

a) Make a list of all the sports offered at your school.

b) Using Notepad, create an HTML document that includes:
- a comment with your name
- the title School Sports
- an appropriate background and text color
- your school name in Heading 1 format
- Sports in Heading 2 format
- a horizontal rule across 50% of the page, aligned left
- the sports offered, each displayed on a separate line, in Heading 3 format

c) Save the HTML document naming it school_sports.htm and print a copy.

d) View the document in a Web browser and print a copy.

Introducing HTML

Exercise 7 —————————————————————— movie.htm

Create an HTML document about your all time favorite movie by completing the following steps:

a) Using Notepad, create an HTML document that includes:

- the title All Time Favorite Movie
- an appropriate background and text color
- the name of your all time favorite movie in Heading 1 format
- by in Heading 4 format
- your name in Heading 2 format
- a horizontal rule across the width of the page
- a paragraph containing at least three sentences that explains why you liked the movie

b) Save the HTML document naming it movie.htm and print a copy.

c) View the document in a Web browser and print a copy.

Exercise 8 —————————————————————— table.htm

Create an HTML document that displays the instructions for setting a table by completing the following steps:

a) Using Notepad, create an HTML document that includes:

- a comment with your name
- the title Table Etiquette
- an appropriate background and text color
- Setting the Table in Heading 1 format
- the following content in appropriate paragraphs:

    Forks go on the left

    Spoons and knives go on the right

    Utensils should be placed from the outside in towards the plate in the order in which they'll be used: the first utensil outside, the second utensil closer toward the plate, and so on.

b) Save the HTML document naming it table.htm and print a copy.

c) View the document in a Web browser and print a copy.

Exercise 9 —————————————————————— book.htm

Create four HTML documents that detail a book you have recently read by completing the following steps:

a) Using Notepad, create the first HTML document that includes:

- the title Book Report
- an appropriate background and text color
- the title and author of the book in Heading 3 format

- your name in Heading 1 format
- at least one paragraph and at least 30 words summarizing the book
- a list of hyperlinks below the summary paragraph that link to the characters page (use the label Characters and link to characters.htm), the author page (use the label Author and link to author.htm), and the favorite part page (use the label Favorite Part and link to fav_part.htm)

b) Save the HTML document naming it book.htm and print a copy.

c) Using Notepad, create a new HTML document that contains:
- the title Characters
- an appropriate background and text color
- the title of the book in Heading 3 format
- Characters in Heading 2 format
- your name in Heading 1 format
- one paragraph for each important character in the book. There should be at least 40 words total on this page.
- a hyperlink below the character paragraphs with the label Home that links to the home page (book.htm)

d) Save the HTML document naming it characters.htm and print a copy.

e) Using Notepad, create a new HTML document that contains:
- the title Author
- an appropriate background and text color
- the title of the book in Heading 3 format
- Author in Heading 2 format
- your name in Heading 1 format
- one paragraph describing the author. Include the author's date of birth, education, and other pertinent information. This paragraph should contain at least 12 words.
- a hyperlink below the author paragraph with the label Home that links to the home page (book.htm)

f) Save the HTML document naming it author.htm and print a copy.

g) Using Notepad, create a new HTML document that contains:
- the title Favorite Part
- an appropriate background and text color
- the title of the book in Heading 3 format
- Favorite Part in Heading 2 format
- your name in Heading 1 format
- at least one paragraph describing your favorite part of the book. This paragraph should contain at least 20 words.
- a hyperlink below the favorite part paragraph(s) with the label Home that links to the home page (book.htm)

h) Save the HTML document naming it fav_part.htm and print a copy.

i) View the first document in a Web browser. Test the links.

Exercise 10 — event.htm

Create three HTML document that detail upcoming events at your school or in your community by completing the following steps:

   a) Using Notepad, create the first HTML document that includes:
   - a comment with your name
   - the title Events
   - an appropriate heading
   - links to documents that contain specific details about two different events

   b) Save the HTML document naming it event.htm and print a copy.

   c) Using Notepad, create a second HTML document. This document should contain an appropriate title, heading, and specific details about an event. Save this HTML document naming it event1.htm. and print a copy.

   d) Using Notepad, create a third HTML document. This document should contain an appropriate title, heading, and specific details about a second event. Save this HTML document naming it event2.htm. and print a copy.

   e) View the first document in a Web browser. Test the links.

Exercise 11 — vacation.htm

Create two HTML documents that detail the last vacation you took by completing the following steps:

   a) Using Notepad, create the first HTML document that includes:
   - a comment with your name
   - the title Vacation
   - an appropriate background and text color
   - an appropriate heading
   - a link to a document that contains details about the vacation destination

   b) Save the HTML document naming it vacation.htm and print a copy.

   c) Using Notepad, create a second HTML document. This document should contain an appropriate title, colors, heading, and specific details about the vacation destination. Save this HTML document naming it destination.htm and print a copy.

   d) View the first document in a Web browser. Test the link.

Exercise 12 ——————————————— courses.htm

Create HTML documents that detail information about your school courses by completing the following steps:

a) Using Notepad, create the first HTML document that includes:
- the title School Courses
- an appropriate background and text color
- your name in Heading 1 format
- your school name in Heading 2 format
- the current school year in Heading 3 format
- links to documents that contain specific information about each of your courses, such as assignment due dates, topic of study, and evaluation procedures

b) Save the HTML document naming it courses.htm and print a copy.

c) Using Notepad, create the appropriate number of HTML documents for each of your courses. Each document should include an appropriate titles, headings, and content. Save the HTML documents naming them appropriately. Print a copy of each document.

d) View the first document in a Web browser. Test the links.

Chapter 4
Introducing Dreamweaver

Chapter 4 Expectations

After completing this chapter you will be able to:

1. Define a Web site.
2. Create a home page and change the page title.
3. Display a Web page in different document views.
4. Understand why tables are used to organize and control the arrangement of content in a Web page.
5. Create tables and modify table properties.
6. Edit the content of Web page documents and check spelling.
7. Print and close a Web page document.
8. Quit Dreamweaver.
9. Edit a Web site.
10. Create and open Web page documents.
11. Create text hyperlinks.

This chapter introduces Dreamweaver and discusses how to create a Web site and Web page documents, add tables and special characters, and create hyperlinks. Printing a Web page, checking spelling, using help, and viewing a Web page document in a browser are also covered.

4.1 Dreamweaver MX

Web Sites

A Web site consists of one or more Web page documents with content such as text, graphics, and links used to navigate through the Web site.

Dreamweaver MX is the Web development application that is part of the Macromedia Studio MX suite. Dreamweaver is used to create Web sites. Also part of the MX suite is Fireworks and Flash. These applications are introduced later in the text.

workspace

The windows, toolbars, and panel groups that are displayed when Dreamweaver MX is running are collectively called the *workspace*. In the Dreamweaver workspace below, a new Web page document window is displayed, and the Site panel displays the folder for the current Web site:

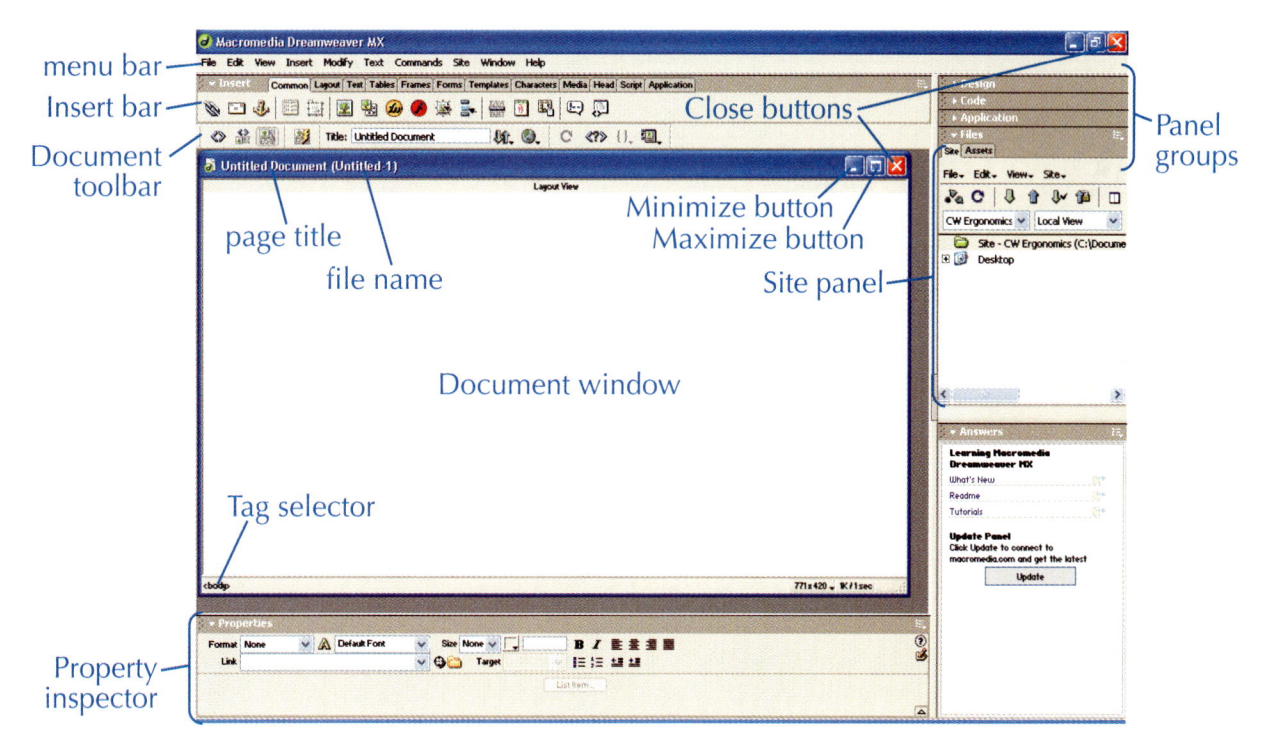

- The **menu bar** displays the names of menus that contain commands.
- The **Insert bar** contains buttons for adding objects to a Web page document.

Introducing Dreamweaver 4 – 1

- The **Document toolbar** contains buttons and menus for changing views and working with a document.
- The **page title** is the title that will be displayed in the title bar of the browser window when a user views the Web page.
- The **file name** is the name of the file that stores the Web page document.
- The **Minimize button** ( ) is clicked to reduce the Document window to a button in the Dreamweaver window.
- The **Maximize button** ( ) is clicked to expand the Document window in the Dreamweaver window.
- A **Close button** ( ) is clicked to remove the Document window or the Dreamweaver window.
- The **Site panel** displays files and folders in the Web site.
- The **Panel groups** are other tools used in developing a Web site. The Site panel is in the Files panel group.
- The **Document window** displays the Web page document.
- The **Tag selector** is used to select a tag and its contents.
- The **Property inspector** is used to change properties of the selected text or object.

Starting Dreamweaver

Dreamweaver is started by selecting Start → All Programs → Macromedia → Macromedia Dreamweaver MX. Dreamweaver may also be started by double-clicking the Dreamweaver icon on the Desktop:

4.2 Defining a Web Site using Dreamweaver

In Dreamweaver, a Web site needs to be defined before creating any Web page documents. A new Web site is defined by selecting Site → New Site using the Site menu on the menu bar or the Site menu in the Site panel. A series of dialog boxes are displayed for defining the site. A folder for the Web site is created and the name, server technology, file locations, and remote server options are specified. Refer to Practice 1 for the dialog boxes that are displayed during site definition.

Practice 1

In this practice you will create a new Web site.

① *START DREAMWEAVER*

Select Start → All Programs → Macromedia → Macromedia Dreamweaver MX. Dreamweaver is started and a new Web page document is displayed. Note the Insert bar, Document window, Property inspector, and Site panel.

② *DEFINE A NEW SITE*

a. From the menu bar or Site panel, select Site → New Site. A dialog box is displayed.
   1. Select the Basic tab if those options are not already displayed.
   2. In the What would you like to name your site? box, type: Computer Ergonomics

[Screenshot: Site Definition for Computer Ergonomics — Basic tab, Editing Files, "What would you like to name your site?" field contains "Computer Ergonomics"]

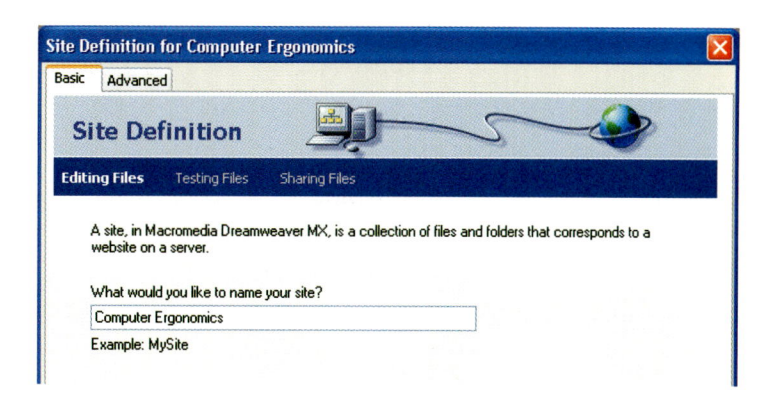

3. Select Next. More options are displayed.
4. Select the No, I do not want to use a server technology option:

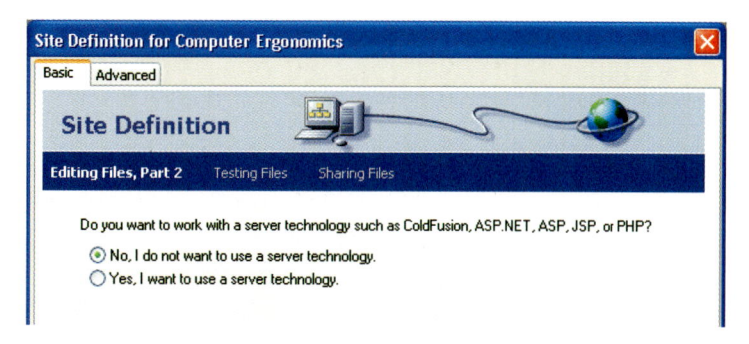

[Screenshot: Site Definition, Editing Files, Part 2 — "Do you want to work with a server technology such as ColdFusion, ASP.NET, ASP, JSP, or PHP?" with "No, I do not want to use a server technology." selected]

5. Select Next. More options are displayed.
6. Select the Edit local copies on my machine, then upload to server when ready option:

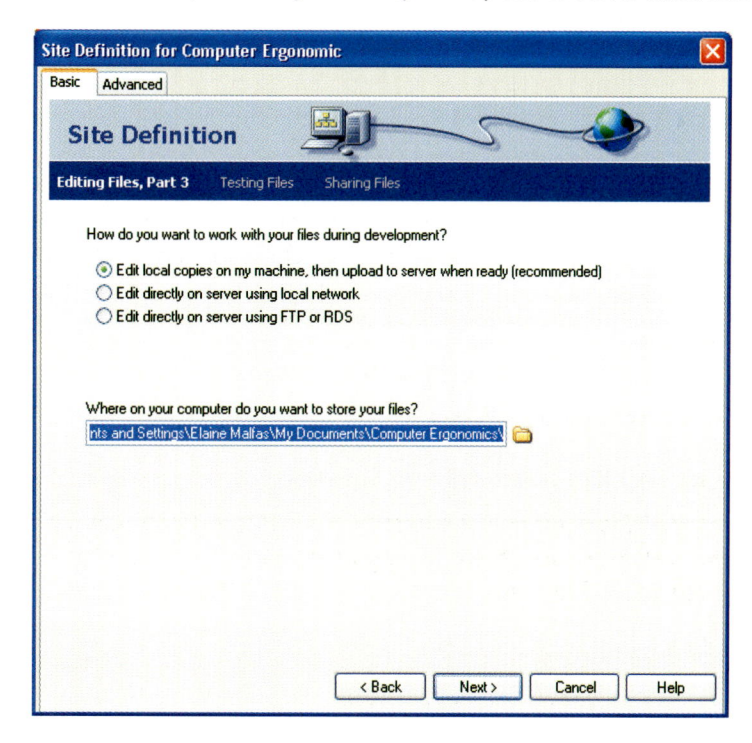

[Screenshot: Site Definition, Editing Files, Part 3 — "How do you want to work with your files during development?" with "Edit local copies on my machine, then upload to server when ready (recommended)" selected; storage path shown: nts and Settings\Elaine Malfas\My Documents\Computer Ergonomics\]

7. Click the folder icon (📁). A dialog box is displayed for browsing the local disk.
    a) Navigate to the appropriate location to create the folder which will store the Web site.
    b) Click the Create New Folder button:

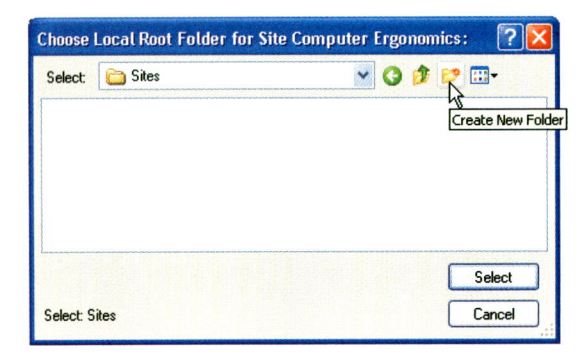

c) Type Computer Ergonomics to replace the New Folder name.
d) Press Enter. The Computer Ergonomics folder appears in the Select list.
e) Select Open.
f) Select Select to choose the new folder as the Web site folder.
8. Select Next. More options are displayed.
9. In the How do you connect to your remote server? list, select None:

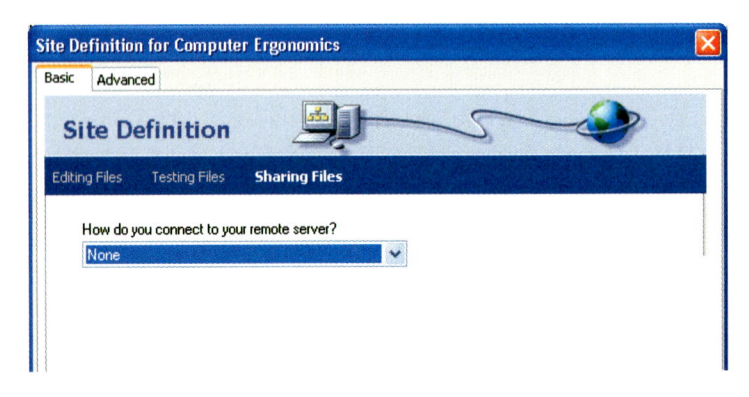

10. Select Next. A summary is displayed:

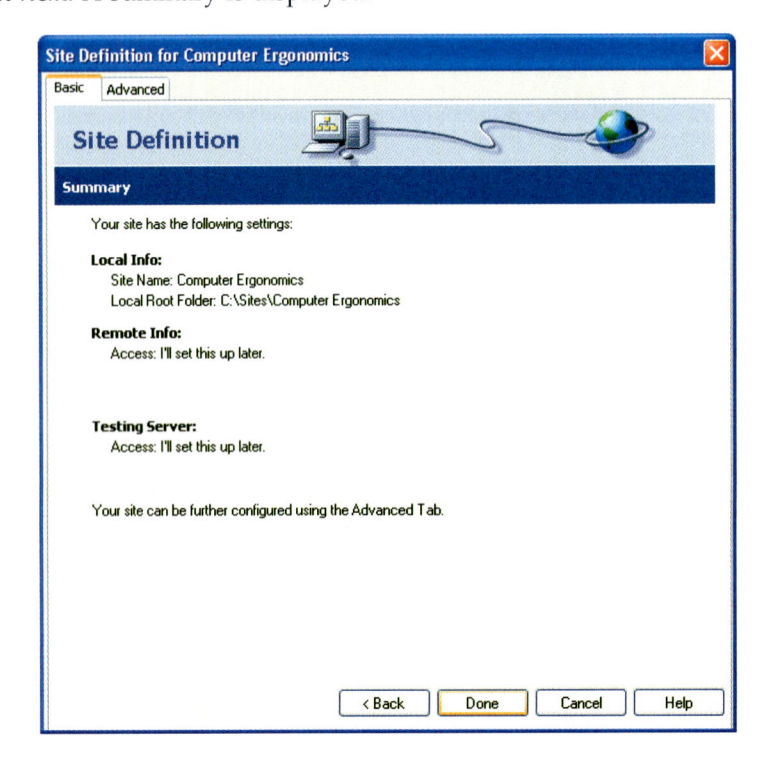

11. Select **Done** to create the site and return to the untitled Web page document. Note the Site folder is displayed in the Site panel:

Why Save Often?

Saving often when working on a document can help prevent accidental loss. A power interruption may erase the document in the computer's memory. Saving before printing can also prevent accidental loss.

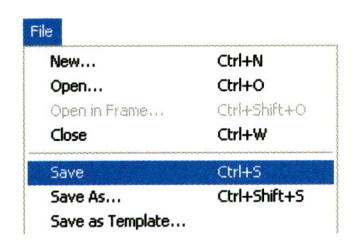

Resizing the Document Window

Clicking the Maximize button (□) in the Document window expands the window, changes the Maximize button to the Restore button (⧉), and moves the Document window's buttons to the upper-right corner of the screen:

Clicking the Restore button (⧉) resizes the Document window to the previous dimensions.

4.3 Saving and Naming a Web Page Document

To add a Web page document to a Web site, the document must be saved to the Web site's folder that was created during site definition. When a Web page document is saved, it must be given a name. File names for Web page documents can contain lowercase letters, numbers, and underscores (_). Do not use spaces or uppercase letters, and it is best to not start the file name with a number. These file name guidelines will ensure that the Web site can be viewed by most users once it is posted to a server and available on the Internet. A file name should also be descriptive of the page contents.

A Web page document is saved by selecting File → Save. The Save As dialog box is displayed the first time a Web page document is saved:

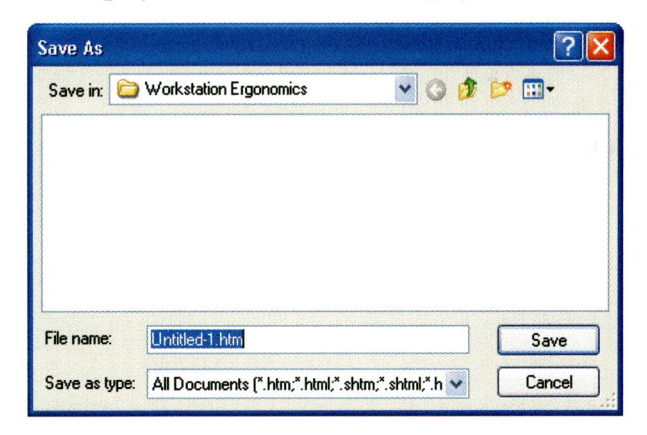

The **Save in** list and the contents box below it are used to navigate to the location where the file is to be saved. A Web page document should be saved in the appropriate Web site folder. Typing a descriptive file name in the **File name** box and selecting **Save** saves the document. The extension .htm is automatically added to the file name.

Introducing Dreamweaver   4 – 5

> **Home Page File Name**
>
> index.htm is usually the best choice for the home page file name because Web servers automatically recognize it as the home page of a Web site.

4.4 Creating the Home Page

The *home page* of a Web site is the main page or starting point of the Web site. A Web page document that is saved with the file name index.htm is automatically designated by Dreamweaver as the home page of the Web site.

4.5 Changing the Page Title

The *page title* of a Web page is the text displayed in the title bar of the browser window when a user views the Web page. The page title also appears in the title bar of the Document window in Dreamweaver. The page title of a Web page document is changed by selecting Modify → Page Properties which displays a dialog box. Typing a new title in the Title box and selecting OK changes the page title. Page titles can contain spaces.

A fast way to change the page title is to type the new title in the Title box on the Document toolbar and press Enter:

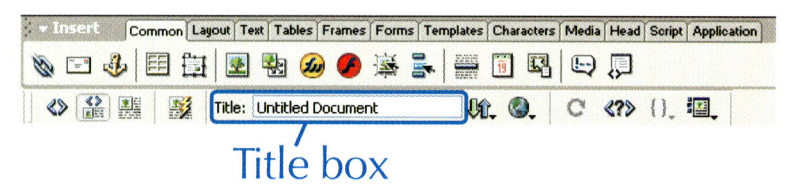

Title box

4.6 Web Page Document Views

Design view

Code view

Code and Design view

In Dreamweaver, Web page documents are displayed in *Design view* by default, which displays the document as it will appear in a browser window. Changing to *Code view* displays the code generated for the Web page, which is useful for studying the HTML. Tags and code can be edited in Code view. A document can also be displayed in *Code and Design view*, a combination of both views. The view can be changed using commands in the View menu or by clicking buttons on the Document toolbar:

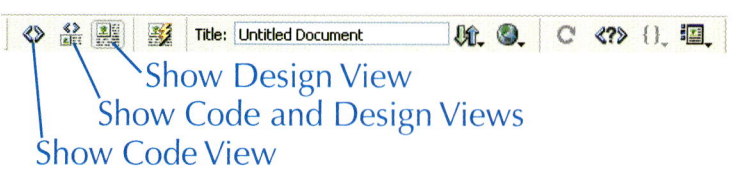

Show Design View
Show Code and Design Views
Show Code View

viewing a Web page document in a browser

A Web page document is viewed in a browser by pressing the F12 key or selecting File → Preview in Browser and then selecting a browser from the submenu. A Web page document cannot be modified in the browser window. Changes are made by switching back to the Dreamweaver window where the document can be modified. Pressing F12 after making the changes updates the browser window with the modified document. The browser window is closed by clicking the Close button (☒).

Practice 2

In this practice you will save a Web page document as the home page, change the page title, and display the document in different views. A new Web page document should already be displayed in the workspace.

① DESIGNATE THE WEB PAGE DOCUMENT AS THE SITE'S HOME PAGE

a. Select File → Save. A dialog box is displayed.

1. Use the Save in list to navigate to the Computer Ergonomics folder, if that is not the current location displayed.
2. In the File name box, replace the existing text with index.htm.
3. Select Save. The file is saved in the Computer Ergonomics folder with the file name index.htm. Note the file name is now displayed in the title bar of the Document window and the Web page document is listed in the Site panel:

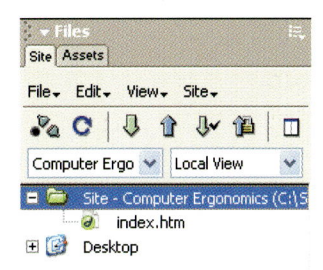

② CHANGE THE PAGE TITLE

a. Select Modify → Page Properties. A dialog box is displayed.

1. In the Title box type: Computer Ergonomics Home Page
2. Select OK. Note that the page title in the Document window now reads "Computer Ergonomics Home Page."

b. Press F12. The document is displayed in a browser window. Note that the page title is displayed in the browser's title bar.

c. Click the Close button (X) to close the browser window.

③ CHANGE VIEWS

a. On the Document toolbar click the Show Code View button (<>). The code for the Web page document is displayed in the Document window. Note the title tags and the page title:

   <title>Computer Ergonomics Home Page</title>

b. On the Document toolbar click the Show Code and Design Views button. The Document window is split, with code displayed in the upper half.

c. On the Document toolbar click the Show Design View button. The Web page document is again displayed in Design view.

Introducing Dreamweaver   4 – 7

4.7 Using a Table to Arrange Content

content

table

cell

The *content* in a Web page is the information presented to the user. Tables should always be used to organize and control the arrangement of content in a Web page. A *table* consists of rows and columns. A row runs horizontally and a column runs vertically with the intersection of a row and column called a *cell*:

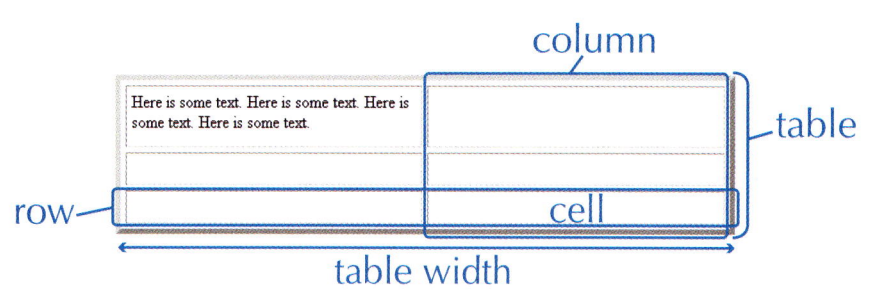

pixel

The width of a table can be specified either in pixels or as a percentage of the width of the browser window. A *pixel* is a unit of measurement related to screen resolution. For example, a monitor set to 800x600 displays 800 pixels across the screen. Newer monitors can display 1024 or more pixels across the screen.

table width

A table width specified in pixels is called *fixed width* because the width of the table will not change when a user resizes the browser window. The content will always look the way it was arranged in Dreamweaver during the development of the Web page document. However, some content may be hidden if the browser window is sized smaller than the table:

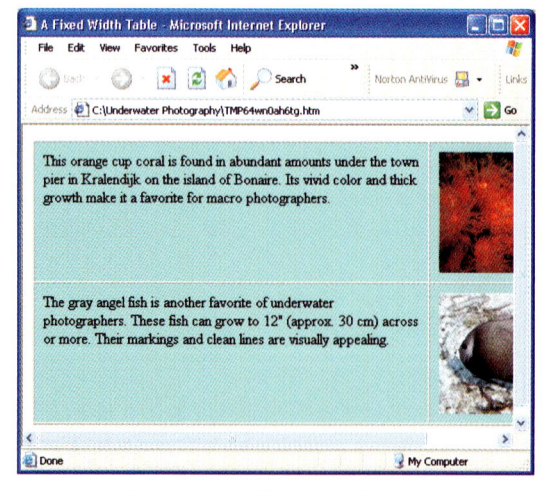

Why Use Tables?

When a Web page is viewed on the Web, there are millions of potential users. These users have different monitor sizes, different screen resolutions, and different browsers. Tables are used to control the layout of the content, so that the Web page the users view looks similar no matter what monitor size, resolution, or browser they have.

The user now has to scroll vertically and horizontally to view the Web page content

To allow a table width to vary, the table width should be specified as a percentage. For example, a table set to 95% will resize to 95% of the browser window width when the browser window is resized. As the user resizes the browser window, the table expands or contracts:

Liquid Design

Tables with widths specified in percentages are sometimes called *liquid* or *fluid* because they change to fill the available space.

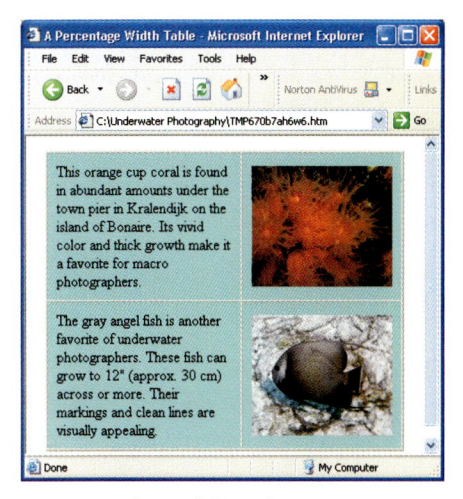

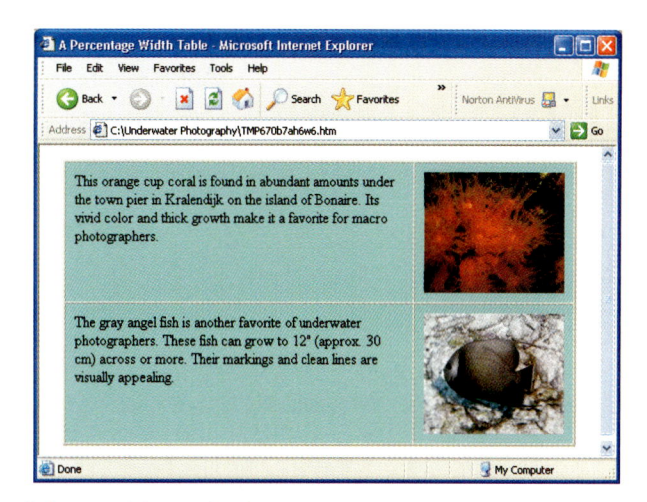

The table adjusts to occupy 95% of the width in the browser window, regardless of window size

However, changing the size of the browser window affects the arrangement of content in a table with widths in percentages. Changing the individual cell widths allows more control of the layout and is discussed in Section 4.10.

more table properties

Other table properties include border, cell padding, and cell spacing:

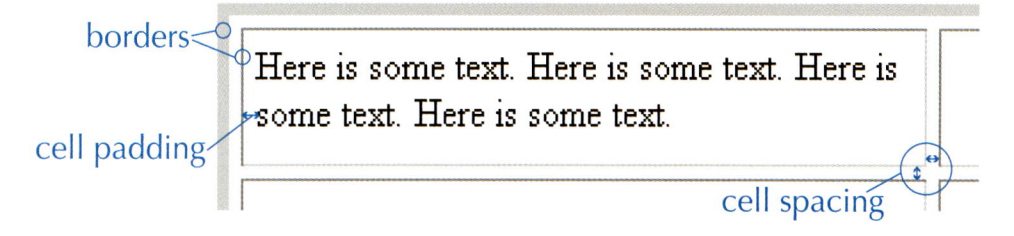

When to use Borders

A table used for presenting numeric data is best formatted with a border. The border helps the user understand the numeric data. A table used for controlling the layout of text and graphics usually does not have a border.

- **Borders** are the lines around the table and the cells. A border size of 0 specifies that no border is displayed. A border size of 1 or more defines the table border thickness in pixels and outlines each cell.

- **Cell padding** is the number of pixels of blank space between the content in the cell and the cell's boundary. If a cell padding amount is not specified, browsers may assign a value. To avoid this, an amount should be specified. 0 is used if the content should be against the cell boundaries. A larger setting, such as 6 or 10, is used to add space.

- **Cell spacing** is the number of pixels between cells. If a cell spacing amount is not specified, browsers may assign a value. To avoid this, an amount should be specified. 0 specifies no spacing.

Introducing Dreamweaver   4 – 9

> **Layout View**
>
> Tables may also be created in Layout view, which includes advanced formatting features. Layout view is best used by experienced Dreamweaver users.

4.8 Creating a Table

Tables are best created in *Standard view*. Clicking the Layout tab in the Insert bar and then clicking the Standard View button displays the document in Standard view.

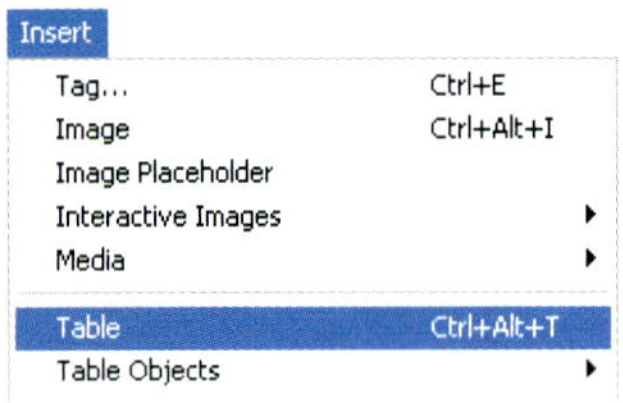

Selecting Insert → Table or clicking the Insert Table button in the Insert bar displays a dialog box:

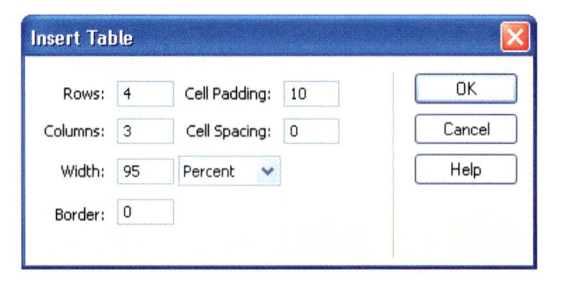

The number of rows and columns for the table is specified in the Rows and Columns boxes. To create a table with a variable width, 95 and Percent is selected for the Width. The Border, Cell Padding, and Cell Spacing boxes are values in pixels. Selecting OK creates the table in the Document window.

selecting a table

A table is selected in the Document window by pointing to a corner or the top border of the table until the pointer changes to ✥ and then clicking. A selected table has a thick black border around it and square black handles on the bottom and right sides:

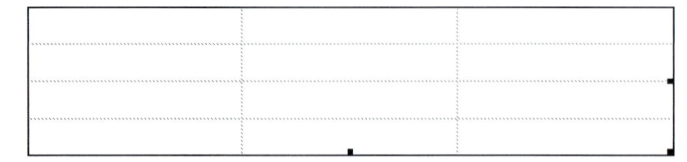

A table is automatically selected after being created

using the Tag selector

A table may also be selected by placing the insertion point in any cell in the table and then clicking the <table> tag in the Tag selector: 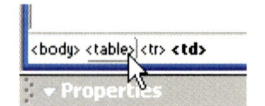

> **Viewing HTML**
>
> When an object in Design view is selected, the corresponding HTML is automatically selected and can be viewed in Code view or Code and Design view.

4 – 10   A Guide to Web Development Using Macromedia Dreamweaver MX

When a table is selected, the Property inspector at the bottom of the Dreamweaver workspace displays table properties:

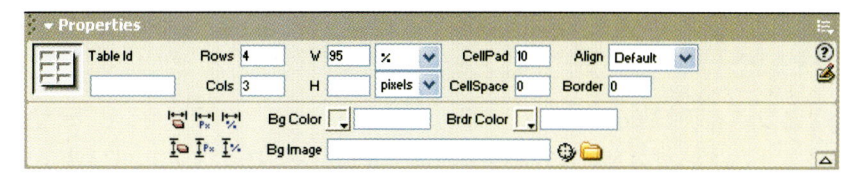

- W is the table width. A new value can be typed. The unit for the value is selected from the adjacent list.

table alignment

- Align is the position of the table within the Web page document. A table that has a percentage width is best center aligned so that the table has equal amounts of space on the right and left side. A new alignment can be selected from the list.

4.9 Changing Cell Width and Height

Placing the insertion point in a cell displays the cell properties in the Property inspector at the bottom of the Dreamweaver window:

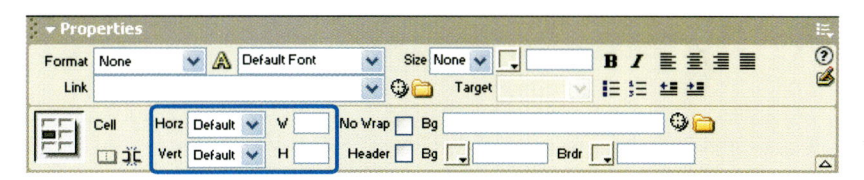

- W is the width of a cell either in a percentage of the table's width or in a number of pixels. A new value can be typed. The value typed is in pixels unless a percent sign (%) is typed as well.

- H is the height of a cell in a percentage or in pixels. A new value can be typed. If a percent sign (%) is not included when H is set, the amount is in pixels.

Cell widths can be specified as either pixels or percentages, regardless of how a table's width is specified. A single table may contain both cells with widths in pixels and cells with widths in percentages. Note that changing the width of a cell may affect the entire column, because the column's width will be the same as the widest cell in that column. To control the layout of a Web page, an amount should always be specified for the width to avoid browser window defaults.

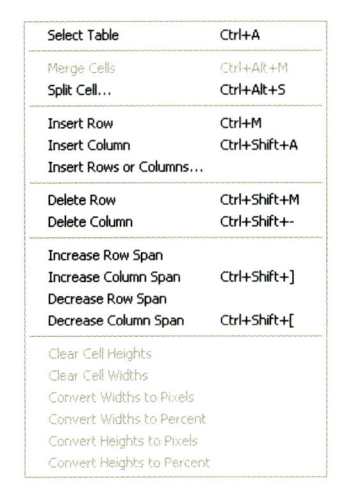

4.10 Adding and Deleting Rows and Columns in a Table

A row or column can be added to a table by first placing the insertion point in a cell and then selecting Modify → Table → Insert Row or Insert Column. A row is added above the cell and a column is added to the left of the cell. A row or column is deleted by first placing the insertion point in a cell and then selecting Modify → Table → Delete Row or Delete Column. The row or column containing the cell is deleted. Be cautious when deleting rows or columns because a warning is not displayed if the cells have content.

Introducing Dreamweaver

Practice 3

In this practice you will add a table to the home page and edit the properties of the table. The index.htm Web page document should be displayed.

① ADD A TABLE

    a. In the Insert bar, click the Layout tab. The Layout buttons are displayed.

    b. On the Layout tab, click the Standard View button if it is not already selected. The Web page document is displayed in Standard view.

    c. Select Insert → Table. A dialog box is displayed.

        1. In the dialog box, specify the following:

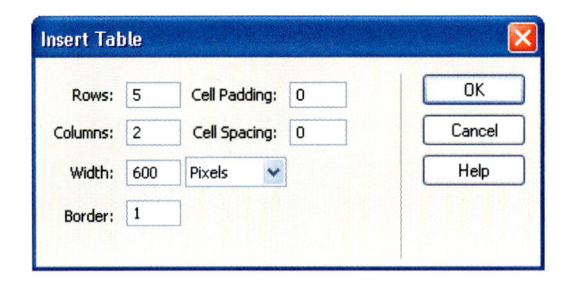

Insert Table
- Rows: 5
- Columns: 2
- Width: 600 Pixels
- Cell Padding: 0
- Cell Spacing: 0
- Border: 1

        2. Select OK. A table is inserted. Note the table properties that are displayed in the Property inspector.

Check—Your Document window should look similar to:

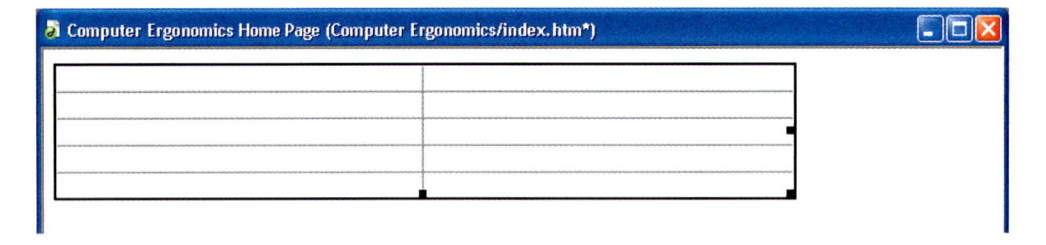

Computer Ergonomics Home Page (Computer Ergonomics/index.htm)*

② VIEW THE WEB PAGE DOCUMENT IN A BROWSER

    a. Press F12. The document is displayed in a browser window. Note that the border is visible because the table was created with a border of 1.

    b. Size the browser window much smaller by dragging the bottom-right window corner (). (If the window is maximized, you need to click the Restore button () in the upper-right corner of the browser window before you can size the window.) Note how the table does not change when the window is sized smaller.

③ CHANGE THE TABLE WIDTH AND ALIGNMENT

    a. Using the taskbar, switch to Dreamweaver.

    b. In the table, click in any cell. The insertion point is placed.

    c. In the Tag selector in the bottom-left corner of the Document window, click the <table> tag. A thick border is displayed around the table indicating that it is selected.

    d. In the Property inspector, set W to 95%. The table width is 95% of the window.

    e. In the Property inspector, set Align to Center. The table is centered between the left and right sides of the window.

④ **VIEW THE WEB PAGE DOCUMENT IN A BROWSER**
   a. Press F12. The document is displayed in the browser window. Note that the table now fits across most of the window.
   b. Size the browser window larger and then smaller by dragging the bottom-right window corner (▨). Note how the table changes to fit the window.

⑤ **CHANGE THE TABLE BORDER AND CELL PADDING**
   a. Switch to Dreamweaver.
   b. If the table is no longer selected, point to the top border of the table until the pointer changes to ✥ and then click. The table displays a thick, black border indicating that it is selected.
   c. In the Property inspector, set **Border** to 0 and press Enter. The border changes to a dotted line around the cells.
   d. Click in any cell of the table. Note the insertion point is against the left cell border.
   e. Select the table, and then in the Property inspector, set **CellPad** to 4 and press Enter.
   f. Click in any cell of the table. Note the insertion point is a several pixels away from the left cell border. With cell padding, content added to cells will be spaced.
   g. Press F12. The document is displayed in the browser window. Note the border is no longer visible because the Border property was changed to 0.
   h. Close the browser window.

⑥ **SAVE THE CHANGES TO THE WEB PAGE DOCUMENT**
   Select File → Save. The changes are saved.

4.11   Adding Text Content to a Table

Text is added in a table cell by clicking in the cell to place the insertion point and then typing. Pressing the Enter key creates a new paragraph in the same cell. HTML paragraphs automatically have a blank line after.

line break

Lines of text that should be displayed without blank lines between are created by inserting a line break at the end of each line. A line break is placed at the insertion point by pressing Shift+Enter. However, an easier method may be to click the Line Break (⏎) button on the Characters tab in the Insert bar:

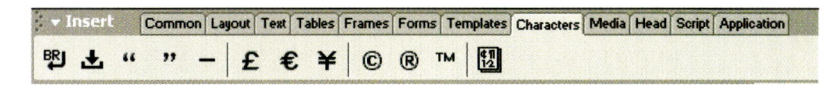

The Characters tab is used to insert special characters

inserting special characters

The **Characters** tab includes buttons for inserting other commonly used symbols. For example, proper quotation marks (" and "), the em dash (—), currency symbols (£, €, ¥), and the copyright (©), registered trademark (®), and trademark (™) symbols. Additional symbols are inserted by clicking the Other Characters button (▦) and then selecting from a displayed dialog box:

Introducing Dreamweaver   4 – 13

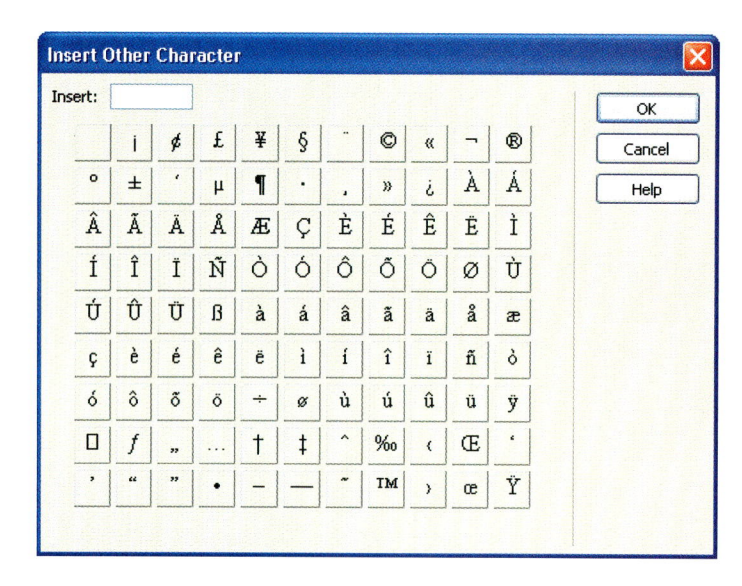

Clicking a symbol and then OK inserts the symbol at the insertion point in the Web page document.

editing content

The Edit menu contains the Undo (Ctrl+Z) and Repeat (Ctrl+Y) commands, which are used to cancel or redo an action. The Edit menu also contains the Cut (Ctrl+X), Copy (Ctr+C), Paste (Ctrl+V), and Clear commands for deleting, duplicating, and moving content.

moving the insertion point in a table

The insertion point is moved to other cells using the arrow keys, or by pressing the Tab key to move to the next cell or Shift+Tab for the previous cell. Note that pressing the Tab key when the insertion point is in the last cell of a table adds a new row to the table.

> **History Panel**
>
> The History panel displays performed actions and can be used to undo or repeat actions. The History panel is displayed be selecting Window → Others → History.

4.12 Checking Spelling

Dreamweaver includes a spelling checker that can help find misspelled words in a Web page document. Selecting Text → Check Spelling or pressing Shift+F7 starts checking the spelling from the insertion point in the Web page document. A misspelled word causes a dialog box to be displayed:

> **Checking Spelling in Part of a Document**
>
> Selecting text before starting to check spelling examines the selected text first, then displays a dialog box asking if you want to continue checking the rest of the document.

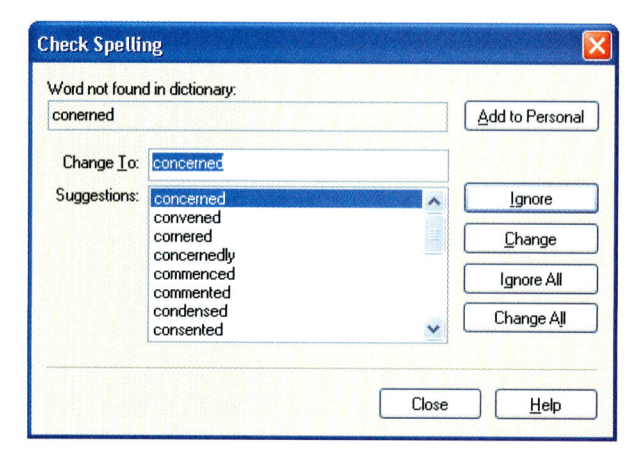

Selecting the correct spelling in the Suggestions list and then Change changes the word and continues checking spelling. Selecting Ignore leaves

4 – 14 *A Guide to Web Development Using Macromedia Dreamweaver MX*

the word spelled as it was, which is useful for proper names that are not in Dreamweaver's dictionary. Selecting Ignore All skips over all occurrences of the word.

When Dreamweaver is done checking the entire document, a dialog box is displayed with a message "Spelling check completed." Selecting OK removes the dialog box.

Practice 4

In this practice you will add and edit content and check the spelling in a Web page document. The index.htm Web page document should be displayed.

① ADD CONTENT

a. Click in the second cell in the top row (the upper-right cell) in the table. The insertion point is placed in the cell.

b. Type: Computer Workstation Ergonomics

c. On the Characters tab in the Insert bar, click the Line Break button ( ). The insertion point moves to the next line.

d. Type the following text. Do NOT press the Enter key to end lines of text; allow the text to wrap in the cell:

Ergonomics, also known as human engineering, is the science of designing working environments to be safe and efficient during interaction. Improper ergonomics can lead to injuries such as MSDs. The ergonomics of a computer workstation include input device ergonomics and posture ergonomics.

e. Press Enter. The insertion point remains in the cell and creates a new paragraph.

f. Type Research by Student Name. replacing Student Name with your name.

② EDIT CONTENT

a. Select the "Research by Student Name." text by dragging or triple-clicking in the text.

b. Select Edit → Cut. The text is cut and no longer appears in the document.

c. Click in the last cell in the table (the lower-right cell). The insertion point is placed.

d. Select Edit → Paste. The text is pasted into the last cell in the table.

e. Click in the blank area below the table to place the insertion point outside of the table. The table adjusts to fit the content:

> Computer Workstation Ergonomics
> Ergonomics, also known as human engineering, is the science of designing working environments to be safe and efficient during interaction. Improper ergonomics can lead to injuries such as MSDs. The ergonomics of a computer workstation include input device ergonomics and posture ergonomics.
>
>
>
> Research by Renny Beiderman.

③ FORMAT THE CELL WIDTHS

a. In the table, click anywhere in the paragraph about ergonomics. The insertion point is placed.

b. In the Property inspector, set W to 70% and press Enter. The width of the cell is formatted as 70% of the table's width.

c. Click in the last cell in the table (the lower-right cell). The insertion point is placed.

d. In the Property inspector, set W to 35% and press Enter. The width of the cell does not change because the widest cell in that column is formatted as 70%.

④ DELETE ROWS

a. Click in the empty cell below the cell that contains the "Computer Workstation Ergonomics" text. The insertion point is placed.

b. Select Modify → Table → Delete Row. The row is deleted.

c. Select Modify → Table → Delete Row again. Another row is deleted.

d. Select Modify → Table → Delete Row again. The table now only has 2 rows.

Check—Your Document window should look similar to:

	Computer Workstation Ergonomics Ergonomics, also known as human engineering, is the science of designing working environments to be safe and efficient during interaction. Improper ergonomics can lead to injuries such as MSDs. The ergonomics of a computer workstation include input device ergonomics and posture ergonomics.
	Research by Renny Beiderman.

⑤ CHECK THE SPELLING

a. Place the insertion point before the first word in the table.

b. Select Text → Check Spelling. A dialog box is displayed. Dreamweaver finds that the word "MSDs" is not in its dictionary and suggests changing it to "MSD's."

  1. Since the word is correctly spelled as is, select Ignore.
  2. Select Ignore if Dreamweaver questions the spelling of your name.
  3. Select OK when Dreamweaver displays a message "Spelling check completed."

⑥ SAVE THE CHANGES AND VIEW THE DOCUMENT IN A BROWSER

a. Select File → Save. The changes are saved.

b. Press F12. The document is displayed in a browser window. Note the modified table.

c. Close the browser window.

4.13 Printing a Web Page Document

printing from a browser   A Web page document can be printed from a browser. In Internet Explorer, selecting File → Print displays a dialog box. Selecting Print in the dialog box prints the Web page using the default options. In Internet Explorer, the Print button ( ) on the toolbar can be clicked to print one copy of a Web page without first displaying the Print dialog box.

previewing before printing   Long Web pages may require several sheets of paper for a printout. In Internet Explorer, selecting File → Print Preview displays the Web page as it will appear when printed, which can help to check how many pages will print. The Print dialog box contains options for specifying just the current page for printing or a range of pages.

headers in Internet Explorer   When printing from Internet Explorer, the header of a printout automatically contains the Web page title and the page number of the printout. The footer contains the URL information. The header and footer are changed by selecting File → Page Setup, which displays the Page Setup dialog box. Information such as your name and the date can be added.

printing from Dreamweaver   The code for a Web page document can be printed in Dreamweaver by selecting File → Print Code (Ctrl+P). A footer with the full path and file name and the page number and number of pages is included on the printout.

4.14 Closing a Web Page Document and Quitting Dreamweaver

When a Web page document is not being worked on, it should be saved and then closed. *Closing a Web page* means that its window is removed from the Dreamweaver workspace and the file is no longer in the computer's memory. A Web page document is closed by selecting File → Close or by clicking the Close button (☒) in the Document window.

Attempting to close a Web page that has been edited but not saved displays a reminder dialog box with the message "Save changes to file name?" Selecting Yes saves the changes in a file and then removes the Document window. Selecting No removes the Document window without saving changes. Selecting Cancel leaves the Web page document open.

When Dreamweaver is no longer needed, it should be quit properly. *Quitting Dreamweaver* means that its window is removed from the Desktop and the program is no longer in the computer's memory. Dreamweaver is quit by selecting File → Exit. Attempting to quit Dreamweaver with an open document that has been edited but not saved displays a reminder dialog box.

Clicking the Close button (☒) in the upper-right corner of the Dreamweaver window closes the application window. Closing an application window quits the application. Attempting to close the Dreamweaver application window with an open Web page that has been edited but not saved displays a warning message dialog box.

4.15 Editing a Web Site

In the Site panel, Dreamweaver maintains a list of Web sites created:

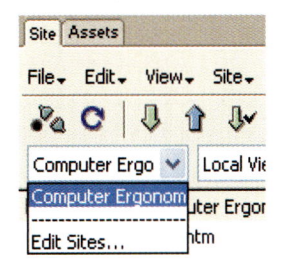

A Web site selected from this list will become the active Web site. If a Web site is not listed, it can be opened by selecting Site → New Site which

Introducing Dreamweaver   4 – 17

displays the Site Definition dialog box. Selecting the Advanced tab displays options for defining an existing site:

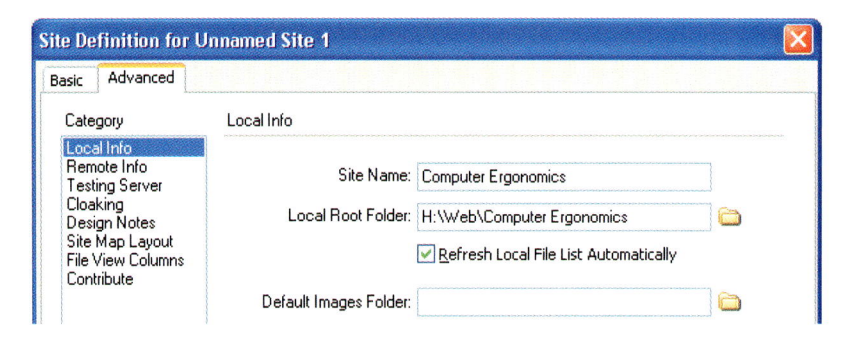

The site name is typed in the Site Name box and the Local Root Folder folder icon (📁) is clicked to navigate to the location of the Web site folder. Selecting OK at the bottom of the dialog box opens the site for editing in Dreamweaver and adds its name to the Site list.

Practice 5

In this practice you will print a Web page two different ways, close a Web page, quit Dreamweaver, and open an existing Web site for editing. The index.htm Web page should be open.

① PRINT THE CODE FOR THE INDEX.HTM WEB PAGE
   a. Select File → Print Code. A dialog box is displayed.
      1. Select OK. The dialog box is removed and the code is printed.

② PRINT THE WEB PAGE DOCUMENT FROM A BROWSER
   a. Press F12. The document is displayed in a browser window.
   b. Select File → Print. A dialog box is displayed.
      1. Select Print. The dialog box is removed and the Web page is printed.
   c. Close the browser window.

③ CLOSE THE WEB PAGE DOCUMENT AND QUIT DREAMWEAVER
   a. Select File → Close. The Document window is removed from the Dreamweaver workspace.
   b. Select File → Exit. The Dreamweaver application window is removed from the Desktop.

④ OPEN A SITE FOR EDITING
   a. Start Dreamweaver. The Site panel may already show Computer Ergonomics as the working Web site.
   b. If Computer Ergonomics is not the active Web site, select Site → New Site. A dialog box is displayed.
      1. Select the Advanced tab.
      2. In the Site Name box, type: Computer Ergonomics
      3. Next to the Local Root Folder box, click the folder icon (📁). A dialog box is displayed.
         i. Navigate to the Computer Ergonomics Web site folder.
         ii. Click Select.
      4. Select OK. A dialog box may be displayed. Select OK. The Computer Ergonomics Web site is the active Web site.

4 – 18   A Guide to Web Development Using Macromedia Dreamweaver MX

4.16 Opening a Web Page Document

Opening a file transfers a copy of the file contents to the computer's memory and displays the file contents in an appropriate window. In Dreamweaver, a Web page document is opened by double-clicking the file name in the Site panel:

Double-clicking index.htm displays the home page document.

Web page documents may also be opened by selecting File → Open (Ctrl+O) or by clicking the Open button ( ) on the toolbar, which displays the Open dialog box. Navigating to the file, clicking the file name, and then selecting Open transfers a copy of the file to a Document window in Dreamweaver.

Window menu

Several documents can be open at the same time, which makes it easy to cut and paste between documents or quickly view different documents. To view a document, double-click the document's file name in the Site panel or select the file name from the Window menu on the menu bar. The Window menu lists all of the open documents.

4.17 Creating a New Web Page Document

A new Web page document is created by selecting File → New, which displays the New Document dialog box:

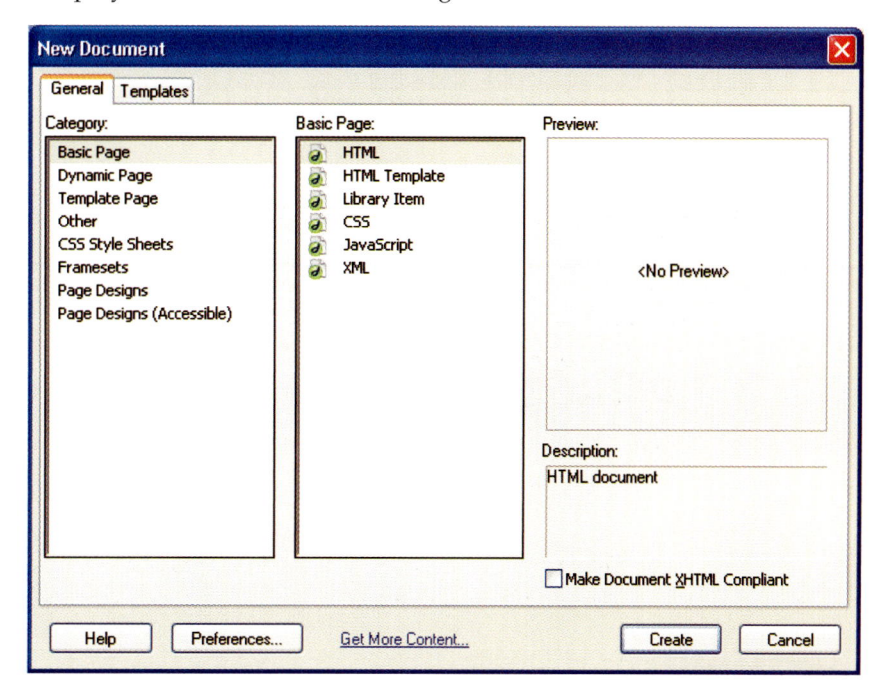

Introducing Dreamweaver 4 – 19

Selecting Basic Page in the Category list, HTML in the Basic Page list, and then Create displays a new Web page document in a Document window.

A new document should be saved with a descriptive file name in the site's folder. A descriptive page title should also be added to a new Web page document.

New Web page documents can also be created and added to a Web site by selecting File → New File in the Site panel. This method is useful for quickly creating many pages in a new Web site at the beginning of the Web site's development. A new document is added to the list of documents in the Site panel and the untitled.htm name is selected and ready to be replaced with a new file name:

A name for the document can be typed

When renamed the extension .htm must be typed as part of the file name. New Web page documents created in this manner are not automatically displayed in a window. The name of the new Web page document must be double-clicked in the Site panel to open the document and display it in a window.

Practice 6

In this practice you will open an existing Web page document, create two new Web page documents, add content, and view different Web page documents. Dreamweaver should be started and the Computer Ergonomics Web site should be the working site.

① OPEN THE INDEX.HTM WEB PAGE DOCUMENT

In the Site panel, double-click the index.htm file name. The index.htm Web page document is opened in a Document window.

② CREATE AND SAVE A NEW WEB PAGE DOCUMENT

a. Select File → New. A dialog box is displayed.
   1. In the Category list, select Basic Page, if it is not already selected.
   2. In the Basic Page list, select HTML, if it is not already selected.
   3. Select Create. A new Web page document is displayed in a Document window.
b. Select File → Save. A dialog box is displayed.
   1. Use the Save in list to navigate to the Computer Ergonomics folder, if that is not the current location displayed.
   2. In the File name box, replace the existing text with: input_device.htm
   3. Select Save. The file is saved and is listed in the Site panel.

③ CREATE AND SAVE ANOTHER NEW WEB PAGE DOCUMENT

   a. From the Site panel, select File → New File. A new file is added to the list of documents.
   b. Rename the document: posture.htm

④ CHANGE THE PAGE TITLES AND DISPLAY DIFFERENT DOCUMENTS

   a. In the Site panel, double-click posture.htm. The Web page document is displayed.
   b. Select Modify → Page Properties. A dialog box is displayed.
      1. In the Title box, type Posture Ergonomics by Student Name replacing Student Name with your name.
      2. Select OK.
   c. Select Window → input_device.htm. The input_device.htm Web page Document is displayed.
   d. On the Document toolbar, in the Title box, replace the text Untitled Document with Input Device Ergonomics by Student Name replacing Student Name with your name.

⑤ ADD CONTENT

   a. In the Site panel, double-click the posture.htm file name. The posture.htm Web page document is displayed.
   b. On the Insert bar, select the Layout tab and then select the Standard View button, if it is not already selected.
   c. On the Insert bar, click the Insert Table button. A dialog box is displayed.
      1. In the dialog box, specify the following:

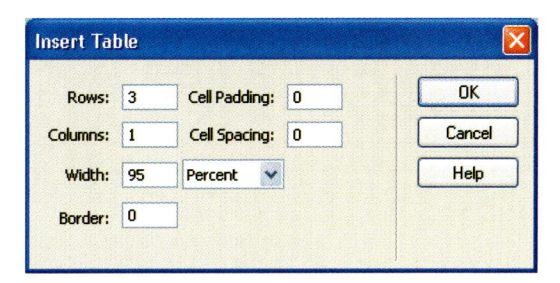

         Insert Table
         Rows: 3   Cell Padding: 0
         Columns: 1   Cell Spacing: 0
         Width: 95   Percent
         Border: 0

      2. Select OK. A table is inserted.
   d. Add content as shown below. Allow the text to wrap:

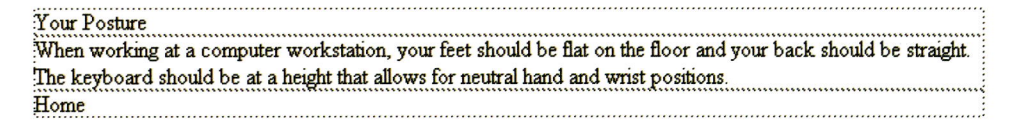

      Your Posture
      When working at a computer workstation, your feet should be flat on the floor and your back should be straight. The keyboard should be at a height that allows for neutral hand and wrist positions.
      Home

   e. Save the modified posture.htm.
   f. Display the input_device.htm Web page document.
   g. Add a table with the following specifications:

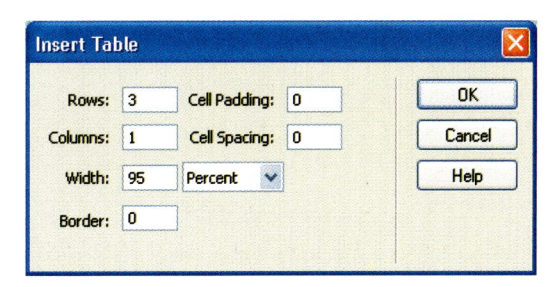

      Insert Table
      Rows: 3   Cell Padding: 0
      Columns: 1   Cell Spacing: 0
      Width: 95   Percent
      Border: 0

h. Add content as shown below. Press the Enter key to create new paragraphs where needed:

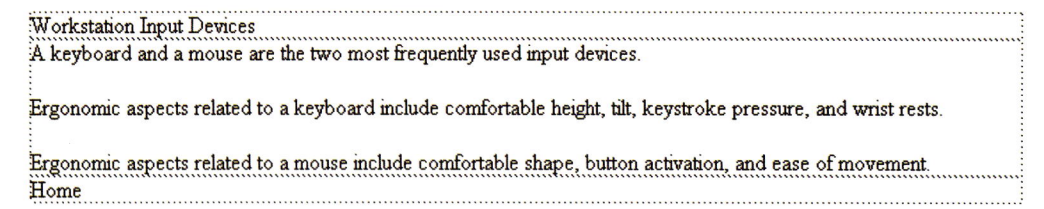

> Workstation Input Devices
> A keyboard and a mouse are the two most frequently used input devices.
>
> Ergonomic aspects related to a keyboard include comfortable height, tilt, keystroke pressure, and wrist rests.
>
> Ergonomic aspects related to a mouse include comfortable shape, button activation, and ease of movement.
> Home

i. Save the modified input_device.htm.

4.18 Text Hyperlinks

One form of hyperlink is text that can be clicked to display a different Web page document in the browser window. A hyperlink that displays a Web page document that is from the same Web site is called a *document-relative hyperlink*.

document-relative hyperlink

The Property inspector can be used to link text to a Web page document. After selecting the text for the hyperlink, the Browse for File icon is clicked:

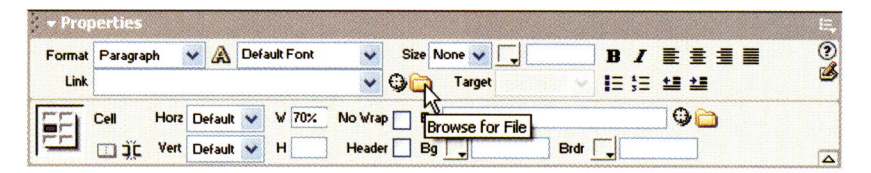

The Select File dialog box is displayed:

> **Right-Clicking Text**
>
> Right-clicking text displays a menu with the Make Link command. Right-clicking linked text displays Change Link or Remove Tag <a> commands.

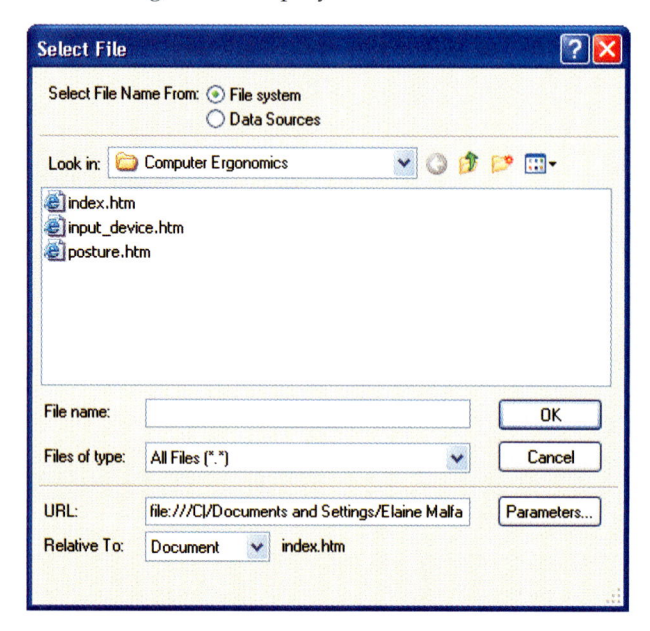

The current Web site and its Web page documents are displayed. Clicking a file name links the selected text to that Web page document. Selecting OK displays the link text as blue and underlined.

4 – 22   A Guide to Web Development Using Macromedia Dreamweaver MX

⊕ The Point to File icon in the Property inspector can also be used to create a hyperlink. After selecting text, the Point to File icon (⊕) is dragged to a Web page document's file name in the Site panel:

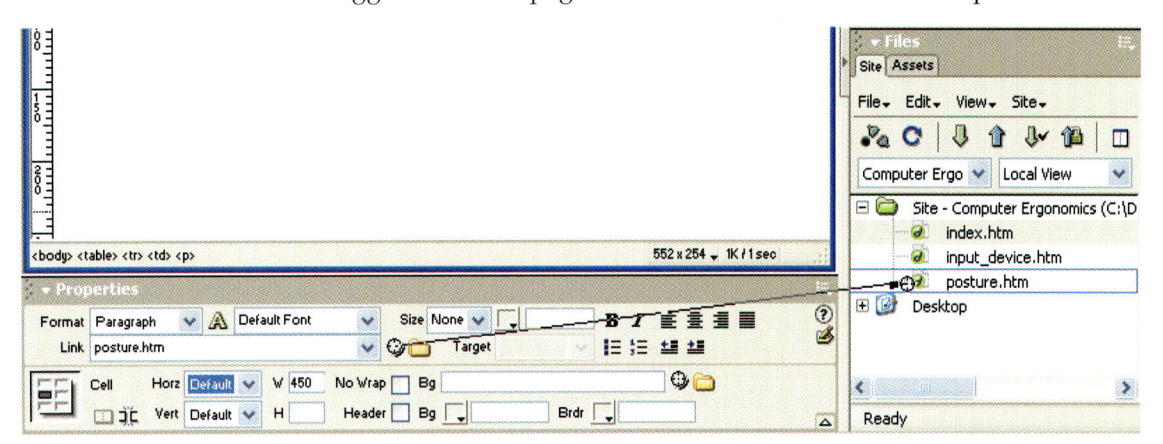

The selected file name has a blue outline when the Point to File icon is used to select a Web page document in the Site panel

The Link list in the Property inspector displays the file name of the linked Web page document when the insertion point is in a hyperlink.

testing and modifying a hyperlink

Links should be tested in a browser window. Links are modified in Dreamweaver by selecting the link text and then selecting Modify → Change Link or Modify → Remove Link.

Practice 7

In this practice you will create hyperlinks, test the hyperlinks, and print Web pages. Dreamweaver should be started and the Computer Ergonomics Web site should be the working site.

① ADD HYPERLINKS TO THE INDEX PAGE

a. Display the index.htm Web page document.

b. Select the text input device ergonomics.

c. In the Property inspector, next to the Link box, click the Browse for File icon (📁). A dialog box is displayed.

   1. Click the input_device.htm file name.
   2. Select OK. The dialog box is removed.

d. Click anywhere to deselect the text. The hyperlink is blue and underlined.

e. In the same sentence, select the text posture ergonomics.

f. Click the Browse for File icon (📁) and link the text to the posture.htm Web page document.

g. Click in the input device ergonomics hyperlink to place the insertion point. Note that the Link box in the Property inspector displays the file name for the link, which is the input_device.htm Web page document.

h. Click in the posture ergonomics hyperlink to place the insertion point. Note that the Link box in the Property inspector displays posture.htm.

i. Save the modified index.htm Web page document.

② ADD HYPERLINKS TO OTHER PAGES

a. Display the posture.htm Web page document.

b. Select the text Home.

Introducing Dreamweaver   4 – 23

c. Link Home to the index.htm Web page document.
d. Save the modified posture.htm Web page document.
e. Display the input_device.htm Web page document.
f. Link the text Home to the index.htm Web page document.
g. Save the modified input_device.htm Web page document.

③ TEST THE HYPERLINKS
a. Display the index.htm Web page document.
b. Press F12. The document is displayed in a browser window.
c. Click the input devices ergonomics hyperlink. The Input Device Ergonomics Web page is displayed.
d. Click the Home link. The index.htm Web page is again displayed.
e. Click posture ergonomics. The Posture Ergonomics Web page is displayed.
f. Click Home. The index.htm Web page is again displayed.

④ PRINT THE WEB PAGES
a. Select File → Print. A dialog box is displayed.
   1. Select Print. The dialog box is removed and the index.htm Web page is printed.
b. Click input devices ergonomics. The Input Device Ergonomics Web page is displayed.
c. Print a copy of the Input Device Ergonomics Web page.
d. Click Home. The index.htm Web page is again displayed.
e. Click posture ergonomics. The Posture Ergonomics Web page is displayed.
f. Print a copy of the Posture Ergonomics Web page.
g. Close the browser window.

⑤ CLOSE THE WEB PAGE DOCUMENT AND QUIT DREAMWEAVER
a. Select File → Close for each of the open Web page documents.
b. Select File → Exit.

Chapter Summary

Dreamweaver MX is an application used for creating Web sites. A Web site is defined in Dreamweaver before creating any Web page documents. To be added to a Web site, a Web page document must be saved to the Web site's folder. A Web page document that is saved using the file name index.htm is automatically designated by Dreamweaver as the home page of the Web site. The page title is the text displayed in the title bar of the browser window.

By default, Dreamweaver displays Web page documents in Design view, which displays the document as it will look in a browser window. Code view displays the code generated for the Web page. Code and Design view displays both views. To view a Web page document in a browser window, press the F12 key or select File → Preview in Browser.

Content is the information presented to the user. Tables are used to organize and control the arrangement of content in a Web page and are best created in Standard view. Table properties include width, rows, columns, border, cell padding, and cell spacing. The width of a table can be specified either in pixels, which is a fixed width, or as a percentage. A table width specified as a percentage expands or contracts as the user resizes the browser window. Table properties such as width and alignment are changed in the Property inspector. Tables can be selected by clicking the border or clicking <table> in the Tag selector.

Cell properties are changed in the Property inspector at the bottom of the Dreamweaver window. The W and H boxes are used to set the width and height of a cell, respectively.

Content is added by clicking in a table and typing. Special characters can be added at the insertion point by using buttons on the Characters tab in the Insert bar. Content can be edited using the Undo, Repeat, Cut, Copy, Paste, and Clear commands in the Edit menu. Dreamweaver also includes a spelling checker that can help find misspelled words in a Web page document.

A Web page document can be printed from a browser. In Internet Explorer, the Print Preview command displays the Web page as it will appear when printed. The code for a Web page document can be printed in Dreamweaver.

Closing a Web page removes its window from Dreamweaver and means that the file is no longer in the computer's memory. Quitting Dreamweaver means that its window is removed from the Desktop and the program is no longer in the computer's memory.

A Web page document is opened by double-clicking the file name in the Site panel. A new Web page document is created by selecting File → New. Several documents can be open at the same time. A document is viewed by double-clicking its file name in the Site panel or selecting it from the Window menu. A Web site is opened for editing by selecting the Web site name from the Site panel list. If a Web site name is not listed, the Site → New Site command displays the Site Definition dialog box where an existing site can be designated in the Advanced tab.

A hyperlink is created in Dreamweaver with the Browse for File or Point to File icons in the Property inspector and then tested in a browser. A document-relative hyperlink is a link from one Web page document to another Web page document in the same Web site. Hyperlink text is displayed as blue and underlined.

Vocabulary

Cell The intersection of a row and column in a table.

Cell padding The pixels of blank space between the content in the cell and the cell's boundary.

Cell spacing The pixels of blank space cells.

Closing a Web page The process of removing the Web page window from the Dreamweaver workspace, which removes the file from the computer's memory.

Code and Design view A combination of Code and Design view.

Code view Displays the code generated for the Web page.

Content The information presented to the user in a Web page.

Design view Displays the Web page document as it will appear in a browser window.

Document-relative hyperlink A hyperlink from one Web page document to another Web page document in the same Web site.

Document toolbar Area of the Dreamweaver workspace that contains buttons and menus for changing views and working with a document.

Document window Area of the Dreamweaver workspace that contains the Web page document.

Dreamweaver An application used to create Web sites.

File name The name of the file that stores the Web page document.

Fixed width A table width that is specified in pixels. A fixed width will not change when a user resizes the browser window.

Home page The main page or starting point of the Web site.

Horizontal alignment A cell property used to align the cell contents relative to the left and right sides of the cell.

Insert bar Area of the Dreamweaver workspace that contains buttons for adding objects to a Web page document.

Menu bar Area at the top of the Dreamweaver workspace that displays the names of menus that contain commands.

Opening a file The process of transferring a copy of the file contents to the computer's memory, which displays the file in an appropriate window.

Page title The text displayed in the title bar of the browser window when a user views the Web page. The page title also appears in the title bar of the Document window in Dreamweaver.

Panel groups Tools used in developing a Web site. The Site panel is in the Files panel group.

Pixel A unit of measurement related to screen resolution.

Property inspector Area of the Dreamweaver workspace that is used to change properties of the selected text or object.

Quitting Dreamweaver The process of removing the Dreamweaver window from the Desktop, which removes the program from the computer's memory.

Site panel Area of the Dreamweaver workspace that displays files and folders in the Web site.

Standard view A view used to create tables.

Table A structure that consists of rows and columns that can be used to organize and control the arrangement of content in a Web page.

Tag selector Area at the bottom of the Document window that is used to select a tag and its contents.

Vertical alignment A cell property used to align the cell contents relative to the top and bottom of the cell.

Workspace The Dreamweaver application interface, which contains windows, toolbars, and panel groups.

Dreamweaver Commands and Buttons

Change Link command Displays a dialog box used to modify a hyperlink. Found in the Modify menu.

Check Spelling command Finds misspelled words in a Web page document. Found in the Text menu.

Clear command Used to delete selected content. Found in the Edit menu.

Close command Removes a Web page document from the Dreamweaver workspace or quits Dreamweaver. Found in the File menu. The button in the upper-right of the window can be used instead of the command.

Copy command Used to duplicate selected content. Found in the Edit menu.

Cut command Used to move selected content. Found in the Edit menu.

Delete Column command Deletes columns from a table. Found in the Table submenu in the Modify menu.

Delete Row command Deletes rows from a table. Found in the Table submenu in the Modify menu.

Exit command Removes the Dreamweaver window from the Desktop.

Insert Column command Inserts columns into a table. Found in the Table submenu in the Modify menu.

Insert Row command Inserts rows into a table. Found in the Table submenu in the Modify menu.

Line Break button Clicked to add a line break at the insertion point. Found on the Characters tab in the Insert bar.

Maximize button Expands the Document window in the Dreamweaver window.

Minimize button Reduces the Document window to a button in the Dreamweaver window.

New command Displays a dialog box used to create a new Web page document. Found in the File menu on the menu bar.

New File command Creates a new Web page document. Found in the File menu in the Site panel.

New Site command Used to define a new Web site. Found in the Site menu on the menu bar or the Site menu in the Site panel.

Open command Displays a dialog box that is used to open a Web page document. Found in the File menu. The Open button on the toolbar can be used instead of the command.

Other Characters button Clicked to display a dialog box for selected special characters to add at the insertion point. Found on the Characters tab in the Insert bar.

Page Properties command Displays a dialog box used to change the page title for a Web page document. Found in the Modify menu.

Paste command Used to move selected content. Found in the Edit menu.

Preview in Browser command Displays a submenu used to view the Web page document in a browser window. Found in the File menu. The F12 key can be used instead of the command.

Print Code command Prints the code for a Web page document. Found in the File menu.

Remove Link command Removes an existing link. Found in the Modify menu.

Repeat command Used to redo an action. Found in the Edit menu.

Save command Displays a dialog box that is used to save a Web page document to the Web site's folder. Found in the File menu.

Show Code and Design Views button Splits the Document window to display both the code and layout of a Web page document. Found on the Document toolbar.

Show Code View button Displays the code for a document in the Document window. Found on the Document toolbar.

Show Design View button Displays the document in the Document window as it will appear in a browser. Found on the Document toolbar.

Introducing Dreamweaver

Standard View button Displays a Web page document in Standard view. Found on the Layout tab in the Insert bar.

Table command Displays a dialog box used to create a table. Found in the Insert menu. The Insert Table button in the Insert bar can be used instead of the command.

<table> tag Selects the table containing the insertion point. Found in the Tag selector.

Undo command Used to cancel an action. Found in the Edit menu.

Window menu Contains a list of open Web page documents.

Review Questions

Sections 4.1 — 4.6

1. a) What is Dreamweaver?
   b) What is the Dreamweaver workspace?

2. a) What does the Insert bar contain?
   b) What does the Site panel display?
   c) What can be changed using the Property inspector?

3. a) During site definition, what is created?
   b) List three options that are specified during site definition.

4. What characters can a Web page document file name contain?

5. a) What is the home page?
   b) What file name is used to designate a document as the home page of a Web site?

6. a) What two places is the page title displayed?
   b) Can page titles contain spaces?
   c) List the steps required to change the page title using the fastest method.

7. a) What view displays a Web page document as it will appear in a browser window?
   b) Which view displays the code generated for a Web page?

8. a) What key is pressed to view a Web page document in a browser window?
   b) Is it possible to modify a Web page document in a browser window?

Sections 4.7 — 4.18

9. a) What is a table used for?
   b) What does a table consist of?
   c) What is a cell?

10. a) What are two ways the width of a table can be specified?
    b) What is a pixel?

11. a) What does a border size of 0 specify?
    b) What is cell padding?
    c) What is cell spacing?

12. a) Which view should be used to create tables?
    b) List the steps required to create a table.

13. a) List two ways to select a table.
    b) List the steps required to center align a table.

14. List two cell properties that can be set in the Property inspector.

15. List the steps required to add a row to a table.

16. a) List the steps required to add text to a cell.
    b) How can a line break be inserted?
    c) How is a © symbol added to content?
    d) List two ways the insertion point can be moved to the next cell in the table.

17. Which command in the Edit menu is used to cancel an action?

18. Give an example of when you might select Ignore in the Check Spelling dialog box.

19. a) List the steps required to print a Web page document from a browser.
    b) What Internet Explorer command can be selected to determine how many sheets of paper a Web page requires?
    c) List the step required to print the code for a Web page document from Dreamweaver.

20. What is the difference between closing a Web page and quitting Dreamweaver?

21. List the steps required to open a Web site not listed in the Site panel.

22. List two ways a Web page document can be opened in Dreamweaver.

23. List the steps required to create a new Web page document.

24. a) Where are Web page documents in a Web site listed?
    b) Which menu lists all of the open documents in a Web site?

25. List the steps required to create a hyperlink to another Web page in the Web site.

Exercises

Exercise 1 ——————————————————— Cooking Herbs

Create a new Web site about cooking with herbs by completing the following steps:

a) Define a new site named Cooking Herbs in a folder named Cooking Herbs.

b) Add three Web page documents to the Cooking Herbs Web site naming them index.htm, popular_herbs.htm, and recipes.htm.

c) Modify the index.htm Web page document as follows:

   1. Change the page title to: Cooking Herbs Home Page
   2. Add a table with 3 rows and 1 column, a width of 95%, no border, a cell padding of 4, and no cell spacing.
   3. Add content as shown below. Allow the text to wrap and replace Student Name with your name:

Cooking Herbs
People have made use of herbs in cooking for centuries. Cooking herbs like parsley, thyme, mint, garlic, and chives are among popular herbs to cook with. There are numerous recipes that call for cooking herbs: vinegars, oils, salads, appetizers, entrees, and desserts.
Research by Student Name

   4. Link the text popular herbs to popular_herbs.htm.
   5. Link the text recipes to recipes.htm.

d) Modify the popular_herbs.htm Web page document as follows:

   1. Change the page title to: Popular Herbs
   2. Add a table with 5 rows and 1 column, a width of 95%, no border, a cell padding of 4, and no cell spacing.
   3. Add content as shown below. Allow the text to wrap:

Popular Herbs
There are so many herbs to cook with. Listed below are just a few:
Garlic
The garlic bulb is used to flavor all sorts of cooking. It is usually added to olive oil to flavor dishes. It is a member of the onion family, and varieties vary in flavor considerably.
Chives
You usually see chives sprinkled on salads, soups, meats, and on sour cream with a baked potato. Chives are also a member of the onion family. They are used in egg and cheese dishes as a garnish. Cooking chives destroys their flavor, so they are best added to dishes at the end of the cooking process.
Dill
Dill leaves are used in salads, fish dishes, and sauces. They are also used to flavor pickles. The seed oil is used in making gripe water also. Dill keeps its flavor even when frozen.
Home

   4. Link the text Home to index.htm.

e) Modify the recipes.htm Web page document as follows:
   1. Change the page title to: Recipes
   2. Add a table with 3 rows and 2 columns, a width of 95%, no border, a cell padding of 8, and no cell spacing.
   3. Add content as shown below. Insert line breaks after each of the ingredients and allow the instructions to wrap:

Recipes	
Dill Salad Dressing	Sage Flavored Rice
Lemon juice Salad oil Dijon mustard Minced fresh dill Combine the juice and the oil slowly by whisking. Add the mustard and the dill and refrigerate. This dressing can be used on sliced tomatoes or on a salad. Try it with fish or chicken also!	Beef or chicken bouillon Rice Butter Chopped fresh sage Parmesan cheese Boil the bouillon, add rice, lower heat and cook 15 - 20 minutes covered. Melt the butter in a separate pan and add the sage. Stir the melted sage butter into the rice. When serving, sprinkle the rice with parmesan cheese. This dish is excellent served with chicken or veal.
Home	

   4. Link the text Home to index.htm.

f) Check the spelling in each of the Web page documents.

g) View each Web page document in a browser window and test the hyperlinks.

h) Print a copy of each Web page document from the browser.

Exercise 2 — Clouds

Create a new Web site about clouds by completing the following steps:

a) Define a new site named Clouds in a folder named Clouds.

b) Add four Web page documents to the Clouds Web site naming them index.htm, high_clouds.htm, middle_clouds.htm, and low_clouds.htm.

c) Modify the index.htm Web page document as follows:
   1. Change the page title to: Clouds Home Page
   2. Add a table with 3 rows and 1 column, a width of 95%, no border, a cell padding of 10, and no cell spacing.
   3. Add content as shown below. Allow the text to wrap and replace Student Name with your name:

Clouds
Clouds are made up of millions of tiny droplets of water and ice. Clouds can be separated into three categories: high clouds, middle clouds, and low clouds.
Research by Student Name

Introducing Dreamweaver

4. Link the text high clouds to high_clouds.htm.
5. Link the text middle clouds to middle_clouds.htm.
6. Link the text low clouds to low_clouds.htm.

d) Modify the high_clouds.htm Web page document as follows:

1. Change the page title to: High Clouds
2. Add a table with 3 rows and 1 column, a width of 95%, no border, a cell padding of 5, and no cell spacing.
3. Add content as shown below. Allow the text to wrap.

High Clouds
These are clouds with bases starting at an average of 20,000 feet. Three types of high clouds are Cirrus, Cirrostratus, and Cirrocumulus. Cirrus are thin feather-like crystal clouds. Cirrostratus are thin white clouds that resemble veils. Cirrocumulus are thin clouds that appear as small "cotton patches."
Home

4. Link the text Home to index.htm.

e) Modify the middle_clouds.htm Web page document as follows:

1. Change the page title to: Middle Clouds
2. Add a table with 3 rows and 1 column, a width of 95%, no border, a cell padding of 5, and no cell spacing.
3. Add content as shown below. Allow the text to wrap.

Middle Clouds
These are clouds with bases starting at about 10,000 feet. Two types of middle clouds are Altostratus and Altocumulus. Altostratus are a grayish or bluish layer of clouds that can obscure the Sun. Altocumulus are a gray or white layer of patches of solid clouds with rounded shapes.
Home

4. Link the text Home to index.htm.

f) Open low_clouds.htm and modify the Web page document as follows:

1. Change the page title to: Low Clouds
2. Add a table with 3 rows and 1 column, a width of 95%, no border, a cell padding of 5, and no cell spacing.
3. Add content as shown below. Allow the text to wrap.

Low Clouds
These are clouds with bases starting near Earth's surface to 6,500 feet. Three types of low clouds are Stratus, Stratocumulus, and Cumulus. Stratus are thin, gray sheet-like clouds with low bases and bring drizzle and snow. Stratocumulus are rounded cloud masses that form on top of a layer. Cumulus are fair-weather clouds with flat bases and dome-shaped tops.
Home

4. Link the text Home to index.htm.

g) Check the spelling in each of the Web page documents.

h) View each Web page document in a browser window and test the hyperlinks.

i) Print a copy of each Web page document from the browser.

Exercise 3 ———————————————————— Sharks

Create a new Web site about sharks by completing the following steps:

a) Define a new site named Sharks in a folder named Sharks.

b) Add four Web page documents to the site naming them index.htm, nurse_shark.htm, zebra_shark.htm, and whale_shark.htm.

c) Modify the index.htm Web page document as follows:

   1. Change the page title to: My Favorite Sharks
   2. Add a table with 3 rows and 1 column, a width of 95%, a border of 1, a cell padding of 4, and no cell spacing.
   3. Add content as shown below. Insert line breaks after each shark name and replace Student Name with your name:

Sharks
I love sharks and have researched my three favorites for this Web site:
Nurse Shark Zebra Shark Whale Shark
Research by Student Name

   4. Link the text Nurse Shark to nurse_shark.htm.
   5. Link the text Zebra Shark to zebra_shark.htm.
   6. Link the text Whale Shark to whale_shark.htm.

d) Modify the nurse_shark.htm Web page document as follows:

   1. Change the page title to: Nurse Shark
   2. Add a table with 3 rows and 1 column, a width of 95%, a border of 1, a cell padding of 4, and no cell spacing.
   3. Add content as shown below. Allow the text to wrap:

Nurse Shark
Scientific name: Ginglymostoma cirratum
This shark is common particularly in the Caribbean. It is sluggish during the day but active at night. It feeds on bottom-dwelling lobsters and other crustaceans, as well as snails, clams, octopus, squid, and any fish slow enough to be caught by its great gulping and inhaling style of feeding. It is a harmless shark unless it is provoked.
Home

   4. Link the text Home to index.htm.

Introducing Dreamweaver

e) Modify the zebra_shark.htm Web page document as follows:
   1. Change the page title to: Zebra Shark
   2. Add a table with 3 rows and 1 column, a width of 95%, a border of 1, a cell padding of 4, and no cell spacing.
   3. Add content as shown below. Allow the text to wrap:

Zebra Shark
Scientific name: Stegostoma fasciatum
The zebra shark is found over tropical coral reefs. It is distinctive because of its very long, broad tail and its coloring. The juvenile shark has zebra-like stripes of yellow on black. It takes on a yellowish brown color with dark brown spotting as it reaches adulthood. It has pointed teeth, with each tooth having two smaller points. It poses no harm to humans.
Home

   4. Link the text Home to index.htm.

f) Modify the whale_shark.htm Web page document as follows:
   1. Change the page title to: Whale Shark
   2. Add a table with 3 rows and 1 column, a width of 95%, a border of 1, a cell padding of 4, and no cell spacing.
   3. Add content as shown below. Allow the text to wrap:

Whale Shark
Scientific name: Rhincodon typus
The whale shark is the world's largest living fish. Its appearance is unique: it has alternating thin white vertical bars and columns of spots on a dark background. This shark swims slowly near the surface, and it has a huge mouth for consuming small crustacean plankton and small and large fish. The whale shark is found in all tropical and subtropical oceans, along coastal regions, and enters lagoons on tropical islands. Divers and snorkelers can swim with this shark because it is gentle and curious.
Home

   4. Link the text Home to index.htm.

g) Check the spelling in each of the Web page documents.

h) View each Web page document in a browser window and test the hyperlinks.

i) Print a copy of each Web page document from the browser.

Exercise 4 ——————————————— Swallowtail Butterflies

Create a new Web site about swallowtail butterflies by completing the following steps:

a) Define a new site named Swallowtail Butterflies in a folder named Swallowtail Butterflies.

b) Add two Web page documents to the Swallowtail Butterflies Web site naming them index.htm and black_swallowtail.htm.

c) Modify the index.htm Web page document as follows:

1. Change the page title to: Swallowtail Butterflies Home Page
2. Add a table with 3 rows and 2 columns, a width of 95%, a border of 1, a cell padding of 4, and no cell spacing.
3. Set the width of the left cell in the second row to 60%, and set the width of the right cell in the second row to 40%.
4. Add content as shown below. Allow the text to wrap and replace Student Name with your name:

Swallowtail Butterflies	
Swallowtail butterflies are found all over the world but live mostly in the tropics. They are brightly colored and have characteristic tail-like projections from their hind wings. The females look different from the males in many of the species. They are often spotted near flowers and are attracted to wet soil, puddles, or ponds.	There are many Swallowtail species. The one I find the most interesting is the Black Swallowtail.
	Research by Student Name

5. Link the text Black Swallowtail to black_swallowtail.htm.

d) Modify the black_swallowtail.htm Web page document as follows:

1. Change the page title to: Black Swallowtail
2. Add a table with 2 rows and 2 columns, a width of 95%, a border of 1, a cell padding of 4, and no cell spacing.
3. Set the width of the left cell in the first row to 20% and set the width of the right cell in the first row to 80%.
4. Add content as shown below. Allow the text to wrap:

Black Swallowtail	This species of butterfly is usually found in open fields and woodland meadows. They frequent clover and flower gardens and always fly near the ground. They have variable markings, but they are mostly black with blue and yellow coloring along the edge of the wings. Some colored spots on the butterfly may be larger and may be orange instead of yellow.
Home	

5. Link the text Home to index.htm.

e) Check the spelling in each of the Web page documents.

f) View each Web page document in a browser window and test the hyperlinks.

g) Print a copy of each Web page document from the browser.

Introducing Dreamweaver   4 – 35

Exercise 5 — Quotations

Create a new Web site that contains inspirational quotes by completing the following steps:

a) Define a new site named Quotations in a folder named Quotations.

b) Add two Web page documents to the Quotations Web site naming them index.htm and inspirational_quotes.htm.

c) Modify the index.htm Web page document as follows:

1. Change the page title to: Quotations Home Page
2. Add a table with 3 rows and 1 column, a width of 95%, a border of 1, a cell padding of 4, and no cell spacing.
3. Add content as shown below. Allow the text to wrap and replace Student Name with your name:

Quotations
A quotation is a phrase spoken or written by another person. This person is usually famous. It is always nice to have an inspirational quote to live by or to remember when times get tough. There are quotes from people about success, commitment, overcoming obstacles, failure, discipline, and knowledge.
Student Name

4. Link the text inspirational quote to inspirational_quotes.htm.

d) Modify the inspirational_quotes.htm Web page document as follows:

1. Change the page title to: Inspirational Quotes
2. Add a table with 6 rows and 2 columns, a width of 95%, a border of 2, a cell padding of 3, and no cell spacing.
3. Set the width of the left cell in the first row to 20% and set the width of the right cell in the first row to 80%.
4. Add content as shown below. Allow the text to wrap:

Success	Mistakes are stepping stones to success. --Charles E. Popplestone The only time you'll find success before work is in the dictionary. --Mary B. Smith
Commitment	Commitment is what transforms a promise into reality. --Abraham Lincoln A somebody was once a nobody who wanted to and did. --Anonymous
Overcoming Obstacles	The greater the difficulty, the more glory in surmounting it. --Epicurus Success is to be measured not so much by the position that one has reached in life as by the obstacles which one has overcome while trying to succeed. --Booker T. Washington
Failure	What would you attempt to do if you knew you would not fail? --Robert Schuller Failure is only the opportunity to more intelligently begin. --Kenny Ford
Discipline	If you don't leap, you'll never know what it's like to fly. --Guy Finley Vision without action is a daydream. Action without vision is a nightmare. --Japanese proverb
Home	

5. Link the text Home to index.htm.

e) Check the spelling in each of the Web page documents.

f) View each Web page document in a browser window and test the hyperlinks.

g) Print a copy of each Web page document from the browser.

Advanced

h) Add a Web page document to the Quotations Web site naming it proverbial_quotes.htm.

i) Modify the proverbial_quotes.htm Web page document as follows:
    1. Change the page title to: Proverbial Quotes
    2. Add a table with 6 rows and 2 columns, a width of 95%, a border of 2, a cell padding of 3, and no cell spacing.
    3. Set the width of the left cell in the first row to 20%, and set the width of the right cell in the first row to 80%.
    4. Add content that should include one proverbial quotation from each of the six categories listed on the Inspirational Quotes Web page: Success, Committment, Overcoming Obstacles, Failure, and Discipline. Use the Internet and the library as sources for finding appropriate proverbial quotes.
    5. In the lower-left cell of the table, add the text Home and link it to index.htm.

j) Modify the index.htm Web page document to include appropriate content and a link to proverbial_quotes.htm.

k) Add a Web page document to the Quotations Web site naming it murphys_law_quotes.htm.

l) Modify the murphys_law_quotes.htm Web page document as follows:
    1. Change the page title to: Murphy's Law Quotes
    2. Add a table with 6 rows and 2 columns, a width of 95%, a border of 2, a cell padding of 3, and no cell spacing.
    3. Set the width of the left cell in the first row to 20% and set the width of the right cell in the first row to 80%.
    4. Add content that should include one quotation from each of the six categories listed in the Inspirational Quotes Web page: Success, Commitment, Overcoming Obstacles, Failure, and Discipline. Use the Internet and the library as sources for finding appropriate Murphy's Law quotes.
    5. In the lower-left cell of the table, add the text Home and link it to index.htm.

m) Modify the index.htm Web page document to include appropriate content and a link to murphys_law_quotes.htm.

n) Check the spelling in the two new Web page documents.

o) View each Web page document in a browser window and test the hyperlinks.

p) Print a copy of the two new Web page documents from the browser.

Chapter 5
Web Site Development

Chapter 5 Expectations

After completing this chapter you will be able to:
1. Outline the steps involved in developing a Web site.
2. Define the purpose and target audience of a Web site.
3. Determine the Web pages and navigation structure of a Web site.
4. Determine the content of Web site.
5. Distinguish between different types of navigation bars.
6. Implement usability standards for Web page layout.
7. Apply design concepts to a Web page.
8. Organize files and folders.
9. Use the Assets panel.
10. Merge and split table cells.
11. Create and edit Library items.
12. Insert a time stamp.
13. Create e-mail hyperlinks.
14. Describe how copyright applies to Web sites.

This chapter introduces the overall process of developing a Web site. Determining the purpose, audience, navigation structure, and content of a Web site is discussed, as well as implementing design concepts in the Web page layout. Creating page headers and bottom shared borders is also discussed.

5.1 Web Site Development

Web site development is the process of planning and creating a Web site. Planning includes determining the Web site's purpose, audience, navigation structure, content, and page layout. Dreamweaver is then used to set up the Web site and create the Web pages. Web site development can be divided into two stages, planning and implementation:

Planning

1. Define the purpose and target audience.
2. Determine the Web pages that will be in the Web site by sketching the navigation structure. Review and revise the sketches as needed.
3. Determine the content and navigation for each Web page.
4. Determine the design of the Web pages by sketching the page layouts. Review and revise the sketches, keeping the four design concepts in mind: appropriateness, placement, consistency, and usability.

Implementation

5. Using Dreamweaver, set up the Web site and organize the files and folders.
6. Create the Web pages using Dreamweaver.
7. Review the Web site both in a browser and printed on paper.
8. Make any necessary changes or corrections.
9. Repeat steps 7 and 8 until complete.

Notice that most of the development process is repetitious: start with something, review it, revise it, review it again, etc. With experience, you may only need to revise once or twice.

5.2 Defining the Purpose and Target Audience

purpose

The first step in planning a Web site is to define the purpose and target audience. The *purpose* is the intent of the Web site. For example, the purpose of a restaurant's Web site could be to provide the phone number, location, hours of operation, and a menu. Clearly defining the purpose helps to make decisions about the Web site navigation structure and the content for each Web page. Most Web sites have more than one purpose, so it is best to list as many as possible:

Purposes for a fast-food restaurant's Web site:

- provide location and contact information
- provide the hours of operation
- provide a fun page for kids
- describe the menu
- provide information about specials and promotions

Purposes for a children's theater Web site:

- list rehearsal and show times
- describe the theater production company
- provide location and contact information

target audience

Once the purpose is identified, the target audience of the Web site needs to be defined. The *target audience* is composed of the individuals who are intended to use the Web site. The content of the Web site is tailored to the target audience. To define the target audience, describe the intended users. Ask questions such as how old are they, where do they live, what are their interests, and what is their level of education. Answers to these and other questions related to the site can be listed as characteristics which define the target audience, as in the following examples:

Target audience characteristics for a fast-food restaurant Web site:

- adults, local residents, and travelers
- children who already know and like the restaurant
- people looking for the particular foods offered at the restaurant
- people in a hurry
- people on a budget

Target audience characteristics for a children's theater Web site:

- parents of children interested in being in or attending the productions
- children interested in being in or attending the productions

> **Information Architect**
>
> Information architects create a vision of what a Web site will look like and defines how it will work. Their job involves all aspects of planning the site and may include helping with the implementation.

Practice 1

In this practice you will determine the purpose and target audience for a pasta restaurant Web site and a bicycling club Web site. Write your answers on paper.

① DETERMINE THE PURPOSE AND TARGET AUDIENCE FOR A PASTA RESTAURANT

You have been asked to develop a Web site for a pasta restaurant. The owners want to include the address, hours, phone number, lunch and dinner menus, and a few recipes from the head chef. The restaurant is unique in that all of the pasta and sauces are made fresh daily. The restaurant is family-owned and has become popular with tourists as well as local residents.

a. What are the purposes of the Web site? List as many as possible.

b. Who is the target audience for the Web site? List characteristics of the audience.

② DETERMINE THE PURPOSE AND TARGET AUDIENCE FOR A BICYCLING CLUB

You have been asked to develop a Web site for a local bicycling club. The club meets once a month for a breakfast meeting followed by a group ride. They want to have the club president's contact information and a schedule of events on the home page, and other pages with photos and reviews of past rides.

a. What are the purposes of the Web site? List as many as possible.

b. Who is the target audience for the Web site? List characteristics of the audience.

5.3 Determining the Web Pages and Navigation Structure

navigation structure

The Web pages that need to be included in a Web site are determined from the purpose and target audience. The home page contains general information and links to other Web pages that contain specific information. The organization of a Web site is called its *navigation structure*. For example, the following sketch represents the navigation structure of a fast-food restaurant's Web site that has three levels of pages:

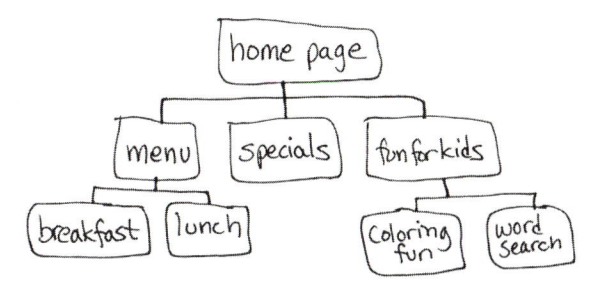

top-level page

same-level page

The home page is referred to as a *top-level page* because it is at the highest level in the structure. At the second level in this example there are three pages, which are *same-level pages*. This example also has Web pages at a third level. These third-level pages, such as breakfast and lunch, are also same-level pages with respect to each other.

parent page

child page

In a navigation structure, Web pages may also be described in terms of parent and child pages. A *parent page* has at least one page below it, called a *child page*. In the example above, the home page is a parent page

> **Sticky Notes as a Design Tool**
>
> When working on the navigation structure of a Web site, sticky notes can help. Using one sticky note for each Web page, the notes can be arranged on a table or wall in a hierarchy like the rectangles in a navigation structure sketch. The notes can be re-arranged many times to find the best structure.

and pages below it are child pages. The menu page is both a parent page and a child page.

A navigation structure shows the pages of the Web site and how they relate to each other. During the planning stage of the Web site development, the navigation structure should be sketched. Rectangles are commonly used to represent each Web page in a site, as in the example sketch in this section.

Sketches of the navigation structure usually go through several revisions before the Web pages and their arrangement are finalized. The arrangement of the pages in a navigation structure should be from general to specific. For example, the menu page is more general than the specific pages for breakfast and lunch. The hierarchy should not be too deep or too shallow and each page should be about one topic.

5.4 Determining the Content

The *content* of each Web page is the text, images, and other objects such as Flash movies presented to the user. Content is defined using the navigation structure of a Web site as an outline and then listing on paper the text and objects for each page. For example, the content for a fast-food restaurant's Web site may be:

- **Home page**   Location information, hours of operation, contact information, and a brief introduction about what this Web site offers. Objects include the restaurant's logo and a picture of the restaurant.

- **Menu page**   A brief description of breakfast and lunch hours and links to the breakfast and lunch pages. Objects include the restaurant's logo and pictures of food.

- **Specials page**   A description of the current specials. Objects include the restaurant's logo.

- **Fun for kids page**   A brief description of what the user will find in the kids pages and links to the coloring fun page and word search page. Objects include the restaurant's logo and a cartoon.

- **Breakfast page**   The breakfast menu. Objects include the restaurant's logo and pictures of breakfast menu items.

- **Lunch page**   The lunch menu. Objects include the restaurant's logo and pictures of lunch menu items.

- **Coloring fun page**   An image that kids can color on a printout of the Web page. Objects include the restaurant's logo and the coloring image.

- **Word Search page**   An image of a word search puzzle that kids can complete on a printout of the Web page. Objects include the restaurant's logo and the word search image.

Practice 2

In this practice you will determine the navigation structure and content of a pasta restaurant Web site. Write your answers on paper.

① SKETCH THE NAVIGATION STRUCTURE OF THE PASTA RESTAURANT SITE

a. Draw a rectangle on a piece of paper and label the rectangle "home page." The home page is at the top level.

b. Below the home page, draw two rectangles in a row and label them "menus" and "recipes" to represent the pages on the second level.

c. Below the menus page, draw two rectangles in a row and label them "lunch" and "dinner" to represent pages on the third level.

Check—Your sketch should look similar to:

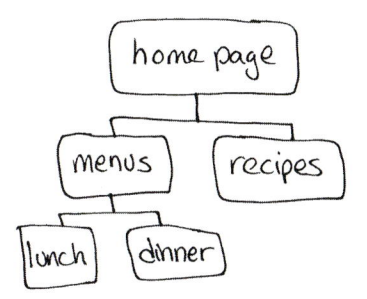

② DETERMINE THE PAGE CONTENT OF THE PASTA RESTAURANT SITE

a. List each of the Web pages from the navigation structure created in step 1.

b. Write down the information each Web page should present.

c. List possible images for each page. Refer to Section 5.4 for examples.

5.5 Defining Navigation Bars

A *navigation bar* is a set of hyperlinks that give users a way to display the different pages in a Web site. A Web site can contain several types of navigation bars and usually contains more than one type for better usability. For example, this Web page includes navigation bars and a breadcrumb trail:

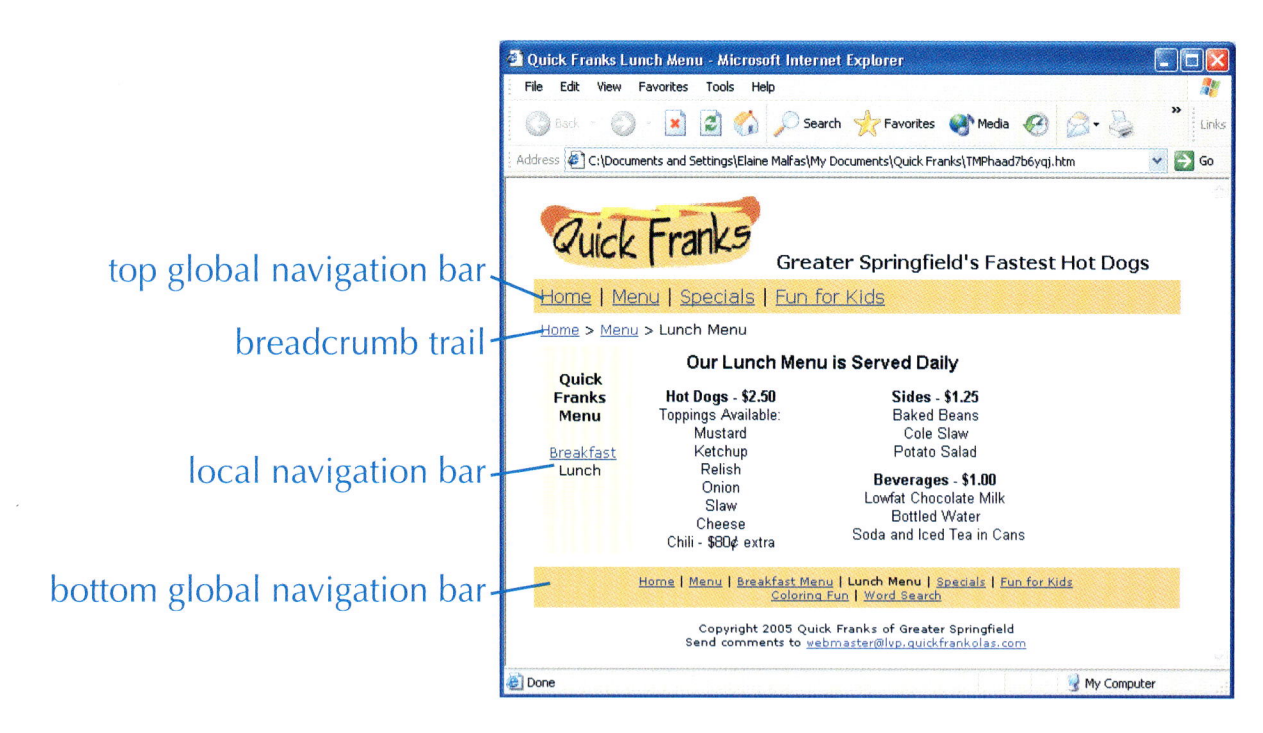

[Screenshot of Quick Franks Lunch Menu web page with labels pointing to: top global navigation bar, breadcrumb trail, local navigation bar, bottom global navigation bar]

top global navigation bar — The *top global navigation bar* typically contains a link to each page on the first and second levels of the Web site's navigation structure. The links can be text or images. A top global navigation bar should be placed near the top of each page and should not contain more than eight links.

bottom global navigation bar — The *bottom global navigation bar* should appear near the bottom of the page. This one should only use text links, in a small size, and should contain links to all of the pages in the Web site if possible.

the | symbol — Each link in the global navigation bars should be clearly separated. The pipe symbol (|) is often used as a separator. The pipe symbol is created with the | key above the Enter key.

local navigation bar — A *local navigation bar* can be positioned below the top global navigation bar or vertically along the left side of a page. A local navigation bar typically contains links to the child pages of the current page. It may also contain links to pages at the current level of the navigation structure or to locations on the current page. The local navigation bar may not be needed on Web sites with only a few pages.

breadcrumb trail, path — A *breadcrumb trail*, also called the *path*, is a navigation bar that displays the page names in order of level, from the home page to the current page, based on the navigation structure. Each of the page names, except for the current page name, is a link to the appropriate page. This path gives the user a point of reference and allows the user to navigate by backtracking through the site. Each page name in the path should be separated by a symbol, most commonly the greater than sign (>). A breadcrumb trail usually doesn't appear on the home page.

the > symbol

links to the home page — There should always be at least one link on each page to the home page. Users may be directed to a Web page in the Web site by a link at a search engine, and therefore need a way to find the home page. Home page links are always included in the breadcrumb trail and in the bottom global navigation bar. A logo at the top of a Web page is also typically a link to the home page.

5.6 The Web Page Layout

A *Web page layout* refers to the placement of the elements on the page. *Elements* can be in the form of text, images, Flash movies, or other media and include navigation bars, a logo or heading, copyright information, and content. A Web page layout should be based on usability standards, which dictate the placement of navigation bars and other elements:

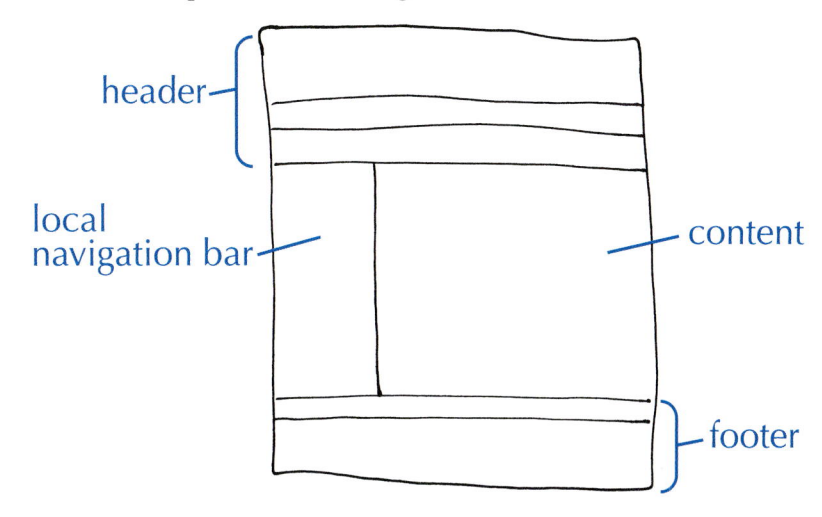

> **Widths of the Navigation Bar**
>
> To control the layout of a table with a percentage width, it is common that the cells in the left column have a fixed width (pixels). This left column often contains links to other pages in the Web site, and by specifying pixels as the cell width the layout of these links remains constant as the user resizes the browser window. Depending on the layout of the Web page, at least one other cell width should be a percentage, which allows the table to change size.

header   The top area of a Web page is called the *header* and includes a logo or heading, top global navigation bar, and possibly a breadcrumb trail.

footer   The bottom area of the page is called the *footer* and includes a bottom global navigation bar and other information such as copyright, the date of the last update, and a link to contact the author.

sketching the layout   A page layout should be sketched for each page of a Web site. The sketches should show the general placement of the content elements. The links in the navigation bars can be listed separately or written on the sketch where the links will appear.

Page layout should be similar for each page. By consistently placing elements in the same location, the user quickly becomes familiar with the Web site and can navigate easily. Because the home page acts as the starting point of a Web site, it should have a slightly different layout than the other Web pages to quickly identify it as the home page.

Practice 3

In this practice you will sketch layouts of Web pages for a pasta restaurant Web site and determine the links for the navigation bars. You will need to refer to the navigation structure created in Practice 2. Write your answers on paper.

① **SKETCH THE HOME PAGE AND DETERMINE THE NAVIGATION BARS**

    a. Sketch the home page. The header includes a logo and a top global navigation bar and the footer includes a bottom global navigation bar and copyright information. Content includes text and a picture.

    b. List the links for the top global navigation bar, which are links to the second level pages.

    c. List the links for the bottom global navigation bar, which are links to the all the pages.

Check—Your sketch should look similar to:

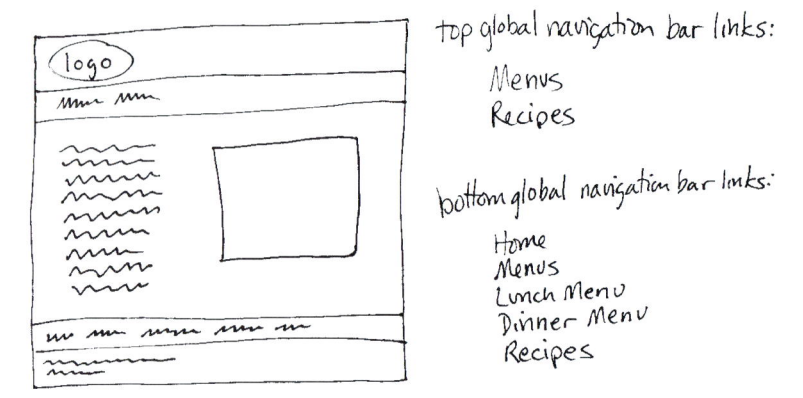

top global navigation bar links:
- Menus
- Recipes

bottom global navigation bar links:
- Home
- Menus
- Lunch Menu
- Dinner Menu
- Recipes

② **SKETCH THE MENUS PAGE AND DETERMINE THE NAVIGATION BARS**

   a. Sketch the menus page. The header includes a logo, top global navigation bar, and a breadcrumb trail. The footer includes a bottom global navigation bar and copyright information. Content includes text and three pictures.
   b. List the links for the top global navigation bar, which are links to the other pages on the second level of the Web site and the home page.
   c. List the links for the bottom global navigation bar, which are links to all the pages.
   d. The breadcrumb trail should display Home > Menus, with Home as a link to the home page. Write this information down on your sketch.

③ **SKETCH THE REMAINING PAGES AND DETERMINE THEIR NAVIGATION BARS**

   Refer to Section 5.6 and steps ① and ② above to sketch the recipes, lunch menu, and dinner menu pages. List appropriate links for navigation bars.

Using Metaphors in a Web Site

Metaphors can be useful by providing a familiar way for the user to think about concepts at a Web site. For example, e-commerce Web sites use a shopping cart metaphor by providing links such as "add to cart," "view cart," and "check out" so that users feel as if they were in a retail store. However, metaphors only work if they are obvious to the majority of users. If there is a slight possibility that a user may not understand it, then do not use a metaphor.

5.7 Concepts of Design

There are four basic concepts to consider when designing a Web page: appropriateness, placement, consistency, and usability. *Web page design* includes the Web page's layout, as explained in Section 5.6, and the content elements.

There are no absolute rules for Web site design, only guidelines that come from design concepts. Although the concepts discussed in this chapter are used frequently to create successful Web site designs, there are times when they may not yield the best design. With experience, the better choices will become obvious. Keep in mind that a Web site goes through many changes before it is finished, and good designs result from numerous revisions.

5.8 Design Concepts: Appropriateness

The *appropriateness* of a design is how well the elements in the Web site match the purpose and target audience. Is the text appropriate for the audience? Do the images fit the purpose of the Web site? Are they appropriate for the audience? What other content would the audience expect to find at this Web site?

Examine the differences in these two home pages:

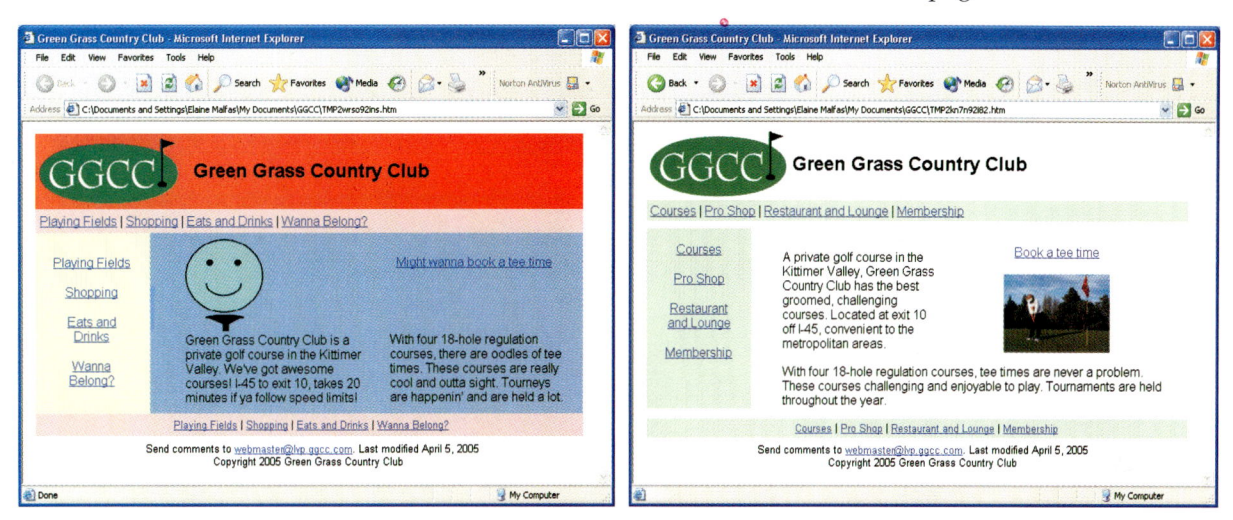

Two different designs of the same home page

The home page on the left conveys immaturity because of inappropriate wording, odd colors, confusing hyperlinks, and a childish smiling golf ball image. Note the link near the top of the page, which reads "Might wanna book a tee time," and compare it to the same link on the right page "Book a tee time." The wording "Might wanna" is too casual and inappropriate for the target audience of the country club. The page on the right has appropriate wording in the links and other text and quiet colors. This page invokes a calm, sophisticated feeling, more appropriate for a country club.

5.9 Design Concepts: Placement

As discussed in Section 5.6, the placement of Web page elements should follow generally accepted standards, with a header, a footer, and content in between. These standards are based on user expectations.

expectations

The expectations continue as the user browses the Web site. After clicking a link, the user expects to see a Web page with similar design but different content. If the design suddenly changes, the links are moved, or the placement is different, they may click away from the Web site in frustration or confusion.

above the fold

Within the content are additional elements that require careful placement. The most important elements, those that the user should see first, need to be near enough to the top of a Web page so that they are visible without requiring the user to scroll. This placement is called *above the fold*, which originally referred to the headlines placed on the top half of a newspaper's front page, above where it is folded in half. News items in this location were sure to be seen first. On a Web page, any elements that can be viewed without scrolling are seen first and can influence whether the user clicks on a link to another page in the site or leaves the site.

Web Sites are Always Under Construction

The words "under construction" or graphics that imply a construction zone are unnecessary and unprofessional on a Web page. The nature of the Web is that it is always changing and that the content of most pages will be updated when necessary. Adding the "under construction" notation could imply that the content on the page is false or fake.

white space

Another factor in the placement of elements is white space. *White space* is any blank area on a page, regardless of the color. Jamming a page full of elements with little space between them causes visual noise and influences users to click away, as demonstrated by the page below:

Testing Layout

Clicking the Window Size button in the status bar of a Web page document window displays a menu:

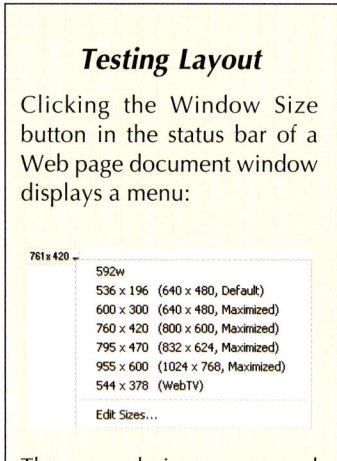

```
761 x 420
        592w
        536 x 196   (640 x 480, Default)
        600 x 300   (640 x 480, Maximized)
        760 x 420   (800 x 600, Maximized)
        795 x 470   (832 x 624, Maximized)
        955 x 600   (1024 x 768, Maximized)
        544 x 378   (WebTV)

        Edit Sizes...
```

The menu choices correspond to monitor sizes and their typical screen resolution. Selecting a size modifies the Document window to reflect how a Web page will look when viewed on that monitor. This allows the page layout to be checked without having to change computers or switch from Design view.

The shape of white space can emphasize elements and influence the direction that the user's eye travels around the page. Although white space is blank, it is just as important as other elements in determining the layout of a Web page.

5.10 Design Concepts: Consistency

Consistency upholds the user's expectations. Repetition in the placement of elements creates and maintains expectations for the user. For example, a breadcrumb trail is repeated on every page except the home page. After viewing a couple of pages, the user expects this as a point of reference and no longer needs to look for it. The user also subconsciously uses it as a visual cue to know which pages are not the home page. A *visual cue* is a pattern or object that the user sees and identifies quickly after repeated use.

visual cue

The importance of consistency increases with the number of pages in a Web site. In a one-page Web site, consistent visual cues are not needed. In a Web site with fifteen pages, consistent visual cues help the user navigate and provide a point of reference.

5.11 Design Concepts: Usability

Although all of the design concepts are important, if a Web site isn't usable, it won't get used. The object is to keep users at a Web site long enough to find information useful to them.

The usability of a Web site is how well the user can navigate through the pages of a Web site to find desired information. Including navigation bars makes the site easier to explore. A breadcrumb trail also helps the user understand the current page location in relation to the rest of the Web site.

printer-friendly version

Text content should be limited to only necessary words and paragraphs. The less text there is for users to scan, the faster they will be able to find what they need. Information should be carefully edited to convey the desired message without wordiness.

Will the user be likely to print out the Web page? If so, you may need to have a link to a *printer-friendly version* of the page. This allows for a Web page that may not print attractively but looks great in the browser, yet the user can click the link to display another Web page with the same content that will print correctly.

Practice 4

In this practice you will analyze the design of a home page for appropriateness, placement, consistency, and usability. You will also sketch the content layout for the Web pages of a pasta restaurant Web site based on the content determined in Practice 2.

① ANALYZE THE DESIGN OF A WEB PAGE

The navigation structure for a strawberry farm's Web site is:

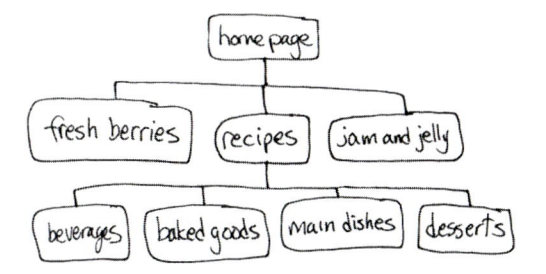

The Recipes page for the strawberry farm Web site is shown below:

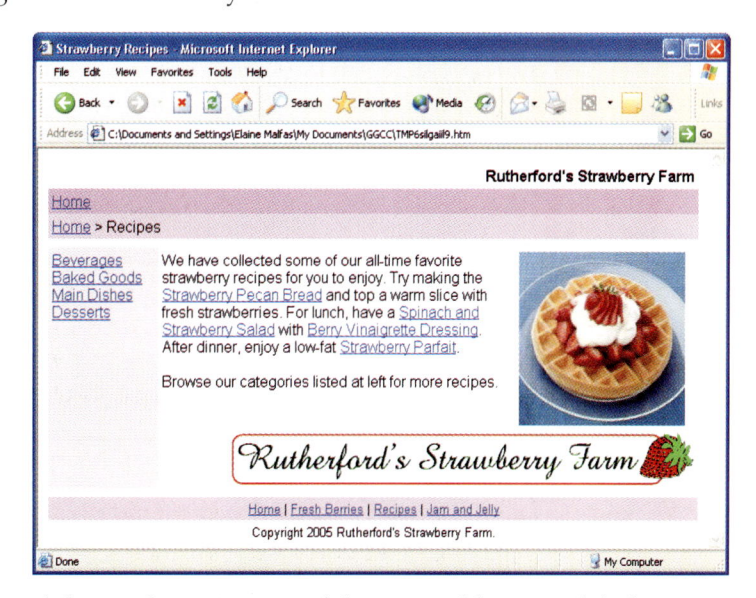

a. Describe the usability and consistency of the top and bottom global navigation bars.
b. Are the links in the local navigation bar appropriate? Explain why or why not.
c. Where is the logo? Where is a more appropriate location for the logo? Why?
d. Describe the appropriateness of the paragraph in the content area.
e. Describe the appropriateness and usability of the links in the content area.
f. How could the footer be improved?

Web Site Development

② DESIGN THE PASTA RESTAURANT WEB SITE HOME PAGE

Refine the content layout of the home page for the pasta restaurant. The content of the home page should include:

- a brief statement about the pasta restaurant
- an image related to the restaurant
- the restaurant address, phone number, and hours of business

Check—Your sketch could look similar to:

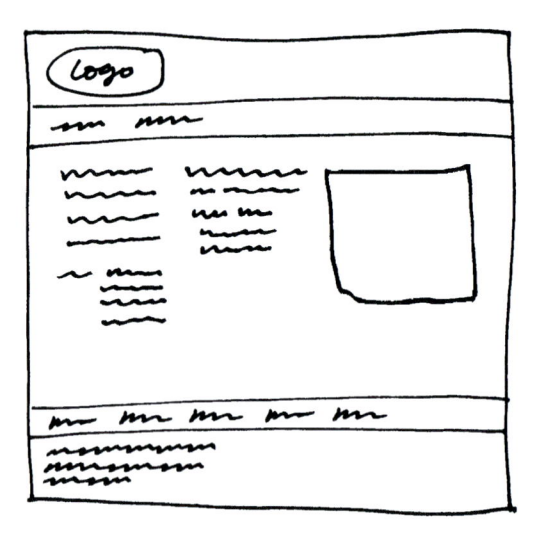

5.12 Organizing Files and Folders

Once the planning stage for a new Web site is complete, the Web site can be defined in Dreamweaver as discussed in Chapter 4. The Site panel is then used to create and organize files and folders for the Web site. The *root folder* is created during site definition for storing files and folders. A new folder can be added by selecting the root folder in the Site panel and then selecting File → New Folder. After adding the new folder, it can be renamed:

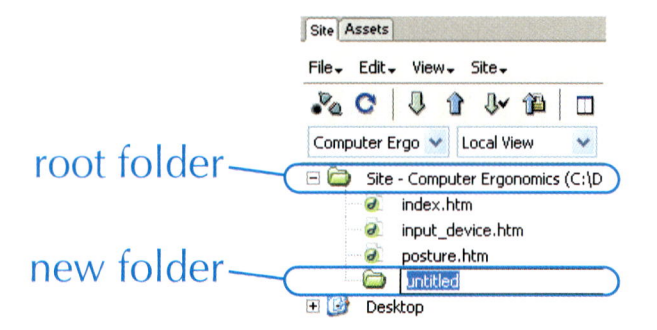

Folder Structures

Large Web sites may use several folders to organize all of the files needed. Use as many folders as needed to maintain organization.

Folders are used to organize files. Web page documents have many elements, including images. For better organization, all the image files for a Web site should be stored together in a folder named *images*.

A Guide to Web Development Using Macromedia Dreamweaver MX

adding a file to the site   A file is added to a site by copying it to a folder in the root folder. The Desktop icon is used to display files outside the Web site root folder:

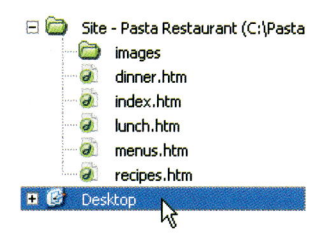

Double-clicking the Desktop icon expands it for navigating to a file needed for the Web site. After navigating to a file, selecting Edit → Copy in the Site panel places a copy of the file in the computer's memory. Selecting a folder in the Web site and then selecting Edit → Paste copies the file to the folder.

copying several files   To copy several files at once, hold down the Ctrl key while selecting the files. The Copy and Paste commands can then be used to copy all the selected files.

Practice 5

In this practice you will create a new Web site and organize the files and folders for the Web site.

① CREATE A NEW SITE

a. Start Dreamweaver.

b. From the Menu bar or Site panel, select Site → New Site. A dialog box is displayed.

1. Select the Basic tab if those options are not already displayed.
2. In the What would you like to name your site? box, type: Pasta Restaurant
3. Select Next. More options are displayed.
4. Select the No, I do not want to use a server technology option.
5. Select Next. More options are displayed.
6. Select the Edit local copies on my machine, then upload to server when ready option.
7. Click the folder icon (📁). A dialog box is displayed for browsing the local disk.
   a) Navigate to where you want the folder that stores the Web site.
   b) Click the Create New Folder button.
   c) Type Pasta Restaurant to replace the New Folder name and press Enter.
   d) Select Open. The Pasta Restaurant folder appears in the Select list at the top of the dialog box.
   e) Select Select.
8. Select Next. More options are displayed.
9. In the How do you connect to your remote server? list, select None.
10. Select Next. A summary is displayed.
11. Select Done to create the site. The Site folder is displayed in the Site panel:

Web Site Development   5 – 13

② CREATE THE HOME PAGE

a. Select File → Save. A dialog box is displayed.
   1. Use the Save in box to navigate to the Pasta Restaurant folder, if that is not the current location displayed.
   2. In the File name box, replace the existing text with: index.htm
   3. Select Save.
b. On the Document toolbar, in the Title box replace the text Untitled Document with Pasta Restaurant Home Page and press Enter.

③ CREATE MORE WEB PAGE DOCUMENTS

a. In the Site panel, click the Site root folder to select it:

```
□ 📁 Site - Pasta Restaurant (C:\Pasta
        index.htm
   ⊞ 🖥 Desktop
```

b. In the Site panel, select File → New File. A new file is added in the Site panel.
c. Replace the selected file name with menus.htm and press Enter.
d. In the Site panel, select the Site root folder.
e. In the Site panel, select File → New File. A new file is added in the Site panel.
f. Replace the selected file name with lunch.htm and press Enter.
g. Create two more Web page documents in the root folder naming them: recipes.htm and dinner.htm

④ CREATE A FOLDER

a. In the Site panel, click the Web site root folder, the Pasta Restaurant folder, to select it.
b. In the Site panel, select File → New Folder. A new folder is added in the Site panel.
c. Replace the selected folder name with images and press Enter. This folder will be used to store the images for the Web site.

Check—Your Site panel should look similar to:

```
□ 📁 Site - Pasta Restaurant (C:\Pasta
        dinner.htm
        index.htm
        lunch.htm
        menus.htm
        recipes.htm
     📁 images
   ⊞ 🖥 Desktop
```

⑤ ADD IMAGE FILES TO THE IMAGES FOLDER

a. In the Site panel, use the Desktop icon to navigate to the folder containing data files for this text.
b. Click the pasta_drawing.gif file to select it.
c. Hold down the Ctrl key and click the pasta_logo.gif file. Two files are now selected.
d. In the Site panel, select Edit → Copy.
e. In the Site panel, select the images folder in the Pasta Restaurant site.
f. In the Site panel, select Edit → Paste. Two images are added to the images folder.

5.13 Maintaining Consistency in a Web Site

Assets panel

Dreamweaver includes the *Assets panel* to help maintain consistency of content throughout a Web site. The Assets panel helps Web site development by listing objects, such as images, that are available in the site. The Assets panel is located in the Files panel group:

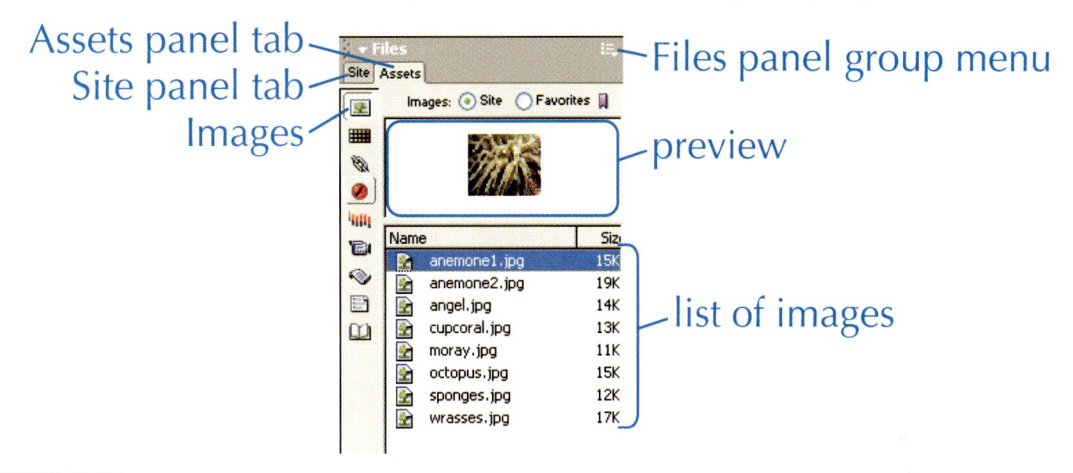

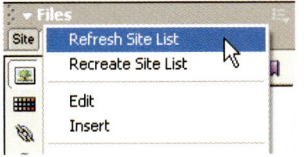

Assets panel tab — Files panel group menu
Site panel tab
Images — preview
— list of images

placing an image in a Web page document

Clicking the Images icon ( ) displays a list of all the image files in the site. The selected image, anemone1.jpg in the example above, is displayed in the preview. Selecting → Refresh Site List in the Files panel group may be necessary to update the list of images.

An image in the Assets panel is placed in an open Web page document by dragging it from the panel into the Document window or by clicking Insert at the bottom of the Assets panel to place the image at the insertion point.

5.14 Merging and Splitting Cells

Cells in a table may be merged into one cell or split into separate cells to help layout a Web page. The Merge cells button ( ) and the Split cell button ( ) in the Property inspector are used to modify selected cells in a table:

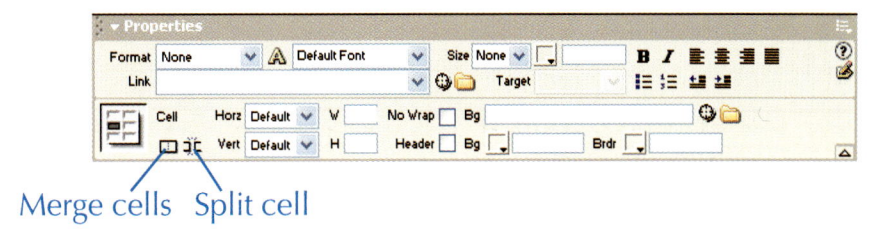

Merge cells Split cell

merging cells   Several cells can be merged into one, while leaving the rest of the table as is. For example, selecting the top two cells in a table:

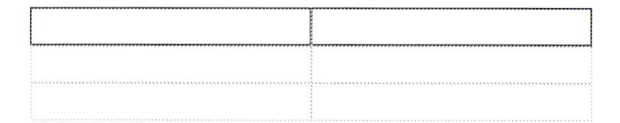

and then clicking the Merge cells button (▢) combines the cells into one cell:

The Tag Selector

In the Tag selector, clicking <td> selects the cell containing the insertion point. Clicking <tr> selects the row containing the insertion point.

Cells selected vertically can also be merged:

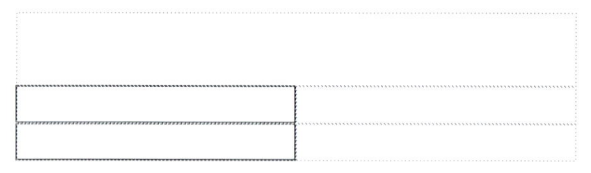

Two cells selected

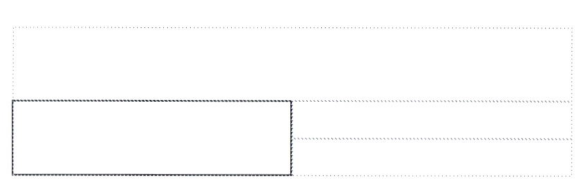

Clicking the Merge cells button combines the cells

splitting cells   One cell can be split into more cells in a specified number of rows or columns. For example, placing the insertion point in the lower-right cell in the table example above and clicking the Split cell button (ⓙⓒ) in the Property inspector displays a dialog box:

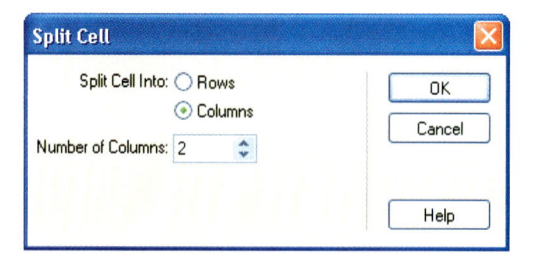

Rows or Columns is selected and then the number of rows or columns to split the cell into is specified, for example 2 columns in the dialog box shown above. Selecting **OK** divides the cell:

The bottom-right cell is split into two cells

5 – 16   *A Guide to Web Development Using Macromedia Dreamweaver MX*

Practice 6

In this practice you will add a table to a Web page document, merge and split cells, and add content using the Assets panel. Dreamweaver should be started and the Pasta Restaurant Web site should be the working site.

① ADD A TABLE TO THE HOME PAGE

a. Display the index.htm Web page document.
b. Insert a table with the following specifications:

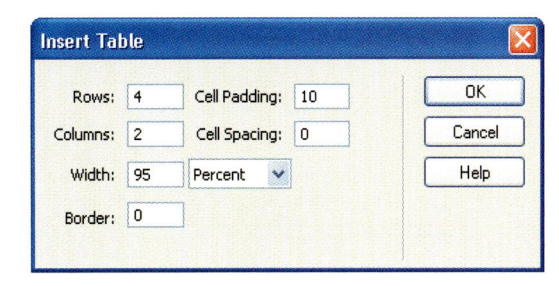

> **Insert Table**
> Rows: 4   Cell Padding: 10
> Columns: 2   Cell Spacing: 0
> Width: 95 Percent
> Border: 0

c. Save the modified index.htm.

② MERGE CELLS

a. Select the two cells in the top row by placing the insertion point in one cell and dragging to the other cell.
b. In the Property inspector, click the Merge cells button (▫). The cells are combined:

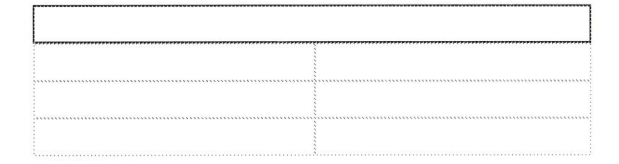

c. Select the two cells in the second row.
d. In the Property inspector, click the Merge cells button (▫). The cells are combined.
e. Merge the two cells in the bottom row. Click in a cell. The table should look similar to:

③ SPLIT A CELL

a. Place the insertion point in the second cell in the third row (the far-right cell).
b. In the Property inspector, click the Split cell button (ⵝ). A dialog box is displayed.
   1. In the dialog box, specify the following:

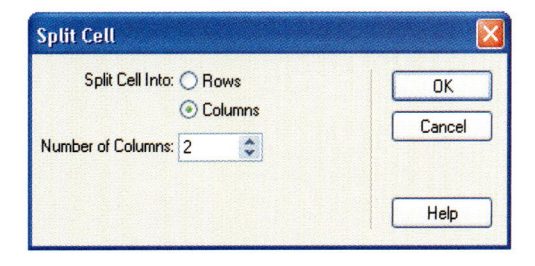

> **Split Cell**
> Split Cell Into: ○ Rows
>   ⊙ Columns
> Number of Columns: 2

Web Site Development   5 – 17

2. Select **OK**. The cell is split into two:

④ VIEW THE ASSETS PANEL

   a. In the Site panel, click the Assets panel tab. The Assets panel is displayed.

   b. In the Assets panel, click the Images icon (▣) if it is not already selected. The images in the site are displayed. If no files are displayed, select ▤ → Refresh Site List from the Files panel group.

   c. In the Assets panel, click the pasta_logo.gif file. The file is displayed in the preview.

⑤ USE THE ASSETS PANEL TO INSERT IMAGES

   a. In the Assets panel, drag the pasta_logo.gif file name to the top cell in the table. The logo now appears in the table.

   b. Drag the pasta_drawing.gif file name to the far-right cell in the third row in the table. The drawing now appears in the table:

⑥ SAVE THE MODIFIED INDEX.HTM

⑦ PRINT THE INDEX.HTM WEB PAGE DOCUMENT

   a. Press F12. The document is displayed in a browser window.

   b. Print a copy of the document displayed in the browser window.

   c. Close the browser window. Dreamweaver is displayed.

⑧ CLOSE INDEX.HTM

   a. Close the index.htm document window. There should be no open document windows.

5.15 Creating Library Items

library item

The Library category in the Assets panel lists the library items that are available in the Web site. A *library item* is content placed in a separate file and given a descriptive name. For example, copyright information that appears on every page of a Web site could be created as a library item named copyright. This library item can be added to each Web page, rather than retyping the copyright information on each page. Using library items helps maintain consistency in a Web site because modifying a library item automatically updates each occurrence in a Web site.

Assets panel

Clicking the Library icon ( ) in the Assets panel displays the Library category. Selecting → New Library Item creates a new, empty library item:

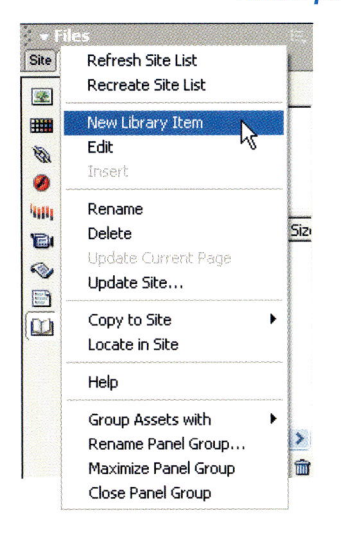

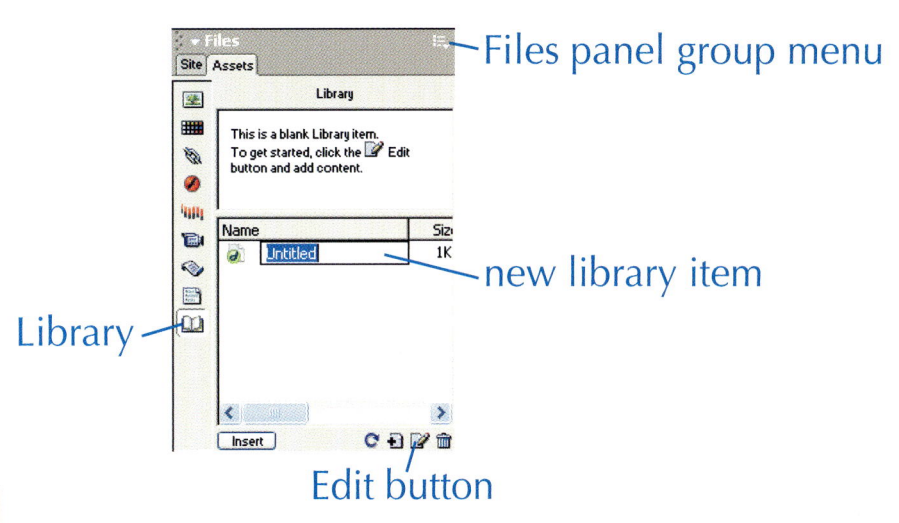

— Files panel group menu

— new library item

Library —

Edit button

LBI

A library item is an LBI file. The extension .lbi is automatically added to the file name.

After adding a new library item, it can be renamed. Clicking the Edit button ( ) at the bottom of the Assets panel opens a window with <<Library Item>> in the title bar. The content for the library item is created in the <<Library Item>> window and then File → Save selected to save the changes. The library item window is closed by clicking the Close button. The content of a selected library item appears in the preview of the Assets panel. Dreamweaver automatically adds a Library folder to the Web site root folder when a library item is created.

Library folder

A library item may also be created from existing content. For example, content on the home page of a Web site can be made into a library item by selecting the content before selecting → New Library Item from Assets panel in the Files panel group. After the new library item is named, the selected content appears with a yellow background to indicate that it is a library item.

yellow background

placing a library item in a Web page document

A library item is placed in an open Web page document by dragging it from the panel into the Document window or by clicking Insert at the bottom of the Assets panel to place the library item at the insertion point. In a Web page document, a library item appears with a yellow background. Its does not appear with a yellow background in a browser.

deleting a library item

A library item is deleted by selecting it in the Assets panel and then pressing the Delete key.

Web Site Development　　5 – 19

> **Opening Library Items**
>
> A library item can be opened by right-clicking the item and selecting Edit from the displayed menu.

5.16 Editing Library Items

An existing library item can be edited by selecting the library item and then clicking the Edit button ( ) at the bottom of the Assets panel, which opens the item in a window. When changes are saved, a dialog box is displayed that lists all of the Web page documents that contain the library item. Clicking Update updates all of the occurrences of the library item in the Web site.

A library item in a Web page document cannot be changed unless the link between it and the original library item is broken. To break the link between a selected library item in a Web page document and the original library item, click [Detach from Original] in the Property inspector. The selected library item will no longer have a yellow background and can now be edited in the Web page document. Note that once the link has been broken, the library item in the Web page document will not be updated if the original library item is changed.

breaking a library item link

5.17 Inserting a Date

The footer of a Web page should contain a date indicating when the page was last updated so that users know how current the information is. This date can be in the form of a *time stamp* that changes automatically when a page is modified. Selecting Insert → Date or clicking the Date button ( ) on the Common tab in the Insert bar displays the Insert Date dialog box:

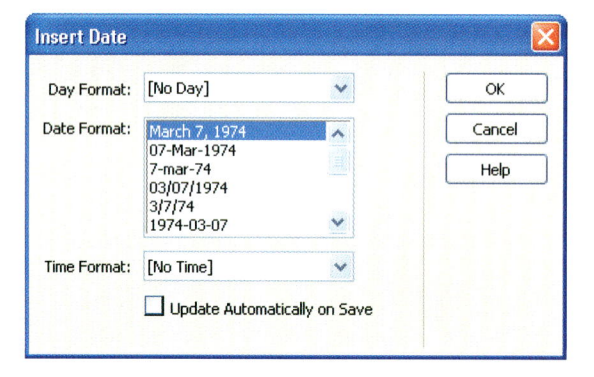

time stamp

The Day Format, Date Format, and Time Format lists are used to select the format of the information that will appear at the insertion point. The Update Automatically on Save check box must be selected if the information is to be updated each time the Web page document is saved. Selecting OK places the time stamp at the insertion point.

5.18 E-mail Hyperlinks

A link to the Webmaster is usually provided in the footer of a Web page. This link is an *e-mail hyperlink* that allows the user to send an e-mail message. When the user clicks an e-mail hyperlink, a new e-mail message window is displayed with the To: address that was specified when the hyperlink was created. After composing the message, the user clicks the Send button to send the message.

> **Outlook Express**
>
> Outlook Express is an e-mail software package that is accessible from Internet Explorer. Outlook Express is discussed in Chapter 2.

Including an e-mail hyperlink to the Webmaster is good design. It allows for feedback, so that improvements can be made to a Web site to better meet the needs of its users.

An e-mail hyperlink is created by selecting text and then typing mailto: followed by the e-mail address in the Link box in the Property inspector:

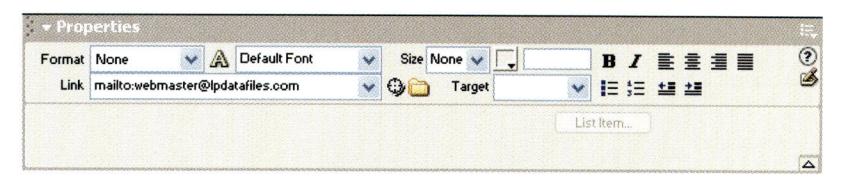

Webmaster

A Webmaster is the person who maintains a Web site. The Webmaster may also create or design the site. Webmaster and other careers are discussed in Chapter 2.

An e-mail hyperlink can be tested in a browser window.

5.19 Copyright Information

All forms of published work, including a Web site you may create, are entitled to copyright protection. A Web page should include copyright information with a *copyright notice* that contains the text Copyright *year*, with the year of publication. In addition to a copyright notice, copyright information may also include other statements regarding the use of the Web site's material and an e-mail hyperlink for sending a request for permission to use the material.

Published work that displays a copyright notice, in this case a Web site, is protected work and not intended for the public domain. Copyrighted material can be reproduced only with written permission from the owner. However, a Web site that does not contain a copyright notice is still entitled to copyright protection. Published work should be treated as copyright protected unless explicitly stated as material for the public domain.

Copyright Symbol

The © symbol may used in place of the word Copyright. Inserting special characters is discussed in Chapter 4.

Certificate of Copyright

A publication, such as a Web site, can be submitted to the United States Copyright Office in order to receive an official certificate of copyright. This certificate can be used in cases of copyright infringement, but it is not required.

Practice 7

In this practice you will create a library item for a footer and navigation bars. Dreamweaver should be started and the Pasta Restaurant Web site should be the working site.

① CREATE A LIBRARY ITEM

a. Close any open document windows if necessary.

b. In the Assets panel, click the Library icon (). No library items exist yet, so the listing is empty.

c. Select → New Library Item from the Files panel group. A new item is added to the list.

d. Replace the selected library item name with footer and press Enter.

e. At the bottom of the Assets panel, click the Edit button (). A new Library Item window is opened with <<Library Item>> in the title bar.

f. Type the text:

   Send comments to webmaster@pasta.lpdatafiles.com. Last modified

g. Insert a line break after the word "modified" and then type the text:

   Copyright 2005 Pasta Restaurant.

h. Select File → Save. In the Assets panel, the content of the saved selected library item appears in the preview.

i. Click the Close button in the Library Item window. The window is closed.

② EDIT THE FOOTER LIBRARY ITEM

a. In the Assets panel, select the footer library item and click the Edit button (📝) at the bottom of the Assets panel. The library item is displayed in a Library Item window.

b. Select the text webmaster@pasta.lpdatafiles.com.

c. In the Property inspector, in the Link box type: mailto:webmaster@pasta.lpdatafiles.com

d. Press Enter. The text webmaster@pasta.lpdatafiles.com is now an e-mail hyperlink.

e. Place the insertion point after the "d" in the text Last modified

f. Type a space.

g. On the Common tab in the Insert bar, click the Date button (📅). A dialog box is displayed.

   1. In the Day Format list, select Thursday,
   2. In the Date Format list, select March 7, 1974
   3. In the Time Format list, select 10:18 PM
   4. Select the Update Automatically on Save check box.
   5. Select OK. A time stamp is placed at the insertion point.

h. Select File → Save. The library item is saved.

i. Close the library item window.

③ CREATE ANOTHER LIBRARY ITEM

a. Be sure there are no open Web page document windows and then select 📋 → New Library Item. A new item is added to the list.

b. Replace the selected library item name with navbar and press Enter.

c. At the bottom of the Assets panel, click the Edit button (📝). A library item window is opened.

d. Type the following text, using the | key above the Enter key to create the "pipe" symbol:

   Menus | Recipes

e. In the text just typed, link the text Menus to the menus.htm Web page document.

f. In the text just typed, link the text Recipes to the recipes.htm Web page document.

g. Select File → Save. In the Assets panel, the content of the saved selected library item appears in the preview.

h. Close the library item window.

④ PLACE LIBRARY ITEMS

a. Open the index.htm Web page document.

b. From the Assets panel Library category, drag the navbar library item to the cell in the second row in the table. The Menus and Recipes links in the library item now appear in the cell. Click in a cell to deselect the library item. Note the yellow background behind the links to indicate a library item.

c. Click in the bottom cell of the table to place the insertion point.

d. In the Assets panel, click the navbar library item and then click [Insert] at the bottom of the Assets panel to place the library item at the insertion point. The Menus and Recipes links now appear in the bottom row of the table.

e. Drag the footer library item to the right of the table. The footer appears, with a yellow background, below the table:

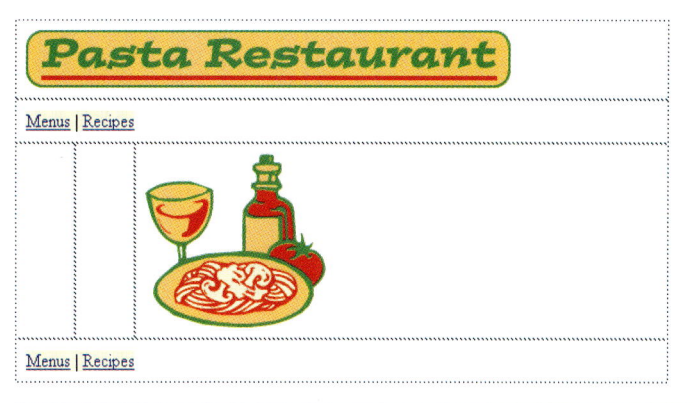

5 EDIT A LIBRARY ITEM

a. In the bottom row, click the Menus and Recipes links library item to select it.

b. In the Property inspector, click [Detach from Original]. Select OK in the warning dialog box. The yellow background no longer appears and the text can be edited.

c. Place the insertion point to the right of Menus and then type: | Lunch Menu Make sure the navigation items are all separated by a pipe symbol (|).

d. Link the text Lunch Menu to: lunch.htm

e. Add the text Dinner Menu | between the Lunch Menu hyperlink and the Recipes hyperlink.

f. Link the text Dinner Menu to dinner.htm and make sure the links are all separated by a pipe symbol (|).

6 SAVE THE MODIFIED INDEX.HTM

7 PRINT THE INDEX.HTM WEB PAGE DOCUMENT

a. Press F12. The document is displayed in a browser window.

b. Print a copy of the document displayed in the browser window.

c. Close the browser window.

8 QUIT DREAMWEAVER

Chapter Summary

Web site development has two stages: planning and implementation. Planning includes determining the Web site's purpose, audience, navigation structure, content, and page layout. Implementation includes using Dreamweaver to set up the Web site and create the Web pages.

The purpose is the intent of the Web site. The target audience is the individuals who will use the Web site. The Web pages in a Web site are determined from the purpose and target audience.

The navigation structure of a Web site shows the pages of the Web site and how they relate to each other. The navigation structure should be sketched using rectangles to represent each Web page in a site. The home page is referred to as a top-level page. Web pages may also be described in terms of parent and child pages. A parent page has at least one page below it, called a child page. The content of a Web page is the text, images, and other objects. Content is determined by using the Web site's navigation structure as an outline and then listing the elements for each page.

A navigation bar is a set of hyperlinks that give a user a way to display the different pages in a Web site. A top global navigation bar contains a link to each page on the second level of a Web site and should appear near the top of a Web page. A bottom global navigation bar contains links to every page in the Web site and should appear near the bottom of a Web page. A local navigation bar typically contains links to the child pages of the current page and can be positioned below the top global navigation bar or vertically along the left side of a page. A breadcrumb trail displays the page names in order of level, from the home page to the current page.

A Web page layout refers to the arrangement of the elements on the page and should follow standards for usability. The header includes a logo, global navigation bar, and possibly a breadcrumb trail. The footer includes a global navigation bar, copyright, date of last update, and a contact link. A page layout should be sketched for each page of a Web site, and the layout should be similar on each page.

There are four basic concepts for designing a Web page: appropriateness, placement, consistency, and usability. Appropriateness is how well the elements in the Web site match the purpose and target audience. Placement of Web page elements should follow the accepted standards of a header, footer, and content in between. Consistency upholds the user's expectations through repetition in the placement of elements on each Web page. The usability of a Web site is how well the user can navigate through the pages of a Web site to find the desired information.

Once the planning stage is complete, the new Web site is defined in Dreamweaver. The Site panel is used to create files and folders for the Web site, which are added to the root folder. Images should be kept in a folder in the Web site's root folder.

Cells in a table may be merged into one cell or split into separate cells using the Merge cells button ( ) and Split cell button ( ) in the Property inspector.

The Assets panel helps maintain consistency in a Web site. Two categories in the Assets panel are Images, which lists the image files that are contained in the Web site folder, and Library, which lists library items that are available in the Web site. Objects in the Assets panel are placed in an open Web page document by dragging the object from the panel to the Document window.

Library items are elements that are used repeatedly in a Web site. A library item can be edited by selecting the item and clicking the Edit button ( ) in the Assets panel. A library item that has been placed in a Web page document can be edited by clicking Detach from Original in the Property inspector. In a Web page document, a library item appears with a yellow background to indicate that it is a library item.

The footer of a Web page should contain a date indicating when the page was last updated. Selecting Insert → Date or clicking the Date button ( ) on the Common tab of the Insert bar displays the Insert Date dialog box, which is used to specify the appearance of the date and time.

The footer of a Web page usually includes an e-mail hyperlink to the Webmaster. An e-mail hyperlink is created by selecting text and then typing mailto: followed by the e-mail address in the Link box in the Property inspector. An e-mail hyperlink can be tested in a browser window.

A Web page should include copyright information including the year of publication. Copyrighted material can be reproduced only with written permission from the owner.

Vocabulary

Above the fold Refers to the placement of the most important elements near the top of a Web page so that they are visible without requiring the user to scroll.

Appropriateness A design concept that refers to how well the elements in the Web site match the purpose and target audience.

Assets panel A panel that helps Web site development by gathering a list of objects, such as images, that are available in the site.

Bottom global navigation bar A navigation bar near the bottom of a Web page, which contains links to every page of a Web site.

Breadcrumb trail A navigation bar that displays the page names in order of level, from the home page to the current page, based on the navigation structure.

Child page A Web page that has at least one page above it in the navigation structure of a Web site.

Consistency A design concept that refers to repetition in the placement of elements.

Content The text, images, and other objects presented to the user on a Web page.

Copyright notice The text Copyright year, which includes the year of publication.

Elements Text, images, or other media. Elements on a Web page include navigation bars, a logo or heading, copyright information, and content.

E-mail hyperlink A link that allows the user to send an e-mail message.

Footer The bottom area of a Web page which includes a global navigation bar and other information such as copyright, the date of the last update, and a link to contact the author.

Header The top area of a Web page which includes a logo or heading, global navigation bar, and possibly a breadcrumb trail.

Library item Content placed in a separate file and given a descriptive name so that it can be used repeatedly in a Web site.

Local navigation bar A navigation bar that typically contains links to the child pages of the current page.

Navigation bar A set of hyperlinks that give a user a way to display the different pages in a Web site.

Navigation structure The organization of a Web site.

Parent page A Web page that has at least one page below it in the navigation structure of a Web site.

Path *See* Breadcrumb trail.

Placement A design concept that refers to the arrangement of Web page elements.

Printer-friendly version A Web page with the same content as another Web page, except this page will print correctly.

Purpose The intent of the Web site.

Root folder The folder created during site definition for storing files and folders.

Same-level page Web pages at the same level in a navigation structure of a Web site.

Target audience The individuals that are intended to use the Web site.

Time stamp A date or time that changes automatically when a page is modified.

Top global navigation bar A navigation bar near the top of a Web page, which contains links to the first and second level pages of a Web site.

Top-level page A Web page at the highest level in the navigation structure of a Web site, usually the home page.

Usability A design concept that refers to how well the user can navigate through the pages of a Web site to find desired information.

Visual cue A pattern or object that the user sees and identifies quickly after repeated use.

Web page design The Web page's layout and the content elements.

Web page layout The arrangement of the elements on the page.

Web site development The process of planning and creating a Web site.

White space Any blank area on a page, regardless of the color.

Dreamweaver Commands and Buttons

Copy command Places a copy of the selected file in the computer's memory. Found in the Edit menu in the Site panel.

Date command Used to insert a time stamp in a Web page document. Found in the Insert menu. The Date button on the Common tab in the Insert bar can be used instead of the command.

Edit button Opens a window that contains the selected library item. Found at the bottom of the Assets panel when the Library category is displayed.

Images icon Displays the Images category in the Assets panel, which is a list of all the images in the site. Found in the Assets panel.

Library icon Displays the Library category in the Assets panel, which is a list of all the library items in the site. Found in the Assets panel.

Merge cells button Combines selected cells into one cell. Found in the Property inspector.

New File command Creates a new Web page document file and adds it to the list of files in the Site panel. Found in the File menu in the Site panel.

New Folder command Creates a new folder and adds it to the list of files and folders in the Site panel. Found in the File menu in the Site panel.

New Library Item command Creates a new library item. Found in the Files panel group menu in the Assets panel.

Paste command Places a copy of the file in the computer's memory in the selected folder. Found in the Edit menu in the Site panel.

Refresh Site List command Updates the list of images in the Assets panel. Found in the Files panel group menu in the Assets panel.

Split cell button Displays a dialog box used to divide the selected cell into rows or columns. Found in the Property inspector.

Review Questions

Sections 5.1 — 5.11

1. a) List the four planning stage steps of Web site development.
   b) List the five implementation stage steps of Web site development.

2. Consider a Web site for a high school soccer team:
   a) List several purposes for the Web site.
   b) Describe the target audience for the Web site.

3. Sketch the navigation structure for an ice cream store's Web site that contains the following Web pages:
   - a home page
   - two second-level pages, one for flavors and one for store hours and other information
   - two child pages of the flavors page, one for ice cream flavors and one for frozen yogurt flavors

4. What is the content of a Web page?

5. a) List three types of navigation bars used on a Web page.
   b) Where should global navigation bars be placed?
   c) How is a breadcrumb trail helpful to the user?

6. List three places on a Web page that may have a link to the home page.

7. What does Web page layout refer to?

8. a) List three elements that can be found in the header of a Web page.
   b) List three elements that can be found in the footer of a Web page.

9. List the four basic concepts of design to consider when designing a Web page.

10. Would a photograph of a car be appropriate for a Web page about gardening? Why or why not?

11. Where do elements need to be placed on a Web page in order to be above the fold?

12. What is white space?

13. a) What does consistency in a Web site do?
    b) What is a visual cue?

14. a) What is usability?
    b) List two ways to increase the usability of a Web site.

Sections 5.12 — 5.19

15. Where does the root folder appear?

16. a) List the steps required to create a new folder named photos.
    b) List the steps required to add a file named puppies.gif from a folder on your computer's Desktop to the photos folder of a Web site.

17. a) List the steps required to display a list of the images contained in a Web site.
    b) What can be done if there are images contained in a Web site but they are not displayed in the Images category in the Assets panel?

18. Describe how to use the Assets panel to place an image in a Web page document.

19. a) List the steps required to merge two cells in a table into one cell.
    b) List the steps required to split a cell into three rows.

20. a) List the steps required to create a new library item named homephone that contains the text 883-555-0303.
    b) What does Dreamweaver automatically add to the root folder after the first library item is created?

21. List the steps required to create a new library item named myname that is created from your name that is already typed into a Web page document.

22. a) List the steps required to place a library item in a Web page document using the Assets panel.
    b) What will a library item placed in a Web page document have that other elements will not have?
    c) List the steps required to edit a library item in a Web page document.

23. Why should a time stamp be used in a Web page document instead of typing the date?

24. List the steps required to insert a time stamp in a Web page document.

25. a) What happens when the user clicks an e-mail hyperlink?
    b) List the steps required to create an e-mail hyperlink with the e-mail address testing@lpdatafiles.com.

26. If a Web page does not contain a copyright notice, is the information on the Web page entitled to copyright protection?

Exercises

Exercise 1 ——————————————————————Hockey League

Create a new Web site for a local hockey league by completing the following steps:

a) Define a new site named Hockey League in a folder named Hockey League. The purpose of the Web site is to provide information about the Lake Worth Hockey League Association, rules, and a game schedule. The target audience is current and prospective league members and hockey fans of all ages.

b) Add three files to the Web site, naming them index.htm, rules.htm, and schedule.htm.

c) In the Hockey League root folder, create a folder named images. Into the new folder, copy the following image files from the folder containing data files for this text:

- lwhl_logo.gif
- lwhl_map.gif
- lwhl_player.gif

d) Modify the index.htm Web page document as follows:

1. Change the page title to: Lake Worth Hockey League Association
2. Insert a table with 6 rows, 1 column, a width of 95%, no border, a cell padding of 6, and no cell spacing.
3. In the top cell, insert the lwhl_logo.gif image.
4. Split the cell in the third row into 2 columns.
5. Split the cell in the fourth row into 2 columns.
6. In the left cell of the third row, insert the lwhl_player.gif image.
7. In the right cell of the third row, type the following text. Allow the text to wrap and replace Student Name with your name:

   Student Name organized the Lake Worth Hockey League Association in 1973 to accommodate the growing interest in the sport of ice hockey. Leagues are organized by age, ranging from the Tom Thumb League (5 to 6 years) to the Men's League (35+). For more information, call (561) 555-PUCK.

8. In the right cell of the fourth row, insert the lwhl_map.gif image.
9. In the left cell of the fourth row, type the following text. Allow the text to wrap:

   The Lake Worth Arena was built in 1972 through a joint effort of the city and private fund raising. It is a state-of-the-art facility with two Olympic-size sheets of ice. Services include ice time rentals, open skating, open hockey, and a pro shop with skate rental, skate sharpening, and hockey supplies.

e) Create a new library item named navbar that looks similar to:

   Home | Rules | Schedule

Link the text Home to index.htm, the text Rules to rules.htm, and the text Schedule to schedule.htm.

f) Create a new library item named footer that is similar to the following, inserting a line break where needed. The date after the text Last modified should be a time stamp that will automatically update when the Web page document is saved:

> Send comments to the webmaster. Last modified Monday, March 7, 2005 10:18 AM
> Copyright 2005 Lake Worth Hockey League Association.

Link the text webmaster to the e-mail address webmaster@lpdatafiles.com.

g) Modify the index.htm Web page document as follows:
   1. In the second row, place the navbar library item. Break the link to the library item and delete the text Home |
   2. In the fifth row, place the navbar library item. Break the link to the library item and delete the text Home |
   3. In the last row, place the footer library item.

h) Modify the rules.htm Web page document as follows:
   1. Change the page title to: LWHLA - Rules
   2. Insert a table with 5 rows, 1 column, a width of 95%, no border, a cell padding of 6, and no cell spacing.
   3. In the top cell, insert the lwhl_logo.gif image.
   4. In the second row, place the navbar library item. Break the link to the library item and remove the link from the text Rules.
   5. In the third row, type the following text. Allow the text to wrap and replace Student Name with your name:

   > Rules are in dispute at this time. Please call Student Name at (561) 555-PUCK with any questions or comments you may have on the rules.

   6. In the fourth row, place the navbar library item. Break the link to the library item and remove the link from the text Rules.
   7. In the last row, place the footer library item.

i) Modify the schedule.htm Web page document as follows:
   1. Change the page title to: LWHLA - Schedule
   2. Insert a table with 5 rows, 1 column, a width of 95%, no border, a cell padding of 6, and no cell spacing.
   3. In the top cell, insert the lwhl_logo.gif image.
   4. In the second row, place the navbar library item. Break the link to the library item and remove the link from the text Schedule.
   5. In the third row, type the following text. Allow the text to wrap and replace Student Name with your name:

   > The new season schedule will be posted any day now. Please call Student Name at (561) 555-PUCK with any questions or comments you may have.

   6. In the fourth row, place the navbar library item. Break the link to the library item and remove the link from the text Schedule.
   7. In the last row, place the footer library item.

j) Check the spelling in each of the Web page documents.

j) View each Web page document in a browser window and test the hyperlinks.

k) Print a copy of each Web page document from the browser.

Exercise 2 — Volcanoes

Create new Web site about volcanoes by completing the following steps:

a) Define a new site named Volcanoes in a folder named Volcanoes.

b) Add three files to the Web site, naming them index.htm, lava.htm, and vol_types.htm.

c) In the Volcanoes root folder, create a folder named images. Into the new folder, copy the following image files from the folder containing data files for this text:

- vol_close.jpg
- vol_gas.jpg
- vol_logo.gif
- vol_splash.jpg

d) Modify the index.htm Web page document as follows:

1. Change the page title to: About Volcanoes
2. Insert a table with 5 rows, 1 column, a width of 95%, no border, a cell padding of 10, and no cell spacing.
3. In the top cell, insert the vol_logo.gif image.
4. Split the cell in the third row into 2 columns.
5. In the right cell of the third row, insert the vol_close.jpg image.
6. In the left cell of the third row, type the following text. Allow the text to wrap:

   A volcano is a location on the surface of the Earth where magma has erupted out of the interior of the planet. Magma is molten rock, which has melted from the extreme heat and pressure inside the Earth. Molten rock on the Earth's surface is called lava. As lava cools, it builds up and forms mountains.

   Volcanoes are classified as active or inactive. Inactive volcanoes are older and have usually erupted many times. A volcano is active if it is currently erupting or expected to erupt eventually.

   A volcanic eruption occurs when lava, gasses, and other matter come out of a vent. A volcano usually has more than one vent. Violent eruptions often include chunks of rock that were blown off the interior walls of the vent. Quiet eruptions consist of lava flowing out of vents.

   Eventually, the volcano reaches the cooling stage. While the volcano cools, it reduces in size from erosion.

e) Create a new library item named navbar that looks similar to:

   Home | Lava Types | Volcano Types

Link the text Home to index.htm, the text Lava Types to lava.htm, and the text Volcano Types to vol_types.htm.

f) Create a new library item named footer that is similar to the following, inserting a line break where needed and replacing Student Name with your name. The date after the text Last modified should be a time stamp that will automatically update when the Web page document is saved:

> Send comments to the webmaster. Last modified Monday, March 7, 2005 10:20 AM Copyright 2005 Student Name.

Link the text webmaster to the e-mail address webmaster@lpdatafiles.com.

g) Modify the index.htm Web page document as follows:

1. In the second row, place the navbar library item. Break the link to the library item and delete the text Home |
2. In the fourth row, place the navbar library item. Break the link to the library item and delete the text Home |
3. In the last row, place the footer library item.

h) Modify the lava.htm Web page document as follows:

1. Change the page title to: Types of Lava Rocks
2. Insert a table with 6 rows, 1 column, a width of 95%, no border, a cell padding of 10, and no cell spacing.
3. In the top cell, insert the vol_logo.gif image.
4. In the second row, place the navbar library item. Break the link to the library item and remove the link from the text Lava Types.
5. In the third row, insert the vol_splash.jpg image.
6. In the fourth row, type the following text. Allow the text to wrap:

   Types of Lava Rocks: Basalt, Obsidian, Andesite

   Basalt (pronounced buh-SALT) is rock composed of mostly feldspar and pyroxene. Dark in color, basalt is considered to be a fine-grained rock. Some varieties of basalt contain iron, silica, or aluminum.

   Obsidian (pronounced ub-SID-ee-en) is semi-translucent glass that contains a large amount of silicon. Obsidian is usually black or dark gray in color and occasionally red or brown. Obsidian is formed when lava cools so quickly that it does not have time to crystallize.

   Like basalt, andesite (pronounced AN-deh-site) is composed of feldspar and pyroxene and is a fine-grained rock. However, andesite is usually light to medium gray in color. Andesite is one of the most common volcanic rocks.

7. In the fifth row place the navbar library item. Break the link to the library item and remove the link from the text Lava Types.
8. In the last row place the footer library item.

i) Modify the vol_types.htm Web page document as follows:

1. Change the page title to Types of Volcanoes
2. Insert a table with 6 rows, 1 column, a width of 95%, no border, a cell padding of 10, and no cell spacing.
3. In the top cell, insert the vol_logo.gif image.
4. In the second row, place the navbar library item. Break the link to the library item and remove the link from the text Volcano Types.

5. In the third row, type the following text. Allow the text to wrap:

   Types of Volcanoes: Cinder Cones, Shield Volcanoes, Composite Volcanoes

   Cinder cone volcanoes are formed from explosive eruptions where materials are ejected high in the air and cool before they hit the ground. Fine-grained rocks are blown away by winds. Coarser rock fragments remain in a cone-shaped pile, which can be hundreds of meters tall.

   Shield volcanoes are formed by frequent, quiet eruptions and are much larger in width than in height. As smooth lava flows build up, a dome shape is formed. Shield volcanoes usually change shape when eruptions become explosive late in the life of the volcano.

   Composite volcanoes are very large and are formed from alternating explosive eruptions and quiet eruptions. This results in layers of ejected material covered by smooth lava flows. Composite volcanoes are usually symmetrical in shape and can be as high as several kilometers.

   6. In the fourth row insert the vol_gas.jpg image.
   7. In the fifth row place the navbar library item. Break the link to the library item and remove the link from the text Volcano Types.
   8. In the last row place the footer library item.

j) Check the spelling in each of the Web page documents.

k) View each Web page document in a browser window and test the hyperlinks.

l) Print a copy of each Web page document from the browser.

Exercise 3 — Baby Sitter

Create new Web site for a baby-sitting service by completing the following steps:

a) Define a new site named Baby Sitter in a folder named Baby Sitter.

b) Add three files to the Web site, naming them index.htm, credentials.htm, and references.htm.

c) In the Baby Sitter root folder, create a folder named images. Into the new folder, copy the following image files from the folder containing data files for this text:

   - baby_blocks.gif
   - baby_bottle.gif
   - baby_hold.gif
   - baby_logo.gif

d) Modify the index.htm Web page document as follows:

   1. Change the page title to: Smiley's Baby-Sitting Service
   2. Insert a table with 5 rows, 1 column, a width of 95%, no border, a cell padding of 8, and no cell spacing.
   3. In the top cell, insert the baby_logo.gif image.
   4. Split the cell in the third row into 2 columns.
   5. In the left cell of the third row, insert the baby_hold.gif image.

6. In the right cell of the third row, type the following text. Allow the text to wrap:

Need a baby sitter? Call me! Hi, I'm Smiley, and I have been baby-sitting for several years. I have a long list of credentials, which include many certifications. I am prepared for any situation and have years of experience with children of all ages. I have a long list of happy customers that are willing to tell you all about me as a baby sitter.

The best feature you will find is that I will work any hour, including overnight. Baby-sitting is my only job, and I have plenty of time to adjust to your schedule. You will find that I am never late and can usually stay later than scheduled if the need arises.

Call Smiley at 903-555-7979 or e-mail me. I have mobile e-mail capabilities and will get your message immediately!

7. Link the text list of credentials in the first paragraph to credentials.htm, the text happy customers in the first paragraph to references.htm, and the text e-mail me to the e-mail address smiley@lpdatafiles.com.

e) Create a new library item named navbar that looks similar to:

<u>Home</u> | <u>Credentials</u> | <u>References</u>

Link the text Home to index.htm, the text Credentials to credentials.htm, and the text References to references.htm.

f) Create a new library item named footer that is similar to the following, inserting a line break where needed and replacing Student Name with your name. The date after the text Last modified should be a time stamp that will automatically update when the Web page document is saved:

Send comments to <u>Smiley</u>. Last modified Monday, March 7, 2005 9:30 AM
Copyright 2005 Student Name.

Link the text Smiley to the e-mail address smiley@lpdatafiles.com.

g) Modify the index.htm Web page document as follows:

1. In the second row place the navbar library item. Break the link to the library item and delete the text Home |
2. In the fourth row place the navbar library item. Break the link to the library item and delete the text Home |
3. In the last row place the footer library item.

h) Modify the credentials.htm Web page document as follows:

1. Change the page title to: Smiley's Baby-Sitting Service - Credentials
2. Insert a table with 5 rows, 1 column, a width of 95%, no border, a cell padding of 8, and no cell spacing.
3. In the top cell, insert the baby_logo.gif image.
4. In the second row, place the navbar library item. Break the link to the library item and remove the link from the text Credentials.
5. Split the cell in the third row into 2 columns.
6. In the left cell of the third row, insert the baby_blocks.gif image.

Web Site Development 5 – 35

7. In the right cell of the third row, type the following text. Insert a line break after each credential:

   Smiley's Credentials

   2003 Baby Sitter Course
   2003 CPR Certification
   2003 Lifeguard Certification
   2003 Psychology of Babies Course
   2003 Parenting Course
   2004 CPR Refresher Course
   2004 Caregiver Course
   2004 Baby Nutrition Course

8. In the fourth row place the navbar library item. Break the link to the library item and remove the link from the text Credentials.
9. In the last row place the footer library item.

i) Modify the references.htm Web page document as follows:

   1. Change the page title to: Smiley's Baby-Sitting Service - References
   2. Insert a table with 5 rows, 1 column, a width of 95%, no border, a cell padding of 8, and no cell spacing.
   3. In the top cell, insert the baby_logo.gif image.
   4. In the second row, place the navbar library item. Break the link to the library item and remove the link from the text References.
   5. Split the cell in the third row into 2 columns.
   6. In the left cell of the third row, insert the baby_bottle.gif image.
   7. In the right cell of the third row, type the following text. Insert a line break after each reference:

      The parents listed below are willing to speak to anyone about my services:

      Frank and Jill Kravis, son Jeffrey 555-0779
      Bill and Lee Haas, daughter Tina and son Hans 555-8080
      Venus Perez, daughter Cherise 555-2233
      Lou Mackey, daughters Ginny and Linda 555-1108

   8. In the fourth row place the navbar library item. Break the link to the library item and remove the link from the text References.
   9. In the last row place the footer library item.

j) Check the spelling in each of the Web page documents.
k) View each Web page document in a browser window and test the hyperlinks.
l) Print a copy of each Web page document from the browser.

Exercise 4 —————————————————————————— METEOROLOGY

Modify the METEOROLOGY Web site by completing the following steps:

a) Open the METEOROLOGY Web site for editing, a Web site provided with the data files for this text.

b) In the Web site's root folder, create a folder named images. Into the new folder, copy the following image files from the folder containing data files for this text:
   - weather_clouds.gif
   - weather_logo.gif
   - weather_storms.gif
   - weather_wind.gif

c) Modify the navigation library item to include the text Wind that is a link to wind.htm. The library item should be similar to:

   Home | Clouds | Storms | Wind

   Allow Dreamweaver to update all occurrences of the library item.

d) Modify the footer library item as follows:
   1. Change the Student Name to your name.
   2. After the text Last modified insert a time stamp that will automatically update when the Web page document is saved. Use a format similar to Monday, March 7, 2005 10:20 AM.

   Allow Dreamweaver to update all occurrences of the library item.

e) Modify the index.htm Web page document as follows:
   1. Change the page title to: Meteorology Home Page
   2. In the top cell, insert the weather_logo.gif image.
   3. Break the link to the library items in the second row and the last row. Remove the link from the text Home in each of the two rows.

f) Modify the clouds.htm Web page document as follows:
   1. In the top cell, insert the weather_clouds.gif image.
   2. Break the link to the library items in the second row and the last row. Remove the link from the text Clouds in each of the two rows.

g) Modify the storms.htm Web page document as follows:
   1. In the top cell, insert the weather_storms.gif image.
   2. Break the link to the library items in the second row and the last row. Remove the link from the text Storms in each of the two rows.

h) Modify the wind.htm Web page document as follows:
   1. In the top cell, insert the weather_wind.gif image.
   2. Break the link to the library items in the second row and the last row. Remove the link from the text Wind in each of the two rows.

i) Check the spelling in each of the Web page documents.

j) View each Web page document in a browser window and test the hyperlinks.

k) Print a copy of each Web page document from the browser.

Exercise 5 — SEVEN WONDERS

Modify the SEVEN WONDERS Web site by completing the following steps:

a) Open the SEVEN WONDERS Web site for editing, a Web site provided with the data files for this text.

b) In the Web site's root folder, create a folder named images. Into the new folder, copy the following image files from the folder containing data files for this text:
- wonder_logo.gif
- wonder_map.gif

c) Modify the navbar library item by finishing linking all the text to the appropriate Web page documents in the Web site. Save the library item, and allow Dreamweaver to update all occurrences of the library item.

d) Modify the footer library item as follows:
1. Change the Student Name to your name.
2. After the text Last modified type a space and then insert a time stamp that will automatically update when the Web page document is saved. Use a format similar to Monday, March 7, 2005 10:18 AM.
3. Link the text webmaster to the e-mail address: webmaster@lpdatafiles.com

Allow Dreamweaver to update all occurrences of the library item.

e) Modify the index.htm Web page document as follows:
1. Change the page title to: The SEVEN WONDERS of the Ancient World
2. Insert a table with 5 rows, 1 column, a width of 95%, no border, a cell padding of 10, and no cell spacing.
3. In the top cell, insert the wonder_logo.gif image.
4. In the second row place the navbar library item. Break the link to the library item and delete the text Home |
5. Split the cell in the third row into 2 columns.
6. In the left cell of the third row, insert the wonder_map.gif image.
7. In the right cell of the third row, type the following text. Insert a line break after each wonder:

   The Seven Wonders of the Ancient World are architectural and sculptural accomplishments. Only one of the seven (the pyramids) survives today. The Seven Wonders of the Ancient World are:

   Temple of Artemis (Diana) at Ephesus
   Mausoleum at Halicarnassus
   Colossus of Rhodes
   Hanging Gardens of Babylon
   Pyramids of Egypt
   Lighthouse of Alexandria
   Statue of Zeus (Jupiter) at Olympia

8. In the fourth row place the navbar library item. Break the link to the library item and delete the text Home |
9. In the last row place the footer library item.

f) In each of the other Web page documents in the Web site, break the link to the library items in the second row and the last row, and remove the link from the appropriate text in both rows. Save the modified Web page documents.

g) Check the spelling in the index.htm Web page document.

h) View each Web page document in a browser window and test the hyperlinks.

i) Print a copy of each Web page document from the browser.

Exercise 6 (advanced) — Local Club

Develop a Web site that is for a local club, such as a bicycling club or a debate club. The Web site should include news about the club, club events, and appropriate topics for the club. Complete the following steps to finish the Web site development, writing on paper when appropriate:

a) Determine the purpose and target audience.

b) Determine the Web pages and then sketch the navigation structure.

c) Determine the content and navigation links for each page.

d) Sketch the design for each page. Include details about tables.

e) Create the Web site naming it Local Club.

f) Create Web page documents, appropriately named, and add the content.

g) Check the spelling in the Web page documents.

h) View each Web page document in a browser window and test the hyperlinks.

i) Print a copy of each Web page document from the browser.

Exercise 7 (advanced) — Dentist

Develop a Web site that is for a dentist. The Web site should include office hours and location, information about the dentist, and educational information about dental hygiene. Complete the following steps to finish the Web site development, writing on paper when appropriate:

a) Determine the purpose and target audience.

b) Determine the Web pages and then sketch the navigation structure.

c) Determine the content and navigation links for each page.

d) Sketch the design for each page. Include details about tables.

e) Create the Web site naming it Dentist.

f) Create Web page documents, appropriately named, and add the content.

g) Check the spelling in the Web page documents.

h) View each Web page document in a browser window and test the hyperlinks.

i) Print a copy of each Web page document from the browser.

Chapter 6
Images in Dreamweaver and Fireworks

Chapter 6 Expectations

After completing this chapter you will be able to:

1. Determine when to use GIF and JPG graphic file formats.
2. Explain why alternative text should be added to an image.
3. Create a graphic hyperlink.
4. Create an image map.
5. Align, resize, and resample images.
6. Demonstrate the basic features and functions of Fireworks.
7. Draw objects and add text in Fireworks.
8. Optimize and Export a Fireworks Document.
9. Create and modify a button symbol in Fireworks.
10. Distinguish between the four states of a button symbol and change the behavior of a state.
11. Export HTML and images from Fireworks.
12. Use an exported HTML document in Dreamweaver.
13. Crop images.
14. Edit an image in Fireworks from Dreamweaver.

This chapter introduces graphic file formats and discusses adding graphics to a Web page document. Fireworks MX is introduced, as well as rollover behaviors, exporting HTML, and cropping images.

6.1 Graphic File Formats for Web Pages

Images and Graphics

The terms "images" and "graphics" are both used to refer to pictures. Pictures may be photographs or drawings.

GIF

JPG

PNG

Images on Web pages are usually a GIF or JPG file because these formats are widely supported. The *GIF* format is best used with graphics that do not contain many colors, such as clip art or logos. GIF graphics are limited to 256 colors. The *JPG* format supports millions of colors and is best used for photographs. JPEG is also used to refer to a JPG. A third format, *PNG* format was created in the mid-1990s during a controversy over copyright of the GIF format. The PNG format has advantages over GIF and JPG, but is only supported by the newest browsers and therefore is currently not a good choice for an image on a Web page.

Both GIF and JPG formats are *bitmap graphics*, which are based on rows and columns of tiny dots that are square in shape. Each square is a *pixel* and is made up of one solid color. Many pixels of varying color create a graphic:

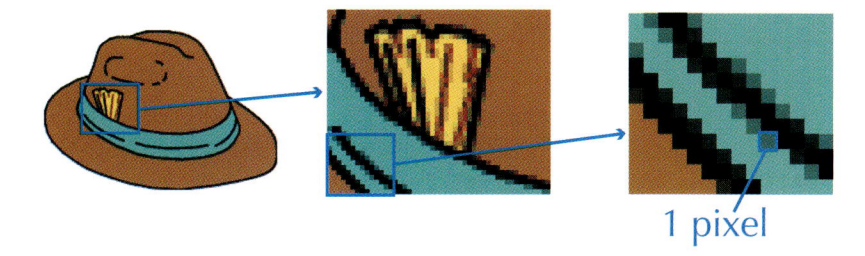

GIF, JPG, and PNG

GIF (Graphics Interchange Format) format is pronounced either giff with a hard g or jiff. JPG (Joint Photographic Experts Group) format is pronounced jay-peg. PNG (Portable Network Graphic) format is pronounced ping.

1 pixel

The number of *dots per inch* (*dpi*) is called the *resolution*. The larger the number of dpi, the better the quality of the graphic.

The GIF format allows one color in the graphic to be chosen as the transparent color, a feature not available for JPG graphics. This allows the background color to show through a graphic:

Background Image

Although there are options in the Page Properties dialog box for displaying an image as the background of a Web page, it is usually not recommended. Text may become difficult to read, which decreases the usability of the Web page.

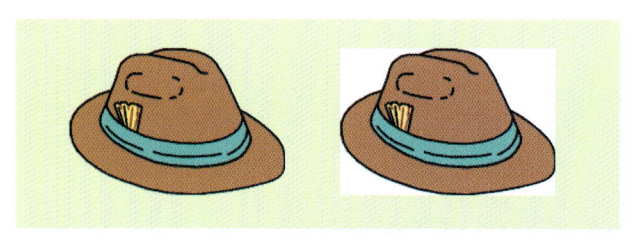

Two hat graphics on a colored background

The GIF on the left has the color white selected as the transparent color. The GIF on the right does not have any transparent color selected. Transparency is not always used in GIF files, but it is a useful option to have.

interlaced

GIF files can be *interlaced*, which means that a low resolution version of the graphic appears first and becomes clearer in four horizontal passes as the Web page fully loads. This allows the user to see that a graphic is going to be displayed.

compression

Compression is a file format feature that reduces file size, which is helpful because smaller files load faster in a browser window. GIF graphics are compressed but retain all of the original information, which is called *lossless compression*. For JPG graphics the compression is *lossy*, which means that some data in the file is lost or removed in order to reduce the file size. The more compression, the smaller the file, but the lower the image quality:

lossless, lossy

> **Editing Graphics**
>
> Double-clicking a graphic's file name in the Site panel opens the file in an editing program. The program that is used depends on the preferences set in Dreamweaver, but will probably be Fireworks MX for GIF, JPG, and PNG graphics.

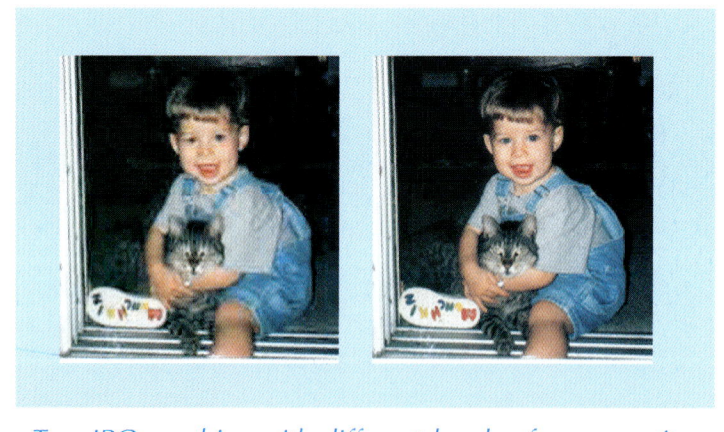

Two JPG graphics with different levels of compression

The JPG on the left has more compression and has a lower image quality, with a small file size of 4 KB. The JPG on the right has less compression and has a higher image quality, with a larger file size of 20 KB.

progressive

JPG files can be *progressive*, which is similar to an interlaced GIF. When a Web page is first loaded into a browser window, a low resolution version of a progressive JPG graphic appears. The graphic becomes clearer as the page fully loads. This allows the user to see that a graphic is going to be displayed.

> **Images from Digital Cameras**
>
> Images from digital cameras are discussed in Appendix C.

6.2 Alternative Text

One consideration for images in a Web page is that some users may not be able to view the images. The user may be visually impaired, or they may have a slow modem connection and therefore turned images off. Adding alternative text to an image provides text for a voice

> **Accessibility**
>
> The ADA (Americans with Disabilities Act), enacted in 1990, called for accessibility for all persons with disabilities. In response, the W3C developed guidelines called the Web Accessibility Initiative (WAI). Among other issues, these guidelines call for alternative text to be provided for any content on a Web page that is not text. Alternative text helps a Web site become accessible to all persons. Ending the alternative text with a period helps voice synthesizers stop or pause, which helps users better understand the content.

synthesizer to "read" in place of the image. Alternative text is also displayed as the screen tip that appears when the pointer is paused over an image. In some browsers, alternative text is displayed in place of an image before it loads.

Alternative text is added to an image by selecting the image in the Web page document and typing the text in the Alt box in the Property inspector:

"Gray Angel fish." is the alternative text for this image

The alternative text can be tested in a browser window by pausing the pointer on the image. A screen tip with the text should appear next to the pointer:

6.3 Graphic Hyperlinks

A hyperlink can be in the form of a graphic that is clicked to display a different Web page document. A graphic hyperlink is created in the same manner as a text hyperlink, using either the Browse for File icon (📁) or the Point to File icon (⊕) in the Property inspector. A graphic hyperlink does not change to blue and underlined. However, when the pointer is moved over a graphic hyperlink in a browser window, the pointer changes to 👆 and the image's alternative text is displayed.

testing and modifying a graphic hyperlink

Links can be tested in a browser window. Links are modified in Dreamweaver by selecting the image and then selecting Modify → Change Link or Modify → Remove Link.

Practice 1

In this practice you will add images and graphic hyperlinks to Web page documents and set alterative text for the images.

① **OPEN THE SCUBA WEB SITE FOR EDITING**
   a. Start Dreamweaver.
   b. In the Site panel, open the SCUBA Web site for editing, a Web site provided with the data files for this text.
   c. In the Site panel, familiarize yourself with the files and folders for this Web site.

Images in Dreamweaver and Fireworks

d. Open the index.htm Web page document and then view the page in a browser.
e. Click the links to explore the other Web pages of the Web site.

② EDIT THE FOOTER LIBRARY ITEM TO INCLUDE YOUR NAME

a. Switch back to Dreamweaver.
b. In the Assets panel, click the Library icon (). A list of library items is displayed.
c. In the Assets panel, double-click the footer library item. A Library Item window is displayed.
d. In the Library Item window, replace the text Student Name with your name.
e. Select File → Save. A dialog box is displayed.
  1. Select Update. The occurrence of the library item on each page in the Web site is updated and a dialog box is displayed with a summary of the changes.
    a) Select Close.
f. Close the Library Item window.

③ ADD AN IMAGE TO THE INDEX.HTM WEB PAGE DOCUMENT

a. Open the index.htm Web page document, if it is not already displayed.
b. In the Assets panel, click the Images icon (). A list of the images in the Web site is displayed.
c. Drag the sketch.gif file from the Assets panel to the empty cell in the table.

Check—Your Web page document should look similar to:

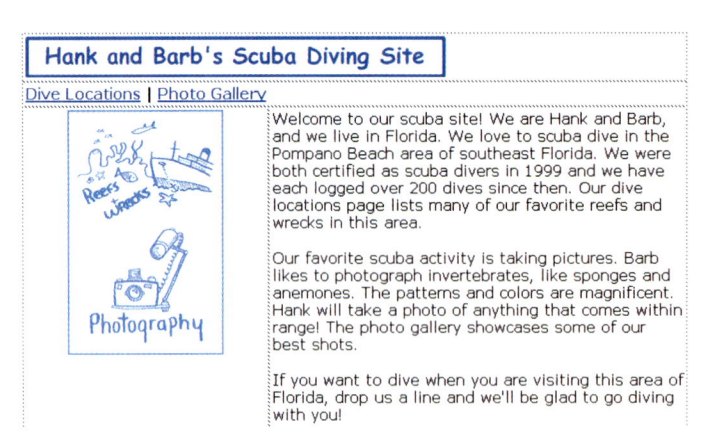

④ ADD ALTERNATIVE TEXT

a. In the Web page document, click the image to select it if it is not already displaying handles.
b. In the Property inspector, set Alt to A drawing of a reef and a wreck and a camera. and press Enter.
c. Save the modified index.htm.
d. Press F12 to switch back to the browser window. The image is included in the Web page.
e. Move the pointer over the image and stop for a moment. The alternative text appears.
f. Print a copy of the Web page.
g. Switch back to Dreamweaver.
h. Close index.htm.

⑤ MAKE A GRAPHIC HYPERLINK

a. Open the photos.htm Web page document.
b. In the top cell of the table, click the blue and white logo that reads "Hank and Barb's Scuba Diving Site" to select it.

c. In the Property inspector, click the Browse for File icon (📁). A dialog box is displayed.
   1. Click the index.htm file name.
   2. Select OK. A graphic hyperlink is created.
d. In the Property inspector, set Alt to Link to home page. and press Enter.
e. Save the modified photos.htm.
f. Press F12 to switch back to the browser window.
g. Click the logo at the top of the Web page to test the hyperlink. The home page is displayed.
h. Switch back to Dreamweaver.
i. Close photos.htm.

⑥ MAKE ANOTHER GRAPHIC HYPERLINK

a. Open the locations.htm Web page document.
b. Link the logo in the top cell of the table to the index.htm Web page document.
c. Set alternative text for the graphic to: Link to home page.
d. Save the modified locations.htm and then test the graphic hyperlink in a browser.
e. Switch back to Dreamweaver and close locations.htm.

6.4 What is an Image Map?

hotspot An *image map* is a graphic that contains one or more hotspots. A *hotspot* is an invisible, defined area on a graphic that is a hyperlink. Just like a graphic hyperlink, when the pointer is moved over a hotspot on an image in a browser window the pointer changes to 👆 and the hotspot's alternative text is displayed:

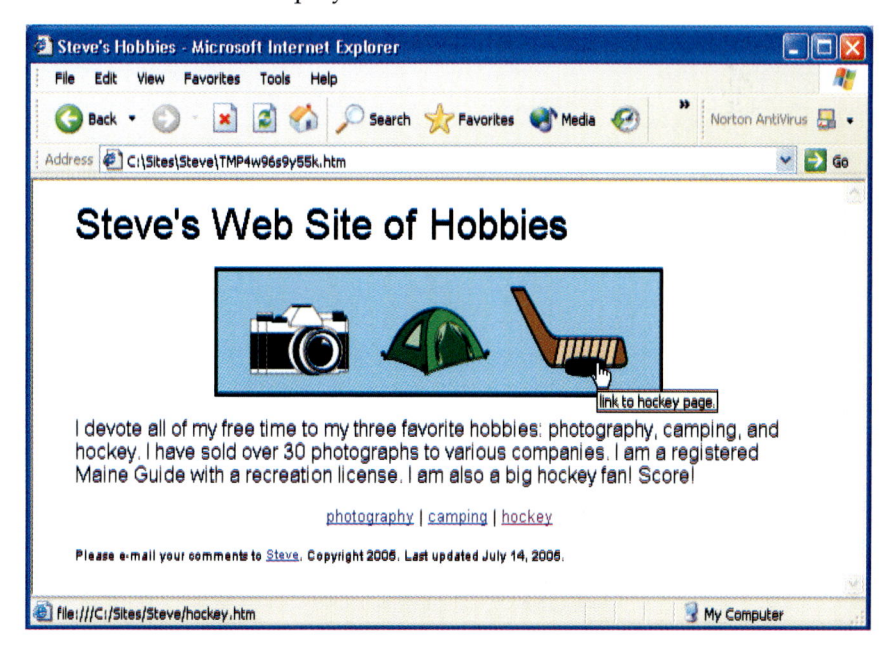

For example, the graphic in the Web page above contains three hotspots. The pointer was moved over one of the hotspots, the pointer changed shape, and the alternative text "link to hockey page." appeared.

Images in Dreamweaver and Fireworks   6 – 5

6.5 Creating an Image Map

An image map is created by adding a graphic to a Web page document and then defining hotspots on the graphic. Selecting a graphic in a Web page document displays image properties in the Property inspector at the bottom of the Dreamweaver window:

Map box —
hotspot tools —

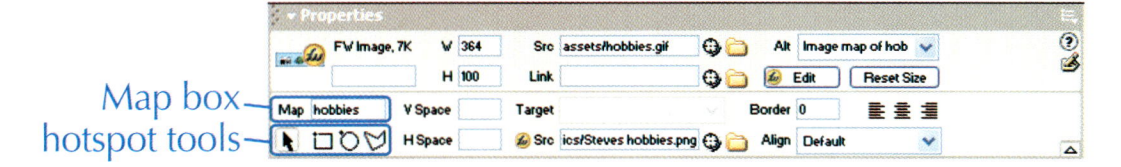

creating a hotspot

A Web page document can have more than one image map, so each image map should be given a unique name in the Map box. The hotspot tools are then used to draw hotspots on the selected graphic. Hotspots can be created using the Rectangular Hotspot tool (□), Oval Hotspot tool (○), or Polygon Hotspot tool (∨), each of which creates a different shaped hotspot. The Pointer Hotspot tool (▶) is used to select and edit the shape of hotspots once they are created.

To draw a hotspot on a selected graphic, first click a Hotspot tool in the Property inspector. The pointer changes to + when it is moved over the graphic. If the Rectangular Hotspot or Oval Hotspot tool is selected, dragging draws the hotspot. To draw with the Polygon Hotspot tool, click to create the corner points of a shape. With each click, the area between the clicked locations fills in. Double-clicking finishes the hotspot. Note that hotspots do not have to perfectly cover an area of the graphic:

Image Maps and Text Hyperlinks

When an image map is used on a Web page, the page should also contain text hyperlinks to the same pages that the hotspots are linked to. This avoids usability problems if a browser is not displaying graphics.

From left to right: a rectangle, oval, and polygon hotspot

Hotspot properties are displayed for a selected hotspot in the Property inspector at the bottom of the Dreamweaver window:

Moving a Hotspot

The arrow keys may also be used to move a selected hotspot.

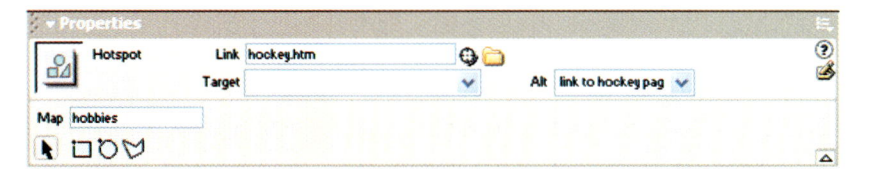

- Link is the Web page document file linked to the hotspot. A new file name is specified using the Browse for File icon (📁) or the Point to File icon (⊕).

- Alt is the alternative text for the hotspot. New text can be typed.

selecting a hotspot

- The Pointer Hotspot Tool button (▶) is clicked to allow hotspot to be selected and edited.

editing, deleting, testing a hotspot

The shape of a selected hotspot is changed by dragging a handle. A selected hotspot is deleted by pressing the Delete key. Hotspots are tested in a browser window.

Practice 2

In this practice you will create an image map. Dreamweaver should be started and the SCUBA Web site should be the working site.

① NAME THE IMAGE MAP

a. Open the index.htm Web page document.

b. Select the image in the left cell of the third row of the table. Image properties are displayed in the Property inspector.

c. In the Property inspector, set **Map** to sketch and press Enter.

② CREATE A RECTANGLE HOTSPOT

a. In the Property inspector, click the Rectangular Hotspot tool (▭).

b. Move the pointer over the image. The pointer changes to +.

c. Starting in the upper-left corner of the image, drag down and to the right to draw a rectangle shape on the top half of the sketch, the part with "Reefs and Wrecks." Do not include the camera. If you make a mistake, press the Delete key to delete the shape and try again.

Check—Your image should look similar to:

d. In the Property inspector, click the Browse for File icon (📁). A dialog box is displayed.
  1. Click the locations.htm file name.
  2. Select **OK**. The dialog box is removed.

e. In the Property inspector, set **Alt** box to Link to dive locations information. and press Enter.

③ CREATE A POLYGON HOTSPOT

a. In the Property inspector, click the Polygon Hotspot tool (▽).

b. Move the pointer over the image. The pointer changes to +.

c. Draw a polygon as follows: click near the "P" at the beginning of the word "Photography," then click at the tallest point of the camera drawing, then double-click near the "y" in the word "Photography." A polygon hotspot is created in the shape of a triangle. If you make a mistake, press the delete key to delete the shape and try again.

Check—Your image should look similar to:

Images in Dreamweaver and Fireworks 6 – 7

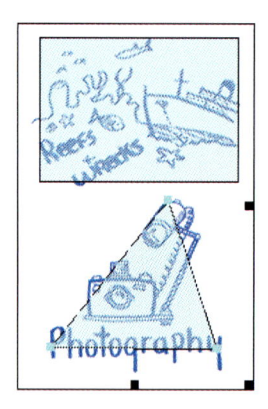

d. Link the hotspot to the photos.htm Web page document.

e. In the Property inspector, set **Alt** to Link to the photo gallery. and press Enter.

④ SELECT AND MOVE HOTSPOTS

a. In the Property inspector, click the Pointer Hotspot tool ( ).

b. In the Web page document, click the rectangle hotspot. Handles are displayed indicating that it is selected.

c. In the Web page document, click the polygon hotspot. Handles are displayed indicating that it is selected.

d. Drag the hotspot, adjusting its position over the camera drawing. Drag its handles to edit the shape. Move it to cover as much of the camera and "Photography" word as possible.

e. Save the modified index.htm.

⑤ TEST THE IMAGE MAP IN THE BROWSER WINDOW

a. Press F12. The Web page document is displayed in a browser window.

b. Move the pointer over the image, noting where the pointer changes to .

c. Pause the pointer over each hotspot area, and check that the alternative text is displayed.

d. Click the top hotspot. The Dive Locations Web page is displayed. Click the logo at the top of the page to return to the home page.

e. Click the bottom hotspot. The Photo Gallery Web page is displayed. Click the logo at the top of the page to return to the home page.

f. Print a copy of the Web page.

g. Close the browser window. Dreamweaver is displayed.

h. Close index.htm.

6.6 Using a Spacer GIF

Why use a spacer GIF?

Even though a cell may be set to a specified pixel width, a browser may still resize the cell smaller than the specified number of pixels if the cell contains text that can be wrapped.

A *spacer GIF* is a transparent GIF image that consists of only 1 pixel. It is transparent so that it is not visible in a browser window. A spacer GIF is used to control the layout of a table by forcing table cells to a specified width. This is done by inserting a spacer.gif file in a cell, and then changing the width of the image to the minimum that the cell should be if the browser window is resized. For example, the left cell in the following table gets very narrow as the browser window is sized smaller:

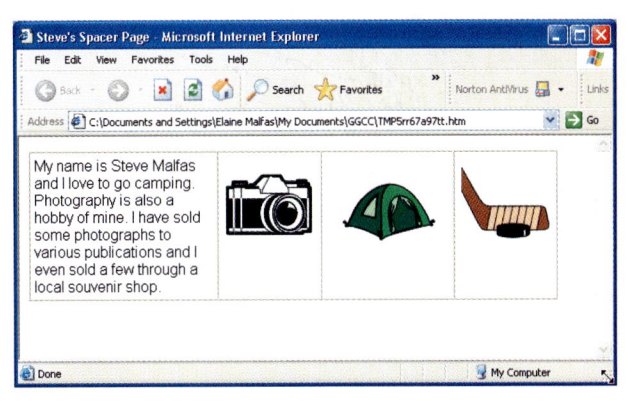

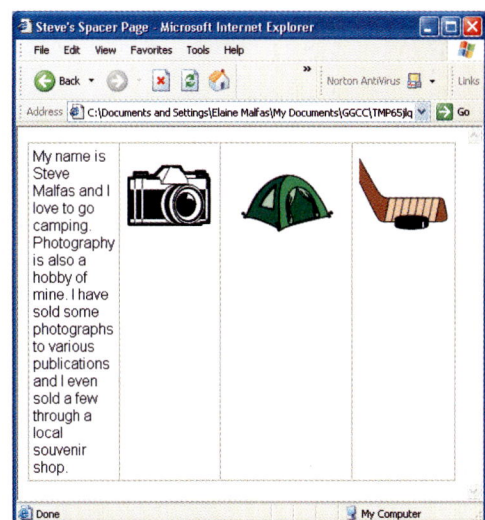

A browser tries to accommodate the entire table by sizing a cell with text smaller than specified

Adding a spacer gif to the left cell and changing the width of the GIF to 200 affects how narrow the table can appear, even when the browser window is very narrow:

Practice 3

In this practice you will add images and a spacer.gif file to control the layout of a Web page document. Dreamweaver should be started and the SCUBA Web site should be the working site.

① ADD IMAGES AND ALTERNATIVE TEXT TO A WEB PAGE DOCUMENT

a. Open the photos.htm Web page document. There are four empty cells in the table.

b. In the Assets panel, click the Images icon ( ) if images are not already displayed.

c. Drag the anemone.jpg file from the Assets panel to the upper-left empty cell.

d. Select the anemone image, if it is not already selected.

e. In the Property inspector, set **Alt** to Anemone photograph. and press Enter.

f. Drag the sponges.jpg file from the Assets panel to the cell just to the right of the anemone image.

g. Set the sponges alternative text to: Purple sponges photograph.

h. Add the octopus.jpg file to the lower-left empty cell and set its alternative text to: Octopus eyes photograph.

Images in Dreamweaver and Fireworks   6 – 9

i. Add the seahorse.jpg file to the last empty cell and set its alternative text to: Red seahorse photograph.
   j. Save the modified photos.htm.

Check—Your Web page document should look similar to:

② TEST THE TABLE IN THE BROWSER WINDOW

   a. Press F12. The photos.htm Web page document is displayed in a browser.
   b. Resize the browser window much smaller and observe how the text in the cell next to the photos changes when the window is very narrow.
   c. Switch back to Dreamweaver.

③ ADD A SPACER GIF

   a. Place the insertion point to the right of the ! at the bottom of the paragraph that ends "…important!" and insert a line break. Note the location of the insertion point, just below the paragraph of text.
   b. In the Assets panel, select the spacer.gif file
   c. At the bottom of the Assets panel, click Insert.
   d. In the Property inspector, set W to 200 and press Enter. The image is resized to 200 pixels wide.
   e. Save the modified photos.htm.

④ TEST THE TABLE IN THE BROWSER WINDOW

   a. Press F12 to switch back to the browser window. The photos.htm Web page document is displayed.
   b. Resize the browser window much smaller and observe how the text in the cell next to the photos changes when the window is very narrow. It doesn't get any narrower than 200 pixels.
   c. Move the pointer over each image and pause, testing that the alternative text appears.
   d. Print a copy of the Web page.
   e. Close the browser window. Dreamweaver is displayed.

6.7 Aligning an Image

The horizontal alignment of a selected image can be changed using the alignment buttons in the Property inspector. Selecting an image and then clicking either the Align Left button ( ), Align Center button ( ), or the Align Right button ( ) aligns the image. Alignment buttons are also available in the Property inspector when the insertion point is next to an image in a Web page document.

6.8 Resizing an Image

resampling

If the width and height of an image in a Web page document needs to be reduced, it can first be resized in the Web page document to determine the exact dimensions in pixels, and then the image can be edited in Fireworks to the determined size. An image should not be resized in a Web page document in Dreamweaver and left that way because the image file has not been properly resampled. *Resampling* changes the size of the file and correctly adjusts the pixels in the image.

Once an image is inserted into a Web page document, clicking it once selects it and displays handles:

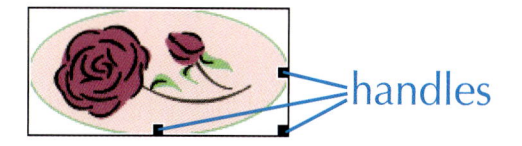

Images can be resized by dragging on a handle

proportionately resize

stretch

Pointing to a handle changes the pointer to , and dragging resizes the image. Dragging the corner handle while pressing the Shift key sizes the image *proportionately*, which means that the width and height remain in the same ratio, preventing distortion. Dragging a handle without pressing and holding Shift *stretches* the image, causing distortion:

A stretched image is distorted

An image that has been resized to a size other than the actual file dimensions will display bold numbers in the W and H boxes in the Property inspector. Note that images should not be sized larger than the original size. The quality of the image decreases as the image is sized larger.

resetting image size

If a mistake is made when resizing an image in Dreamweaver, clicking Reset Size in the Property inspector returns an image to its original dimensions.

editing a resized image

Once a selected image has been resized, the image's file can be quickly edited in Fireworks by selecting Commands → Optimize Image in Fireworks, which displays the image in a window with Fireworks optimization options. Selecting the File tab in the window displays image dimensions:

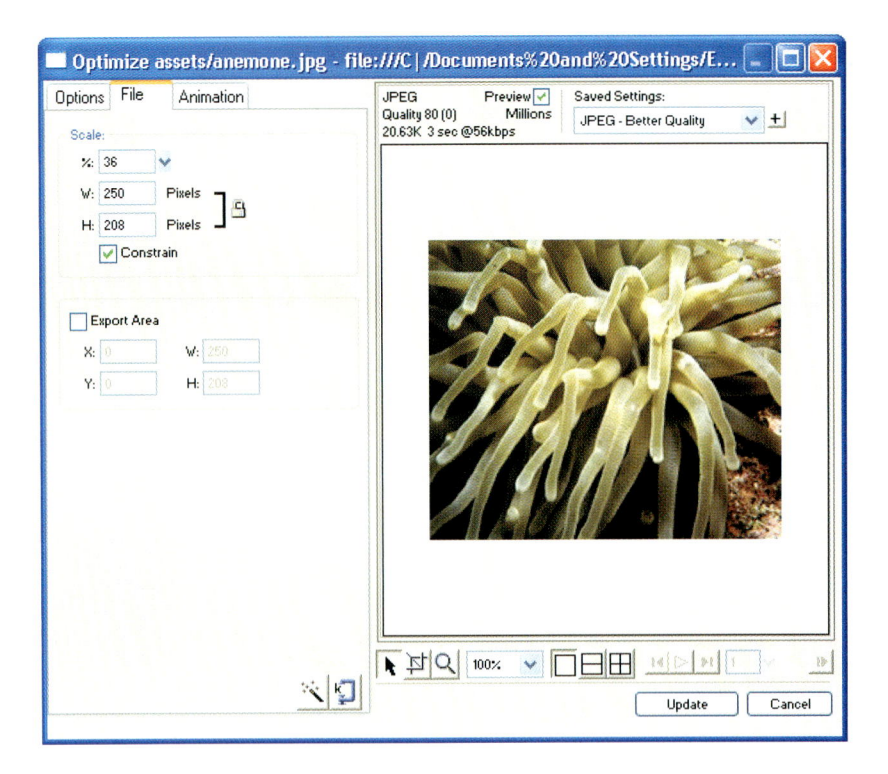

Selecting Update changes the image to the new dimensions, saves the changes to the file, and updates the image in the Web page document in Dreamweaver.

Practice 4

In this practice you will align and resize images. Dreamweaver should be started and the SCUBA Web site should be the working site.

① CHANGE THE ALIGNMENT OF IMAGES

a. Open the photos.htm Web page document, if it is not already displayed.

b. In the Web page document, click the anemone image (first image) to select it. Handles are displayed.

c. In the Property inspector, click the Align Center button (≡). The image is centered in the cell.

d. In the Web page document, center align the three other photograph images. The center alignment improves the layout of the table since it contains images of varying widths.

② RESIZE AN IMAGE AND OPTIMIZE IT IN FIREWORKS

a. Click the anemone image to select it. Handles are displayed. In the Property inspector, note that W is 200, because this image is 200 pixels wide.

b. Select the octopus image and note the image is 220 pixels wide.

c. Drag the corner handle to make the octopus smaller. In the Property inspector, the W and H values are now bold because the image's size is different from its actual file's size.

d. In the Property inspector, click [Reset Size]. The image changes back to its original size and proportions and W and H values are no longer bold.

e. Hold down the Shift key and drag the corner handle of the octopus image until W in the Property inspector is 200. If you have difficulty, click [Reset Size] in the Property inspector and try again.

f. Select **Commands** → **Optimize Image** in Fireworks. If a dialog box appears, select **No**. The image is displayed in a window with Fireworks optimization options.

g. In the window, select the **File** tab to display the image size information. 200 should be in the W box.

h. Select **Update**. The window is removed and the image in the Web page document is resampled to 200 pixels wide, just like two of the other images. The octopus image was resized to match the other images because it was bigger. The seahorse image cannot be changed to match because as images are resized larger they lose quality.

i. Save the modified photos.htm.

Check—Your Web page document should look similar to:

③ TEST THE TABLE IN THE BROWSER WINDOW

a. Press F12. The photos.htm Web page document is displayed in a browser.

b. Print a copy of the Web page.

c. Close the browser window. Dreamweaver is displayed.

d. Close photos.htm.

④ QUIT DREAMWEAVER

6.9 Introducing Fireworks MX

Fireworks MX is the image editing application that is part of the Macromedia Studio MX suite. Fireworks is used to create and edit images specifically for use on the Web. Fireworks documents are PNG files, which can be exported in the file format of choice for use in a Web page document. Image of other file types, such as GIF and JPG, can also be opened and edited directly in Fireworks.

A new document is created in Fireworks by selecting **File** → **New**, which displays a dialog box:

Starting Fireworks

Fireworks is started by selecting **Start** → **All Programs** → **Macromedia** → **Macromedia Fireworks MX**. Fireworks may also be started by double-clicking the Fireworks icon on the Desktop:

Images in Dreamweaver and Fireworks   6 – 13

Image Placeholders

A Web page document that is designed to include an image usually has a specific amount of space alloted for the image. In Dreamweaver, a placeholder for an image is added to a Web page document by clicking the Image Placeholder button ( ) in the Insert bar and then typing a descriptive name in the displayed dialog box. A gray box is added to the open Web page document and can be moved and resized to take up the area alloted for the image. Right-clicking the placeholder and selecting **Create Image in Fireworks** starts Fireworks with a new document of the exact dimensions of the placeholder. After creating the image, selecting the Done button in the Document window saves, exports, and places the new image.

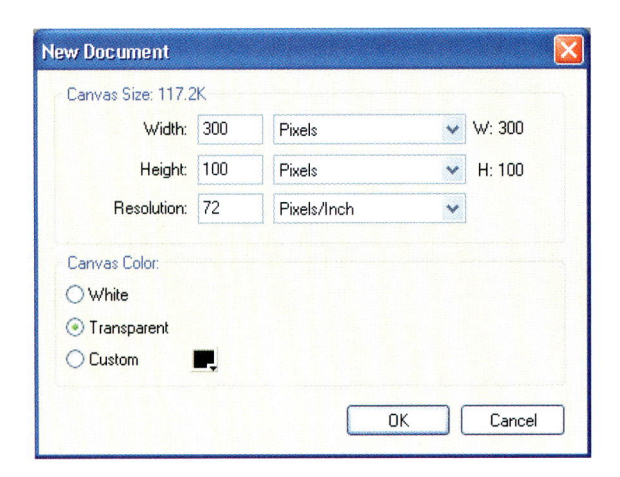

The *canvas* is the rectangular area in which an image will be created. Ideally the canvas is the exact size of the image, but the canvas can be modified as discussed in Section 6.13. Options in this dialog box specify characteristics of the canvas in the new document:

- The Width and Height are usually specified in pixels.
- The Resolution for an image used in a Web page should be 72 Pixels/Inch. A larger number would only increase the file size, and not affect how the image looks when viewed on a monitor.
- The Canvas Color can be transparent, white, or a different color. Transparent is often used for an image that will be exported as a GIF, because the GIF file format supports one transparent color. The JPG file format does not support transparency.

Selecting OK creates a new document and displays it in a window in Fireworks:

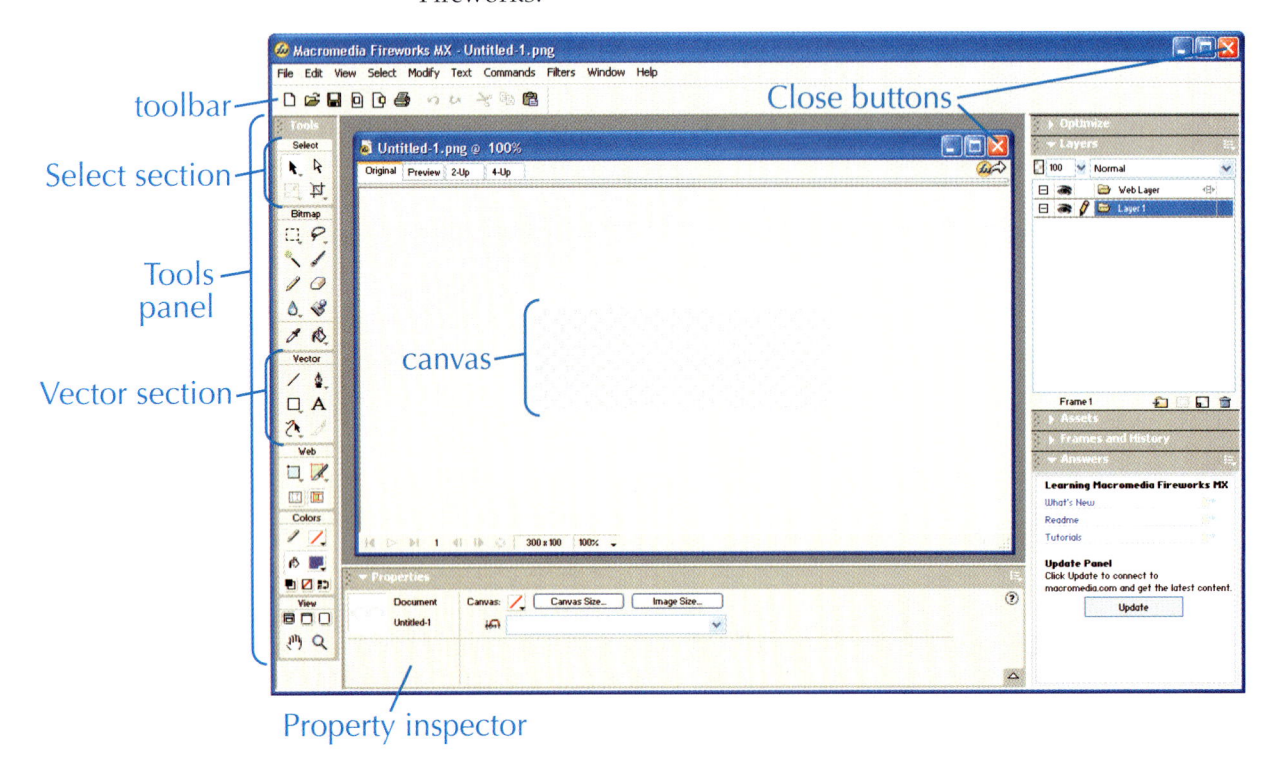

A Guide to Web Development Using Macromedia Dreamweaver MX

> **Vector Graphics**
>
> A vector image is mathematically configured, which allows for an exceptionally small file size.

- The **toolbar** contains buttons for working with a document.
- A **Close button** is clicked to remove the document window or the Fireworks window.
- The **Tools panel** contains tools for creating and editing images. The tools are divided into sections.
- The **Select section** contains tools used to select an image or parts of an image in various ways.

vector graphic

- The **Vector section** contains tools used to draw vector images. A *vector graphic* is composed of lines connected by points, which allows the image to be resized smoothly. Fireworks can be used to create vector graphics and bitmap graphics.
- The **canvas** is the area where the image is created and edited. A canvas that is specified as transparent appears as a checkerboard pattern. The pattern does not appear in an image once it has been exported.
- The **Property inspector** is used to change properties of the selected text or object.

saving a Fireworks document

A new Fireworks document is saved by selecting File → Save, which displays a dialog box where a location outside of the site folder should be selected. A good practice is to keep related files that are not directly used in a Web site together in a folder outside the Web site root folder. Fireworks documents are automatically saved in PNG format. The PNG file should not be used in a Web page document. Fireworks documents can be exported to a different format for use in a Web site. The PNG file is saved in case the file later needs to be edited and exported again. Exporting is discussed in Section 6.14.

> **Native File Format**
>
> The native file format in Fireworks is PNG. A *native file format* is the default format that an application saves files in. Files may be saved and exported in other formats, but are worked on in the native file format.

6.10 Drawing Objects in Fireworks

Objects such as shapes and lines can be drawn on the canvas by selecting a tool in the Vector section in the Tools panel and dragging across the canvas. The Line tool (/) can be selected by clicking it. Clicking and holding down the mouse button on a tool displays a menu from which a shape tool can be selected:

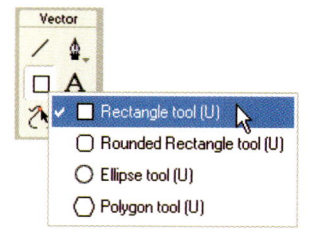

> **Drawing Squares and Circles**
>
> Holding down the Shift key while dragging the Rectangle, Rounded Rectangle, or Ellipse tool draws a square or circle shape, respectively.

When any shape tool or the line tool is selected, the pointer changes to + when it is moved over the canvas. Dragging draws the shape or a straight line. Options in the Property inspector can be set before an object is drawn, or afterwards for a selected object:

> **Constraining Lines**
>
> Holding down the Shift key while dragging with the Line tool constrains the line to 45° angles.

Images in Dreamweaver and Fireworks 6 – 15

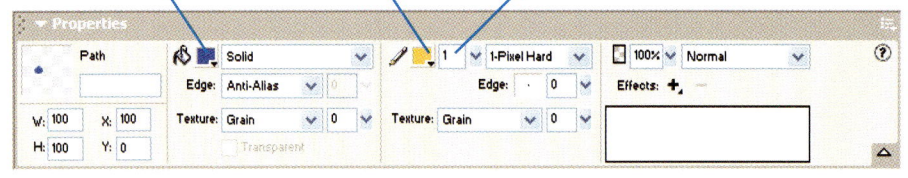

Fill Color box   Stroke Color box   Tip size

- The **Fill Color box** is the color that will fill the shape. A ✎ indicates transparent, or no color. A new color can be selected by clicking the Fill Color box and selecting a color.

- The **Stroke Color box** is the color that will outline the shape. A ✎ indicates transparent, or no color. A new color can be selected by clicking the Stroke Color box and selecting a color.

- The **Tip size** is the thickness of an outline or a straight line in pixels. A new thickness is selected from the list.

Drawing from the Center

Holding down the Alt key while dragging draws the center of the shape or line at the starting location of the pointer.

The rectangle, rounded rectangle, and polygon shapes have additional options that become available in the Property inspector:

- Rectangle Roundness is the roundness of the corners of a rectangle or rounded rectangle. The roundness is changed by typing a value from 1 to 100.

- For a polygon, the Shape can be either polygon or star. The number of Sides can be specified, as well as the degrees of Angle between the sides of the polygon.

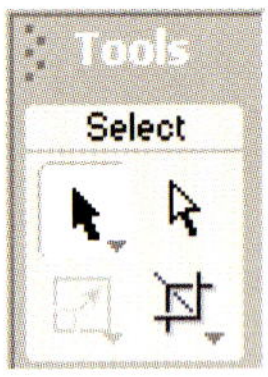

moving objects

An object is moved on the canvas by selecting the Pointer tool (▶) in the Select section in the Tools panel and dragging the object. An object can be precisely moved by changing the values in the X and Y boxes in the Property inspector.

resizing objects

Objects are resized using several methods:

- A selected object is resized by setting the values in the W (width) and H (height) boxes in the Property inspector.

- A rectangle is resized by selecting the Pointer tool (▶) in the Select section in the Tools panel and then dragging a corner handle of the rectangle. Holding down the Shift key while dragging the corner handle proportionately resizes the rectangle.

- Selecting the Scale tool (▦) in the Select section in the Tools panel and clicking an object in the canvas displays handles. Dragging a corner handle resizes the shape proportionately, and dragging a side handle distorts the shape.

6.11 Adding Text in Fireworks

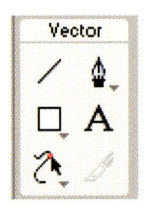

Text can be added to the canvas as a separate object by selecting the Text tool (**A**) from the Vector section in the Tools panel, which changes the pointer to ꭞ when it is moved over the canvas. Clicking creates a text block that changes size to accommodate text as it is typed:

a new, empty text block    the text block after typing

6 – 16   *A Guide to Web Development Using Macromedia Dreamweaver MX*

Options in the Property inspector can be changed before a text block is created. After text is typed, changing properties in the Property inspector affects either all the text in a selected text block, or just text that has been selected in the text block:

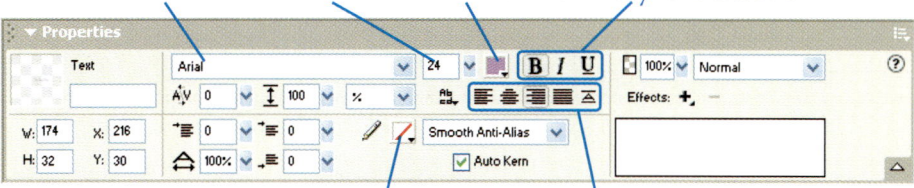

Font list   Size box   Fill Color box   style buttons

Stroke color   alignment buttons

Fonts

Fonts, sizes, and text color are discussed in Chapter 7.

- The **Font list** is the name that describes the shape and style of the letters in the text. A new font can be selected from the list.
- The **Size box** is the size of the text. Larger numbers produce larger letters. A new size can be typed or set using the slider.
- The **Fill Color box** is the text color. A new color can be selected by clicking the Fill Color box and selecting a color.
- The **style buttons** (**B** *I* U) indicate a of **bold**, *italic*, and underlined. Styles are applied by clicking a button. Clicking a selected button removes a style.
- The **alignment buttons** are used the same way style buttons are used. Alignment buttons indicate the arrangement and position of text in the text block:

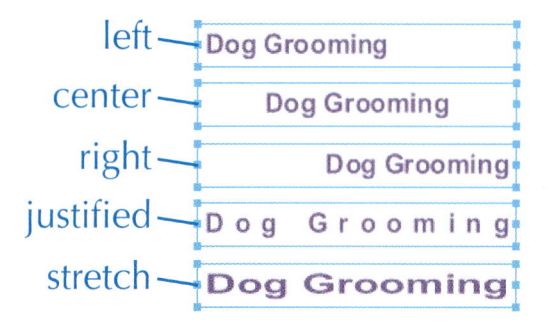

left — Dog Grooming
center — Dog Grooming
right — Dog Grooming
justified — D o g   G r o o m i n g
stretch — Dog Grooming

Fixed-Width Text Block

Selecting the Text tool and dragging the pointer on the canvas creates a fixed-width text block that does not resize to accommodate text.

moving and resizing text blocks

Text blocks are objects and are moved and resized in the same manner as shapes. Note that resizing a text block by dragging a corner handle changes the text block to a fixed width block, and it will no longer change size as more text is typed. However, it can be resized repeatedly by dragging on its handles.

modifying text in a text block

Text is added or deleted in a text block by selecting the Text tool and clicking in the text block to place the insertion point. Text is then typed or deleted. Text is selected by dragging the Text tool over text.

6.12 Aligning Objects in Fireworks

Objects can be aligned with respect to each other by first selecting the objects and then selecting commands in the Modify menu.

selecting objects

More than one object is selected using the Pointer tool ( ) in the Select section in the Tools panel. The pointer is dragged to draw a rectangle that touches all the objects to select them, or the Shift key is held down as each object is clicked:

Once all of the objects are selected, commands in the Align submenu in the Modify menu are selected to align the objects. For example, selecting Modify → Align → Center Vertical aligns the objects as follows:

Selecting Modify → Align → Center Horizontal aligns the objects as follows:

6.13 Modifying the Canvas

When work is complete on an image, selecting Modify → Canvas → Trim Canvas reduces the canvas to exactly fit the objects. Other commands in the Canvas submenu can also be used to modify the canvas:

- The dimensions of the canvas size in pixels can be changed by selecting Canvas Size.
- The canvas color can be changed by selecting Canvas Color.
- If the objects are too small for the canvas, Trim Canvas decreases the size of the canvas to just fit all the objects.
- If the objects are too large for the canvas, Fit Canvas increases the size of the canvas enough to fit all the objects.

6.14 Optimizing and Exporting a Fireworks Document

To use a Fireworks document in Dreamweaver, it should be exported in a format other than PNG. But before exporting, the images should be optimized. *Optimizing* means to choose a graphic file format that has as much compression as possible while maintaining good image quality. This also helps to create the smallest possible files, which allow a Web page to load faster in a browser window.

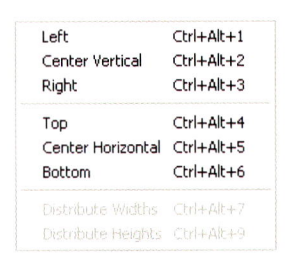

Export Wizard

The Export Wizard can be used to choose the best optimization settings and to then export the document. Selecting File → Export Wizard displays a dialog box. The **Select an export format** option should be selected:

> **Target File Size**
>
> The target file size is the size, in kilobytes, of the exported file. If an approximate file size is known, select **Target export file size** in the first Export Wizard dialog box and type the amount of kilobytes in the k box.

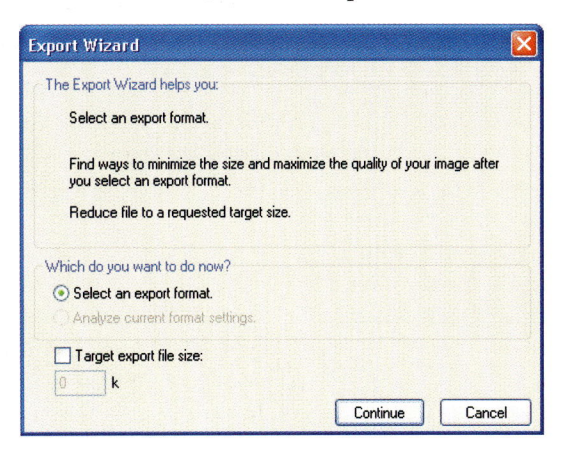

Select **Continue** to display the next dialog box. Select **Dreamweaver** since the file will be used in Dreamweaver:

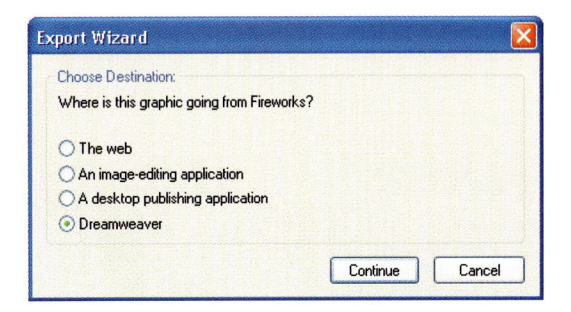

Select **Continue** to display the next dialog box, which recommends file formats:

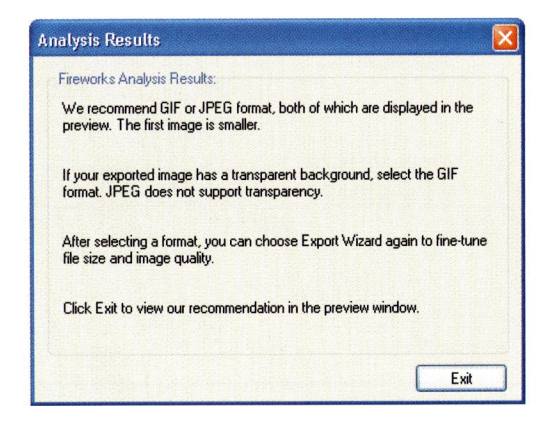

Select **Exit** to display the Export Preview window, where optimization options are selected:

Images in Dreamweaver and Fireworks   6 – 19

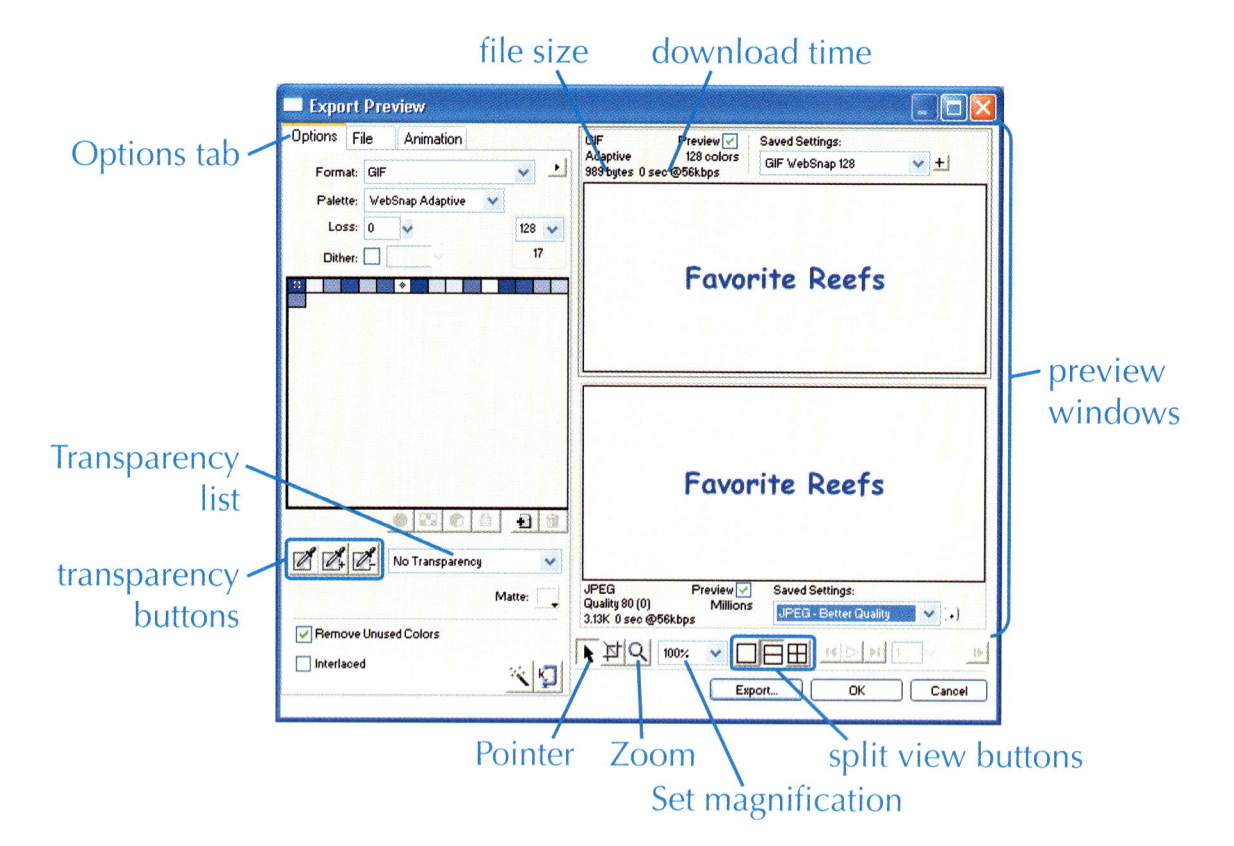

Annotated screenshot of the Export Preview dialog box with the following labels: file size, download time, Options tab, preview windows, Transparency list, transparency buttons, Pointer, Zoom, Set magnification, split view buttons.

- The **file size** and **download time** are displayed in each preview window. These can be used to help choose between the suggested file formats.

- The **preview windows** display the image in the suggested file formats. Settings can be changed in the previews, but remember that the window opens with the best choices.

- The **split view buttons** are used to change the number of preview windows displayed to one, two, or four. The window opens with the number of preview windows needed to display suggested file formats.

- The **Set magnification** box is used to change the magnification of the previews with precision. 100% is the best magnification when viewing an image for quality.

- Selecting the **Zoom button** changes the pointer to ⊕ when it is moved over a preview. Clicking ⊕ magnifies the previews. Holding down the Alt key while moving the pointer over a preview changes the pointer to ⊖. Clicking ⊖ zooms out the previews.

- Selecting the **Pointer button** and dragging an image moves it within the preview.

- Clicking a **transparency button** changes the pointer to ✒ when it is moved over a color in the **color list**, and clicking a color selects the transparency color (✒), adds the color to the transparency (✒), or removes the transparency color (✒).

6 – 20   A Guide to Web Development Using Macromedia Dreamweaver MX

- The **Transparency list** is used to set transparency for a GIF image by selecting Index transparency. In the example above, the image should have a transparent background so GIF would be the best file format choice and the transparency should be changed to Index transparency. Alpha transparency is only supported by newer browsers, so it is not a good choice yet.

- Triple-clicking a preview displays the preview's optimization settings in the Options **tab**, where options can be set.

With the best preview selected, clicking Export displays the Export dialog box with a file name already selected:

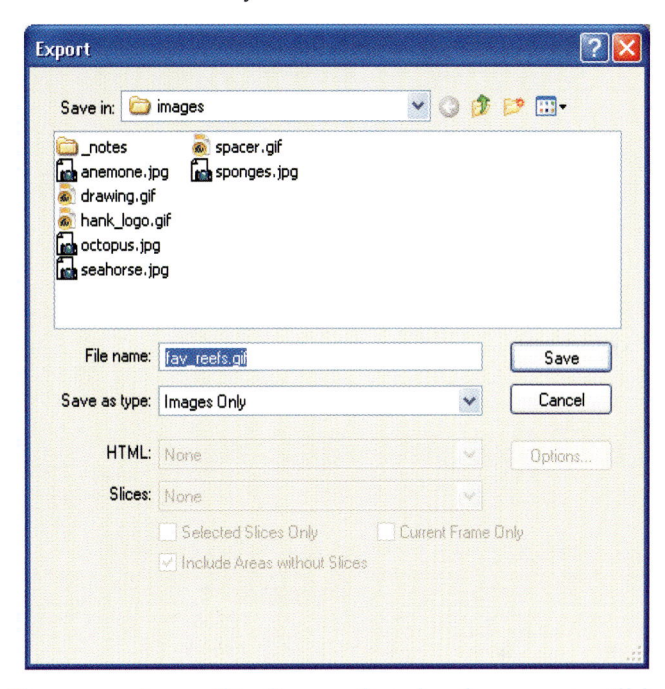

The extension .gif indicates that the document will be exported as a GIF

The Save in list and the contents box below it are used to navigate to the location where the file is to be saved. A Fireworks image exported for use in a Web site should be saved in the site's images folder. A descriptive file name for the image is typed in the File name box, and the Save as type is set to Images Only by the Export Wizard. Selecting Save exports the image in the appropriate format to the Web site folder. In Dreamweaver, the exported image can then be inserted into a Web page document.

Practice 5

In this practice you will create two Fireworks documents, export them as GIFs, and insert them into Web page documents.

① *START FIREWORKS*

a. Select Start → All Programs → Macromedia → Macromedia Fireworks MX. Fireworks is started. Note the canvas, Tools panel, and Property inspector.

Images in Dreamweaver and Fireworks

② CREATE AND SAVE A NEW FIREWORKS DOCUMENT

a. Select File → New. A dialog box is displayed.

   1. In the dialog box, specify the following:

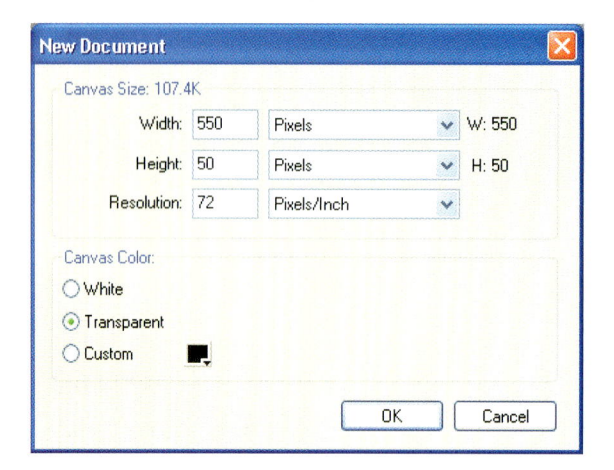

   2. Select OK. A new document is created with a transparent canvas that appears as a checkerboard pattern.

b. Select File → Save.

   1. Use the Save in list to navigate to a folder that is outside of any Web site folder.
   2. In the File name box, replace the existing text with: fav_reefs
   3. Select Save. Fireworks automatically adds the .png extension, so the document is saved with the file name fav_reefs.png.

③ ADD A TEXT OBJECT AND FORMAT THE TEXT

a. In the Tools panel, in the Vector section, click the Text tool (A).
b. Move the pointer over the canvas. The pointer changes to Ĭ.
c. On the canvas (not the gray document area), click to create a new, empty text block.
d. Type: Favorite Reefs and click in the canvas outside of the text block. The text block is selected.
e. If necessary, in the Tools panel, in the Select section, click the Pointer tool (▶) and then drag the text block so that it is entirely on the canvas.
f. In the Property inspector, in the Font list, select Comic Sans MS if it is available or else select Arial. The font of the text is changed.
g. In the Property inspector, in the Size box, set the value to 20 and press Enter. The size of the text is changed.
h. In the Property inspector, click the Fill Color box. The Fill Color options are displayed:

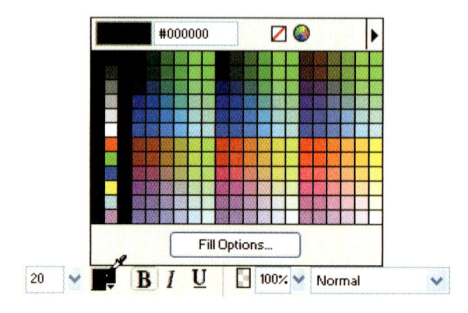

   1. Edit the existing hexadecimal value to #0000CC and press Enter. The text is now a blue color.

i. In the Property inspector, set the stroke color to transparent (✎❘), if it is not already set.

6 – 22   A Guide to Web Development Using Macromedia Dreamweaver MX

Check—Your canvas should look similar to:

Favorite Reefs

④ MODIFY THE CANVAS

Select Modify → Canvas → Trim Canvas. The canvas is reduced in size to exactly fit the text.

⑤ SAVE THE MODIFIED FAV_REEFS.PNG

⑥ EXPORT THE IMAGE

a. Select File → Export Wizard. A dialog box is displayed.
   1. Select the Select an export format option if it is not already selected.
   2. Select Continue. The next dialog box is displayed.
   3. Select Dreamweaver since the file will be used in Dreamweaver.
   4. Select Continue. The next dialog box is displayed.
   5. Read the information in the dialog box and then select Exit. The Export Preview window is displayed.
      a) Note the top preview has GIF settings and the bottom preview is JPG. Triple-click the GIF preview. The GIF settings appear in the Options tab in the left side of the Export Preview window.
      b) In the Transparency list, select Index Transparency.
      c) Click the Zoom button.
      d) Hold down the Alt key and move the pointer over a preview. The pointer changes to 🔍.
      e) Click the preview. The preview is zoomed out and more of the image is displayed in the preview.
   6. Select Export. The Export dialog box is displayed.
      a) Use the Save in list to navigate to the images folder in the Scuba folder.
      b) In the File name box, type the file name: fav_reefs.gif
      c) In the Save as type list, the Export Wizard has already selected Images Only.
      d) Select Save. A GIF is exported to the SCUBA Web site.

⑦ ADD AN IMAGE TO A WEB PAGE

a. Start Dreamweaver. The SCUBA Web site should be the working Web site.
b. In the Site panel, open the locations.htm Web page document.
c. In the left cell of the third row of the table, delete the text: FAVORITE REEFS
d. In the Assets panel, click the Images icon (🖼) if it is not already selected. The images in the site are displayed. Select ☰ → Refresh Site List. The fav_reefs.gif image is displayed in the list.
e. Drag the fav_reefs.gif file from the Assets panel to the location that contained the deleted text.

Check—Your document should look similar to:

Hank and Barb's Scuba Div

Home | Dive Locations | Photo Gallery

Favorite Reefs

Boca Trench, max depth 60', North of Boca Inlet
Boca Ledge, 55-82', South of Boca Inlet
Separated Rocks, 40', South of Boca Inlet
Hillsboro Ledge, 59-72', North of Hillsboro Inlet
Twin Ledges, 36-49', South of Hillsboro Inlet
Pompano Dropoff, 10-26', South of Hillsboro Inlet

⑧ CREATE A SECOND GIF

a. Switch back to Fireworks.

b. Follow steps ② through ⑥ to create a second Fireworks document named fav_wrecks.png that looks similar to:

Favorite Wrecks

c. Save the document and then export it to the images folder of the SCUBA Web site naming it: fav_wrecks.gif

d. Follow step ⑦ to insert the fav_wrecks.gif image into the locations.htm Web page document in the right cell of the third row of the table:

Hank and Barb's Scuba Diving Site

Home | Dive Locations | Photo Gallery

Favorite Reefs	Favorite Wrecks
Boca Trench, max depth 60', North of Boca Inlet	Sea Emperor, max depth 70', South of Boca Inlet
Boca Ledge, 55-82', South of Boca Inlet	Noula Express, 70', South of Boca Inlet
Separated Rocks, 40', South of Boca Inlet	Berry Patch Tug, 65', South of Boca Inlet
Hillsboro Ledge, 59-72', North of Hillsboro Inlet	Ancient Mariner, 70', South of Boca Inlet
Twin Ledges, 36-49', South of Hillsboro Inlet	Captain Dan, 110', South of Hillsboro Inlet
Pompano Dropoff, 10-26', South of Hillsboro Inlet	Copenhagen, 20-35', South of Hillsboro Inlet

e. Save the modified locations.htm.

6.15 Creating a Button Symbol in Fireworks

button   In a Web page document, a *button* is an element that indicates to the user that it is a graphic hyperlink by its appearance. A button can be created easily in Fireworks, and then several copies placed together in a Fireworks document to form a navigation bar that can be exported to Dreamweaver.

A button is created by drawing the objects that make up the button, for example a rounded rectangle and a text block:

symbol

The objects are then selected together and made into a single object called a *symbol*. A symbol is similar to a library item in Dreamweaver, except a symbol placed on a canvas does not have to have its link broken to be edited. In Fireworks, symbols appear in the Library panel in the Assets panel group.

Selecting Modify → Symbol → Convert to Symbol displays a dialog box where a descriptive name should be typed for the symbol:

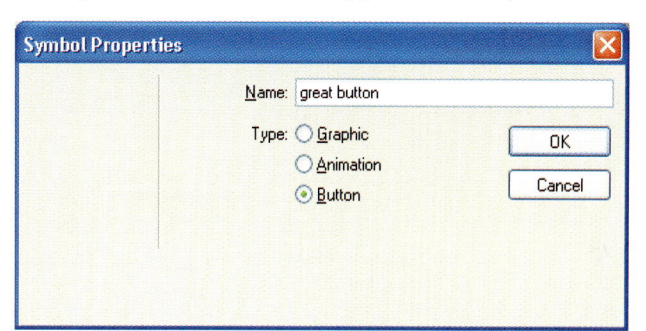

Selecting Button and then OK converts the selected objects to a button symbol and adds the symbol to the Library panel:

Items in the Library panel are stored with the open Fireworks document.

instance

When a symbol is created, the selected objects on the canvas are changed into an *instance* of the symbol, which is a copy of the button symbol:

slice

A symbol is also automatically sliced. *Slicing* is the way Fireworks divides an image so that interactivity can be assigned. The red lines on the canvas are slice boundaries. A button symbol has only one slice— the entire object itself. Therefore interactivity is assigned to the entire button object.

Images in Dreamweaver and Fireworks 6 – 25

adding instances

Navigation bars usually have more than one button. More instances can be added to the canvas by dragging the button symbol from the Library panel to the canvas. Another way to create an instance is to select an instance on the canvas and then select Edit → Clone, which places another button on top of the selected one. The arrow keys can then be used to position the button, or the Pointer tool can be used to drag the button. A document can contain many clones of a symbol:

modifying an instance

Each instance of a symbol can be selected individually and its properties changed in the Property inspector:

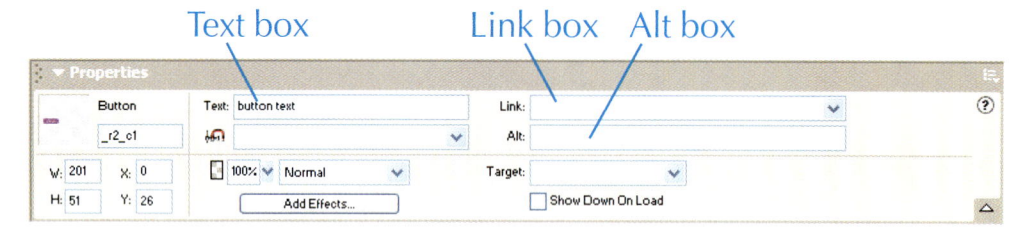

- Text is the text displayed on the button. New text can be typed.
- Link is the file name of the document linked to the button. A new file name can be typed or selected from the list.
- Alt is the alternative text for the button. New alternative text can be typed.

previewing and testing buttons

Buttons on a canvas can be previewed by clicking the Preview tab at the top of the Document window. The preview is interactive, so hovering and clicking the mouse displays the assigned interactivity.

6.16 Button Symbol Rollover Behavior

JavaScript

Rollover behavior is defined with JavaScript code. Fireworks automatically generates the JavaScript for a button.

A *behavior* is how a symbol interacts with the user. The default behavior for a button symbol is a *rollover*, which allows each state of a button symbol to display a different image. In Fireworks, a button symbol has four states:

Up state
- The *Up state* is also called the normal state. A button is in this state when a pointer is not over it or it is not clicked.

Over state
- The *Over state* is when the pointer is moved over a button.

Down state
- The *Down state* is when a button is clicked.

Over While Down state
- The *Over While Down state* is when the pointer is moved over a button that is in the Down state.

The images for each state of a button symbol are modified by double-clicking a button instance on the canvas or the button symbol's preview in the Library panel to open the Button Editor window:

tabs — (callout to tabs in screenshot)

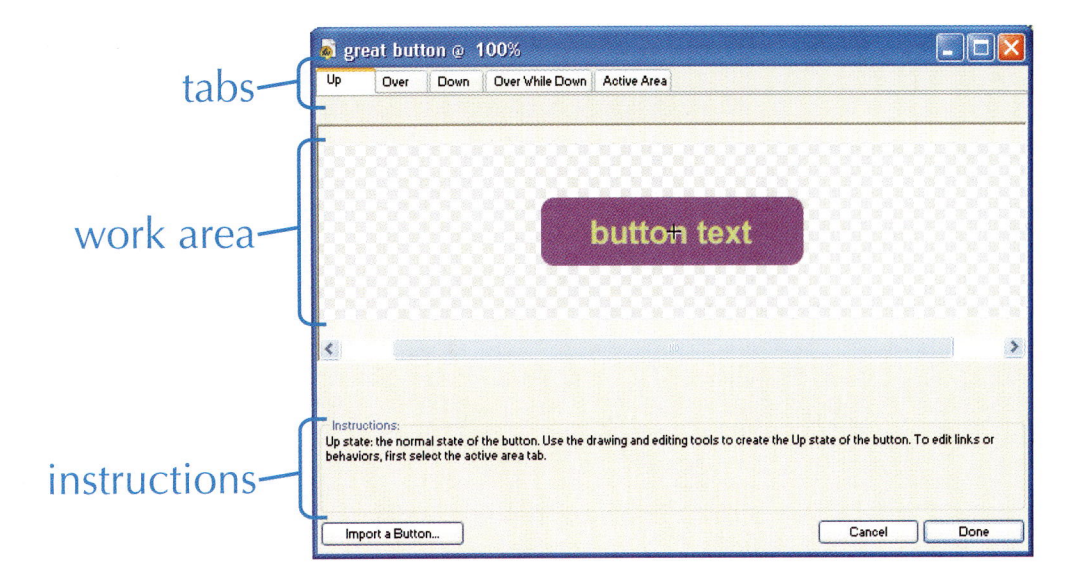

work area — (callout to work area in screenshot)

instructions — (callout to instructions in screenshot)

- The **work area** is where the button appears and can be edited.
- The Up tab, Over tab, Down tab, and the Over While Down tab displays the image for the states. Each state can be edited separately by clicking the tab for the state.
- The Active Area tab displays the hotspot area on the button that will trigger the button action.
- The **instructions** area displays descriptions and instructions.

Clicking a state tab displays the button as it will appear in that state. If the work area is empty, clicking the Copy Graphic button copies the button from the previous state into the work area where edits such as color changes can be made. Clicking Done makes the changes to the button symbol and to all the instances on the canvas. Edits in the Button Editor window do not affect text, alternative text, and links that were set for each button instance on the canvas.

previewing and testing buttons

Clicking the Preview tab at the top of the document window displays the button as it will appear in a Web site. In the Preview tab view, the images for each button state can be tested by moving the pointer over the button and clicking.

Practice 6

In this practice you will create and edit a button symbol in Fireworks and use it to create a navigation bar. Start Fireworks if it is not already running.

① **CREATE AND SAVE A NEW FIREWORKS DOCUMENT**

   a. Select File → New. A dialog box is displayed.

      1. In the dialog box, specify the following:

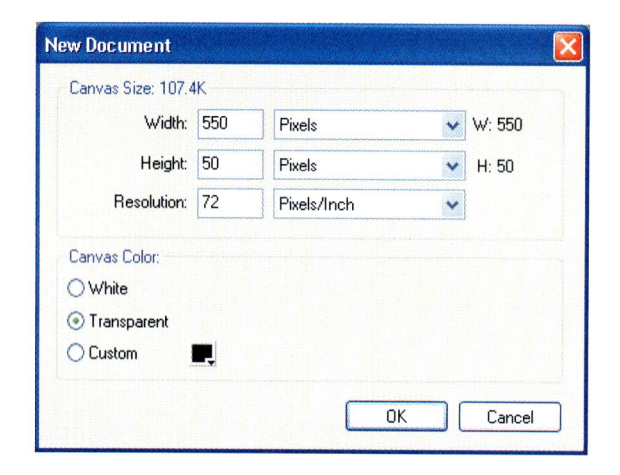

2. Select OK. A new document is created with a transparent canvas.

b. Select File → Save. Save the document in a folder that is outside of any Web site folder, naming it: divebar.png

② CREATE OBJECTS

a. In the Tools panel, in the Vector section, click the Rectangle tool ( ).

b. On the canvas, draw a rectangle of any size.

c. In the Property inspector, set W to 150 and H to 30 and press Enter. The rectangle is resized.

d. In the Property inspector, click the Fill Color box ( ). Replace the existing hexadecimal value with #0000CC and press Enter. The rectangle is now a blue color.

Check—Your canvas should look similar to:

e. In the Tools panel, in the Vector section, click the Text tool (A).

f. On the canvas, click to create a new, empty text block with a blinking insertion point.

g. In the Property inspector:

　1. In the Font box, select Comic Sans MS if it is available or else select Arial.

　2. In the Size box change the value to 20 and press Enter.

　3. Click the Center alignment button ( ) if it is not already selected.

　4. Click the Fill Color box ( ). Replace the existing hexadecimal value with #FFFFFF and press Enter.

h. Type: button text and then click in the canvas outside of the text block. White, centered, Comic Sans MS, size 20 text is displayed.

③ ALIGN THE OBJECTS

a. In the Tools panel, in the Select section, click the Pointer tool ( ).

b. On the canvas, click the rectangle to select it.

c. Hold down the Shift key, and on the canvas, click the text block to select it. Both objects are selected.

d. Select Modify → Align → Center Vertical. The objects are aligned vertically.

e. With both objects still selected, select Modify → Align → Center Horizontal. The objects are aligned horizontally.

f. With both objects selected, drag the objects to the left side of the canvas.

Check—Your canvas should look similar to:

④ SAVE THE MODIFIED DIVEBAR.PNG

⑤ CONVERT THE OBJECTS TO A BUTTON SYMBOL

a. Select the rectangle and the text block if they are not already selected. Note that handles are displayed for both objects:

b. Select Modify → Symbol → Convert to Symbol. A dialog box is displayed.

   1. In the Name box, type: blue button
   2. Select Button.
   3. Select OK. The objects are converted to a Button symbol, which is added to the Library panel. The canvas displays an instance of the button symbol and slice boundaries are displayed. The instance is a different color to indicate a symbol.

⑥ PREVIEW THE BUTTON AND CREATE MORE INSTANCES OF THE BUTTON

a. In the Document window, click the Preview tab. A preview of the button with correct colors is displayed.

b. In the Document window, click the Original tab. The editing view is again displayed.

c. On the canvas, select the instance if it is not already selected.

d. Select Edit → Clone. Another instance is added to the canvas.

e. Hold down the right arrow key until the two instances are next to each other:

f. Select Edit → Clone. Another instance is created.

g. Hold down the right arrow key until the three instances are in a row:

⑦ CHANGE THE PROPERTIES OF EACH INSTANCE

a. On the canvas, click the far-left instance to select it.

b. In the Property inspector, set Text to Home and press Enter.

c. In the Property inspector, set Link to index.htm and press Enter.

d. In the Property inspector, set Alt to Link to home page. and press Enter.

e. On the canvas, select the middle button instance and set its properties to:
   - Text: Dive Locations
   - Link: locations.htm
   - Alt: Link to dive locations information.

f. On the canvas, select the far-right button instance and set its properties to:
   - Text: Photo Gallery
   - Link: photos.htm
   - Alt: Link to the photo gallery.

⑧ EDIT THE OVER BUTTON STATE IMAGES

a. On the canvas, double-click any button symbol instance. The Button Editor opens and the blue button button symbol is displayed.

b. In the Button Editor, click the Over tab. No image yet exists for this state.

   1. Click Copy Up Graphic. The Up state image is copied to the Over state.
   2. In the Button Editor work area, click the text block to select it.
   3. In the Property inspector, click the Fill Color box ( ) and replace the existing hexadecimal value with #FFFF00 and then press Enter. The text is now yellow for the Over state.

⑨ EDIT THE DOWN STATE AND THE OVER WHILE DOWN STATE

a. In the Button Editor, click the Down tab. No image yet exists for this state.

   1. Click Copy Over Graphic. The Over state image is copied to the Down state.
   2. In the Button Editor work area, click the text block to select it.
   3. In the Property inspector, change the Fill Color to #FFFFFF. The text is now white for the Down state.
   4. In the Button Editor work area, click the rectangle to select it.
   5. In the Property inspector, change the Fill Color to #66CCFF. The rectangle is now light blue for the Down state.

b. In the Button Editor, click the Over While Down tab. No image yet exists for this state.

   1. Click Copy Down Graphic. The Down state image is copied to the Over While Down state. This state will remain as is so that nothing changes when the pointer is moved over a button displayed in the Down state.

c. In the Button Editor, click Done. The changes are made to the button symbol and all instances of the symbol on the canvas.

⑩ MODIFY THE CANVAS

a. Select Modify → Canvas → Trim Canvas. The canvas is reduced in size to exactly fit the instances.

⑪ PREVIEW THE BUTTONS

a. In the Document window, click the Preview tab. A preview is displayed.

b. Move the pointer over the buttons and click each one.

c. In the Document window, click the Original tab. The editing view is again displayed.

⑫ SAVE THE MODIFIED DIVEBAR.PNG

6.17 Exporting HTML and Images from Fireworks

Exporting a Fireworks document with symbol instances generates many files, including a set of image files for rollover behavior states and an HTML file that arranges the objects in the Fireworks document in a table. Also in the HTML file is the code that controls the rollover behavior of the clones. For example, a Fireworks document with a button symbol and three clones generates an HTML document and up to 12 image files, one image file for each state of each button instance.

The Export Wizard can be used to optimize and automatically generate all the files associated with a Fireworks document. Selecting File → Export Wizard displays the same dialog boxes as shown in Section 6.14. When the Export Preview dialog box is displayed, selecting Export displays a dialog box with HTML and Images as the file type:

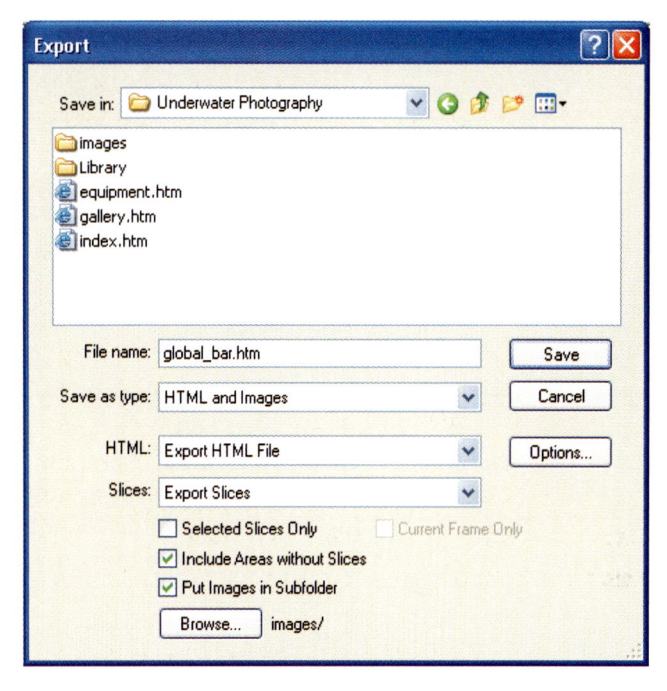

- The Save in list and the contents box below it are used to navigate to the location of the Web site root folder where the HTML document is to be saved.
- A descriptive file name is typed in the File name box.
- The Save as type is set to HTML and Images by the Export Wizard.
- The HTML and Slices lists should be set as shown in the dialog box above.
- The Include Areas without Slices option is selected to ensure that the entire document is exported.
- Selecting Put Images in Subfolder will place image files into the images folder of the Web site root folder specified in the Save in list.
- Selecting Save creates an HTML document and associated image files.

Images in Dreamweaver and Fireworks   6 – 31

6.18 Using an Exported HTML Document in Dreamweaver

A Fireworks document exported as HTML and Images to a Dreamweaver Web site is used by following these steps:

1. Open the HTML document that was exported from Fireworks.
2. Select <body> in the Tag selector to select everything in the document.
3. Select Edit → Copy HTML to make a copy of the HTML.
4. Open a Web page document and place the insertion point where the exported document should appear.
5. Select Edit → Paste HTML to add the HTML to the document.

editing a Fireworks image

source file

In Design view, a selected image from Fireworks can be edited by clicking the Edit button in the Property inspector. Fireworks is started and the PNG *source file*, the PNG file that was created in Fireworks, is displayed. After edits are made and the modified PNG is saved, selecting Done in the Fireworks document window closes the PNG file and changes are automatically made to the exported HTML document in Dreamweaver. The HTML that was copied and pasted in Dreamweaver is also updated. Note that changes to links need to be made in Dreamweaver.

6.19 Changing Behaviors in Dreamweaver

In Dreamweaver, behaviors for a selected button are listed in the Behaviors panel in the Design panel group:

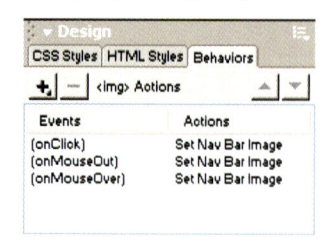

Double-clicking any behavior listed in the Behaviors panel displays a dialog box for all the states set for the selected button:

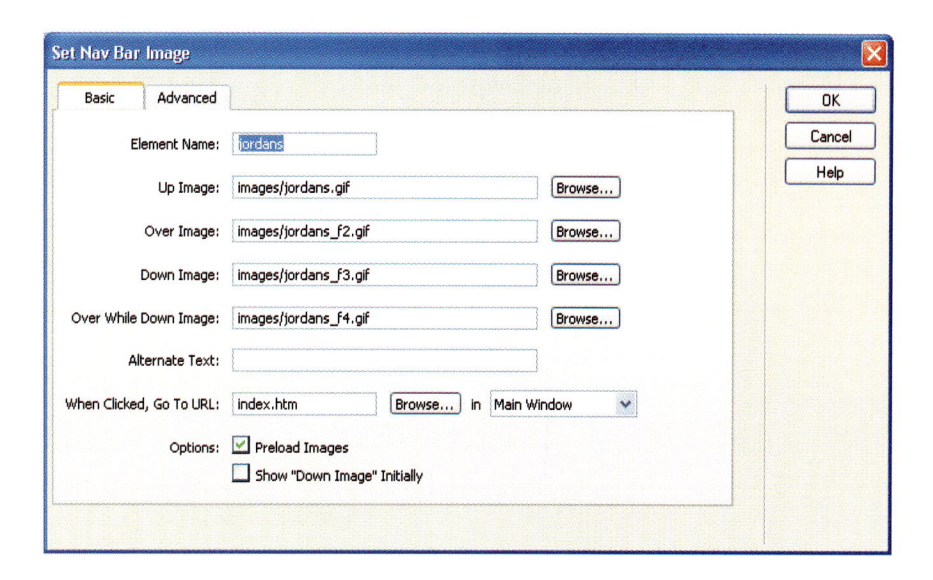

The appearance of the button in a state can be changed by browsing to a different image. The button's link can be changed in the When Clicked, Go To URL box. Selecting the Show "Down Image" Initially option displays the button in the Down state. This option is used to change the appearance of a button on the page that it links to. The When Clicked, Go To URL box will need to be cleared if the button appears in the Down state. Selecting OK applies the changes to the behaviors for the button.

Practice 7

In this practice you will optimize and export a document from Fireworks to Dreamweaver, copy and paste the HTML, and change the behaviors of buttons in Dreamweaver. Open divebar.png in Fireworks if it is not already displayed.

① OPTIMIZE AND EXPORT THE NAVIGATION BAR

    a. Select File → Export Wizard. A dialog box is displayed.

        1. Select the Select an export format option if it is not already selected.

        2. Select Continue. The next dialog box is displayed.

        3. Select Dreamweaver since the file will be used in Dreamweaver.

        4. Select Continue. The next dialog box is displayed.

        5. Read the information in the dialog box and then select Exit. The Export Preview window is displayed.

            a) Note which preview has GIF settings selected and triple-click that preview. The GIF settings appear in the Options tab in the left side of the Export window.

            b) In the Transparency list, select Index Transparency.

            c) Click the Zoom button.

            d) Hold down the Alt key and move the pointer over a preview. The pointer changes to ⊖.

            e) Click the preview. The preview is zoomed out and more of the image is displayed in the preview.

        6. Select Export. The Export dialog box is displayed.

            a) Use the Save in list to navigate to the SCUBA Web site folder.

            b) In the File name box, check that the existing text is divebar.htm.

            c) In the Save as type list, select HTML and Images if it is not already selected.

d) In the HTML list, select Export HTML File if it is not already selected.
e) In the Slices list, select Export Slices if it is not already selected.
f) Make sure that the Selected Slices Only option is not selected.
g) Select the Include Areas without Slices option if it is not already selected.
h) Select the Put Images in Subfolder.
i) Click the Browse button. A dialog box is displayed.
   i. Navigate to the images folder in the root folder of the SCUBA Web site.
   ii. Select Open.
j) Select Save. An HTML document named divebar.htm is created in the SCUBA Web site folder and all the images used in divebar.htm are added to the images folder of the Web site.

② SAVE THE MODIFIED DIVEBAR.PNG AND QUIT FIREWORKS

③ EDIT THE SCUBA WEB SITE

a. Start Dreamweaver. The SCUBA Web site should be the working Web site.
b. In the Site panel, check that the divebar.htm document is there.
c. In the Assets panel, display the Images category. Note the additional images for the site. If only the few images from earlier practices are displayed, select ▯ → Refresh Site List.

④ OPEN DIVEBAR.HTM AND COPY THE HTML TO ANOTHER DOCUMENT

a. Open the divebar.htm Web page document. The document contains the three buttons created in Fireworks in the previous practice.
b. Select the <body> tag in the Tag selector at the bottom of the Document window. The entire document is selected.
c. Select Edit → Copy HTML. A copy is created of the selected content.
d. Open the index.htm Web page document.
e. In the cell in the second row of the table, delete the contents.
f. In the cell in the second row of the table, place the insertion point.
g. Select Edit → Paste HTML. The copied content is pasted into the cell.
h. Save and close the modified index.htm.
i. Close divebar.htm.

⑤ COPY THE HTML TO OTHER DOCUMENTS

a. Open the locations.htm Web page document.
b. In the cell in the second row of the table, delete the contents.
c. In the cell in the second row of the table, place the insertion point.
d. Select Edit → Paste HTML. The copied content is pasted into the cell.
e. Save and close the modified locations.htm.
f. Open photos.htm.
g. In the cell in the second row of the table, delete the contents.
h. In the cell in the second row of the table, place the insertion point if it is not already there.
i. Select Edit → Paste HTML. The copied content is pasted into the cell.
j. Save the modified photos.htm.

⑥ TEST THE BUTTONS IN A BROWSER WINDOW

a. Press F12. The photos.htm Web page document is displayed in a browser window.
b. Move the pointer over the buttons and observe the text changing to yellow for the Over state.
c. Click the Home button. The index.htm Web page document is displayed in the browser window.
d. Test the buttons on this and the other Web page documents.
e. Finish testing the buttons and then switch back to Dreamweaver.

⑦ CHANGE THE BUTTONS IN EACH WEB PAGE DOCUMENT

a. Open photos.htm if it is not already displayed.
b. Click the arrow in the Design panel group if it is not already expanded.
c. Click the Behaviors tab to display the Behaviors panel.
d. In the Document window, click the Photo Gallery button to select it. Note the behaviors listed in the Behaviors panel.
e. In the Behaviors panel, double-click any behavior. A dialog box is displayed.
   1. Select the **Basic** tab if those options are not already displayed.
   2. Select the **Show "Down Image" Initially** option.
   3. Select **OK**. The dialog box is removed and the button is displayed in the Down state.
f. Save and close the modified photos.htm.
g. Open the locations.htm Web page document.
h. In the Document window, click the Dive Locations button to select it.
i. In the Behaviors panel, double-click any behavior. A dialog box is displayed.
   1. In the **Basic** tab, select the **Show "Down Image" Initially** option.
   2. Select **OK**. The dialog box is removed and the button is displayed in the Down state.
j. Save and close the modified locations.htm.
k. Open the index.htm Web page document.
l. In the Document window, click the Home button to select it.
m. In the Behaviors panel, double-click any behavior. A dialog box is displayed.
   1. In the **Basic** tab, select the **Show "Down Image" Initially** option.
   2. Select **OK**. The dialog box is removed and the button is displayed in the Down state.
n. Save the modified index.htm.

⑧ TEST THE BUTTONS IN A BROWSER WINDOW

a. Press F12 to display the index.htm Web page document in the browser window. Note that the Home button is in the Down state, indicating that the displayed Web page document is the home page.
b. Move the pointer over the buttons and observe the text changing to yellow for the Over state.
c. Click the Photo Gallery button. The photos.htm Web page document is displayed, with the Photo Gallery button in the Down state.
d. Test the buttons on this and the other Web page documents.
e. Print a copy of each Web page document from the browser.
f. Close the browser window. Dreamweaver is displayed.
g. Close index.htm.

Images in Dreamweaver and Fireworks

6.20 Cropping Images in Fireworks

There may be occasions when only need part of an image is needed. In Fireworks, an image can be *cropped*, which means to remove parts of an image that are no longer needed. Opening an image in Fireworks, clicking the Crop tool ( ) in the Select section in the Tools panel, and moving the pointer over the canvas changes the pointer to . Dragging the pointer across the image draws a cropping box with handles:

Dragging any handle of the cropping box changes the box. The dimensions of the cropping box can be adjusted precisely by setting the W (width) and H (height) properties in the Property inspector. The arrow keys can be used to move the cropping box. Double-clicking in the box or pressing Enter crops the image to include only the part of the image displayed inside the cropping box:

Cropping an image resizes the canvas to include only the cropped image. If a mistake is made, the cropping can be reversed by selecting Edit → Undo Crop Document.

6.21 Editing an Image in Fireworks from Dreamweaver

There may be occasions when an image in a Web page document in Dreamweaver needs to be edited. Selecting an image and clicking **Edit** in the Property inspector starts Fireworks and may display a dialog box:

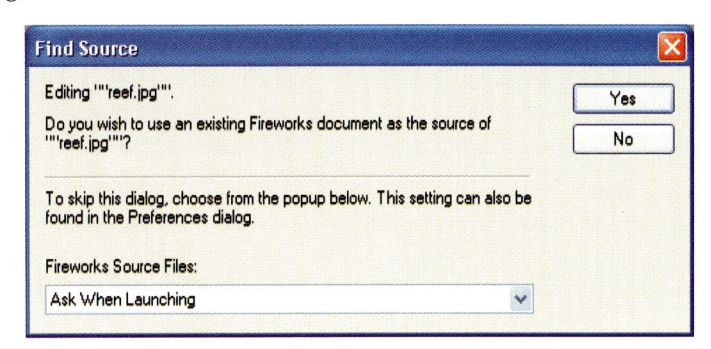

updating the image in Dreamweaver

Selecting **No** opens the image in Fireworks. After edits to the image are made, for example cropping, clicking **Done** in the Document window saves the changes to the image and closes the file. In Dreamweaver, the image is updated in the Web page document where it appears by selecting the image and then clicking **Reset Size** in the Property inspector.

Practice 8

In this practice you will add images to a Web page document in Dreamweaver and crop one of the images in Fireworks. The SCUBA Web site should be the current Web site in the Dreamweaver workspace.

① ADD AN IMAGE TO THE LOCATIONS.HTM WEB PAGE DOCUMENT

a. Open the locations.htm Web page document.
b. In the Assets panel, display the Images category.
c. Drag the a_reef.jpg file from the Assets panel to the blank area below the text in the left cell in the table. The image is quite large.

② OPEN THE IMAGE FOR EDITING IN FIREWORKS

a. Click the image to select it if it is not already selected.
b. In the Property inspector, click **Edit**. A dialog box is displayed.
   1. Select **No**. The image is displayed in a Document window in Fireworks.

③ CROP THE IMAGE IN FIREWORKS

a. Click the image to select it if it is not already selected.
b. In the Tools panel, in the Select section, click the Crop tool.
c. Move the pointer over the canvas. The pointer changes.
d. Drag the pointer. A cropping box is drawn.
e. In the Property inspector, set W to 250 and press Enter. The width of the cropping box is changed.
f. In the Property inspector, set H box to 200 and press Enter. The height of the cropping box is changed.

Images in Dreamweaver and Fireworks

g. Use the arrow keys to move the cropping box to only include the bright fish and the corals beneath it:

h. Press Enter. The image is cropped to the size of the cropping box. Note the width and height of the image in the Property inspector.

④ UPDATE AND FORMAT THE IMAGE IN DREAMWEAVER

a. In the Document window, above the image click Done. The Document window is closed and Dreamweaver is again displayed.

b. In the Property inspector, click [Reset Size]. The image changes to the new size.

⑤ ADD AN IMAGE TO THE LOCATIONS.HTM WEB PAGE DOCUMENT

a. Drag the a_wreck.jpg file from the Images list to the blank area below the text in the right cell in the table. Note in the Property inspector that the image is the same size as the cropped image.

b. Save the modified locations.htm.

⑥ VIEW THE DOCUMENT IN A BROWSER

a. Press F12. The locations.htm Web page document is displayed in a browser window.

b. Print a copy.

c. Close the browser window. Dreamweaver is displayed.

d. Close locations.htm.

⑦ QUIT DREAMWEAVER

Chapter Summary

Images on Web pages are usually a GIF or JPG file because these formats are widely supported. The PNG format has advantages over GIF and JPG, but is only supported by the newest browsers.

Both GIF and JPG formats are bitmap graphics. The number of dots per inch (dpi) is called the resolution. The larger the number of dpi, the better the quality of the graphic. GIF files can be interlaced and JPG files can be progressive, which are methods of displaying the graphic as the Web page fully loads. Compression is a special feature that reduces file size. GIF graphics have lossless compression and JPG graphics have lossy compression.

Adding alternative text to an image provides text for voice synthesizers to "read" in place of the image and text for the screen tip that appears when the pointer is paused over an image.

A hyperlink can be in the form of a graphic. Links can be tested in a browser window and modified in Dreamweaver by selecting the image and then selecting Modify → Change Link or Modify → Remove Link. An image map is a graphic that contains one or more hotspots. A hotspot is an invisible, defined area on a graphic that is a hyperlink. Hotspots can be created using the Rectangular Hotspot tool, Oval Hotspot tool, or Polygon Hotspot tool.

A spacer GIF is a transparent GIF image that consists of only 1 pixel. A spacer GIF is used to control the layout of a table by forcing table cells to a specified width.

The horizontal alignment of a selected image can be changed using either the Align Left button, Align Center button, or the Align Right button in the Property inspector.

If an image size needs to be reduced, the image can first be resized in the Web page document to determine the exact dimensions in pixels, and then the image edited in Fireworks to that size. Resampling changes the size of the file and correctly adjusts the pixels in the image.

Fireworks is used to create and edit images specifically for use on the Web. Fireworks documents are PNG files, but GIF and JPG files can also be opened and edited in Fireworks. A new document is created in Fireworks by selecting File → New. The canvas is the rectangular area in which an image is created. A new Fireworks document is saved by selecting File → Save. To use a Fireworks document in Dreamweaver it must be exported in a format other than PNG.

Objects can be drawn on the canvas by selecting a tool in the Vector section in the Tools panel. The Fill Color box is used to change the color that fills the shape. The Stroke Color box is used to change the color of the outline of the shape. Text objects can be added to the canvas with the Text tool. Selected objects can be aligned with respect to each other by selecting commands in the Modify menu. When work is complete on an image, selecting Modify → Canvas → Trim Canvas reduces the canvas to exactly fit the objects.

The objects that make up a button created in Fireworks are made into a single object called a symbol. A copy of the button symbol is an instance of the symbol. Slicing is the way Fireworks divides an image so that interactivity can be assigned. A behavior is how a symbol interacts with the user. Exporting a Fireworks document with symbol instances generates many files that can be used in a Dreamweaver Web site. In Dreamweaver, behaviors for a selected button are listed in the Behaviors panel in the Design panel group.

Fireworks can be used to crop an image, which means to remove parts of an image that are no longer needed. A selected image in Dreamweaver is edited in Fireworks by clicking Edit in the Property inspector.

Vocabulary

Behavior How a symbol interacts with the user.

Bitmap graphic A graphic based on rows and columns of tiny dots that are square in shape.

Button An element that indicates to the user that it is a graphic hyperlink by its appearance.

Canvas In Fireworks, the rectangular area in which an image is created and edited.

Compression A file format feature that reduces file size.

Cropped The process of removing parts of an image that are no longer needed.

Dots per inch (dpi) The number of dots in an inch, used to measure the resolution of a bitmapped graphic.

Down state The button state when a button is clicked.

GIF A file format best used with graphics that do not contain many colors, such as clip art or logos.

Hotspot An invisible, defined area on a graphic that is a hyperlink.

Image map A graphic that contains one or more hotspots.

Instance A copy of a symbol.

Interlaced A GIF file format feature in which a low resolution version of the graphic appears first and becomes clearer in four horizontal passes as the Web page fully loads.

JPG A file format that supports millions of colors and is best used for photographs.

Lossless compression Type of compression in which all of the original file information is retained. Used for GIF graphics.

Lossy compression Type of compression in which some data in the file is lost or removed in order to reduce the file size. Used for JPG graphics.

Optimizing The process of choosing a graphic file format that has as much compression as possible while maintaining good image quality.

Over state The button state when a pointer is moved over a button.

Over While Down state The button state when a pointer is moved over a button that is in the Down state.

Pixel A square in a bitmap graphic that is made up of one solid color.

PNG A file format created in the mid-1990s during a controversy over copyright of the GIF format. It is only supported by the newest browsers.

Progressive A JPG file format feature in which a low resolution version of the JPG graphic appears when a Web page is first loaded and then becomes clearer as the page fully loads.

Proportionate size The width and height of a graphic are in the same ratio as the original graphic to prevent distortion.

Resampling The process of changing the size of the file and correctly adjusting the pixels in the image.

Resolution The number of dots per inch (dpi) in a graphic. Used to measure the quality of a graphic.

Rollover The default behavior for a button symbol, which allows each state of a button symbol to display a different image.

Select section Area in the Tools panel that contains tools used to select an image or parts of an image.

Slice The way Fireworks divides an image so that interactivity can be assigned.

Source file The PNG file created in Fireworks that is opened when a selected image from Fireworks is edited in Design view by clicking the Edit button in the Property inspector.

Spacer GIF A transparent GIF image consisting of only 1 pixel that is used to control the layout of a table by forcing table cells to a specified width.

Stretched An image distorted by dragging a handle without holding the Shift key.

Symbol A single object that is similar to a library item in Dreamweaver, except a symbol placed on a canvas does not have to have its link broken to be edited.

Tools panel Area in the Fireworks window that contains tools for creating and editing images.

Up state The button state when a pointer is not over it or it is not clicked. Also called the normal state.

Vector graphic A graphic composed of lines connected by points, which allows the image to be resized smoothly.

Vector section Area in the Tools panel that contains tools used to draw vector images.

Dreamweaver Commands and Buttons

Align Left button   Left aligns a selected image. Found in the Property inspector.

Align Center button   Center aligns a selected image. Found in the Property inspector.

Align Right button   Right aligns a selected image. Found in the Property inspector.

Browse for File icon   Displays a dialog box used to locate a destination file for a hyperlink. Found in the Property inspector.

Change Link **command**   Modifies an existing link. Found in the Modify menu.

Copy HTML **command**   Makes a copy of selected HTML. Found in the Edit menu.

Optimize Image in Fireworks **command**   Displays the image in a window with Fireworks optimization options. Found in the Commands menu.

Oval Hotspot tool   Creates an oval shaped hotspot. Found in the Property inspector.

Paste HTML **command**   Pastes copied HTML at the insertion point. Found in the Edit menu.

Point to File icon   Used to point to a destination file for a hyperlink. Found in the Property inspector.

Pointer Hotspot tool   Used to select a hot spot. Found in the Property inspector.

Polygon Hotspot tool   Creates an polygon shaped hotspot. Found in the Property inspector.

Rectangle Hotspot tool   Creates a rectangular shaped hotspot. Found in the Property inspector.

Remove Link **command**   Removes an existing link. Found in the Modify menu.

Fireworks Commands and Buttons

Center Horizontal command Aligns selected objects so that they are horizontally centered with respect to each other. Found in the Align submenu in the Modify menu.

Center Vertical command Aligns selected objects so that they are vertically centered with respect to each other. Found in the Align submenu in the Modify menu.

Clone command Creates an instance of from a selected instance. Found in the Edit menu.

Convert to Symbol command Displays a dialog box used to create a symbol. Found in the Symbol submenu in the Modify menu.

Crop tool Used to remove parts of an image that are no longer needed. Found in the Select section in the Tools panel.

Export Wizard command Displays a series of dialog boxes used to select the best optimization settings and to export a document. Found in the File menu.

Line tool Used to draw a line on the canvas. Found in the Vector section in the Tools panel.

New command Displays a dialog box used to create a new document. Found in the File menu.

Pointer tool Used to move and resize an object. Found in the Select section in the Tools panel.

Rectangle tool Used to add a rectangle to the canvas. Found in the Vector section in the Tools panel.

Save command Displays a dialog box that is used to save a Fireworks document. Found in the File menu.

Scale tool Used to resize a shape. Found in the Select section in the Tools panel.

Text tool Used to add text to the canvas as separate object. Found in the Vector section in the Tools panel.

Trim Canvas command Reduces the canvas to exactly fit the objects. Found in the Canvas submenu in the Modify menu.

Undo Crop Document command Reverse a cropping if a mistake is made. Found in the Edit menu.

Images in Dreamweaver and Fireworks

Review Questions

Sections 6.1 — 6.8

1. a) Why are images on Web pages usually a GIF or JPG file?
   b) Which file format is best used with graphics that do not contain many colors?
   c) How many colors are GIF graphics limited to?
   d) What format is best used with photographs?
   e) Why is the PNG format currently not a good choice for an image on a Web page?

2. a) What is a bitmap graphic based on?
   b) In a bitmap graphic, how is the quality of the graphic measured?

3. What file format allows one color in a graphic to be transparent?

4. Describe how an interlaced GIF graphic is displayed as a Web page is loaded.

5. a) What is compression?
   b) What is lossless compression?
   c) What is lossy compression?

6. Describe how a progressive JPG file is displayed as a Web page is loaded.

7. Why should alternative text be added to an image?

8. What happens when the pointer is moved over a graphic hyperlink?

9. a) What is an image map?
   b) What is a hotspot?

10. a) List the three tools that can be used to create hotspots.
    b) List the step required to delete a selected hotspot.

11. a) What is a spacer GIF?
    b) Why is a spacer GIF used?

12. List the step required to change the horizontal alignment of a selected image to center.

13. a) Why should an image not be resized in a Web page document in Dreamweaver?
    b) What is resampling?

14. How can an image be sized proportionately in Dreamweaver?

15. List the steps required to edit a selected image in Fireworks once it has been resized in Dreamweaver.

Sections 6.9 — 6.21

16. a) What is Fireworks MX?
    b) What type of file are Fireworks documents?

17. a) What is the canvas?
    b) What should the resolution be set to for an image used in a Web page?

18. What is a vector graphic?

19. a) Where should a Fireworks document be saved?
    b) What format are Fireworks documents automatically saved in?

20. Describe how shapes and lines are drawn in Fireworks.

21. a) What is the Stroke Color box used to change?
    b) What does the Tip size change?

22. List the steps required to add text to the canvas as a separate object.

23. List the steps required to align objects so that they are centered vertically with respect to each other.

24. List the step required to reduce the canvas to exactly fit the objects.

25. a) What is optimizing?
    b) What can be used to choose the best optimization settings and to then export the document?

26. a) What is a button in a Web page document?
    b) List the steps required to convert a button to a symbol.

27. What is an instance of a symbol?

28. What is slicing?

29. a) What is a behavior?
    b) What is the default behavior for a button symbol?
    c) List and describe the four states a button symbol has in Fireworks.

30. List the steps required to use an exported HTML document in Dreamweaver.

31. Where are the behaviors for a selected button listed?

32. List the steps required to crop an image.

33. List the steps required to edit an image that is in a Web page document in Dreamweaver.

Exercises

Exercise 1 ──────────────────── GREECE

Use Fireworks and Dreamweaver to modify the GREECE Web site by completing the following steps:

a) In Dreamweaver, open the GREECE Web site for editing, which is a Web site provided with the data files for this text.

b) Edit the footer library item by replacing Student Name with your name. Allow Dreamweaver to update all occurrences of the library item in the Web page documents.

c) Modify the index.htm Web page document as follows:

   1. In the right cell of the third row, insert the map_greece.gif image and add alternative text: Map of Greece.
   2. Resize the image proportionately to 280 pixels wide, and then optimize the image in Fireworks.

d) Modify the photos.htm Web page document as follows:

   1. In the empty cell above the text Cats on the Island of Hydra, insert the image hydra_cats.jpg and add alternative text: Cats on Hydra.
   2. Click **Edit** to edit the image in Fireworks. In Fireworks, crop the image using a cropping box of 250 pixels wide and 154 pixels high. Move the cropping box so that the white cat and the black and white cat are included in the image. Press Enter and then select Done in the Document window to return to Dreamweaver. Click **Reset Size** in the Property inspector to reset the size of the image.
   3. In the other empty cells, insert images and add alternative text as follows:

In the cell above the text	insert the image	and add alternative text
Hydra	hydra_view.jpg	Island of Hydra.
Diros Caves	diros.jpg	Inside the Diros caves.
A Goat	goat.jpg	One of the many goats.
Monemvasia	monemvasia.jpg	The city of Monemvasia.
The Road to Kosmas	road_to_kosmas.jpg	Winding road to Kosmas.

   4. Center align the six images.

e) Switch to Fireworks and create a new document with a width of 660 pixels, a height of 100 pixels, a resolution of 72 pixels/inch, and a transparent canvas. Save the document outside of any Web site folder naming it greeknav.png.

f) Create a button symbol as follows:

   1. Draw a rectangle with a width of 160 pixels and a height of 36 pixels.
   2. Apply a fill color of #3399FF and a transparent stroke color to the rectangle.
   3. Create a text box with the text button and format the text as Verdana font, 24 points in size, center aligned, and #FFFFFF in color.
   4. Select both the rectangle and the text block and align them horizontally and vertically.
   5. With both the rectangle and text block selected, convert them to a button symbol named: greek button

g) Create instances of the button symbol and modify them as follows:

1. Create two more instances of the button symbol on the canvas and then position all three instances next to each other.
2. Change the properties of each instance, from left to right, as follows:

Text	Link	Alt
Home	index.htm	Link to home page.
Photos	photos.htm	Link to photo page.
Itinerary	itinerary.htm	Link to itinerary page.

Your buttons should look similar to:

h) Double-click any instance to display the greek button symbol in the Button Editor. Edit the states of the button symbol as follows:

1. Edit the Over state to be identical to the Up state except change the text color to #FFCCFF.
2. Edit the Down state to be identical to the Over state except change the rectangle fill color to #3300FF.
3. Edit the Over While Down state to be identical to the Down state.

i) Finish and export the navigation bar as follows:

1. Modify the canvas to exactly fit the buttons.
2. Save the modified greeknav.png.
3. Use the Export Wizard to export an HTML file named greeknav.htm to the GREECE Web site. Make sure the images are exported as GIF files, with Index Transparency, to the images folder.

j) In Dreamweaver, modify the GREECE Web site as follows:

1. Open greeknav.htm and click the <body> tag to select the entire document.
2. Copy the HTML.
3. Paste the HTML in the cell in the second row of the index.htm, photos.htm, and itinerary.htm Web page documents.
4. In each Web page document, modify the appropriate button to initially appear in the Down state.

k) In the photos.htm and itinerary.htm Web page documents, link the logo in the top cell to index.htm.

l) View each Web page document in a browser window and test the hyperlinks.

m) Print a copy of each Web page document from the browser.

Exercise 2 ——————————————————————— CACTUS

Use Fireworks and Dreamweaver to modify the CACTUS Web site by completing the following steps:

a) In Dreamweaver, open the CACTUS Web site for editing, which is a Web site provided with the data files for this text.

b) Edit the footer library item by replacing Student Name with your name. Allow Dreamweaver to update all occurrences of the library item in the Web page documents.

c) Modify the index.htm Web page document as follows:

   1. In the left cell of the third row, insert the cactus.gif image and add alternative text: Cute cactus.
   2. Click [Edit] to edit the image in Fireworks. In Fireworks, crop the image to include only one cactus using a cropping box of 140 pixels wide. Select Done in the document window to return to Dreamweaver, and then click [Reset Size] in the Property inspector to reset the size of the image.

d) Modify the gallery.htm Web page document as follows:

   1. In the empty cell above the text Prickly Pear, insert the image prickly_pear.jpg and add alternative text: Prickly pear cactus.
   2. Resize the image proportionately to 300 pixels wide, and then optimize the image in Fireworks.
   3. In the empty cell above the text Agave, insert the image agave.jpg and add alternative text: Agave or century plant.
   4. Resize the image proportionately to 300 pixels wide, and then optimize the image in Fireworks.
   5. In the two remaining cells, insert images and add alternative text as follows:

In the cell above the text	insert the image	and add alternative text
Saguaro	saguaro.jpg	Saguaro cactus.
Cholla	cholla.jpg	Cholla cactus.

   6. Center align the four images.

e) Switch to Fireworks and create a new document with a width of 660 pixels, a height of 100 pixels, a resolution of 72 pixels/inch, and a transparent canvas. Save the document outside of any Web site folder naming it cactusnav.png.

f) Create a button symbol as follows:

   1. Draw an ellipse with a width of 180 pixels and a height of 40 pixels.
   2. Apply a fill color of #009900 and a transparent stroke color to the ellipse.
   3. Create a text box with the text button and format the text as Arial font, 18 points in size, center aligned, bold, and #CCFFCC in color.
   4. Select both the ellipse and the text block and align them horizontally and vertically.
   5. With both the ellipse and text block selected, convert them to a button symbol named: cactus button

g) Create instances of the button symbol and modify them as follows:

   1. Create two more instances of the button symbol on the canvas and then position all three instances next to each other.
   2. Change the properties of each instance, from left to right, as follows:

Text	**Link**	**Alt**
Home	index.htm	Link to home page.
Photo Gallery	gallery.htm	Link to photo page.
Cactus Types	types.htm	Link to page about cactus types.

   Your buttons should look similar to:

h) Double-click any instance to display the cactus button symbol in the Button Editor. Edit the states of the button symbol as follows:

   1. Edit the Over state to be identical to the Up state except change the ellipse fill color to #00CC33.
   2. Edit the Down state to be identical to the Over state except change the text color to #FFFFFF.
   3. Edit the Over While Down state to be identical to the Down state.

i) Finish and export the navigation bar as follows:

   1. Modify the canvas to exactly fit the buttons.
   2. Save the modified cactusnav.png.
   3. Use the Export Wizard to export an HTML file named cactusnav.htm to the CACTUS Web site. Make sure the images are exported as GIF files, with Index Transparency, to the images folder.

j) In Dreamweaver, modify the CACTUS Web site as follows:

   1. Open cactusnav.htm and click the <body> tag to select the entire document.
   2. Copy the HTML.
   3. Paste the HTML in the cell in the second row of the index.htm, gallery.htm, and types.htm Web page documents.
   4. In each Web page document, modify the appropriate button to initially appear in the Down state.

k) In the gallery.htm and types.htm Web page documents, link the logo in the top cell to index.htm.

l) View each Web page document in a browser window and test the hyperlinks.

m) Print a copy of each Web page document from the browser.

Images in Dreamweaver and Fireworks

Exercise 3 — FRUIT

Use Fireworks and Dreamweaver to modify the FRUIT Web site by completing the following steps:

a) In Dreamweaver, open the FRUIT Web site for editing, which is a Web site provided with the data files for this text.

b) Edit the footer library item by replacing Student Name with your name. Allow Dreamweaver to update all occurrences of the library item in the Web page documents.

c) Modify the index.htm Web page document as follows:

1. In the right cell of the third row, select the fruitbowl.gif image and in the Property inspector set Map to fruitbowl and press Enter.
2. Using the Polygon Hotspot tool, create hotspots on the banana, orange, and apple in the fruitbowl.gif image, linking each hotspot and adding alternative text as follows:

The hotspot	should link to	and have alternative text
banana	banana.htm	Banana information.
orange	orange.htm	Orange information.
apple	apple.htm	Apple information.

d) Start Fireworks and create a new document with a width of 400 pixels, a height of 80 pixels, a resolution of 72 pixels/inch, and a transparent canvas. Save the document outside of any Web site folder naming it title_banana.png. Create and export a GIF image as follows:

1. Create a text box with the text About Bananas and format the text as Verdana font, 40 points in size, not bold, and #FF3300 in color. Move the text box, if necessary, so that all of the text is visible on the canvas.
2. Modify the canvas to exactly fit the text.
3. Using the Export Wizard, export the image as a GIF with Index Transparency, named title_banana.gif, saved in the images folder of the FRUIT Web site.

e) In Fireworks create two more GIF images, following the instructions in step (d) above. Name one title_orange.png and use the text About Oranges in the image. Name the other title_apple.png and use the text About Apples in the image. Use all of the same color and font properties as listed in step (d). Export the GIFs using the names title_orange.gif and title_apple.gif.

f) In Dreamweaver, modify the FRUIT Web site as follows:

1. Open banana.htm and in the third row, insert the title_banana.gif image and add alternative text: About bananas.
2. Open orange.htm and in the third row, insert the title_orange.gif image and add alternative text: About oranges.
3. Open apple.htm and in the third row, insert the title_apple.gif image and add alternative text: About apples.

g) Switch to Fireworks and create a new document with a width of 660 pixels, a height of 100 pixels, a resolution of 72 pixels/inch, and a transparent canvas. Save the document outside of any Web site folder naming it fruitnav.png.

h) Create a button symbol as follows:

1. Select the Rounded Rectangle tool and set **Rectangle Roundness** to 70. Draw a rounded rectangle with a width of 120 pixels and a height of 30 pixels.
2. Apply a fill color of #FF9933 and a transparent stroke color to the rectangle.
3. Create a text box with the text button and format the text as Verdana font, 20 points in size, center aligned, bold, and #FFFF00 in color.
4. Select both the rectangle and the text block and align them horizontally and vertically.
5. With both the rectangle and text block selected, convert them to a button symbol named: fruit button

i) Create instances of the button symbol and modify them as follows:

1. Create three more instances of the button symbol on the canvas and then position all three instances next to each other, with a little space in between them.
2. Change the properties of each instance, from left to right, as follows:

Text	**Link**	**Alt**
Home	index.htm	Link to home page.
Bananas	banana.htm	Link to banana page.
Oranges	orange.htm	Link to orange page.
Apples	apple.htm	Link to apple page.

Your buttons should look similar to:

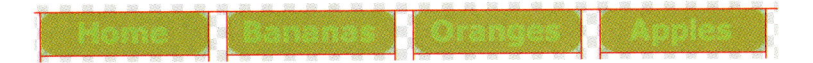

j) Double-click any instance to display the fruit button symbol in the Button Editor. Edit the states of the button symbol as follows:

1. Edit the Over state to be identical to the Up state except change the rectangle fill color to #FF3300.
2. Edit the Down state so that the text color is #FF9933 and the rectangle has a fill color of #FFFF00.
3. Edit the Over While Down state to be identical to the Down state.

k) Finish and export the navigation bar as follows:

1. Modify the canvas to exactly fit the buttons.
2. Save the modified fruitnav.png.
3. Use the Export Wizard to export an HTML file named fruitnav.htm to the FRUIT Web site. Make sure the images are exported as GIF files, with Index Transparency, to the images folder.

l) In Dreamweaver, modify the FRUIT Web site as follows:

1. Open fruitnav.htm and click the <body> tag to select the entire document.
2. Copy the HTML.
3. Paste the HTML in the cell in the second row of the index.htm, banana.htm, orange.htm, and apple.htm Web page documents.
4. In each Web page document, modify the appropriate button to initially appear in the Down state.

m) In the banana.htm, orange.htm, and apple.htm Web page documents, link the logo in the top cell to index.htm.

n) View each Web page document in a browser window and test the hyperlinks.

o) Print a copy of each Web page document from the browser.

Exercise 4 — SEVEN WONDERS

The SEVEN WONDERS Web site was last modified in Chapter 5, Exercise 5. Use Dreamweaver to further modify the SEVEN WONDERS Web site by completing the following steps:

a) In Dreamweaver, open the SEVEN WONDERS Web site for editing.

b) Modify the index.htm Web page document as follows:

1. In the left cell of the third row, select the wonder_map.gif image and in the Property inspector set **Map** to locations and press Enter.

2. Create seven rectangular hotspots, one on each word and its corresponding bullet on the wonder_map.gif image, linking each hotspot and adding alternative text as follows:

The hotspot	**should link to**	**and have alternative text**
Ephesus	temple.htm	Temple of Artemis at Ephesus.
Halicarnassus	mausoleum.htm	Mausoleum at Halicarnassus.
Rhodes	colossus.htm	Colossus of Rhodes.
Babylon	hanging.htm	Hanging Gardens of Babylon.
Giza	pyramids.htm	Pyramids of Egypt.
Alexandria	lighthouse.htm	Lighthouse of Alexandria.
Olympia	statue.htm	Statue of Zeus at Olympia.

c) View the index.htm Web page document in a browser window and test the hyperlinks and alternative text.

d) Print a copy of index.htm from Dreamweaver.

Exercise 5 (advanced) — Logos

Develop a Web site that showcases your talent for creating logos in Fireworks. The Web site should contain at least:

- at least two Web page documents
- at least six logos, created in Fireworks and exported as GIFs
- alternative text
- graphic hyperlinks
- a navigation bar created using button symbols in Fireworks

Preview the Web site in a browser. When satisfied with the Web site, print a copy of each Web page document from the browser.

Exercise 6 (advanced) ——————————————— Nav Bar Expert

Develop a Web site that showcases your talent for creating navigation bars using button symbols in Fireworks. The Web site should contain at least:

- at least four Web page documents, each with a different navigation bar created in Fireworks
- one logo, created in Fireworks and exported as a GIF, placed in the top cell on each page and linked to the home page where appropriate
- alternative text
- graphic hyperlinks

Preview the Web site in a browser. When satisfied with the Web site, print a copy of each Web page document from the browser.

Exercise 7 (advanced) ——————————————— Photographer

Develop a Web site that showcases a photographer's works. The Web site should contain at least:

- two Web page documents
- at least six JPG images—if you do not have images to use, copy JPG images from the data files provided for this text
- a logo created in Fireworks, placed in the top cell in each Web page document, and linked to index.htm
- alternative text
- use of a spacer.gif

Preview the Web site in a browser. When satisfied with the Web site, print a copy of each Web page document from the browser.

Images in Dreamweaver and Fireworks

Chapter 7
Typography, Style Sheets, and Color

Chapter 7 Expectations

After completing this chapter you will be able to:
1. Understand typography and paragraph styles.
2. Explain what a style sheet is using appropriate terminology.
3. Link and create a CSS style sheet document.
4. Create and apply a rule, class, and selector styles.
5. Check the existing HTML tags of a Web page document for inconsistencies.
6. Edit, duplicate, delete, and remove styles.
7. Tag indented text and redefine the blockquote tag.
8. Distinguish between numbered and bulleted lists.
9. Tag list items and redefine either the ul or ol tag.
10. Determine appropriate colors for a Web page document.
11. Change the background and text color of Web page document with a style sheet.
12. Create a hyperlink to a named anchor.
13. Create selector styles to change link colors.

This chapter discusses CSS style sheets for formatting a Web site. Typography, using fonts on the Web, paragraph formats, and formatting backgrounds, text, and hyperlinks in color is discussed. Linking to a named anchor is also explained.

7.1 Typography

Typography refers to the arrangement, shape, size, style, and weight of text. Typography affects the navigation and usability of a Web site and helps to convey the desired message to the audience.

typeface

A *typeface* is a set of letters drawn in a specific style. For example, the letters in "Typography" in the heading of this section are shaped differently than the same word in the first paragraph because each is printed in a different typeface. The word *font* technically refers to a specific size and weight of a single typeface, such as 10 point Verdana bold. However, font and typeface are both commonly used to refer to the set of letters, for example "the Verdana font" or "the Verdana typeface."

font

serif, sans serif

Each font can be grouped into one of two categories: *serif* and *sans serif* (*sans* is French for "without"). Serifs are the small extensions found on the ends of letters:

serif **The**   sans serif **The**

When reading text, our eyes scan whole words and not individual letters. Because the serifs extend towards the neighboring letters, serif fonts appear closer together, scan easier, and are more readable than sans serif. However, on a monitor, small letters with serifs can appear fuzzy, making words more difficult to read. When choosing a font for a Web page, sans serif is a better choice if the text is small.

capitalization

Another consideration is the capitalization of the letters. Text that is in all capital letters is more difficult to read than lowercase, because our eyes scan for shapes:

EXAMPLE   example

Notice that the word in all capitals has a squared shape, whereas the same word in lowercase letters has bumps where the p and l are. All capitals is also a bad choice because in e-mail and on Web pages it is the equivalent of screaming.

type size

The size of printed text is measured vertically in *points*, where one point is $1/72$ of an inch. The text in this paragraph is 10 point. For Web pages, text may be specified in points, but pixels are a good choice to prevent distortion. However, the appearance of the text will still vary because monitor resolutions vary.

type styles

Type *styles* indicate variations of the characters. For example, Times New Roman and Arial can each be displayed in bold, italic, or both styles:

Times New Roman regular, **bold**, *italic*, ***bold italic***

Arial regular, **bold**, *italic*, ***bold italic***

Plain type is called *normal*, although *regular*, *roman*, and *book* are also popular terms that indicate the normal style. Because text stands out when formatted in bold or italic style, these styles are frequently used in headings to indicate a hierarchy. Bold text is said to "weigh" more than normal text. Type styles are powerful statements in design that can visually change the meaning of words and should be used with care.

leading

Leading (pronounced "ledding") is the distance from one line of text to another. Text with greater leading will have more space below it, which gives more separation to lines of text. Leading affects the readability of a document. Lines of text need enough space between them to allow the reader's eye to focus and scan.

7.2 Design Considerations: Text

Although there are thousands of fonts available, the Web is not the place to use them all. A Web site should be as readable as possible, allowing the user to scan the text looking for information. Using six different fonts in three sizes does not accomplish this. Two different fonts should be the maximum for a single Web page. More than two fonts decreases usability, turning users away from your site.

choosing fonts

In order for fonts to display correctly in a browser, the user must have the fonts installed on their computer. For example, if you format text in Khaki font, and the user does not have Khaki installed, the text will be displayed in the default font set in user's browser. Choosing which fonts to use is simple, because there are only a few that most users will have. Fonts available on most computers are:

> **Fireworks and Flash**
>
> Elements, such as a logo or a heading, that make use of uncommon fonts or special effects can be created in Fireworks or Flash. Fonts used in a Fireworks or Flash document are converted to shapes and do not require the font to be installed on the user's computer. However, converting paragraphs of text into a image is not recommended.

Serif Fonts
- Times New Roman
- Georgia
- `Courier New`

Sans Serif Fonts
- Arial
- Verdana
- Geneva (a Macintosh font)

Times New Roman and Arial are two fonts that have been designed for viewing on a monitor. They are the safest choice because more users will have them on their computer.

So how can all those other fonts appear on Web pages you view when you surf the Web? Maybe the special font that was specified in a Web page is installed on your computer. A common method of ensuring that logos and other fancy font usages display as intended is to create a graphic of the logo or text and just place the graphic in the Web page.

choosing sizes

When choosing sizes for the text on a Web page, keep usability in mind. The font size should be big enough so that the user can easily read the text, but not so big that it appears loud. Sizes from 10 point to 14 point are a good guess for large paragraphs of text, and 12 point to 16 point for headings. Other size considerations are:

- Text in the **top global navigation bar** should be in the same size as the text or slightly larger.
- Text in the **breadcrumb trail** and **local navigation bar** should be slightly smaller than the top global navigation bar.
- Page footer elements, including the **bottom global navigation bar**, can be much smaller.
- **Serif fonts** become difficult to read at small sizes, so use **sans serif fonts** for any text in a very small size.

choosing leading

line height

Leading is determined by the type size. The greater the type size, the greater the leading. Another consideration is line length. The longer the lines of text, the greater the leading should be. Leading is also called *line height*.

choosing styles

Bold style text can be used to indicate heading hierarchies. Italic style should only be applied to larger text (at least 12 points), because it is much more difficult to read on a screen at a smaller size. Note that italic text may not display properly in Web pages viewed on a Macintosh computer.

Underline Style

Don't do it. It looks like a hyperlink.

7.3 Paragraph Alignment

Alignment is a paragraph format that refers to the position of the lines of text relative to the sides of a cell: left, centered, right, and justified. The Web page document below demonstrates each of these alignments:

left — The scientific classification of the zebras are as follows: mountain zebra is Equus zebra, Burchell's zebra is Equus burchelli, and Grevy's zebra is Equus grevyi. The scientific classification of the zebras are as follows: mountain zebra is Equus zebra, Burchell's zebra is Equus burchelli, and Grevy's zebra is Equus grevyi.

centered — The scientific classification of the zebras are as follows: mountain zebra is Equus zebra, Burchell's zebra is Equus burchelli, and Grevy's zebra is Equus grevyi. The scientific classification of the zebras are as follows: mountain zebra is Equus zebra, Burchell's zebra is Equus burchelli, and Grevy's zebra is Equus grevyi.

right — The scientific classification of the zebras are as follows: mountain zebra is Equus zebra, Burchell's zebra is Equus burchelli, and Grevy's zebra is Equus grevyi. The scientific classification of the zebras are as follows: mountain zebra is Equus zebra, Burchell's zebra is Equus burchelli, and Grevy's zebra is Equus grevyi.

justified — The scientific classification of the zebras are as follows: mountain zebra is Equus zebra, Burchell's zebra is Equus burchelli, and Grevy's zebra is Equus grevyi. The scientific classification of the zebras are as follows: mountain zebra is Equus zebra, Burchell's zebra is Equus burchelli, and Grevy's zebra is Equus grevyi.

7.4 Design Considerations: Paragraphs

Although there are four paragraph alignments, left alignment is the most readable and therefore provides the highest degree of usability. Right alignment is usually not desirable in long paragraphs of text. Long paragraphs of centered text are difficult to read, so centered alignment should be used only for headings or short amounts of text. Justified alignment is not recommended because browser support for this format varies.

formatting navigation bars

Links in top and local navigation bars are most readable and usable when left aligned. However, centered alignment is also an acceptable and usable choice for formatting the links in navigation bars. The bottom global navigation bar is often formatted as centered.

7.5 What is a Style Sheet?

A *style sheet* defines the type, paragraph, and page formats for a Web page document. A single style sheet can be applied to all the pages in a Web site to achieve a consistent look. Changing the text format of all the Web pages in a Web site is as easy as modifying a single style sheet because updates to the style sheet are automatically applied to linked documents.

> **W3C**
> The World Wide Web consortium (www.w3.org) develops standards in design and accessibility for the Web.

The W3C recommends the CSS2 (Cascading Style Sheets, level 2) style sheet language. Multiple style sheets can be applied to a single Web page, with the rules in one style sheet layering, or *cascading*, those in another style sheet.

cascading

rule

selector, declaration

class

A CSS document can include rules and classes. A *rule* modifies an HTML element and is comprised of a selector and declarations. The *selector* is the HTML element being redefined and the *declarations* are the formats to be applied. A *class* is a set of declarations that can be applied to different tags. Rules are defined using the HTML element name and class names begin with a dot (.):

```
p {  font-family: Georgia, "Times New Roman", Times, serif;
     font-size: 14px;
}

.para_with_space {
     font-family: Georgia, "Times New Roman", Times, serif;
     font-size: 14px;
     line-height: 28px;
     text-align: center;
}
```

> **Publishing Style Sheets**
> Style sheets are posted along with a Web site. The browser displaying the Web page must support CSS1 or CSS2. Most newer browsers support both.

A CSS document with a rule and a class

When the above style sheet is applied to a Web page document, paragraphs will automatically display in 14px Georgia. The para_with_space class can be applied to individual paragraphs. Classes override rules.

font family

Note the font-family declarations in the CSS document above, which indicates the first font that a browser should display, and then alternate fonts if the first is not installed on the user's computer.

7.6 Linking to a CSS Style Sheet

Dreamweaver includes the CSS Styles panel, located in the Design panel group, for linking, creating, and modifying style sheets:

> **Displaying the CSS Styles Panel**
>
> Selecting Window → CSS Styles displays the CSS Styles panel.

The CSS Styles panel shows a style sheet has not yet been linked to the current Web page document

A style sheet is linked to the open Web page document by clicking the Attach Style Sheet button ( ) at the bottom of the CSS Styles panel, which displays a dialog box where the style sheet name including the .css extension is typed:

creating a new style sheet

Selecting OK displays a warning dialog box if the style sheet does not already exist in the Web site root folder:

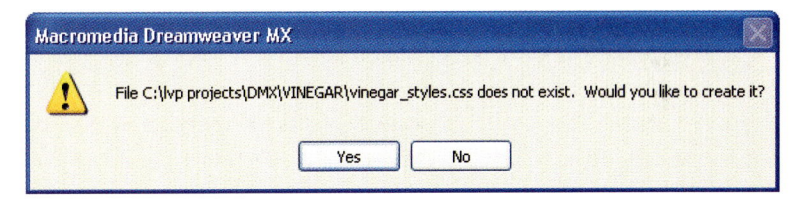

Selecting Yes creates a new style sheet in the Web site root folder. The CSS file name appears after styles are added to the style sheet.

linking to an existing style sheet

To link an existing style sheet, clicking the Browse button in the Link External Style Sheet dialog box displays another dialog box where the style sheet name is selected. The selected style sheet is copied to the Web site root folder.

Dreamweaver style sheets

Dreamweaver includes many themed CSS style sheets. A Dreamweaver style sheet is opened by selecting File → New and then selecting the CSS Style Sheets category. Selecting a style sheet and then Create displays a style sheet document than can be saved to the Web site's root folder with a descriptive name. After saving, the style sheet can be linked to Web pages in the Web site.

Typography, Style Sheets, and Color

7.7 Creating and Applying a CSS Rule

A new style is added to a style sheet by clicking the New CSS Style button ( ) at the bottom of the CSS Styles panel to display the following dialog box. A rule is created by first selecting Redefine HTML Tag and then selecting a tag from the Tag list:

HTML

Refer to Chapter 3 for a discussion on HTML, tags, attributes, and setting attribute values. Refer also to Appendix A for a list of tags and their attributes.

A new rule will be created for the paragraph tag (<p>).

Selecting OK displays a dialog box where formats for a paragraph and text within a paragraph are set:

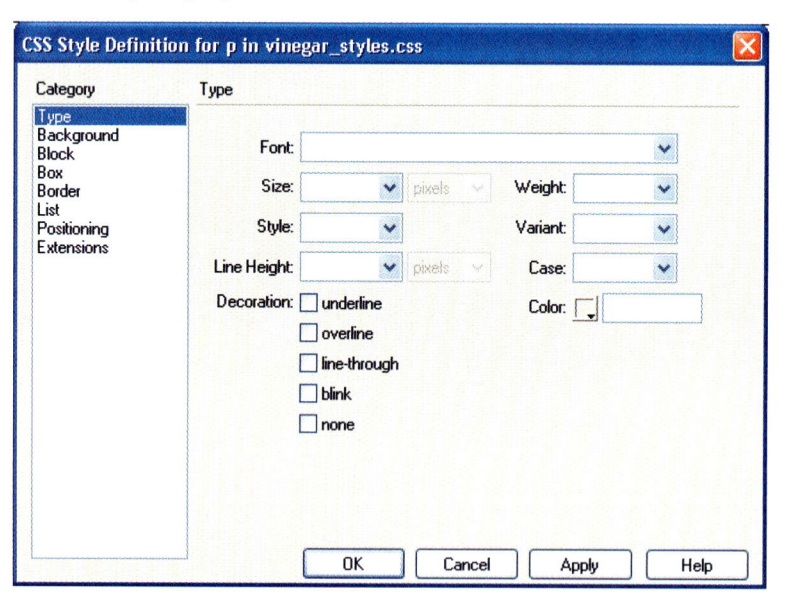

choosing text attributes

Each Category in the CSS Style Definition dialog box contains a different set of attributes. Not every attribute affects the tag being redefined. For example, the List category of attributes has no effect on paragraph text. For the p tag, the Type and Block categories of attributes can be set. The Type attributes include:

- Font for selecting a font family.
- Size for specifying a type size. Selecting a value enables the units list where pixels should be selected.
- Weight for selecting the boldness of text.
- Style for selecting normal, italic, or oblique.
- Line Height for selecting the leading.

choosing paragraph alignment

The Block category displays attributes that include the Text Align list for selecting a paragraph alignment of left, center, right, or justified.

applying a rule Selecting OK in the CSS Style Definition dialog box creates the style. Rules are automatically applied because they redefine HTML tags. Therefore, any text on the linked Web page document that is within <p> and </p> will be formatted.

7.8 Creating and Applying a CSS Class

A new class is added to a style sheet the same way a rule is created, except that Make Custom Style (class) is selected and then a class name typed. Class names must begin with a dot:

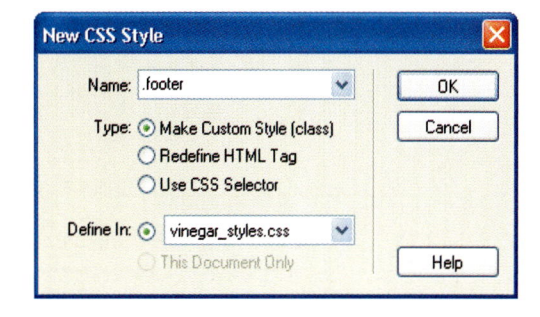

Selecting OK displays the CSS Style Definition dialog box where attributes are set. It is important to keep in mind what the class will be used for. A class that will modify paragraphs should only include attribute settings that apply to paragraphs of text.

applying a class After creating the class style, it must be applied to selected text. Classes are not automatically applied as rules are because they are created to modify tags, not redefine specific tags. A class is applied by selecting the text or table cell to receive it and then clicking the style name in the CSS Styles panel:

The attached style sheet has two classes

Only class names are displayed in Apply Styles of the CSS Styles panel because they can be applied to selected elements. Rules are not listed because they are automatically applied to redefine HTML tags.

Typography, Style Sheets, and Color

7.9 Inserting Tags

The HTML tags in a document become important when using CSS style sheets. For example, a modified p tag affects only text enclosed by <p> and </p>. Although tags are automatically inserted by Dreamweaver, there may be cases where a different tag is wanted. The Web site development process includes checking the tags of a Web page document for inconsistencies. This can be done most easily by switching to Code and Design view:

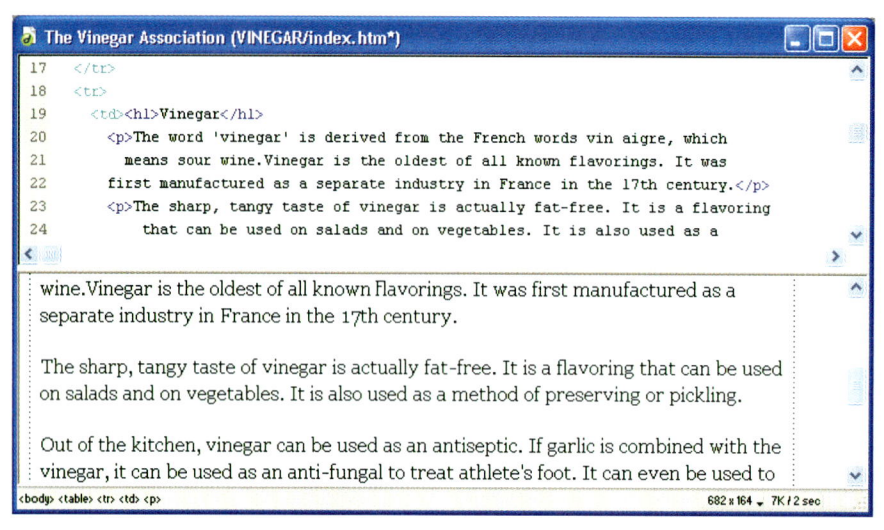

Code and Design view can be used to determine if paragraphs of text are enclosed by <p> and </p>

Text that needs to be tagged differently should be selected and then a tag button on the Text tab in the Insert bar clicked to enclose it. The Text tab includes many commonly used tags:

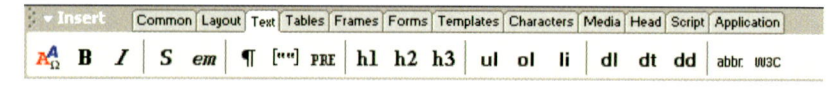

The Text tab is in the Insert bar

Paragraph button   The Paragraph button (¶) is used to insert <p> and </p> around selected text.

Practice 1

In this practice you will attach a new style sheet to the VINEGAR Web site, create and apply three styles, and check for tags.

① **OPEN THE VINEGAR WEB SITE FOR EDITING**

    a. Start Dreamweaver.

    b. In the Site panel, open the VINEGAR Web site for editing, a Web site provided with the data files for this text.

    c. In the Site panel, familiarize yourself with the files and folders for this Web site.

    d. Open the index.htm Web page document, and then view the page in a browser.

    e. Click the links to explore the other Web pages of the Web site.

② ATTACH A NEW STYLE SHEET TO INDEX.HTM

a. Switch to Dreamweaver.

b. Display the index.htm Web page document, if it is not already displayed.

c. Select Window → CSS Styles, if the CSS Styles panel is not already visible.

d. In the bottom of the CSS Styles panel, click the Attach Style Sheet button ( ). A dialog box is displayed.

  1. In the File/URL box, type: vinegar_styles.css
  2. Select OK. A dialog box is displayed.
  3. Select Yes. A new style sheet is linked to the index.htm Web page document.

③ CREATE A NEW STYLE

a. In the bottom of the CSS Styles panel, click the New CSS Style button ( ). A dialog box is displayed.

  1. Select Redefine HTML Tag.
  2. In the Tag list, select p.
  3. Select OK. A dialog box is displayed.

     a) In the Type category, set attributes to:

     CSS Style Definition for p in vinegar_styles.css
     - Font: Georgia, "Times New Roman", Times, serif
     - Size: 16 pixels
     - Line Height: 28 pixels

     b) Select the Block category, and then set Text Align to left.

     c) Select OK. A rule is created and applied to the Web page document.

④ CHECK THE HTML TAGS

a. Scroll the Web page document window and note that the sentence that begins "Many people even use…" has not changed to reflect the new rule. Click in the sentence without formatting.

b. Select View → Code and Design to display the HTML for the Web page document. Note the text is not enclosed by <p> and </p>.

c. Select the entire sentence that begins "Many people even use…."

d. On the Text tab in the Insert bar, click the Paragraph button (¶). <p> and </p> enclose the text, similar to:

```
31        a Jellyfish sting. If 2 liters of vinegar are applied over the skin
32     for more than 30 seconds, the discharge of the venom will cease.</p>
33     <p>Many people even use vinegar as a chemical-free cleaner. It does a great job on
34     windows!
35     </p>
```

Note that in the Design pane, the text displays the formatting of the redefined p tag.

e. Save the modified index.htm.

⑤ CREATE AND APPLY A SECOND STYLE

a. In the bottom of the CSS Styles panel, click the New CSS Style button ( ). A dialog box is displayed.

   1. Select Make Custom Style (class).
   2. In the Name list, type: .footer
   3. Select OK. A dialog box is displayed.

      a) In the Type category, set attributes to:

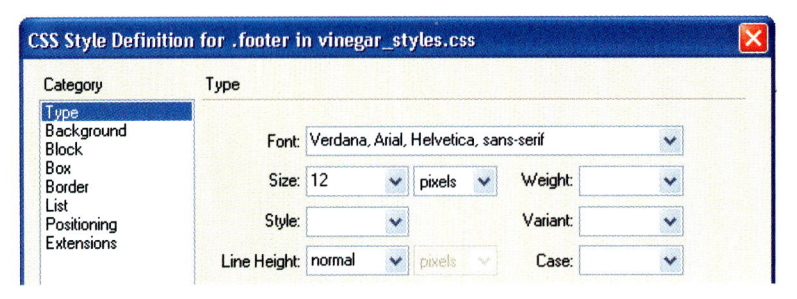

      b) Select the Block category, and then set Text Align to center.
      c) Select OK. A class is created.

b. In the Document window, place the insertion point in the bottom navigation bar.
c. In the CSS Styles panel, select Apply Styles, if it is not already selected, and then in the list of styles, click footer. The bottom navigation bar is formatted.
d. In the Document window, place the insertion point to the left of the library item in the last row of the table.
e. In the CSS Styles panel, click the footer style. The library item is formatted.
f. Save the modified index.htm.

⑥ CREATE AND APPLY A SECOND STYLE

a. In the CSS Styles panel, click the New CSS Style button ( ). A dialog box is displayed.

   1. Select Make Custom Style (class).
   2. In the Name list, type: .topnavbar
   3. Select OK. A dialog box is displayed.

      a) In the Type category, set Font to Verdana, Arial, Helvetica, sans-serif, and set Size to 16 pixels.
      b) Select the Block category, and then set Text Align to left.
      c) Select OK. A class is created.

b. In the Document window, place the insertion point in the top navigation bar.
c. In the CSS Styles panel, click the topnavbar style. The navigation bar is formatted.
d. Save the modified index.htm.

7.10 Working with CSS Styles

editing a style

Styles can be edited, duplicated, deleted, and removed from a document with the CSS Styles panel. A style is modified by first selecting Edit Styles at the top of the CSS Styles panel, which lists style names and attribute settings for each style:

The attached style sheet includes three styles

Next, clicking a style and then clicking the Edit Style Sheet button ( ) in the bottom of the CSS Styles panel displays the CSS Style Definition dialog box where attributes can be modifed. Double-clicking a style name in the panel also opens the CSS Style Definition dialog box.

duplicating a style

A style can be duplicated to create a new, similar style. A style is duplicated by first selecting Edit Styles at the top of the CSS Styles panel. Next, clicking the style sheet name and then clicking the Edit Style Sheet button ( ) displays a dialog box listing all the styles. Selecting a style name and then the Duplicate button displays a dialog box where the new style is given a name. The style can then be edited to customize it.

deleting a style

A style is deleted by selecting its name and then clicking the Delete CSS Style button ( ) in the CSS Styles panel.

removing an applied style

A class style is removed from a document by first clicking in the affected text. Next, selecting Apply Styles at the top of the CSS Styles panel and then clicking No CSS Style removes class styles. Rules can only be removed by deleting the style.

7.11 Strong and Emphasized Text

strong, em tags

Tags are used in a Web page document to indicate that selected text should be displayed as strong (<strong>) or emphasized (<em>). The Web developer usually intends for strong text to be displayed as bold and emphasized text to be displayed as italic. The best way to ensure that text is displayed as intended is to redefine the tags used to format the text with CSS styles.

To insert the appropriate tags for strong or emphasized text, buttons on the Text tab in the Insert bar are used. Selected text will be enclosed by <strong> and </strong> when the Bold button (B) or Strong button (S) is clicked. The <em> and </em> tags enclose selected text when the Italic button (I) or Emphasize button (em) is clicked.

Bold and italic are removed from a selected text by deselecting the Bold and Italic buttons in the Property inspector, respectively.

Typography, Style Sheets, and Color 7 – 11

Practice 2

In this practice you will create emphasized text and redefine the em tag. Dreamweaver should be started and the VINEGAR Web site should be the working site.

① **EMPHASIZE TEXT**

    a. Display the index.htm Web page document.

    b. In the first paragraph below the "Vinegar" title, select the words vin aigre.

    c. On the Text tab in the Insert bar, click the Italic button (*I*). The text is emphasized.

② **CREATE A NEW STYLE**

    a. In the bottom of the CSS Styles panel, click the New CSS Style button ( ). A dialog box is displayed.

        1. Select Redefine HTML Tag.

        2. In the Tag list, select em.

        3. Select OK. A dialog box is displayed.

            a) In the Type category, set Style to italic.

            b) Select OK. A rule is created and applied to the Web page document.

    b. Save the modified index.htm.

7.12 Formatting Headings

Headings are used in text to indicate a hierarchy and help with readability. Different levels of headings can be used to further enhance readability. For example, two heading levels are shown below:

Recipes

Pasta with Balsamic Vinegar

A user can more easily scan a long page of text if topics are divided by headings.

h1 through h6 tags   HTML includes six headings tags, ranging from <h1> through <h6>. The largest font size is typically applied to <h1> to represent the highest level or the topic of greatest importance. <h6> typically has the least importance and the smallest font size.

Dreamweaver does not automatically format text with heading tags. Therefore, text for a heading should be selected in Code and Design view and then the appropriate Heading button on the Text tab in the Insert bar used to insert tags. The h1 and h2 buttons are the most frequently used. The Text tab contains only a few heading tag buttons. Other heading tags can be inserted by selecting Text → Paragraph Format. CSS styles should then be used to redefine the headings tags in a Web site so that heading formats compliment the paragraph styles. In the CSS Style Definition dialog box, both the Type and Block categories have attributes that can apply to headings.

heading buttons

Practice 3

In this practice you will create and modify styles in the vinegar_styles style sheet. Headings will also be added to the VINEGAR Web site. Dreamweaver should be started and the VINEGAR Web site should be the working site.

① ATTACH THE STYLE SHEET AND APPLY STYLES TO RECIPES.HTM

    a. Display the recipes.htm Web page document.

    b. Display the CSS Styles panel if it is not already displayed.

    c. In the CSS Styles panel, click the Attach Style Sheet button ( ). A dialog box is displayed.

        1. Select the Browse button. The Select Style Sheet File dialog box is displayed.

            a) Select: vinegar_styles.css

            b) Select OK. The dialog box is removed.

            c) Select OK. The vinegar_styles.css style sheet is linked to the recipes.htm Web page document.

    d. In the Document window, place the insertion point in the top navigation bar.

    e. In the CSS Styles panel, select Apply Styles, and then click the topnavbar style. The navigation bar is formatted.

    f. Place the insertion point in the bottom navigation bar.

    g. In the CSS Styles panel, click footer. The bottom navigation bar is formatted.

    h. In the Document window, place the insertion point to the left of the library item.

    i. In the CSS Styles panel, click the footer style. The library item is formatted.

    j. Save the modified recipes.htm.

② DUPLICATE A STYLE

    a. In the CSS Styles panel, select Edit Styles. The style sheet name is displayed.

    b. Click the vinegar_styles.css name to select it.

    c. In the CSS Styles panel, click the Edit Style Sheet button ( ). A dialog box is displayed.

        1. Select the .topnavbar style to select it.

        2. Select Duplicate. A dialog box is displayed.

            a) In the Name box, replace the current name with: .btrail

            b) Select OK. The new style is listed in the dialog box.

        3. Select Edit. The CSS Style Definition dialog box is displayed.

            a) In the Type category, set Size to 12 pixels.

            b) Select OK. The dialog box is removed.

        4. Select Save. The dialog box is removed.

    d. In the recipes.htm Document window, place the insertion point in the breadcrumb trail.

    e. In the CSS Styles panel, select Apply Styles, and then in the list of styles, click btrail. The breadcrumb trail is formatted.

③ DUPLICATE ANOTHER STYLE

a. In the CSS Styles panel, select **Edit Styles** and then click the vinegar_styles.css name.
b. In the CSS Styles panel, click the Edit Style Sheet button ( ). A dialog box is displayed.
   1. Select the .btrail style to select it.
   2. Select **Duplicate**. A dialog box is displayed.
      a) In the Name box, replace the current name with: .localnavbar
      b) Select **OK**. The new style is listed in the dialog box.
   3. Select **Edit**. The CSS Style Definition dialog box is displayed.
      a) In the Type category, set **Line Height** to 35 pixels.
      b) In the Block category, set **Vertical Alignment** to top.
      c) Select **OK**. The dialog box is removed.
   4. Select **Save**. The dialog box is removed.

④ FORMAT THE LOCAL NAVIGATION BAR

a. In the recipes.htm Document window, click in the cell to the left of the recipes to place the insertion point in the local navigation bar.
b. In the CSS Styles panel, select **Apply Styles**, and then in the list of styles, click localnavbar. The local navigation bar text is formatted and the text is moved to the top of the cell.
c. Select View → Code and Design to display the HTML for the Web page document, if it is not already displayed.
d. Note that the text for the local navigation bar is enclosed by <td> and </td>. The style is affecting the table data, not paragraph text. Paragraph text will not be affected by a vertical alignment setting, like the one used in the localnavbar style.
e. Save the modified recipes.htm.

⑤ CREATE HEADINGS

a. In the Design pane, click in the text "Recipes" above the sentence that begins "Vinegar is used in…." Note in the Code pane that the text is enclosed by <p> and </p>.
b. In the Design pane, select the Recipes text.
c. On the Text tab in the Insert bar, click the Heading 1 button (**h1**). Note in Code view that the "Recipes" text is now enclosed by <h1> and </h1>.
d. Below the "Recipes" heading text, select the Pasta with Balsamic Vinegar text.
e. On the Text tab in the Insert bar, click the Heading 2 button (**h2**). Note in Code view that the text is now enclosed by <h2> and </h2>.
f. Scroll down to the "Barbeque Sauce with Cider Vinegar" text and make it Heading 2 text.
g. Scroll down to the "Chicken with Malt Vinegar" text and make it Heading 2 text.
h. Save the modified recipes.htm.

⑥ CREATE HEADING STYLES

a. In the CSS Styles panel, click the New CSS Style button ( ). A dialog box is displayed.
   1. Select **Redefine HTML Tag**.
   2. In the Tag list, select h1.
   3. Select **OK**. The CSS Style Definition dialog box is displayed.
      a) In the Type category, set **Font** to Verdana, Arial, Helvetica, sans-serif, **Size** to 32 pixels, and **Weight** to 600.
      b) In the Block category, set **Text Align** to left.
      c) Select **OK**. The dialog box is removed and the heading is formatted.

b. Create a new style that redefines the h2 tag so that the font family is Verdana, Arial, Helvetica, sans-serif, the size is 22 pixels, the weight is 500, and the text alignment is left.

c. Save the modified recipes.htm.

d. Display the index.htm Web page document. Note how the heading is formatted because the style sheet is already attached.

7.13 Using Blockquotes

A paragraph that should be set off from other paragraphs, such as a quotation, can be indented. In a Web page document, a paragraph is indented by making it a blockquote. For example, the Web page document below includes a blockquote:

> We at the Vinegar Association live by the motto:
>
>> We must all revel in the fullness of the taste of vinegar. Vinegar fills your mouth with glorious tingling, and enhances the flavor of any other food. The privilege of using vinegar is one that should be shared, as with the joy of good cooking and fine friendships.

The second paragraph is a blockquote

blockquote tag

A blockquote is a paragraph enclosed by <blockquote> and </blockquote>. Selecting a paragraph and then clicking [***] on the Text tab in the Insert bar inserts tags. Unlike heading tags, the blockquote tag does not replace existing tags. Multiple blockquote tags can be inserted to increase the indentation. A CSS class style can then be created and applied to format the blockquote text, if the text should be formatted differently than that applied by the paragraph tag.

increasing the indent

removing blockquotes

Blockquotes are removed from a paragraph by selecting Text → Outdent. The command may used multiple times to remove levels of blockquotes.

Practice 4

In this practice you will create a blockquote. Dreamweaver should be started and the VINEGAR Web site should be the working site.

① CREATE A BLOCKQUOTE

a. Display the index.htm Web page document.

b. Scroll to the bottom of the Web page to display the Vinegar Association motto.

c. Click in the paragraph that starts "We must all revel…."

d. On the Text tab in the Insert bar, click the Block Quote button ([***]). The paragraph is indented.

e. Click the Block Quote button ([***]) again. The paragraph is further indented.

f. Save the modified index.htm.

Typography, Style Sheets, and Color   7 – 15

7.14 Using Lists

numbered list

Lists are used to indicate features, to-do items, or steps in a procedure. One type of list is the *numbered list*, which shows a priority of importance for each step. Steps are denoted by numbers:

1. Pour the olive oil into a sauté pan and heat over medium heat for about 30 seconds.
2. Sauté the leeks for about 2 minutes until softened.
3. Add the garlic and mushrooms and sauté, stirring frequently.
4. Add the balsamic vinegar, stir well, and season with salt to taste.
5. Pour sauce and mushrooms over cooked pasta, drizzle with black truffle oil and serve.

> **Nested Lists**
>
> A sublist, or nested list, can be created within another list. Selecting the list items to be nested and selecting Text → Indent indents the items and numbers.

ol, li tags

In a Web page document, selected paragraphs are converted to a numbered list by clicking `ol` on the Text tab in the Insert bar to insert tags. Ordered list (<ol>) and list item (<li>) tags replace any tags originally enclosing the text.

bulleted list

ul, li tags

A *bulleted list* contains a set of items where each item is equally important. A solid circle (•) called a bullet is typically used to denote each item. To convert paragraphs to a bulleted list, the Unordered List button (`ul`) on the Text tab in the Insert bar is clicked. Unordered list (<ul>) and list item (<li>) tags replace any tags originally enclosing the text.

creating a list style

Lists are formatted by creating and then applying a CSS class style. The Type category in the CSS Style Definition dialog box can be used to set attributes to match paragraph text. The List category contains attributes that will apply to list items:

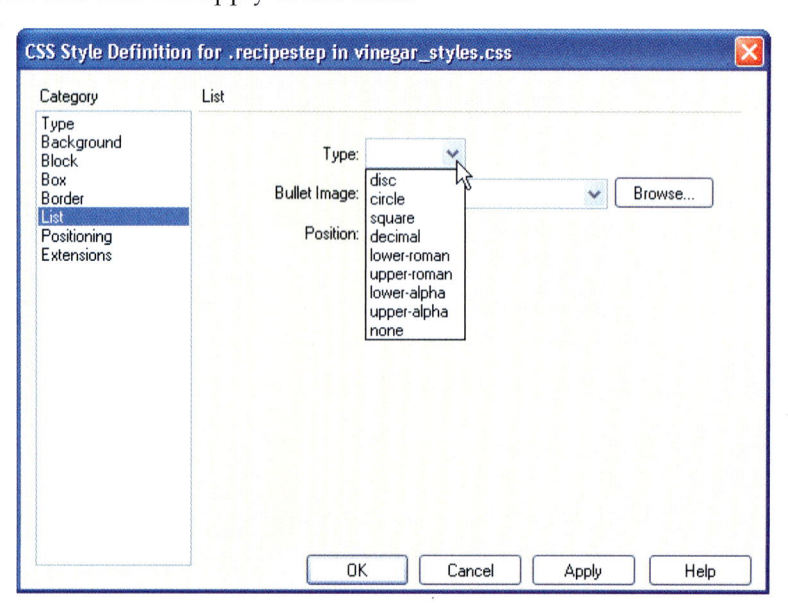

Bullet shapes and number formats can be selected from the Type list.

Practice 5

In this practice you will create numbered lists. Dreamweaver should be started and the VINEGAR Web site should be the working site.

① CREATE A NUMBERED LIST

    a. Display the recipes.htm Web page document.

    b. Scroll to the Pasta with Balsamic Vinegar recipe steps that begin "Pour the olive oil…."

    c. Select all the text that make up the list items:

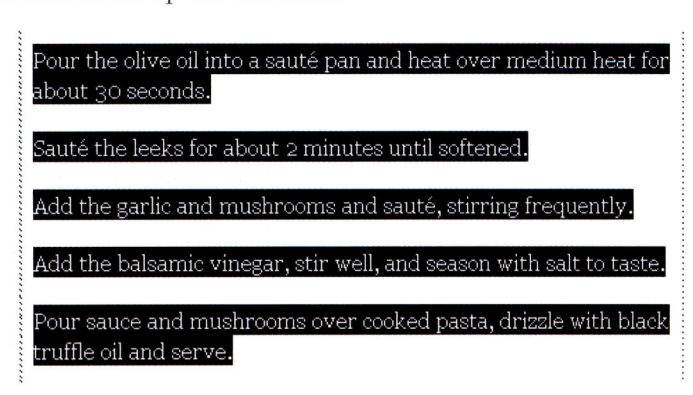

> Pour the olive oil into a sauté pan and heat over medium heat for about 30 seconds.
>
> Sauté the leeks for about 2 minutes until softened.
>
> Add the garlic and mushrooms and sauté, stirring frequently.
>
> Add the balsamic vinegar, stir well, and season with salt to taste.
>
> Pour sauce and mushrooms over cooked pasta, drizzle with black truffle oil and serve.

    d. On the Text tab in the Insert bar, click the Ordered List button (ol). The paragraphs are converted to a numbered list.

    e. Save the modified recipes.htm.

② CREATE AND APPLY A LIST STYLE

    a. In the CSS Styles panel, click the New CSS Style button ( ). A dialog box is displayed.

        1. Select **Make Custom Style (class)**.

        2. In the **Name** box, type: .recipestep

        3. Select **OK**. The CSS Style Definition dialog box is displayed.

            a) In the Type category, set **Font** to Georgia, "Times New Roman", Times, serif, **Size** to 16 pixels, and **Line Height** to 25 pixels.

            b) In the List category, set **Type** to decimal.

            c) Select **OK**. The dialog box is removed.

    b. Select the recipe steps, if they are not already selected.

    c. In the CSS Styles panel, select **Apply Styles**, and then in the list of styles, click recipestep. The steps are formatted similar to the rest of the content.

③ CREATE TWO MORE LISTS

    a. Scroll the recipes.htm Document window to locate the Barbeque Sauce with Cider Vinegar recipe.

    b. Select the two paragraphs that make up the recipe steps.

    c. Convert them to an ordered list and then apply the recipestep CSS style.

    d. Locate the Chicken with Malt Vinegar recipe, convert the four recipe steps to an ordered list, and then apply the recipestep CSS style.

    e. Save the modified recipes.htm.

    f. View the page in a browser and then print a copy.

    g. Switch back to Dreamweaver.

7.15 Using Color in a Web Site

Color can be added to a Web page in many ways: text, page background, and table cells. However, using too many colors on a Web page can make it visually annoying, causing users to click off the site. Color should be used to enhance the design and increase the usability of a Web site by guiding the user through the navigation aids and making the content more scannable.

color wheel

Colors that go together well can be determined with a *color wheel*. On the color wheel, colors from red to violet are arranged chromatically in a circle:

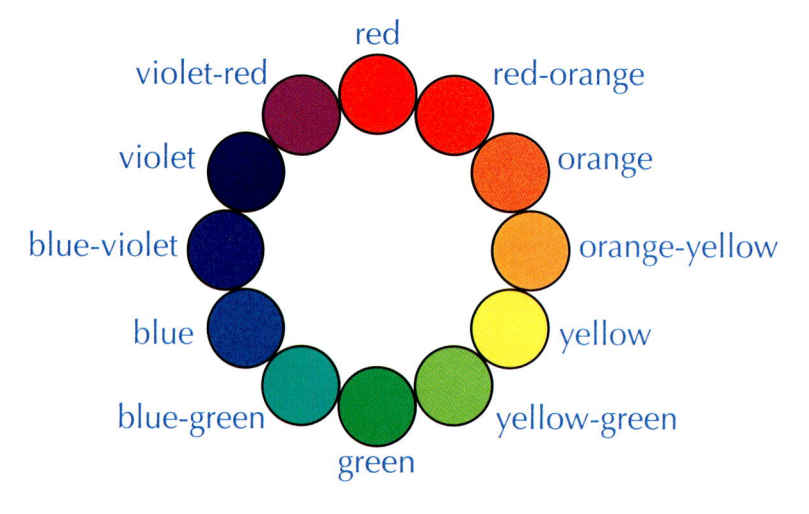

complementary
analogous
triads
warm
cool

The position of a color on the wheel represents its relationship to other colors. For example, red and green are directly opposite each other and said to be *complementary*. Three adjacent colors such as red, red-orange, and orange, are called *analogous*. Three equally-spaced colors, such as red, blue, and yellow, are called *triads*. Colors are also grouped by temperature, where reds, oranges, and yellows are called *warm* colors, and blues, greens, and violets are *cool*. Choosing two or three colors from the color wheel using one of these methods will ensure that the colors go well together.

Other elements on a Web page should also be considered when choosing colors. For example, a company logo may be red, and cannot be changed, so the other colors chosen should go well with red. Also consider the effect of the color on the user. For example, red is a bright, energetic color, and does not appear soothing or relaxing. Therefore, red is usually not the best color choice for a background or text.

How colors interact with each other should also be considered when choosing text color and background color. Black text on a white background is the easiest to read, and white text on a black background is also a readable choice. Colored text can be difficult depending on the background color, especially with light colored text on a light background, or dark on dark:

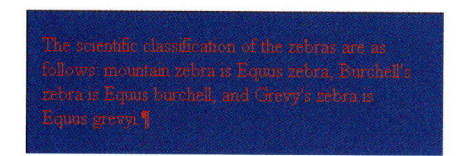

Note the effects of different color combinations

design considerations Colored text needs to be large enough and contrast with the background enough to be easily read. For example, yellow text can be eye-catching and effective, but it has to be in large letters on a dark background to be readable. However, if all the text is yellow, it would get tiring for the user to read. A bright color, for any element, also is tiring for the user to view. The text and background colors should enhance the usability of a Web page, not reduce it.

top, local navigation bars One application of cell background color is the top navigation bar and local navigation bar. The top and local navigation bars should be in a different color than the background for maximum usability. The **breadcrumb trail, bottom navigation rail** breadcrumb trail and the bottom navigation bar should be in the same color as the page background or in a slightly different color as the navigation bars. When choosing a color for the top and local navigation bars, be careful that the color does not conflict with the hyperlink blue and purple colors.

7.16 Changing Background Color

page background color The background of a Web page document is changed by redefining the body tag. The Background category in the CSS Style Definition dialog box includes the **Background Color** attribute:

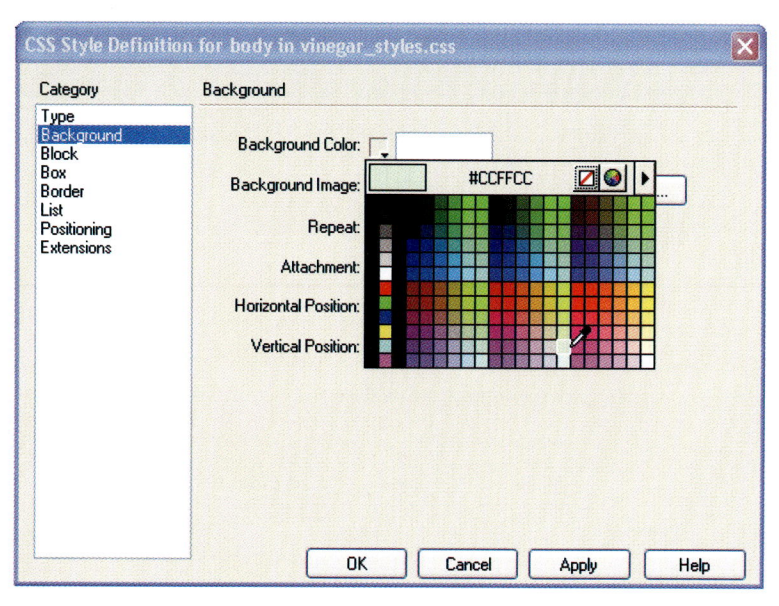

Selecting a color and then selecting **OK** changes the background color for the entire Web page.

Typography, Style Sheets, and Color

The body tag should be redefined with a background color even if the color is white. If the color is not formatted and left as Automatic, the Web page will display with whatever the user has chosen as the default background color for their browser.

cell background color   The background color for a cell is changed with a CSS class style. The Text category contains the Color attribute that will apply to cells.

7.17 Changing Text Color

Text can be displayed in a different color by changing the Color option in the Type category of a CSS style:

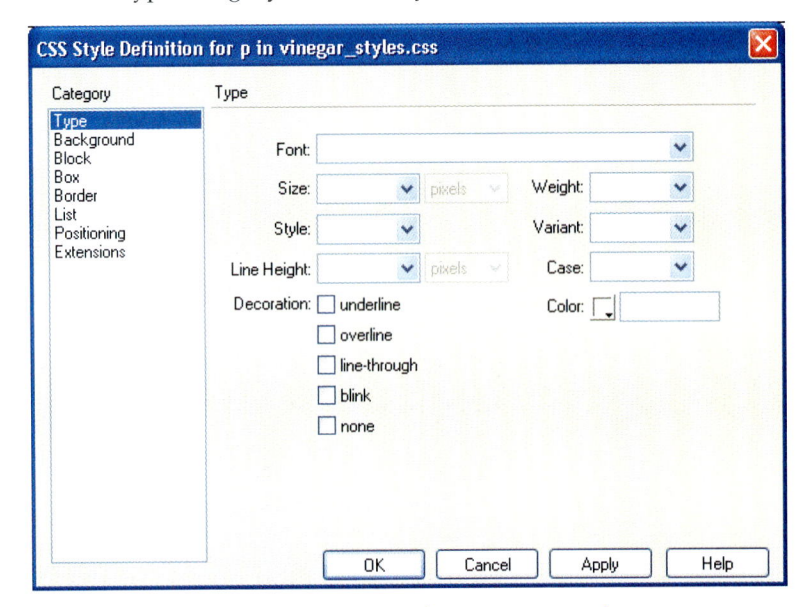

The Color option changes text color

Clicking Color shows available colors. Selecting a color changes the color of text with the applied CSS style.

Practice 6

In this practice you will add color to a Web site. Dreamweaver should be started and the VINEGAR Web site should be the working site.

① CHANGE THE WEB SITE BACKGROUND COLOR

a. Display the recipes.htm Web page document.
b. In the CSS Styles panel, click the New CSS Style button ( ). A dialog box is displayed.
  1. Select Redefine HTML Tag.
  2. In the Tag list, select body.
  3. Select OK. The CSS Style Definition dialog box is displayed.
      a) In the Background category, click the Background Color box and select the light green color, near the bottom, that corresponds to #CCFFCC.
      b) Select OK. A rule is created and applied to the Web site.

② **CHANGE THE LOCAL NAVIGATION BAR COLORS**

    a. In the CSS Styles panel, select Edit Styles and then double-click the .topnavbar class name. You may need to expand the list by clicking + beside the style sheet name. A dialog box is displayed.

        1. In the Background category, click the Background Color box and select the green color that corresponds to #CCFF66.

        2. Select OK. The top local navigation bar color is changed.

    b. Edit the .localnavbar class so that it has a background color that corresponds to #CCFF99.

③ **CHANGE THE FOOTER TEXT COLOR**

    a. In the CSS Styles panel, double-click the .footer class name. A dialog box is displayed.

        1. In the Type category, click the Color box and select the dark green color, near the top, that corresponds to #006600.

        2. Select OK. The text with the applied footer class is displayed in a different color.

7.18 Hyperlinks to Named Anchors

named anchor

A long Web page is easier to navigate if hyperlinks are provided to different parts of the page. For example, hyperlinks in a local navigation bar can link to sections in a Web page. Hyperlinks to different parts of the same page are linked to a *named anchor* that has been created in the page. A named anchor is created by placing the insertion point in the location of the anchor. Next, clicking the Named Anchor button (⚓) on the Common tab in the Insert bar displays a dialog box:

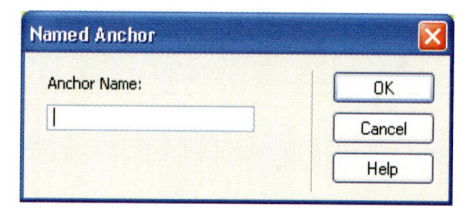

Typing a descriptive name for the anchor and then selecting OK displays an anchor icon in the Web page document:

⚓Pasta with Balsamic Vinegar

The anchor icon is not visible in a browser

Selected text is linked to a named anchor by clicking the Browse for File icon (📁) in the Property inspector and typing the anchor name in the Select File dialog box. Selected text can also be linked to a named anchor by dragging the Point to File icon to the anchor icon:

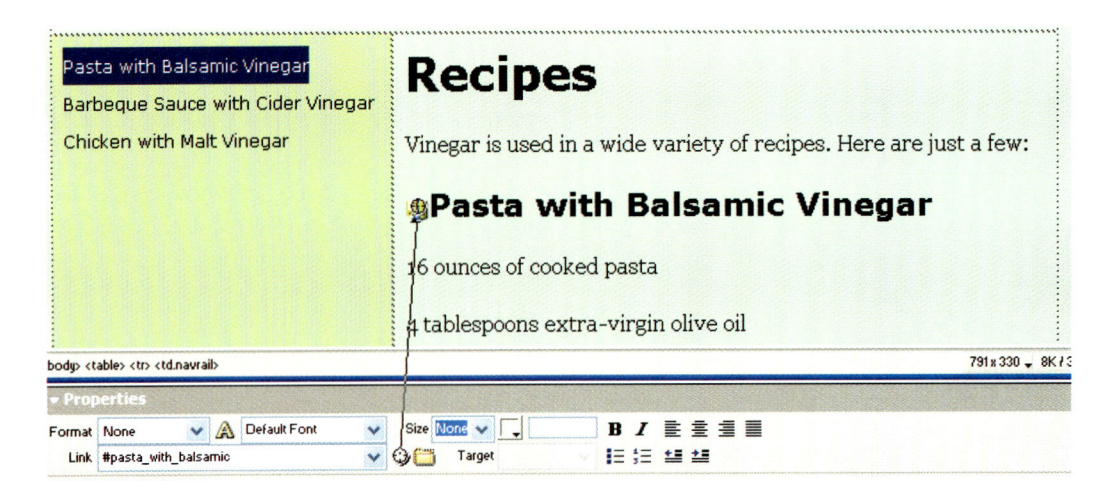

The Link list in the Property inspector displays the anchor name when the insertion point is in a hyperlink.

testing and modifying a hyperlink

Links should be tested in a browser window. Links are modified in Dreamweaver by selecting the link text and then selecting Modify → Change Link or Modify → Remove Link.

design considerations

A hyperlink to a named anchor typically causes a page to scroll. As a matter of good design, there should be a hyperlink near the anchor location that takes the user back to the hyperlink location. For example, including links such as top or Back to top that link to a named anchor near the position of the original hyperlink.

7.19   Changing Hyperlink Colors

A lot of design consideration should go into the decision to change hyperlink colors. Users know the standard colors: blue for a link and purple for a visited link. However, when appropriately done, nonstandard hyperlink colors can enhance a design.

CSS selector style

Hyperlink colors are changed by creating a *CSS selector style*, which defines a style for a tag and attribute combination. A CSS selector style is created by clicking the New CSS Style button ( ) to display the New CSS Style dialog box, selecting Use CSS Selector, and then making a selection from the Selector list:

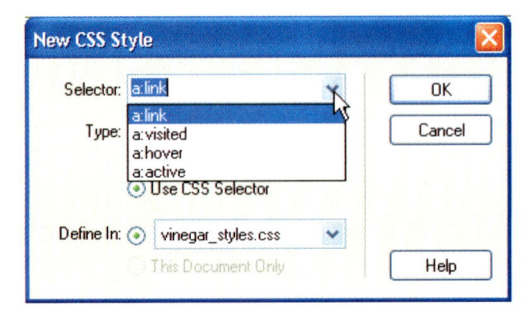

The Selector list contains predefined tag and attribute combinations

Selecting OK displays the CSS Style Definition dialog box where color and other formats can be selected from the Type category:

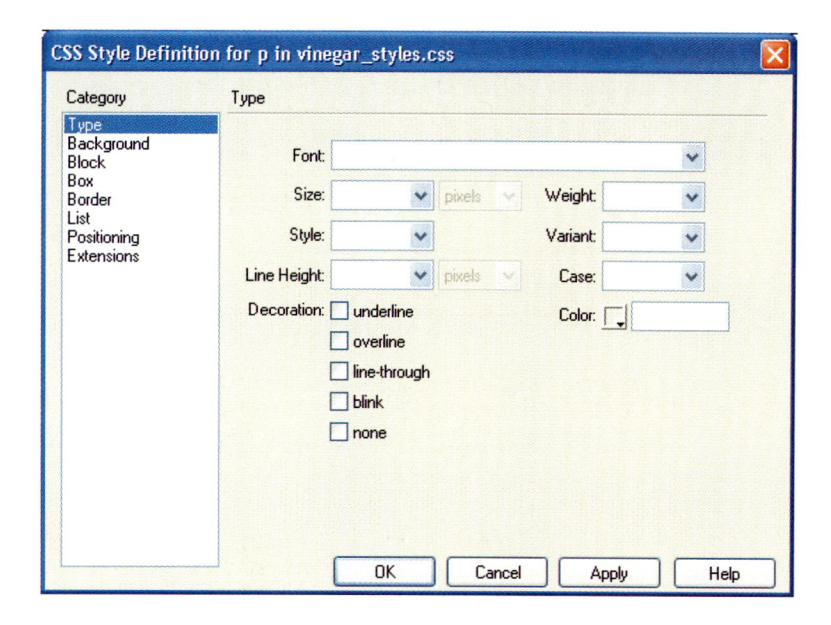

Practice 7

In this practice you will create links to named anchors and change hyperlink colors. Dreamweaver should be started and the VINEGAR Web site should be the working site.

① CREATE NAMED ANCHORS

a. Display the recipes.htm Web page document.

b. Place the insertion point to the left of the recipe heading that reads "Pasta with Balsamic Vinegar."

c. On the Common tab in the Insert bar, click the Named Anchor button ( ). A dialog box is displayed.

   1. In the Anchor Name box, type: pasta_with_balsamic
   2. Select OK. An anchor icon is displayed in the Web page document.

d. Scroll to the recipe heading that reads "Barbeque Sauce with Cider Vinegar" and insert an anchor named bbqsauce_with_cider to the left of the heading.

e. Scroll to the recipe heading that reads "Chicken with Malt Vinegar" and insert an anchor named chicken_with_malt to the left of the heading.

f. Save the modified recipes.htm.

② CREATE HYPERLINKS TO ANCHORS

a. In the local navigation bar, select the text: Pasta with Balsamic Vinegar

b. In the Property inspector, drag the Point to File icon to the anchor next to the "Pasta with Balsamic Vinegar" recipe. A hyperlink is created. In the Property inspector, note the anchor name in the Link box.

c. In the local navigation bar, select the text: Barbeque Sauce with Cider Vinegar

d. Scroll to the recipe heading that reads "Barbeque Sauce with Cider Vinegar" and then drag the Point to File icon to the anchor next to that recipe. A hyperlink is created.

e. In the local navigation bar, select the text: Chicken with Malt Vinegar

f. Scroll to the recipe heading that reads "Chicken with Malt Vinegar" and then drag the Point to File icon to the anchor next to that recipe. A hyperlink is created.

g. Save the modified recipes.htm.

Typography, Style Sheets, and Color

③ CREATE BACK TO TOP HYPERLINKS

a. Scroll to the top of the recipes and place the insertion point to the left of the "Recipes" heading.

b. Insert an anchor named: top

c. Scroll to Step 5 of the recipe for Pasta with Balsamic Vinegar.

d. Place the insertion point just after the period in "…and serve." and then insert a line break.

e. Type the text: Back to top

f. Select the Back to top text, scroll to the top of the Document window, and then in the Property inspector, drag the Point to File icon to the anchor next to "Recipes." A hyperlink is created.

g. Create Back to top hyperlinks below the remaining two recipes.

h. Save the modified recipes.htm.

④ VIEW THE RECIPES.HTM PAGE IN A BROWSER AND TEST THE HYPERLINKS

7.20 Using Content from Other Sources

Web development often involves collaborating with others to get the content for a Web site. For example, one person or department may have the responsibility of providing the images for a site, while others are responsible for the copy. *Copy* is a term that refers to text content.

copy

Copy often comes as a TXT file. In this case, Notepad can be used in a process to copy and paste text to a Dreamweaver Web page document:

1. Open the TXT file, which has the .txt extension, in Notepad.

2. Select the text to be placed in a Web page document.

3. Selecting Edit → Copy. The text is placed on the Windows clipboard.

4. Display the Web page document in Dreamweaver and place the insertion point where the text should be placed.

5. Select Edit → Paste. The copy is pasted into the Web page document.

If files are saved in the native format of the application used to create them, they will need to be opened in the appropriate application before copying and pasting into Dreamweaver.

> **Notepad**
>
> Notepad is introduced in Chapter 3.

Practice 8

In this practice you will paste content into a Web page document. Dreamweaver should be started and the VINEGAR Web site should be the working site.

① ADD COPY FROM A TEXT FILE

a. Start Notepad.
b. Open the RICE.txt file, a text file provided with the data files for this text.
c. Select Edit → Select All. All the text is selected.
d. Select Edit → Copy. The text is copied to the Windows Clipboard.

② PASTE THE TEXT

a. Switch to Dreamweaver.
b. Display the rice.htm Web page document.
c. Place the insertion point in the empty paragraph below the "Rice Vinegar" heading.
d. Select Edit → Paste. The text is pasted.
e. In the CSS Styles panel, attach the vinegar_styles.css style sheet.
f. Apply the topnavbar, localnavbar, btrail, and footer styles appropriately. Remember the footer style will need to be applied to both the bottom navigation bar and the library item.
g. Save the modified rice.htm and then close the Web page document.

③ ATTACH THE STYLE SHEET TO OTHER PAGES

a. Open the balsamic.htm, cider.htm, malt.htm, types_of_vinegar.htm, and wine.htm Web page documents and link the vinegar_styles.css style sheet.
b. Apply the topnavbar, localnavbar, btrail, and footer styles appropriately. Remember the footer style will need to be applied to both the bottom navigation bar and the library item.
c. Save the modified balsamic.htm, cider.htm, malt.htm, types_of_vinegar.htm, and wine.htm.

④ VIEW THE WEB SITE IN A BROWSER

a. Note the consistency between the pages.
b. Close the browser widow.
c. Quit Notepad.
d. Quit Dreamweaver.

Chapter Summary

Typography refers to the arrangement, shape, size, style, and weight of text. A typeface is a set of letters drawn in a specific style. The word font technically refers to a specific size and weight of a single typeface. A font is classified as a serif or sans serif font. Text in all capital letters is more difficult to read than lowercase. The size of printed text is usually measured vertically in points. Type styles indicate variations of the characters. Leading is the distance from one line of text to another.

In order for fonts to display correctly in a browser, the user must have the fonts installed on their computer. Fonts that are available on most computers are Times New Roman, Georgia, Courier New, Arial, Verdana, and Geneva. When choosing sizes for the text on a Web page, keep usability in mind.

In a paragraph, left alignment is the most readable and therefore provides the highest degree of usability. Links in navigation bars and rails are most readable and usable when left aligned.

A style sheet defines the type, paragraph, and page formats for a Web page document. A single style sheet can be applied to all the pages in a Web site to achieve a consistent look. The CSS Styles panel is used for linking, creating, and modifying style sheets. Styles can also be edited, duplicated, deleted, and removed from a document with the CSS Styles panel. A Dreamweaver themed CSS style sheet can be opened by selecting File → New.

A CSS document can have rules, which modify HTML elements and classes, which are a set of declarations that can be applied to different tags. A new style is added to a style sheet by clicking the New CSS Style button. A rule is created by first selecting Redefine HTML Tag and then selecting a tag from the Tag list. A new class is added to a style sheet the same way a rule is created, except that Make Custom Style (class) is selected and then a class name typed.

The HTML tags in a document become important when using CSS style sheets. Text that needs to be tagged differently should be selected and then a tag button on the Text tab in the Insert bar clicked to enclose it. Tags are used in a Web page document to indicate that selected text should be displayed as strong (<strong>) or emphasized (<em>). Headings are used in text to indicate a hierarchy and help with readability. HTML includes six headings tags, ranging from <h1> through <h6>. A paragraph that should be set off from other paragraphs, such as a quotation, can be indented using a blockquote.

A numbered list shows a priority of importance for each step. A bulleted list contains a set of items where each item is equally important. Lists are formatted by creating and then applying a CSS class style.

Color can be added to a Web page in many ways: text, page background, and table cells. Colors that go together well can be determined with a color wheel. Colored text needs to be large enough and contrast with the background enough to be easily read. The background of a Web page document is changed by redefining the body tag.

A long Web page is easier to navigate if hyperlinks are provided to different parts of the page. Hyperlinks to different parts of the same page are linked to a named anchor. A link taking the user back to the original hyperlink location should be included near the anchor location.

Hyperlink colors can be changed. However, a lot of design consideration should go into the decision to change hyperlink colors because users know the standard blue and purple colors.

Web development often involves collaborating with others to get the content for a Web site. This may require copying and pasting text.

Vocabulary

Alignment A paragraph format that refers to the position of the lines of text relative to the sides of a cell. Paragraph alignments include left, centered, right, and justified.

Analogous Three adjacent colors on the color wheel.

Bulleted List A list of items where each item is equally important.

Cascading The effect of applying rules from one style sheet in addition to those in another style sheet.

Class A set of declarations that can be applied to different tags.

Color wheel Colors from red to violet that are arranged chromatically in a circle. Used to determine colors that go together well.

Complementary Colors that are directly opposite each other on the color wheel.

Cool colors Blue, green, and violet colors.

Copy Refers to text content.

CSS Selector Style Defines a style for a tag and attribute combination. Used to change hyperlink colors.

Declarations The formats to be applied in a rule.

Font A specific size and weight of a single typeface. May be used interchangeably with typeface.

Leading The distance from one line of text to another.

Named Anchor A hyperlink destination that is located on the same Web page document as the hyperlink.

Numbered List A list of items where each item has a priority of importance.

Point Unit used to measure the size of text. One point is $1/72$ of an inch.

Regular Text that has no style applied to it.

Rule A single selector and its declaration(s) which are used to modify an HTML element.

Sans serif Letters without the small extensions (serifs) on their ends.

Selector The HTML element being redefined in a rule.

Serif The small extensions on the ends of letters.

Style Variations of characters including bold and italic.

Style Sheet Used to define the type, paragraph, and page formats for a Web page document.

Triad Three equally-spaced colors on the color wheel.

Typeface A set of letters drawn in a specific style.

Typography The arrangement, shape, size, style, and weight of text.

Warm colors Red, orange, and yellow colors.

Dreamweaver Commands and Buttons

Attach Style Sheet button Links a style sheet to the open Web page document. Found in the CSS Styles panel.

Block Quote button Indents a paragraph. Found on the Text tab in the Insert bar.

Bold button Creates strong text, which is displayed as bold text. Found on the Text tab in the Insert bar.

Change Link **command** Displays a dialog box used to modify a hyperlink. Found in the Modify menu.

Copy **command** Copies selected text. Found in the Edit menu.

Delete CSS Style button Deletes a style. Found in the CSS Styles panel.

Edit Style Sheet button Displays a dialog box used to modify attributes or duplicate styles. Found in the CSS Styles panel.

Emphasize button Creates emphasized text, which is displayed as italic text. Found on the Text tab in the Insert bar.

Heading 1 button Formats the selected text in heading 1. Found on the Text tab in the Insert bar.

Heading 2 button Formats the selected text in heading 2. Found on the Text tab in the Insert bar.

Italic button Creates emphasized text, which is displayed as italic text. Found on the Text tab in the Insert bar.

Named anchor button Creates a named anchor at the location of the insertion point. Found on the Common tab in the Insert bar.

New **Command** Displays a dialog box used to open a themed CSS style sheet. Found in the File menu.

New CSS Style button Adds a new style or a new class to a style sheet. Also used to create a CSS selector style. Found in the CSS Styles panel.

No CSS Style button Removes a class style from affected text. Found in the CSS Styles panel.

Ordered list button Converts selected paragraphs to a numbered list. Found on the Text tab in the Insert bar.

Outdent **command** Removes a blockquote from a paragraph. Found in the Text menu.

Paragraph button Inserts <p> and </p> around selected text. Found on the Text tab in the Insert bar.

Paragraph Format **command** Displays a submenu used to insert heading tags. Found in the Text menu.

Paste **command** Pastes copied text. Found in the Edit menu.

Remove Link **command** Removes an existing link. Found in the Modify menu.

Strong button Creates strong text, which is displayed as bold text. Found on the Text tab in the Insert bar.

Unordered list button Converts selected paragraphs to a bulleted list. Found on the Text tab in the Insert bar.

Review Questions

Sections 7.1 — 7.4

1. What does typography refer to?

2. a) What is a typeface?
   b) What is a font?

3. What is the difference between a serif and a sans serif font?

4. Which is easier to read when viewing a Web page, ALL CAPITALS or lowercase text?

5. a) What is the size of printed text measured in?
   b) In Web pages, what are two ways to specify text?

6. List two type styles.

7. What is leading?

8. a) What is the maximum number of fonts that should be used on a single Web page?
   b) List four fonts that are available on most computers.

9. a) What is the recommended size for large paragraphs of text?
   b) What is the recommended size for headings?

10. a) What can bold style text be used to indicate?
    b) What font size should italic style be applied to?

11. a) What does the alignment of text in a paragraph refer to?
    b) List the four paragraph alignments.

12. What paragraph alignment is most readable?

Sections 7.5 — 7.20

13. What does a style sheet define?

14. a) What does a rule modify?
    b) What is a rule comprised of?
    c) What is a selector?
    d) What are declarations?
    e) What is a class?

15. List the steps required to create a new style sheet named school_styles.css.

16. List the steps required to create a rule for the p tag that sets the size attribute to 14 pixels.

17. List the steps required to create a new class named .footer and apply the class style to selected text.

18. List the step required to insert <p> and </p> around selected text.

19. a) What two buttons can be clicked to display selected text as bold?
    b) What two buttons can be clicked to display selected text as italic?

20. a) What are headings used to indicate and help with?
    b) List the six HTML heading tags.

21. List the steps required to indent a paragraph.

22. a) What is a numbered list?
    b) What is a bulleted list?
    c) List the steps required to format three paragraphs as items in a bulleted list.

23. a) What are complementary colors?
    b) What are analogous colors?
    c) List two cool colors.

24. Which color combination would be easier for the user to read: red text on a pink background, or black text on a white background?

25. List the steps required to change the background color of a Web page to #CCFF66.

26. a) What is a named anchor?
    b) What type of Web page would be most likely to use hyperlinks to named anchors?

27. List the steps required to change hyperlink colors.

28. What is copy?

29. List the steps required to copy content from a TXT file into a Web page document.

Exercises

Exercise 1 — GREECE

The GREECE Web site was last modified in Chapter 6, Exercise 1. Use Dreamweaver to further modify the GREECE Web site by completing the following steps:

a) In Dreamweaver, open the GREECE Web site for editing.

b) Modify the index.htm Web page document as follows:
   1. Link a new style sheet named greece_style.css to the Web page.
   2. Select the text in the cell to the left of the map. Tag the text with <p> and </p>.
   3. Create a new style that redefines the p tag as follows:
      a) In the Type category, set Font to Verdana, Arial, Helvetica, sans-serif, Size to 14 pixels, and Line Height to 26 pixels.
      b) In the Block category, set Text Align to left.
   4. Create a new class style named .footer that includes the formats:
      a) In the Type category, set Font to Verdana, Arial, Helvetica, sans-serif, and Size to 12 pixels.
      b) In the Block category, set Text Align to center.
   5. Apply the footer style to the cells containing the bottom navigation bar and the library item.

c) Modify the itinerary.htm Web page document as follows:
   1. Link the greece_style.css to the Web page.
   2. Place the insertion point in the word "Itinerary" in the first paragraph of the content. Tag the text with <h1> and </h1>.
   3. Tag the text "Day 1", "Day 2", "Day 3", "Day 4", "Day 5", "Day 6", and "Day 7" with <h1> and </h1>.
   4. Create a new style that redefines the h1 tag as follows:
      a) In the Type category, set Font to Verdana, Arial, Helvetica, sans-serif, Size to 30 pixels, and Weight to bold.
      b) In the Block category, set Text Align to left.
   5. Create a new style that redefines the h2 tag as follows:
      a) In the Type category, set Font to Verdana, Arial, Helvetica, sans-serif, Size to 24 pixels, and Weight to bold.
      b) In the Block category, set Text Align to left.
   6. Below "Day 1," after the text "Stay in Athens." press Enter and type the text: Back to top
   7. For each of the remaining days, add the text Back to top after the last itinerary item.
   8. Select just the itinerary items (not the text "Back to top") under "Day 1" and tag it as an unordered list (<ul>, </ul> and <li>, </li>).
   9. Create unordered lists for the just the itinerary items in the remaining six days.

10. Create a new style that redefines the ul tag as follows:
    a) In the Type category, set **Font** to Verdana, Arial, Helvetica, sans-serif, **Size** to 14 pixels, and **Line Height** to 30 pixels.
    b) In the List category, set **Type** to square.
11. Below the "Itinerary" heading, create a set of hyperlinks to named anchors by following the steps below the image:

Itinerary

Day 1
Day 2
Day 3
Day 4
Day 5
Day 6
Day 7

Day 1

- Depart Miami, Florida, U.S.A.
- Arrive Athens, Greece.
- Stay in Athens.

Back to top

  a) Below "Itinerary," type the text for the seven hyperlinks shown above, inserting line breaks as needed.
  b) To the left of "Itinerary," insert an anchor named: top
  c) To the left of "Day 1," insert an anchor named: Day_1
  d) To the left of the remaining "Day" headings, insert appropriately named anchors.
  e) Link the "Day 1, "Day 2," "Day 3," "Day 4," "Day 5," "Day 6," and "Day 7," text to the appropriate named anchor.
  f) Link the "Back to top" text under each "Day" heading to the top anchor.
12. Apply the footer style to the cells containing the bottom navigation bar and the library item.

d) Modify the photos.htm Web page document as follows:
   1. Link the greece_style.css to the Web page.
   2. Create a new class style named .caption that includes the formats:
      a) In the Type category, set **Font** to Verdana, Arial, Helvetica, sans-serif, **Size** to 14 pixels, and **Weight** to bold.
      b) In the Block category, set **Text Align** to center.
   3. Apply the caption style to the text below each of the photos.
   4. Apply the footer style to the cells containing the bottom navigation bar and the library item.

e) View each Web page document of the formatted Web site in a browser window.

f) Print a copy of each Web page document from the browser.

Exercise 2 — CACTUS

The CACTUS Web site was last modified in Chapter 6, Exercise 2. Use Dreamweaver to further modify the CACTUS Web site by completing the following steps:

a) In Dreamweaver, open the CACTUS Web site for editing.

b) Modify the index.htm Web page document as follows:
   1. Link a new style sheet named cactus_style.css to the Web page.
   2. Create a new style that redefines the p tag as follows:
      a) In the Type category, set Font to Georgia, "Times New Roman", Times, serif, Size to 14 pixels, and Line Height to 26 pixels.
      b) In the Block category, set Text Align to left.
   3. Create a new selector style that redefines a:link as follows:
      a) In the Type category, set Color to a dark green that corresponds to #009900.
   4. Create a new selector style that redefines a:visited as follows:
      a) In the Type category, set Color to a brown-green that corresponds to #666600.
   5. Create a new class style named .footer that includes the formats:
      a) In the Type category, set Font to Arial, Helvetica, sans-serif, Size to 12 pixels, and Color to a dark green that corresponds to #009900.
      b) In the Block category, set Text Align to center.
   6. Apply the footer style to the cells containing the bottom navigation bar and the library item.

c) Modify the gallery.htm Web page document as follows:
   1. Link the cactus_style.css to the Web page.
   2. Place the insertion point in the text "A Gallery of Cactus Photographs" in the first cell of the content. Tag the text with <h1> and </h1>.
   3. Create a new style that redefines the h1 tag as follows:
      a) In the Type category, set Font to Arial, Helvetica, sans-serif, Size to 32 pixels, Weight to bold, and Color to a dark green that corresponds to #009900.
      b) In the Block category, set Text Align to center.
   4. Create a new class style named .caption that includes the formats:
      a) In the Type category, set Font to Arial, Helvetica, sans-serif, Size to 16 pixels.
      b) In the Block category, set Text Align to center.
   5. Apply the caption style to the text below each of the photos.
   6. For each caption, select only the cactus name (not the pronunciation text) and then tag the text with <strong> and </strong>.
   7. Create a new style that redefines the Strong tag as follows:
      a) In the Type category, set Weight to bold.
   8. Apply the footer style to the cells containing the bottom navigation bar and the library item.

d) Modify the types.htm Web page document as follows:
   1. Link the cactus_style.css to the Web page.
   2. Place the insertion point in the text "Types of Cacti." Tag the text with <h1> and </h1>.
   3. Select and tag each of the cacti names in the remaining paragraphs with <strong> and </strong>.
   4. Apply the footer style to the cells containing the bottom navigation bar and the library item.

e) View each Web page document of the formatted Web site in a browser window.

f) Print a copy of each Web page document from the browser.

Exercise 3 — FRUIT

The FRUIT Web site was last modified in Chapter 6, Exercise 3. Use Dreamweaver to further modify the FRUIT Web site by completing the following steps:

a) In Dreamweaver, open the FRUIT Web site for editing.

b) Modify the index.htm Web page document as follows:
   1. Link a new style sheet named fuit_style.css to the Web page.
   2. Create a new style that redefines the body tag as follows:
      a) In the Background category, set Background Color to a light yellow that corresponds to #FFFFCC.
   3. Select the fruit bowl image and then in the Property inspector, click [Edit] to edit the image in Fireworks. In Fireworks, change the white background of the image to match the new page Web page background color by completing the following steps:
      a) In the Tools panel, click the Paint Bucket tool ( ).
      b) In the Tools panel, change the paint color in the Colors section to a light yellow that corresponds to #FFFFCC:
      c) In the image window, click the Paint Bucket tool ( ) on each of the white background areas. The color changes to match the Web page background color.
      d) In the image window, click Done. The image is updated in Dreamweaver.
   4. Create a new style that redefines the p tag as follows:
      a) In the Type category, set Font to Verdana, Arial, Helvetica, sans-serif, Size to 14 pixels, and Line Height to 28 pixels.
      b) In the Block category, set Text Align to left.
   5. Create a new class style named .footer that includes the formats:
      a) In the Type category, set Font to Verdana, Arial, Helvetica, sans-serif, Size to 12 pixels, and Line Height to 22 pixels.
      b) In the Block category, set Text Align to left.
   6. Apply the footer style to the cells containing the bottom navigation bar and the library item.

c) Modify the apple.htm Web page document as follows:
   1. Link the fruit_style.css to the Web page.
   2. Place the insertion point in the word "Nutrition" in the first paragraph of the content. Tag the text with <h2> and </h2>.
   3. Tag the text "Selection and Storage" and "Common Types" with <h2> and </h2>.
   4. Create a new style that redefines the h2 tag as follows:
      a) In the Type category, set Font to Verdana, Arial, Helvetica, sans-serif, Size to 22 pixels, and Weight to bold.
      b) In the Block category, set Text Align to left.
   5. Select the two paragraphs below the "Nutrition" heading and then tag them as an unordered list (<ul>, </ul> and <li>, </li>).
   6. Select the two paragraphs below the "Selection and Storage" heading and then tag them as an unordered list (<ul>, </ul> and <li>, </li>).
   7. Select the four paragraphs below the text "There are thousands of varieties…" and then tag them as an unordered list (<ul>, </ul> and <li>, </li>).
   8. Create a new style that redefines the ul tag as follows:
      a) In the Type category, set Font to Verdana, Arial, Helvetica, sans-serif, and Size to 14 pixels.
      b) In the List category, set Type to disc.
   9. Apply the footer style to the cells containing the bottom navigation bar and the library item.

d) Modify the banana.htm Web page document as follows:
   1. Link the fruit_style.css to the Web page.
   2. Place the insertion point in the word "Nutrition" in the first paragraph of the content. Tag the text with <h2> and </h2>.
   3. Tag the text "Selection and Storage" and "Common Types" with <h2> and </h2>.
   4. Select the two paragraphs below the "Nutrition" heading and then tag them as an unordered list (<ul>, </ul> and <li>, </li>).
   5. Select the two paragraphs below the "Selection and Storage" heading and then tag them as an unordered list (<ul>, </ul> and <li>, </li>).
   6. Select the four paragraphs below the "Common Types" headings and then tag them as an unordered list (<ul>, </ul> and <li>, </li>).
   7. Apply the footer style to the cells containing the bottom navigation bar and the library item.

e) Modify the orange.htm Web page document as follows:
   1. Link the fruit_style.css to the Web page.
   2. Place the insertion point in the word "Nutrition" in the first paragraph of the content. Tag the text with <h2> and </h2>.
   3. Tag the text "Selection and Storage" and "Common Types" with <h2> and </h2>.
   4. Select the two paragraphs below the "Nutrition" heading and then tag them as an unordered list (<ul>, </ul> and <li>, </li>).
   5. Select the three paragraphs below the "Selection and Storage" heading and then tag them as an unordered list (<ul>, </ul> and <li>, </li>).

6. Select the three paragraphs below the "Common Types" headings and then tag them as an unordered list (<ul>, </ul> and <li>, </li>).
7. Apply the footer style to the cells containing the bottom navigation bar and the library item.

f) View each Web page document of the formatted Web site in a browser window.

g) Print a copy of each Web page document from the browser.

Exercise 4 — SEVEN WONDERS

The SEVEN WONDERS Web site was last modified in Chapter 5, Exercise 5. Use Dreamweaver to further modify the SEVEN WONDERS Web site by completing the following steps:

a) In Dreamweaver, open the FRUIT Web site for editing.

b) Modify the index.htm Web page document as follows:
1. Link a new style sheet named seven_wonders_style.css to the Web page.
2. Create a new style that redefines the p tag as follows:
    a) In the Type category, set Font to Verdana, Arial, Helvetica, sans-serif, Size to 14 pixels, and Line Height to 24 pixels.
    b) In the Block category, set Text Align to left.
3. Create a new class style named .topnavbar that includes the formats:
    a) In the Type category, set Font to Verdana, Arial, Helvetica, sans-serif, Size to 12 pixels, and Line Height to 24 pixels.
    b) In the Block category, set Text Align to left.
4. Apply the topnavbar style to the cell containing the top navigation bar.
5. Create a new class style named .footer that includes the formats:
    a) In the Type category, set Font to Verdana, Arial, Helvetica, sans-serif, Size to 10 pixels, and Line Height to 18 pixels.
    b) In the Block category, set Text Align to left.
6. Apply the footer style to the cells containing the bottom navigation bar and the library item.

c) Modify the colossus.htm Web page document as follows:
1. Link the seven_wonders_style.css style sheet to the Web page.
2. Place the insertion point in the title "SEVEN WONDERS - Colossus of Rhodes." Tag the text with <h1> and </h1>.
3. Create a new style that redefines the h1 tag as follows:
    a) In the Type category, set Font to Verdana, Arial, Helvetica, sans-serif, Size to 28 pixels, and Weight to bold.
    b) In the Block category, set Text Align to left.
4. Apply the footer style to the cells containing the bottom navigation bar and the library item.

d) Modify the hanging.htm Web page document as follows:
   1. Link the seven_wonders_style.css style sheet to the Web page.
   2. Place the insertion point in the title "SEVEN WONDERS - Hanging Gardens of Babylon." Tag the text with `<h1>` and `</h1>`.
   3. Apply the footer style to the cells containing the bottom navigation bar and the library item.

e) Modify the lighthouse.htm Web page document as follows:
   1. Link the seven_wonders_style.css style sheet to the Web page.
   2. Place the insertion point in the title "SEVEN WONDERS - Lighthouse of Alexandria." Tag the text with `<h1>` and `</h1>`.
   3. Apply the footer style to the cells containing the bottom navigation bar and the library item.

f) Modify the mausoleum.htm Web page document as follows:
   1. Link the seven_wonders_style.css style sheet to the Web page.
   2. Place the insertion point in the title "SEVEN WONDERS - Mausoleum at Halicarnassus." Tag the text with `<h1>` and `</h1>`.
   3. Apply the footer style to the cells containing the bottom navigation bar and the library item.

g) Modify the pyramids.htm Web page document as follows:
   1. Link the seven_wonders_style.css style sheet to the Web page.
   2. Place the insertion point in the title "SEVEN WONDERS - Pyramids of Egypt." Tag the text with `<h1>` and `</h1>`.
   3. Apply the footer style to the cells containing the bottom navigation bar and the library item.

h) Modify the statue.htm Web page document as follows:
   1. Link the seven_wonders_style.css style sheet to the Web page.
   2. Place the insertion point in the title "SEVEN WONDERS - Statue of Zeus at Olympia." Tag the text with `<h1>` and `</h1>`.
   3. Apply the footer style to the cells containing the bottom navigation bar and the library item.

i) Modify the temple.htm Web page document as follows:
   1. Link the seven_wonders_style.css style sheet to the Web page.
   2. Place the insertion point in the title "SEVEN WONDERS - Temple of Artemis at Ephesus." Tag the text with `<h1>` and `</h1>`.
   3. Apply the footer style to the cells containing the bottom navigation bar and the library item.

j) View each Web page document of the formatted Web site in a browser window.

k) Print a copy of each Web page document from the browser.

Exercise 5 (advanced)

The Web sites developed in the exercises of Chapters 4 through 6 have no style sheets attached. Use the steps below to attach a style sheet and apply formatting to previously created Web sites:

a) Link a new style sheet with an appropriate name to the index.htm Web page document.

b) Redefine the body tag if a background color is appropriate for the Web site.

c) Redefine the p tag to format paragraph text with an appropriate font, font size, line height, and paragraph alignment.

d) Create selector styles that redefine hyperlink colors where appropriate.

e) Create class styles to format navigation bars, breadcrumb trails, and footer text.

f) Link the style sheet to the other Web page documents in the Web site.

g) For each page of the Web site, do the following:

1. Check the document tags in Code and Design view for text that should be enclosed by <p> and </p>.
2. Create named anchors and links to the named anchors as appropriate.
3. Tag text as appropriate to create headings and then redefine the h1 and h2 tags.
4. Tag text as appropriate to create strong and emphasized text and then redefine the strong and em tags.
5. Tag text as appropriate to create ordered lists and then redefine the ol tag.
6. Tag text as appropriate to create unordered lists and then redefine the ul tag.
7. Tag text as appropriate to create blockquotes and then redefine the blockquote tag.
8. Apply styles as appropriate.

h) Preview the Web site in a browser. When satisfied with the Web site, print a copy of each Web page document from the browser.

Chapter 8
Introducing Flash

Chapter 8 Expectations

After completing this chapter you will be able to:
1. Create Flash buttons and Flash text in Dreamweaver.
2. Use the Assets panel to access Flash movie files.
3. Explain animation.
4. Demonstrate the basic features and functions of Flash MX.
5. Outline the process of creating a Flash movie.
6. Create a frame-by-frame animation.
7. Edit animations.
8. Export Flash documents.
9. Organize and use Flash movie files in Dreamweaver.
10. Create an animation using shape tweening.
11. Optimize a Flash movie by creating symbols.
12. Create an animation using motion tweening.
13. Use layers in a Flash document.
14. Animate text.
15. Import sound files and video.

This chapter introduces Flash MX. Customizing Flash buttons and text in Dreamweaver are discussed. Creating Flash movies is also discussed.

8.1 What is Flash?

Flash is the technology used to create a movie file for a Web site. A Flash movie file can be an animated button, animated text, or an entire Web application. For example, the Web application below was created with Flash:

Flash

Flash was originally called FutureSplash until the company that developed it was purchased by Macromedia, and the name was changed to Flash.

The Flash Player Plug-in

The Flash Player is incorporated into the Windows XP operating system and the latest versions of Netscape Navigator, Internet Explorer, and America Online. It can also be downloaded for free at www.macromedia.com.

Pointing to a trail displays information about the trail and color-codes the level of difficulty

Flash buttons and Flash text can be created directly in Dreamweaver. However, animations beyond these and Web applications must be created in Flash MX, the authoring tool that is part of the Macromedia Studio MX suite.

8.2 Creating Flash Buttons in Dreamweaver

Dreamweaver includes predefined Flash buttons that can be added to a Web page:

Sample of predefined Flash buttons in Dreamweaver

Flash buttons can have customized text, font, size, and color.

The **Media** tab in the Insert bar can be used to add a Flash button to a Web page document. After saving the Web page document and placing the insertion point where the button is to appear, the Flash Button button is clicked:

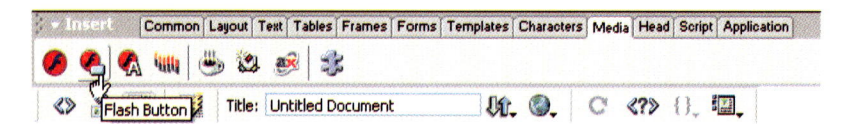

The Insert Flash Button dialog box is displayed:

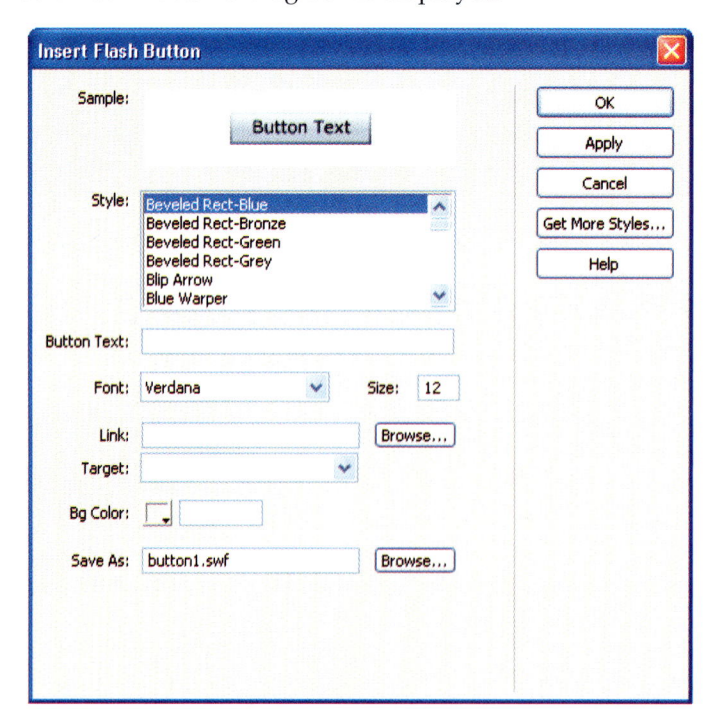

- Pointing to the button in the Sample area previews the button. Clicking the button in the Sample area shows the button behavior for the Down state.

- **Style** is a list with a selected button, which is shown in the Sample area. A different button can be selected by clicking a name in the list.

- **Button Text** is the text displayed on the button. New text can be typed in the box. Some button styles do not allow specified text.

- Font is the font for the button text. A new font can be selected from the list.

- Size is the font size in points for the button text. A new size can be typed.

- Link is the linked Web page document file name. Browse is clicked to display a dialog box where the Web page document file name can be selected.

- Bg Color is the background color of the button. A color that matches the cell background can be selected by clicking the box and choosing a color.

.swf

- Save As displays the location and name of the Flash movie file. Clicking Browse displays the Select File dialog box with a Save in list for selecting the appropriate folder in the root folder of the Web site. The File name box in the dialog box is where a descriptive name is typed. A Flash button is saved as a Flash movie file, which has the extension .swf.

Clicking OK inserts the Flash button into the Web page document. Note that clicking Apply also inserts the Flash button in the Web page document and leaves the dialog box open so that the object can be edited.

previewing a button

A Flash button can be previewed in a browser or in Design view by selecting the button and then clicking [Play] in the Property inspector. Clicking [Stop] in the Property inspector ends the preview.

editing a button

A Flash button is edited by double-clicking the button to display the Insert Flash Button dialog box. Clicking [Edit...] in the Property inspector when a Flash button is selected also displays the Insert Flash Button dialog box.

8.3 Arranging Flash Buttons in a Web Page Document

Flash buttons added to a Web page document should be arranged in a nested table with each button in a separate cell:

Each cell is sized to the width of the button

creating a nested table

A nested table is created by first placing the insertion point in the cell of an existing table and then creating a new table. A nested table sized in pixels with cell widths also in pixels will prevent the buttons from wrapping in a browser when the browser window is resized. The table and cell widths can be determined after creating a button. The W property in the Property inspector displays the width in pixels of a selected button.

determining table and cell widths

aligning buttons

The Align property in the Property inspector can be set to change the alignment within a cell for a selected Flash button.

Introducing Flash   8 – 3

Practice 1

In this practice you will add a Flash button to a Web page document.

① OPEN THE SAMPLER WEB SITE FOR EDITING

a. Start Dreamweaver.
b. In the Site panel, open the SAMPLER Web site for editing, a Web site provided with the data files for this text.
c. In the Site panel, familiarize yourself with the files and folders for this Web site.
d. Open the index.htm Web page document and then view the page in a browser.
e. Click the links to explore the other Web pages in the Web site.

② EDIT THE FOOTER LIBRARY ITEM TO INCLUDE YOUR NAME

a. Switch back to Dreamweaver.
b. In the Assets panel, click the Library icon ( ). A library item is displayed.
c. In the Assets panel, double-click the header library item. The Library Item is displayed in a window.
d. In the Library Item window, replace the text Student Name with your name.
e. Select File → Save. A dialog box is displayed.
   1. Select Update. The occurrence of the library item on each page in the Web site is updated and a dialog box is displayed with a summary of the changes.
      a) Select Close.
f. Close the Library Item window.

③ INSERT A NESTED TABLE

a. Display the index.htm Web page document if it is not already displayed.
b. Place the insertion point in the empty cell in the second row.
c. Add a table with the following specifications:

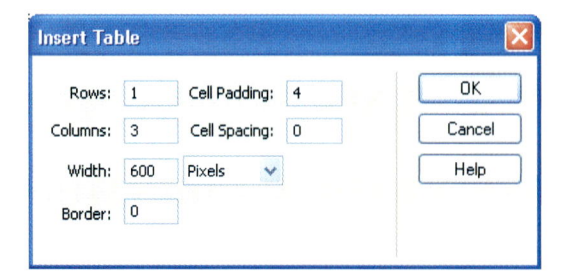

> Insert Table
> Rows: 1   Cell Padding: 4
> Columns: 3   Cell Spacing: 0
> Width: 600   Pixels
> Border: 0

Check—Your index.htm Web page document should look similar to:

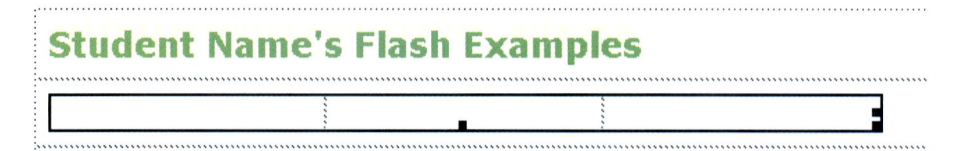

Student Name's Flash Examples

A Guide to Web Development Using Macromedia Dreamweaver MX

④ INSERT A FLASH BUTTON

a. Place the insertion point in the left cell of the nested table.
b. Above the Document window, in the Insert bar, click the **Media** tab. The Media buttons are displayed.
c. On the Media tab, click the Flash Button button ( ). A dialog box is displayed.
   1. In the **Style** list, select Blue Warper. Scroll the list if necessary.
   2. In the **Sample** box, point to the sample button to preview it. Click the button to view the Down state behavior.
   3. In the **Button Text** box, type: Rollover Text
   4. In the **Font** box, select Verdana, if it it is not already selected.
   5. In the **Size** box, type 12 if it it is not already selected.
   6. Next to the **Link** box, click **Browse**. A dialog box is displayed.
      a) Select the rollover.htm Web page document.
      b) Select OK.
   7. Next to the **Save As** box, click **Browse**. A dialog box is displayed.
      a) In the **File name** box, type: rollover_text.swf
      b) Select Save.
   8. Select **OK**. The dialog box is removed and the Flash button is inserted in the cell. Note the nested cell widths may have changed.

⑤ RESIZE THE TABLES AND CELLS

a. Click the Flash button to select it, if it is not already selected.
b. In the Property inspector, note the W property displays 103 for the width of the button.
c. Click beside the Flash button to place the insertion point in the cell. Note that cell properties are displayed in the Property inspector.
d. In the Property inspector, set W to 103 and press Enter. The cell width changes.
e. Resize the remaining two cells by placing the insertion point in each cell and then setting W to 103 for each.
f. Select the entire nested table and set W to 309 and press Enter.

Check—Your Web page document with the nested table should look similar to:

Student Name's Flash Examples

Rollover Text

⑥ VIEW THE DOCUMENT IN A BROWSER

a. Save the modified index.htm.
b. Press F12. The document is displayed in a browser window.
c. Point to the button. Note the animated effect.
d. Click the button. The rollover.htm Web page document is displayed.
e. Close the browser window.

Introducing Flash

8.4 Using Movie Files

Assets panel

Flash movies that are available in a Web site are listed in the Flash category in the Assets panel. Clicking the Flash icon ( ) in the Assets panel displays the list:

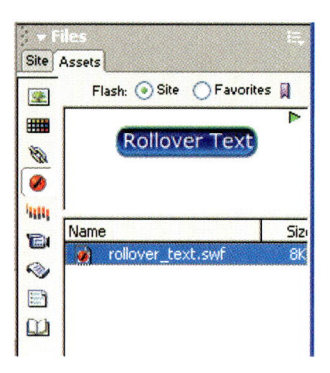

The selected image, rollover_text.swf in the example above, is displayed in the preview. The ▶ button in the preview is clicked to play the Flash movie. When running, the ■ button is displayed. Clicking this button ends the movie. Selecting ≡ → Refresh Site List in the Files panel group may be necessary to update the list of movies in the Assets panel.

placing a movie in a Web page document

A Flash movie is placed in an open Web page document by dragging it from the Assets panel into the Document window or by clicking Insert at the bottom of the Assets panel to place the movie at the insertion point.

creating a navigation bar

Rather than recreating a button from scratch for a Web site, an existing Flash button in the Assets panel can be placed in a Web page document and then modified and saved with a different name. This approach ensures a consistent look among buttons in the same Web site.

Practice 2

In this practice you will complete a navigation bar of Flash buttons. Dreamweaver should be started and the SAMPLER Web site should be the working site.

① VIEW THE ASSETS PANEL

a. In the Site panel, click the Assets panel tab, if it is not already displayed.

b. In the Assets panel, click the Flash icon ( ). The Flash movie file is displayed. If no files are displayed, select ≡ → Refresh Site List from the Files panel group.

② CREATE A SECOND BUTTON IN THE NAVIGATION BAR

a. Open the index.htm Web page document, if it is not already displayed.

b. In the Assets panel, drag the rollover_text.swf file name to the middle cell of the nested table.

c. Double-click the middle Flash button. A dialog box is displayed.
   1. In the **Button Text** box, type: Animation
   2. Next to the **Link** box, click **Browse**. A dialog box is displayed.
       a) Select the animation.htm Web page document.
       b) Select **OK**.
   3. Next to the **Save As** box, click **Browse**. A dialog box is displayed.
       a) In the File name box, type: animation.swf
       b) Select **Save**.
   4. Select **OK**. The dialog box is removed and the Flash button is updated in the cell.
d. In the Assets panel, select ▤ → Refresh Site List from the Files panel group. The animation.swf Flash movie file is displayed in the list.

③ CREATE A THIRD BUTTON IN THE NAVIGATION BAR
a. In the Assets panel, drag the rollover_text.swf file name to the last cell of the nested table.
b. Double-click the last Flash button. A dialog box is displayed.
c. Change the button text to Video/Sound and link the button to the video_and_sound.htm Web page document. Save the button naming it: video_and_sound.swf

④ SAVE THE MODIFIED INDEX.HTM

⑤ VIEW THE DOCUMENT IN A BROWSER AND TEST THE BUTTONS
a. Press F12. The document is displayed in a browser window.
b. Click the Animation button. The animation.htm page is displayed.
c. Click the Home link. The index.htm Web page is again displayed.
d. Test the Video/Sound button.

8.5 Creating Flash Text in Dreamweaver

Flash text allows the use of fonts in Dreamweaver without worrying about whether the user's computer has the font installed. For example, the Flash text below was created with the Harrington font:

Welcome

Flash text can include a rollover color and a link to create a rollover text hyperlink. Text with a rollover behavior changes color when the user points to it in a browser. When the pointer is moved over Flash text that is also a hyperlink, the pointer changes to 👆.

Introducing Flash 8 – 7

The Media tab in the Insert bar can be used to add Flash text to a Web page document. After saving the Web page document and placing the insertion point where the text is to appear, the Flash Text button is clicked:

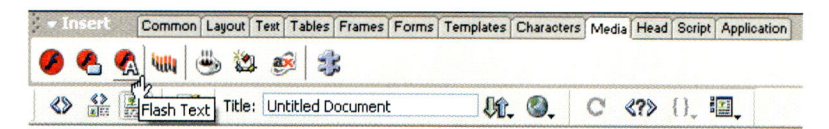

The Insert Flash Text dialog box is displayed:

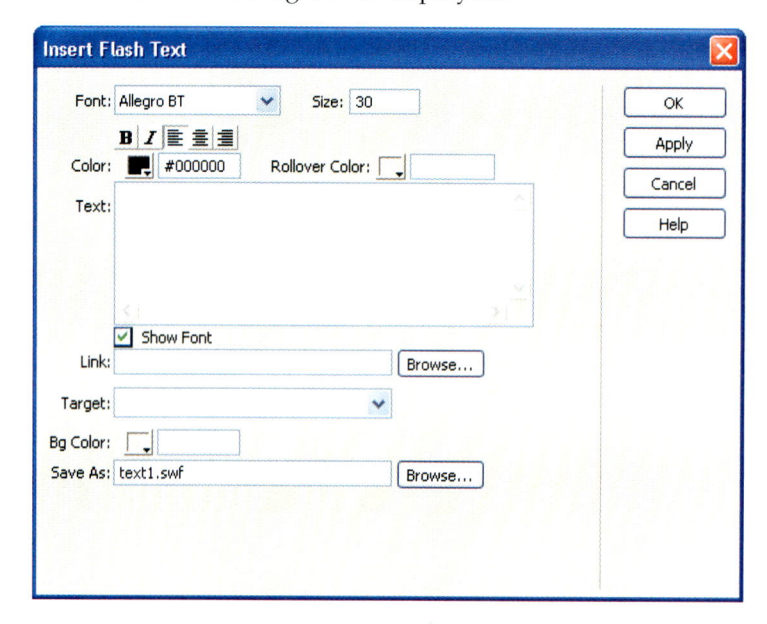

- Font is the font for the text. A new font can be selected from the list.

- Size is the font size in points for the text. A new size can be typed.

- Style and alignment buttons (**B** *I* ≡ ≡ ≡) are selected by clicking the appropriate button.

- Color is the text color. A new color can be selected by clicking the box and choosing a color.

- Rollover Color is the color the text changes to when the user points to the text in a browser. A new color can be selected by clicking the box and choosing a color.

- Text is the text to be displayed. New text can be typed. Note that the size of the text in this box does not correspond to the selected Size.

- Link is the linked Web page document file name. Browse is clicked to display a dialog box where the Web page document file name can be selected.

- Bg Color is the background color of the text. A color that matches the cell background can be selected by clicking the box and choosing a color.

- Save As displays the location and name of the Flash movie file. Clicking Browse displays the Select File dialog box with a Save in list for selecting the appropriate folder in the root folder of the Web site. The File name box in the dialog box is where a descriptive name is typed. Flash text is saved as a Flash movie file, which has the extension .swf.

previewing Flash text Clicking OK inserts the Flash text into the Web page document. Note that clicking Apply also inserts the Flash text in the Web page document and leaves the dialog box open so that the object can be edited.

modifying Flash text Flash text can be previewed in a browser or in Design view by selecting the Flash text and then clicking [Play] in the Property inspector. Clicking [Stop] in the Property inspector ends the preview.

editing Flash text Flash text is edited by double-clicking it to display the Insert Flash Text dialog box. Clicking [Edit...] in the Property inspector when Flash text is selected also displays the Insert Flash Text dialog box.

Practice 3

In this practice you will add Flash text to the rollover.htm page. Dreamweaver should be started and the SAMPLER Web site should be the working site.

① ADD FLASH TEXT TO A TABLE
  a. In the Site panel, open the rollover.htm Web page document.
  b. Place the insertion point in the empty cell.
  c. On the Media tab in the Insert bar, click the Flash Text button ( ). A dialog box is displayed.
    1. Set Font to a font of your choice.
    2. Set Size to 30.
    3. Set Color to a dark color of your choice.
    4. Set Rollover Color to a light color of your choice.
    5. In the Text box, type: Back to the Home Page
    6. Next to the Link box, click Browse. A dialog box is displayed.
       a) Select the index.htm Web page document.
       b) Select OK.
    7. Next to the Save As box, click Browse. A dialog box is displayed.
       a) In the File name box, type: home_link.swf
       b) Select Save.
    8. Select OK. The dialog box is removed and the Flash text is inserted in the cell.
  d. Save the modified rollover.htm.

② VIEW THE DOCUMENT IN A BROWSER
  a. Press F12. The document is displayed in a browser window.
  b. Point to the Flash text. Note the rollover color.
  c. Click the Flash text. The home page is displayed.
  d. Close the browser window.

③ QUIT DREAMWEAVER

Introducing Flash 8 – 9

8.6 What is Animation?

Animation is the result of many images shown quickly one after the other to create the effect of movement. For example, the following images shown quickly one after the other create the effect of a skateboarder going down a hill:

A Flash movie animation can be broken into components. A *Timeline* correlates images to a particular moment in the movie. At any point in a movie, there is a *frame* with an image. The frame can be several images that are layered. *Layering* is done because from frame to frame there may be different animation techniques applied. For example, an animation of a skateboarder going down a hill requires only the position of the skateboarder to change. The hill remains unchanged from frame to frame. The hill can be on one layer and the skateboarder on another.

Starting Flash

Flash is started by selecting Start → All Programs → Macromedia → Macromedia Flash MX. Flash may also be started by double-clicking the Flash icon on the Desktop:

8.7 Introducing Flash MX

Web sites are often designed to include animations beyond rollover text and buttons with special effects. The Flash MX application, which is part of the Macromedia Studio MX suite, is used to create custom animations. When Flash MX is started, a new Flash document is displayed:

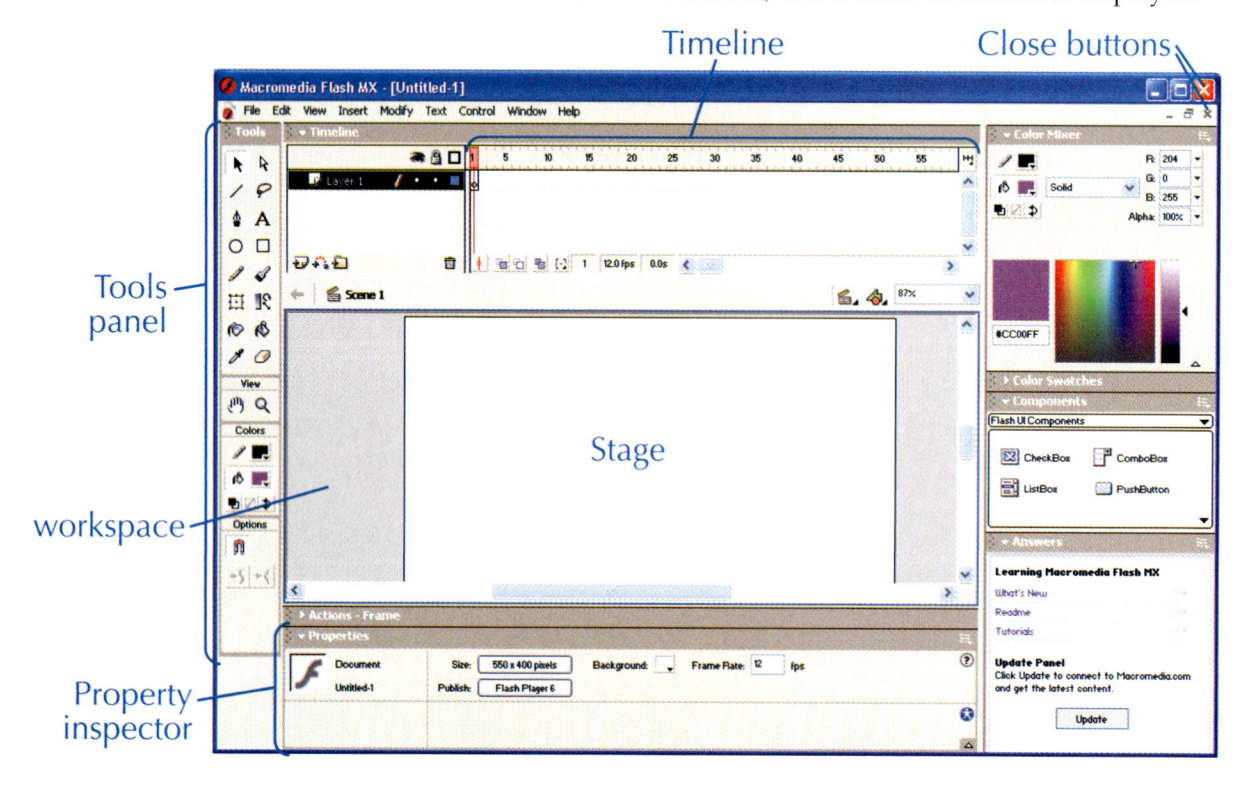

8 – 10   A Guide to Web Development Using Macromedia Dreamweaver MX

- The **Tools panel** contains tools for drawing, painting, and selecting. The tools are divided into sections.
- The **Timeline** correlates images to a frame in the movie.
- A **Close button** is clicked to remove the document window or the Flash window.
- The **Stage** is the area used to create a Flash movie.
- The **workspace** is the gray area around the Stage, which can be used as a temporary storage area while working.
- The **Property inspector** contains options to modify object properties.

saving a Flash document

A new Flash document is saved by selecting File → Save, which displays a dialog box where a location outside of the site folder should be selected. A good practice is to keep related files that are not directly used in a Web site together in a folder outside the Web site root folder. Flash documents are automatically saved in FLA format. The FLA file cannot be used in a Web page document, so the Flash document must be exported as a SWF movie file for use in the Web site. The FLA file is saved in case the file later needs to be edited and exported again. Exporting is discussed in Section 8.11.

> **Native File Format**
>
> The native file format in Flash is FLA. A *native file format* is the default format that an application saves files in. Files may be saved and exported in other formats, but are worked on in the native file format.

8.8 The Flash Tools Panel

vector graphics

Images drawn in Flash are vector graphics. A *vector graphic* is composed of lines connected by points, which allows the image to be resized smoothly. The file size of a vector-based graphic is much smaller than a bitmap graphic.

The tools in the Tools panel are used to create images. Tools include:

Arrow tool selects objects.

Subselection tool adjusts anchor points, which define sections of a line or shape.

Line, Oval, and Rectangle tools draw basic shapes.

Pen tool draws straight or curved lines.

Text tool creates a text block.

Pencil tool draws free-form lines and shapes.

Brush tool paints with brush-like strokes.

Paint Bucket tool fills enclosed areas with a selected color.

Eraser tool deletes parts of a shape.

The View section in the Tools panel includes:

Zoom tool changes the magnification level of the Stage.

The Colors section in the Tools panel is used to set tool colors:

Stroke Color changes the outline color of the tool.

Fill Color changes the fill color of the tool.

Introducing Flash 8 – 11

The Options section contains modifier buttons for the tools. Modifiers for the Brush tool include:

Brush Mode changes what is painted.

Brush Size changes size of the brush stroke.

Brush Shape changes the shape of the brush stroke.

8.9 Creating a Flash Movie

The process of creating a Flash movie includes:

- Setting Flash document properties.
- Creating images.
- Using the Timeline to lay out the sequence of the images.
- Previewing the animation.
- Exporting the document.

setting Flash document properties

A new Flash document is created by selecting File → New. The Property inspector displays the properties for the current Flash document:

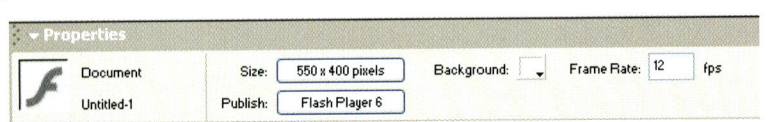

resizing the Stage

- Size is the Stage size in pixels. The size of the Stage is representative of the size of the movie. Clicking the button next to Size displays a dialog box where the Stage size can be specified. Clicking Contents in the dialog box resizes the Stage to just accommodate the objects on the Stage.

The Ruler Scale

The ruler scale is changed to inches or centimeters by using Modify → Document.

- Background is the color of the Stage, which will be the background color of the movie. A new color can be selected by clicking the box and choosing a color.
- Frame Rate is the number of animation frames to be displayed every second. The default frame rate is 12 frames per second (fps). A new frame rate can be typed.

creating images

Images are created using the Tools panel. Rulers and a grid can be displayed to help with the precise placement of objects. Selecting View → Rulers display rulers along the top and left side of the work area. Rulers are scaled in pixels by default. Selecting View → Grid → Show Grid displays a set of gridlines on the Stage.

using the Timeline

The Timeline is used to lay out the sequence of images. The Timeline below is for a movie with 20 frames:

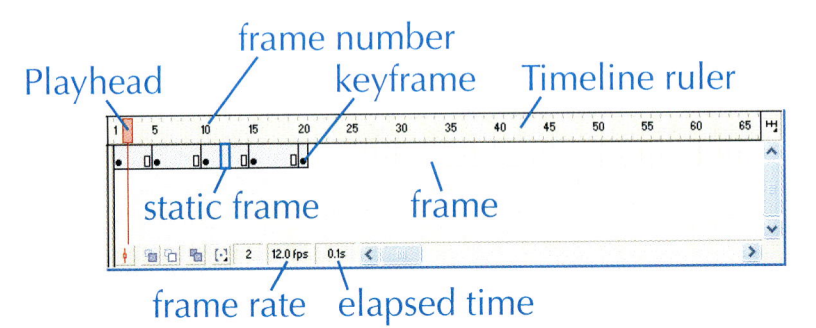

8–12   *A Guide to Web Development Using Macromedia Dreamweaver MX*

- The **Playhead** can be dragged to a specific frame to display the image for that frame on the Stage. When previewing an animation, the Playhead automatically moves through the Timeline.
- A **keyframe** is a frame that contains an image different from the image in the previous frame.
- A **frame** contains an image.
- A **static frame** contains the same image as the previous frame.
- The **elapsed time** is the total length of the animation. When the animation is previewed, the elapsed time starts at 0 and increments to the total time, indicating how many seconds have elapsed.
- **Frame rate** displays how many frames per second will be displayed when the animation is played.

> **Movie Length**
>
> The length of a movie can be calculated by multiplying the number of frames by the frame rate. For example, a movie with 24 frames at a rate of 12 fps will run for 2 seconds.

previewing and rewinding

An animation should be previewed to test it. An animation is previewed by selecting Control → Play. Previewing shows if an animation is moving too slowly or too quickly and demonstrates the smoothness of transition from one keyframe image to another. The Playhead is moved back to frame 1 by selecting Control → Rewind.

exporting

An animation ready for use in a Web site must be exported. Exporting is discussed in Section 8.11.

8.10 Frame-by-Frame Animation

Frame-by-frame animation is a movie created from a set of specified images. In a new Flash document, the first frame in the Timeline is a blank keyframe. Creating an image on the Stage makes it the first keyframe:

> **Printing in Flash**
>
> Selecting File → Print Preview displays the current frame as it will appear on a printed page. A frame is printed by selecting File → Print, which displays the Print dialog box. Selecting Print in the dialog box prints the frame using the default options.

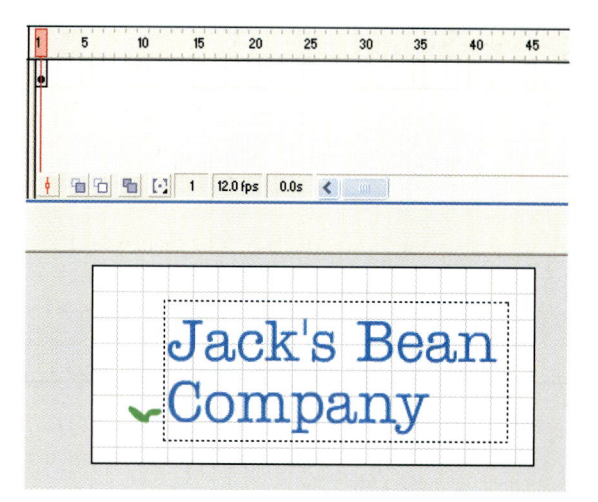

The image for the first frame can be created by drawing an image with tools in the Tools panel. The frame image above was created with the Text and Pencil tools.

adding a keyframe

Clicking a new frame on the Timeline and selecting Insert → Keyframe adds the image from the previous keyframe in the new keyframe and creates static frames in between the two keyframes:

Introducing Flash   **8 – 13**

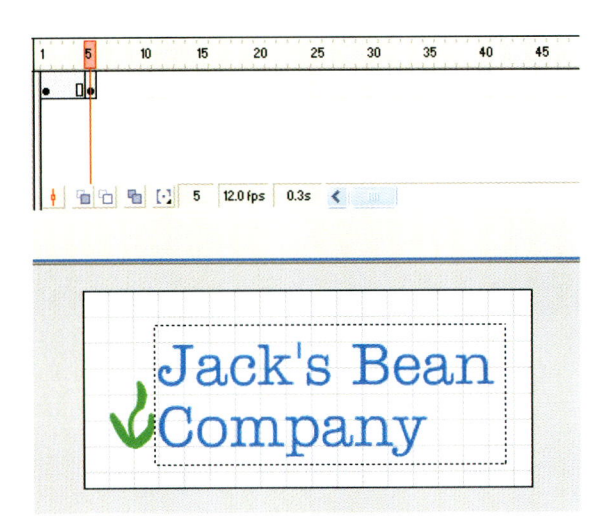

Larger leaves and stem were added to the next keyframe

The image in the new keyframe can then be modified to progress the animation. The gray static frames are needed to control the rate of animation. If there are no static frames, the animation may play too quickly for the viewer to comprehend.

The process of inserting keyframes and modifying the image is repeated until the final frame of the animation:

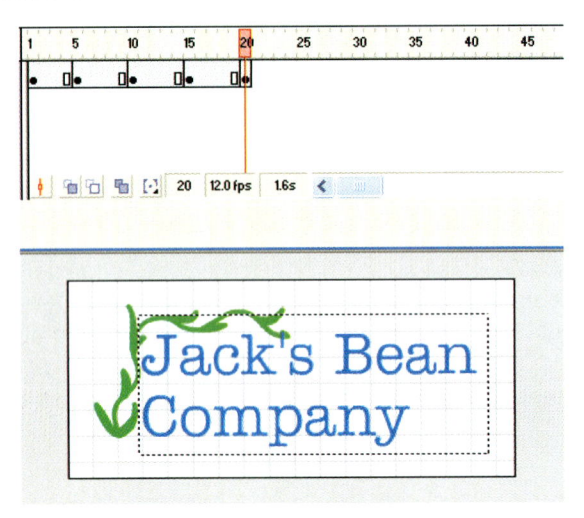

Final keyframe of the animation

8.11 Editing Techniques

removing frames An animation that is moving too slowly should have static frames removed. The same number of static frames should be removed between each keyframe to keep the animation smooth. A static frame is removed by right-clicking the static frame and selecting **Remove Frames** from the menu. If the animation is too fast, frames can be added by right-clicking a frame and selecting **Insert Frame** from the menu.

adding frames

onion skinning To help position and edit images, two or more frames can be displayed at the same time using a technique called *onion skinning*. The Onion Skin button ( ) at the bottom of the Timeline is clicked to display Onion Skin markers. Dragging the right marker in the Timeline ruler displays keyframe images between the markers:

8 – 14   *A Guide to Web Development Using Macromedia Dreamweaver MX*

> **Importing Images**
>
> Artwork created in other applications can be imported and used in Flash. Supported file formats include JPG, GIF, PNG, BMP, EMF, EPS, AI, PIC, and WMF. Selecting File → Import displays a dialog box where a file is selected. Imported images used more than once in an animation should be converted to a symbol. Symbols are discussed in Section 8.14.

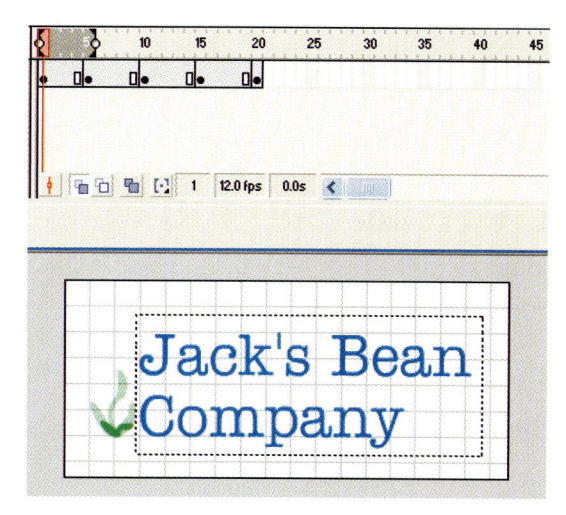

The current keyframe is darker than the other keyframes

Images that are dimmed cannot be edited, but the Playhead can be dragged to change the current keyframe for editing.

the Transform panel

Common ways to modify an image include scaling, rotating, and skewing objects. Selecting an object and then selecting Window → Transform displays the Transform panel:

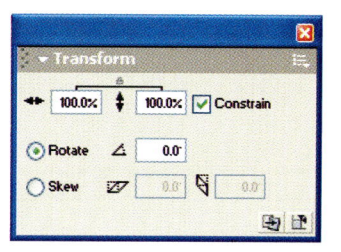

> **The Arrow Tool**
>
> The Arrow tool ( ) is used to select objects. Clicking and double-clicking select the stroke and fill that make up a shape. Multiple shapes can be selected by holding down the Shift key while selecting.

The width and height can be adjusted by typing or selecting a percentage value in the Width (↔) and Height (↕) boxes. The object can be rotated by clicking Rotate and typing a rotation angle. Clicking Skew and typing an angle in the Skew Horizontal and Skew Vertical boxes slants the object.

Practice 4

In this practice you will start Flash MX and open a frame-by-frame animation.

① START FLASH MX

  a. Select Start → All Programs → Macromedia → Macromedia Flash MX. Flash is started. Note the Stage, Tools panel, workspace, Timeline, and Property inspector.

② OPEN A FLASH DOCUMENT

  a. Select File → Open. A dialog box is displayed.
   1. Use the Look in list to navigate to the folder containing data files for this text.
   2. Select the PURPLE_BALL.fla file.
   3. Select Open. The Flash document is opened and the first frame is displayed on the Stage.

Introducing Flash   8 – 15

③ PLAY THE FRAME-BY-FRAME ANIMATION

   a. Select Control → Play. The animation plays. Note that the animation is not complete.
   b. In the Timeline, drag the Playhead back to frame 1. The Playhead is now over frame 1. The image for the first keyframe is displayed.

④ USE ONION SKINNING TO VIEW THE FRAMES

   a. At the bottom of the Timeline, click the Onion Skin button ( ). Onion Skin markers are displayed on the Timeline ruler.
   b. Drag the right Onion Skin marker to the last keyframe (frame 15) to display all of the keyframes. The images are dimmed except the image from the selected frame:

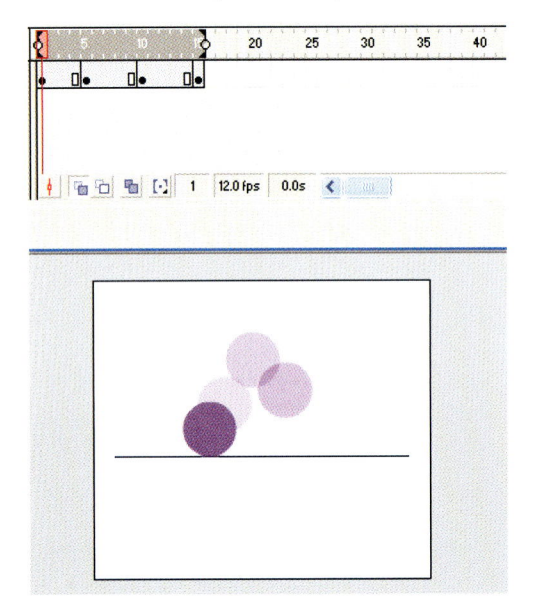

   c. Drag the Playhead to the last keyframe. The image in the last frame is in full color and editable.

⑤ ADD A KEYFRAME

   a. In the Timeline, click frame 20, below the Timeline ruler.
   b. Select Insert → Keyframe. A keyframe is added to the animation and the image from the last keyframe is displayed on the Stage. Note the Onion Skin has advanced to the last frame:

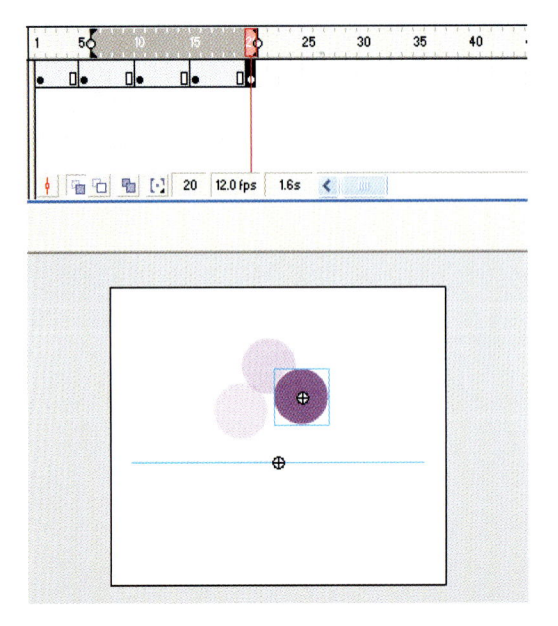

c. Click anywhere in the workspace to remove the selection from the ball and surface object.

d. Drag the ball object so that it is just on the surface and slightly to the right:

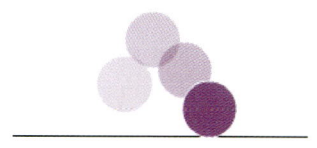

e. Select File → Save. The modified PURPLE_BALL.fla is saved.

⑥ PLAY THE ANIMATION

a. Deselect the Onion Skin button. The Onion Skin images are no longer displayed.

b. Select Control → Play. The animation plays. The ball bounces from one spot to another.

⑦ MODIFY THE ANIMATION

a. In the Timeline, click frame 2, the static frame after the first keyframe, to select it.

b. Select Insert → Remove Frames. A frame is removed.

c. Remove one static frame after each of the other keyframes, so that your Timeline looks similar to:

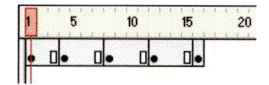

d. Save the modified PURPLE_BALL.fla.

e. Select Control → Rewind. The Playhead moves back to frame 1.

f. Select Control → Play. The animation is faster.

8.12 Exporting a Flash Document

To use a Flash document in Dreamweaver, it must be exported in the SWF format, which can be played with the Flash Player plug-in. A Flash document is exported as a movie by selecting File → Export Movie, which displays the Export Movie dialog box:

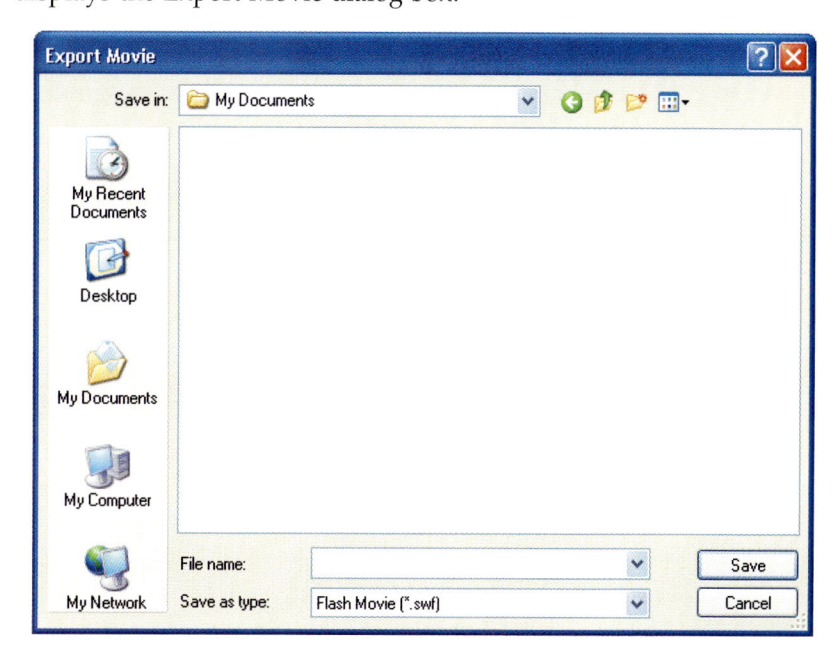

Introducing Flash

The Save in list and the contents box below it are used to navigate to the location where the file is to be saved. A Flash movie exported for use in a Web site should be saved in the site's media folder. A descriptive file name for the movie is typed in the File name box, and the Save as type should be Flash Movie. Selecting Save exports the movie and displays the Export Flash Player dialog box:

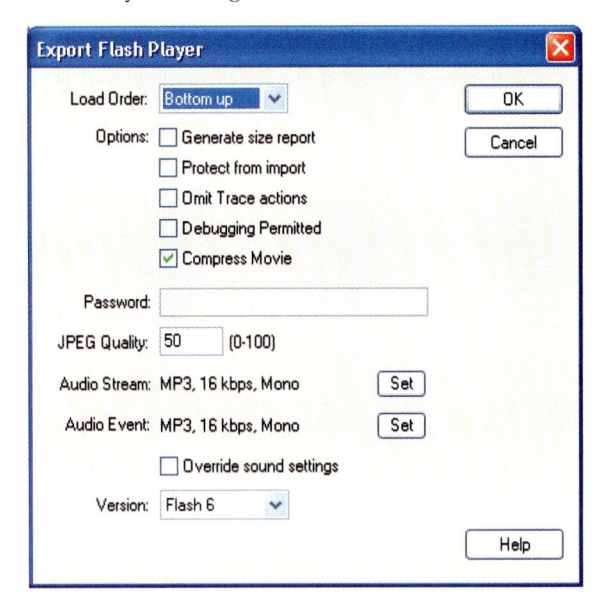

Creating a Media Folder

If a Web site does not have a media folder when the Flash document is exported, the Create New Folder button ( ) in the Export Movie dialog box can be used to create the media folder in the Web site root folder.

Selecting OK completes the export process.

8.13 Organizing and Using Flash Movie Files in Dreamweaver

the media folder

For better organization, Flash movies created in Flash MX for a Web site should be stored together in a media folder that is created in the Web site root folder.

the Assets panel

In Dreamweaver, Flash movie files are displayed in the Assets panel. A selected movie in the Assets panel is displayed in the preview area. The ▶ button in the preview is clicked to play the Flash movie. When running, the ■ button is displayed. Clicking this button ends the preview movie. Selecting → Refresh Site List in the Files panel group may be necessary to update the list of movies in the Assets panel.

inserting a Flash movie

A Flash movie is placed in an open Web page document by dragging it from the Assets panel into the Document window or by clicking Insert at the bottom of the Assets panel to place the movie at the insertion point. When a movie created in Flash is added to a Web page document, a placeholder is displayed:

A Flash placeholder varies in size depending on the movie size

Clicking the Flash placeholder displays the Flash movie properties in the Property inspector:

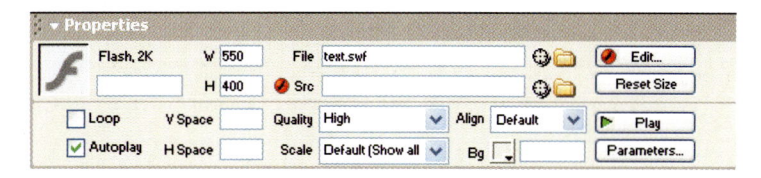

previewing and editing a Flash movie

To have the Flash movie play only once when the Web page document is loaded in a browser, **Loop** must be cleared if it is selected. A Flash movie can be previewed in a browser or in Design view by selecting the placeholder and then clicking **Play** in the Property inspector. Clicking **Stop** in the Property inspector ends the preview. Clicking **Edit** displays a dialog box where the FLA file corresponding to the movie can be opened for editing in Flash.

Practice 5

In this practice you will export a Flash document and insert it into a Web page document. Flash should be started and the PURPLE_BALL.fla document displayed.

① CREATE A MOVIE

a. Select File → Export Movie. A dialog box is displayed.

1. Use the **Look in** list to navigate to the SAMPLER Web site folder. Note that there is no media folder.
2. At the top of the dialog box, click the Create New Folder button ( ). A folder is added to the Web site folder.
3. Replace the existing folder name with: media
4. Open the media folder.
5. In the **File name** box, type: bouncing_ball
6. Select **Save**. A dialog box is displayed.
   a) Select **OK**. The default options are applied and the purple ball animation is exported as an SWF file to the SAMPLER Web site.

② INSERT A FLASH MOVIE IN DREAMWEAVER

a. Start Dreamweaver. Open SAMPLER for editing if it is not the working Web site.
b. Open the animation.htm Web page document.
c. In the Assets panel, click the Flash icon ( ). If bouncing_ball.swf is not listed, select → Refresh Site List from the Files panel group.
d. Drag the bouncing_ball.swf file from the Assets panel to the empty cell next to the text that reads "This example is frame-by-frame animation:" A Flash placeholder is displayed:

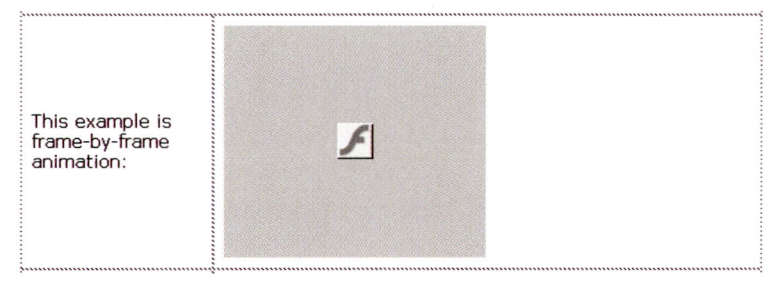

e. Save the modified animation.htm.

Introducing Flash

③ PREVIEW THE FLASH MOVIE

a. Press F12. The Web page document is displayed in a browser. The bouncing ball animation plays continuously.
b. Switch back to Dreamweaver.
c. Click the Flash movie placeholder to select it, if it is not already selected.
d. In the Property inspector, clear the Loop check box.
e. Save the modified animation.htm and then press F12. The movie plays just once in the browser when the page loads.
f. Close the browser window. Dreamweaver is displayed.

8.14 Shape Tweening

tweened animation

morphing

A *tweened animation* is created by starting with one shape in a keyframe and a different shape in a later keyframe. Flash can then generate the shapes in the frames between the first keyframe and the last. One form of tweened animation is *shape tweening*, which is similar to morphing an image. *Morphing* is a technique that turns one shape into another. For example, a square can be turned into a circle:

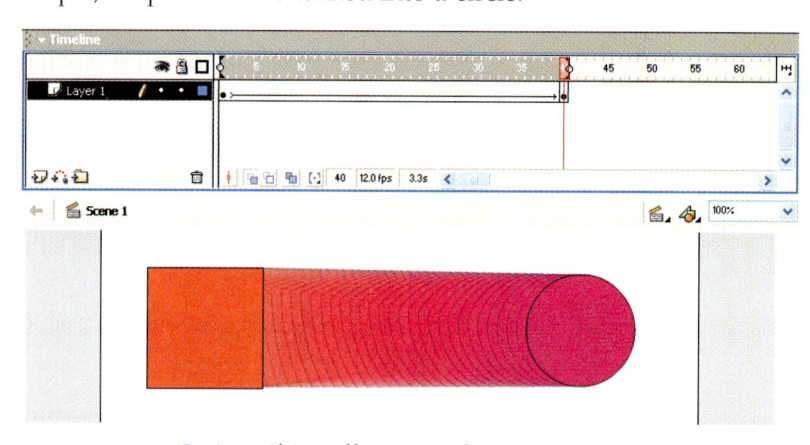

Onion Skins illustrate shape tweening

Shape tweening can only be applied to images composed of simple lines and fills. An image is drawn in the first keyframe and then a second keyframe created and another image drawn. Next, selecting a frame between the keyframes and setting the Tween property to Shape in the Property inspector tweens the keyframes. Shape tweening is indicated by green shading and an arrow in the Timeline:

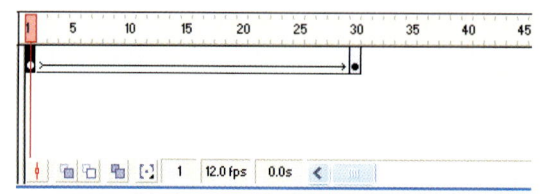

Break Apart

A selected object can be broken down to simple lines and fills by selecting Modify → Break Apart. This command must be applied twice to selected text.

The steps for creating a shape tweened animation include:

1. Create an image in the first keyframe.
2. Create an end keyframe, deleting the image from the first keyframe, and drawing a second image.
3. Select a frame between the keyframes.
4. Set Tween to Shape in the Property inspector.
5. Preview the animation.
6. Export the document.

Practice 6

In this practice you will create a shape tweened animation. Start Flash if it is not already running.

① CREATE A NEW FLASH DOCUMENT

a. In Flash, close any open documents, saving if necessary.
b. Select File → New. A new document with a blank Stage is displayed.

② CREATE KEYFRAMES

a. Scroll so that the upper-left corner of the Stage is visible.
b. In the Tools panel, in the Colors section, select a black Fill color.
c. In the Tools panel, in the Colors section, select a transparent Stroke color ( ).
d. In the Tools panel, click the Rectangle Tool ( ).
e. Near the top-left corner of the Stage draw a rectangle.
f. In the Timeline, click frame 10 to select it.
g. Select Insert → Keyframe. A keyframe is added to the animation with the rectangle image.
h. Press the Delete key to remove the selected rectangle from the Stage.
i. In the Tools panel, select a pink Fill color.
j. In the Tools panel, click the Oval Tool ( ).
k. To the right and level with the rectangle, draw an oval. Use Onion Skin markers to help with placement.
l. In the Timeline, click frame 5.
m. In the Property inspector, set Tween to Shape. An arrow is displayed between the starting and ending frames on the Timeline and the shape in frame 5 is displayed.

③ PLAY THE ANIMATION

a. Save the document in a folder that is outside of any Web site folder, naming it: morph_demo.fla
b. Rewind and then play the animation.

④ CREATE A MOVIE

a. Select the Arrow tool ( ).
b. Click anywhere in the workspace. Document properties are displayed in the Property inspector.

c. In the Property inspector, click the button next to the Size option. A dialog box is displayed.
    1. Click Contents. The dimensions of the Stage are recalculated based on the amount of space needed by the animation.
    2. Select OK. The Stage is resized.
d. Save the modified morph_demo.
e. Select File → Export Movie. A dialog box is displayed.
    1. Navigate to the media folder in the SAMPLER Web site folder.
    2. In the File name box, type: morphing
    3. Select Save. A dialog box is displayed.
        a) Select OK. The default options are applied and the shape tweened animation is exported as an SWF file to the SAMPLER Web site.
f. Close morph_demo.

⑤ INSERT A FLASH MOVIE IN DREAMWEAVER

a. Switch to Dreamweaver.
b. Open the SAMPLER Web site for editing if it is not the working Web site.
c. Open the animation.htm Web page document if it is not already displayed.
d. Scroll the animation.htm Web page document to display the empty cell next to the text that reads "This example is shape tweened animation:"
e. In the Assets panel, display the Flash category. If morphing.swf is not listed, select 📋 → Refresh Site List from the Files panel group.
f. Drag the morphing.swf file from the Assets panel to the empty cell to the right of the text that reads "This example is shape tweened animation:" A Flash placeholder is displayed.
g. Save the modified animation.htm.

⑥ PREVIEW THE FLASH MOVIE

a. Press F12. The Web page document is displayed in a browser and the morphing animation plays continuously, while the frame-by-frame animation plays just once.
b. Switch back to Dreamweaver.

8.15 Creating Symbols to Optimize a Flash Movie

optimization techniques

A Flash movie file should be as small a file size as possible to keep Web page load times as short as possible. Techniques for optimizing an animation for size include using symbols for images that appear more than once, using tweened animation, and using layers for objects that do not change from frame to frame. Layers are discussed in Section 8.17.

instance

Symbols are stored in a Flash Library and used to create instances on the Stage. An *instance* is a reference to a symbol, rather than a copy of an image. Any image that is used more than once in a movie file should be converted to symbol. This allows the movie file size to be much smaller.

A symbol can be created from a single object or multiple objects selected together. The Arrow tool is used to select the objects for the symbol. Dragging to marquee select the object is one way to be sure the entire object is selected:

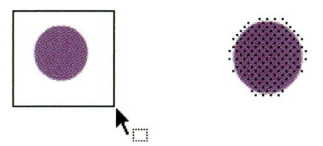

Dragging the Arrow tool selects the objects enclosed by the box (the marquee). On right, the object is selected.

Selecting Insert → Convert to Symbol displays a dialog box where a descriptive name is typed for the symbol and **Graphic** selected to create a graphic symbol:

Selecting **OK** converts the selected objects on the Stage to an instance of the symbol. An instance displays a registration mark (⊕) in the center:

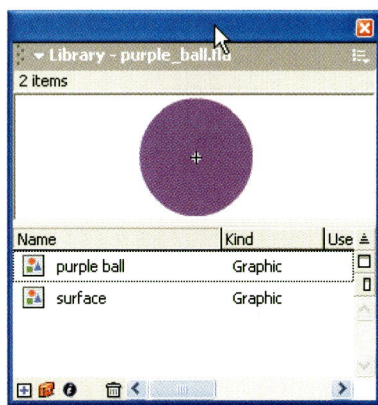

the Flash Library   The Flash Library window is displayed by selecting Window → Library:

adding an instance to the Stage   Dragging the symbol name in the Library window to the Stage creates an instance of the symbol.

Introducing Flash   **8 – 23**

8.16 Motion Tweening

In *motion tweening*, a single symbol is tweened to move from a start location to an end location:

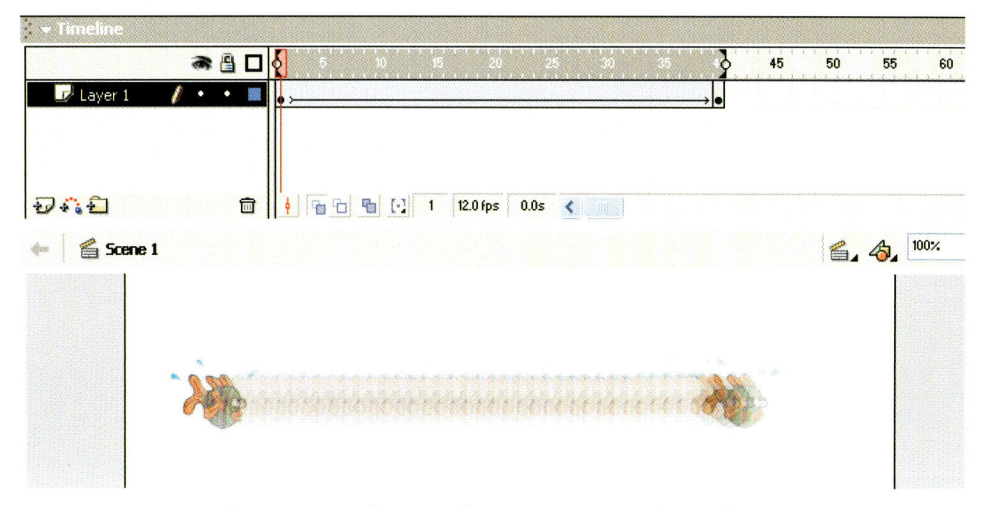

The Onion Skin markers are set to show the keyframes generated by Flash in motion tweening

Motion tweening can only be applied to symbols. The symbol is placed in the start location in the first keyframe and then a second keyframe is created with the symbol in the end position. Next, selecting a frame between the keyframes and setting the **Tween** property to Motion in the Property inspector tweens the keyframes. Motion tweening is indicated by lavender shading and an arrow in the Timeline:

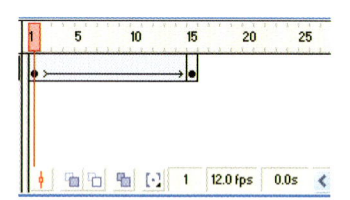

The steps for creating a motion tweened animation include:

1. Create an image.
2. Convert the image to a graphic symbol.
3. Create a start keyframe with an instance at the starting position.
4. Create an end keyframe with an instance at the ending position.
5. Select a frame between the keyframes.
6. Set Tween to Motion in the Property inspector.
7. Preview the animation.
8. Export the document.

modifying the motion path Motion tweening uses the shortest, most direct path from the start position to the end position. This path can be customized by clicking a frame and then dragging the instance in that frame to a new position. For example, in the animation below, frame 20 was clicked and the instance was dragged up to change the straight-line path:

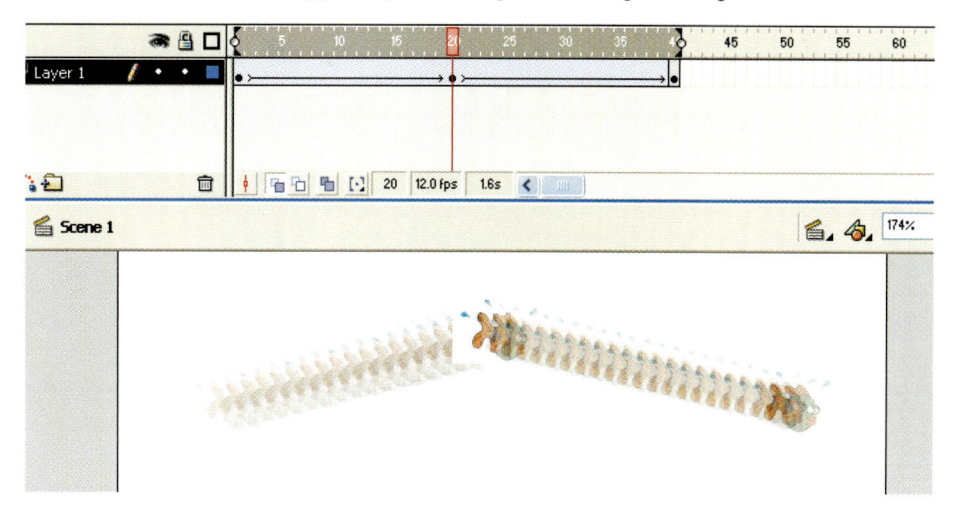

Onion Skins show the change in the motion path. The Timeline includes a new keyframe.

Flash makes each frame that changes the path a keyframe and recalculates the motion path.

Practice 7

In this practice you will create a motion-tweened animation. Start Flash if it is not already running.

① CREATE A NEW FLASH DOCUMENT

a. In Flash, close any open documents, saving if necessary.
b. Select File → New. A new document with a blank Stage is displayed.

② CREATE AN IMAGE

a. Scroll so that the upper-left corner of the Stage is visible.
b. Select View → Rulers to display rulers, if they are not already displayed.
c. In the Tools panel, in the Colors section, change the Stroke color and Fill color to a bright yellow:

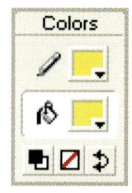

d. In the Tools panel, click the Oval tool (O).
e. Hold down the Shift key and drag on the Stage to create a small circle about 50 pixels in diameter.
f. In the Tools panel, change the Stroke and Fill colors to black.
g. In the Tools panel, click the Brush tool ( ).

Introducing Flash

h. In the Tools panel, in the Options section, set options to:

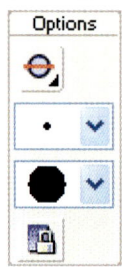

i. Draw eyes and a smile onto the yellow circle to create a smiley face:

Note: Select **Edit** → **Undo** as necessary. Change the brush size if needed.

j. Save the document in a folder that is outside of any Web site folder, naming it: smiley.fla

③ CREATE A SYMBOL

a. In the Tools panel, select the Arrow tool ( ) and then marquee select the smiley face:

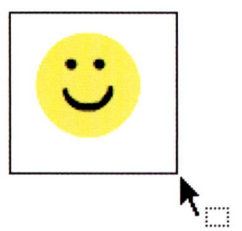

b. Select **Insert** → **Convert to Symbol**. A dialog box is displayed:
   1. In the **Name** box, type: smiley_face
   2. Select **Graphic**.
   3. Select **OK**. The selected image is converted to a symbol and replaced by an instance of the symbol.

c. Select **Window** → **Library**. The Library window is displayed. Note the smiley_face symbol name. Click the smiley_face name to see a preview in the Library window. Drag the Library panel away from the Stage and workspace. Close if needed.

④ CREATE KEYFRAMES

a. In the Timeline, note that the first frame is already a keyframe. Drag the smiley_face instance on the Stage, leaving some room above the image:

b. In the Timeline, click frame 40 to select it.

c. Select **Insert** → **Keyframe**. A keyframe is added to the animation with a smiley_face instance.

d. Drag the smiley_face instance directly across to the right side of the Stage.

e. Save the modified smiley.fla.

⑤ APPLY MOTION TWEENING

a. In the Timeline, click frame 12.

b. In the Property inspector, set Tween to Motion. An arrow is displayed between the starting and ending frames on the Timeline.

c. Save the modified smiley.

d. Select Control → Rewind and then select Control → Play. The smiley face moves horizontally.

⑥ MODIFY THE PATH

a. In the Timeline, click the Onion Skin button ( ). Onion Skin markers are displayed on the Timeline ruler.

b. Drag the Onion Skin markers to display the entire animation. Note the straight path.

c. Deselect the Onion Skin button. The Onion Skins are no longer displayed.

d. Click frame 20. Drag the smiley face up near the top of the Stage. The frame is automatically converted to a keyframe and a symbol is displayed.

e. Display Onion Skins and move the markers as necessary to see the complete motion path. The path is no longer a straight line.

f. Save the modified smiley.fla.

g. Select Control → Rewind and then select Control → Play. The smiley face moves across the stage along the new motion path.

⑦ CREATE A MOVIE

a. Click anywhere in the workspace. Document properties are displayed in the Property inspector.

b. Click the button for the Size option. A dialog box is displayed. Change the dimensions for the Stage by clicking Contents and then selecting OK.

c. Save the modified smiley.

d. Select File → Export Movie. A dialog box is displayed.

    1. Navigate to the media folder in the SAMPLER Web site folder.

    2. In the File name box, type: smiley.swf

    3. Select Save. A dialog box is displayed.

        a) Select OK. The default options are applied and the smiley face animation is exported as an SWF file to the SAMPLER Web site.

⑧ INSERT A FLASH MOVIE IN DREAMWEAVER

a. Switch to Dreamweaver.

b. Open the SAMPLER Web site for editing if it is not the working Web site.

c. Display the animation.htm Web page document.

d. Scroll the animation.htm Web page document to display the empty cell next to the text that reads "This example is motion tweened animation:"

e. In the Assets panel, display the Flash category and refresh the list.

f. Drag the smiley.swf file from the Assets panel to the empty cell to the right of the text that reads "This example is motion tweened animation:" A Flash placeholder is displayed.

g. Save the modified animation.htm.

⑨ PREVIEW THE FLASH MOVIE

a. Press F12. The Web page document is displayed in a browser with the smiley face animation.

b. Switch back to Dreamweaver.

Introducing Flash

8.17 Using Layers

Flash documents of any complexity should be divided into layers. *Layers* can be thought of as images drawn on transparent sheets of paper placed one on top of the other. By working in layers, the image on one layer can be modified without changing the image on a different layer.

tweening on layers

The same is true for animation. An image on one layer can be tweened without affecting the other layers. This allows multiple objects to be motion tweened and for both motion and shape tweening in one document. The document below is divided into layers:

Onion Skins show shape tweening with a caterpillar morphing to a butterfly, and motion tweening with a word moving from top to bottom.

creating a new layer

A layer is added to a document by selecting Insert → Layer. Layer names appear in the Layers list:

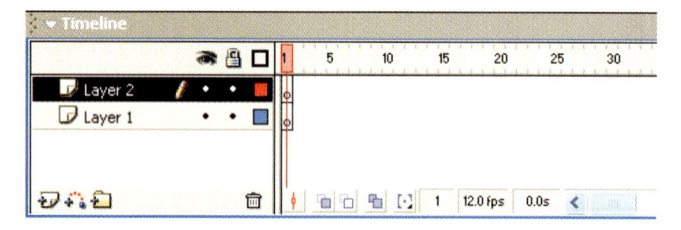

The Layers list is to the left of the Timeline

naming layer

By default, layers are named Layer 1, Layer 2, and so on. The layer names can be changed to a more descriptive name by double-clicking the layer name in the list and typing a new name.

layer order

The layers in the Layer list are ordered top to bottom, with the top layer being layer 1. Images on layer 1 appear on top of any images in the layers below. The order of the layers is changed by dragging a layer to a different location in the list:

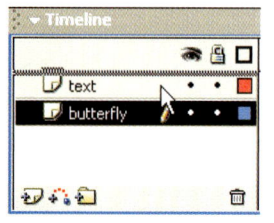

Dragging a layer displays a heavy line in its new location

hiding a layer Working on a layer may require hiding another layer from the Stage. A layer is hidden by clicking to the right of the layer name in the Eye column (👁), which displays an ✗ in the column. In the list below, the text layer is hidden but not the butterfly layer:

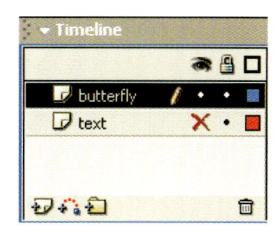

A layer is displayed again by clicking the ✗ in the Eye column in the Layer list.

locking a layer A layer can be locked by clicking to the right of the layer name in the Lock/Unlock All column (🔒). Locking a layer prevents it from being edited.

deleting a layer A layer is deleted by clicking the Layer name in the Layer list and then clicking the Delete Layer button (🗑) below the list.

8.18 Animating Text

Text can be broken apart into separate letters and then placed onto layers so that a word or phrase can be motion tweened. For example, each letter in a word can move onto the Stage from a different direction or the letters of a word could "dance" on Stage.

creating a text block In Flash, a text block is created with the Text tool (**A**) in the Tools panel. Clicking the Text tool and then clicking the Stage and typing a word or phrase creates a text block:

The Property inspector can be used to change font, size, and color properties for a selected text block.

breaking apart a text block The next step in animating text is selecting the text block and then selecting Modify ➔ Break Apart to break the text into separate letter objects:

Introducing Flash   8 – 29

distributing to layers

To allow motion tweening for smooth animation of the text, the letters must be distributed to layers. Selecting Modify → Distribute to Layers automatically distributes each letter to an individual layer and names the layer:

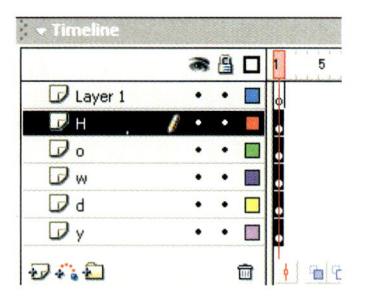

At this point, Layer 1 can be deleted because the entire word is no longer needed. Adding a second keyframe creates the end keyframe. In the first keyframe, position each letter to starting position. Finally, motion tweening is applied to each layer. Below is the animated "Howdy" with the Playhead on the first keyframe:

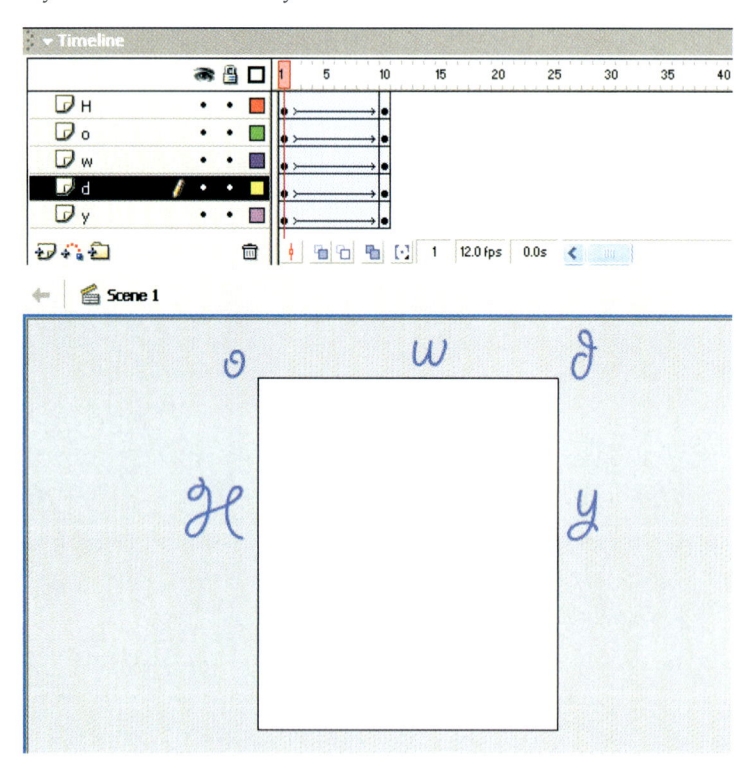

The steps for creating animated text include:

1. Create a text block.
2. Break apart the text block into separate layers.
3. Distribute the letters objects to layers.
4. Delete layer 1.
5. Insert the last keyframe for each letter layer.
6. In the first keyframe, position the letters to a start position.
8. Set Tween to Motion in the Property inspector for each layer.
9. Preview the animation.
10. Export the document.

Practice 8

In this practice you will animate text. Start Flash if it is not already running.

① CREATE A NEW FLASH DOCUMENT

a. In Flash, close any open documents, saving if necessary.
b. Select File → New. A new document with a blank Stage is displayed.

② CREATE A TEXT ANIMATION

a. In the Tools panel, click the Text tool (**A**).
b. Click the Stage to create a text block.
c. In the Property inspector, select an appropriate Font, a Font Size of 72, and a dark Text Fill color.
d. Type: Hola!
e. In the Tools panel, select the Arrow tool and then drag the text block to the center of the Stage.
f. Select Modify → Break Apart. Letters are selected as separate objects.
g. Select Modify → Distribute to Layers. A named layer is created for each letter in the word Hola!
h. In the Layer list, click Layer 1 to select it.
i. At the bottom of the Layer list, click the Delete Layer button (🗑). Layer 1 is deleted.
j. In layer H, click frame 20 and select Insert → Keyframe. A keyframe is added.
k. Add a keyframe at frame 20 for each of the remaining layers.
l. In the Timeline, drag the Playhead back to the first frame.
m. Drag each of the letters to a starting position off the Stage, similar to the letters for "Howdy" on the previous page.
n. In the H layer, click a frame between the keyframes and then set Tween to Motion in the Property inspector.
o. Motion tween the remaining layers.

③ SAVE THE FLASH DOCUMENT

Save the document in a folder that is outside of any Web site folder, naming it: hola.fla

④ REWIND AND THEN PLAY THE ANIMATION

Introducing Flash

8.19 Importing Sound Files

Sound can be added to a Flash movie by importing a sound file and then adding the file to a layer. Supported sound file formats include WAV and MP3. Other file formats are available if QuickTime 4 or DirectX 7 is installed on your computer.

importing a sound file

Sound files are imported to the document's Library to allow the sound file to be used repeatedly without increasing the Flash movie file size. A sound file is imported by selecting File → Import to Library, which displays the Import to Library dialog box:

> **QuickTime Player**
>
> The QuickTime Player can be downloaded for free at www.apple.com.

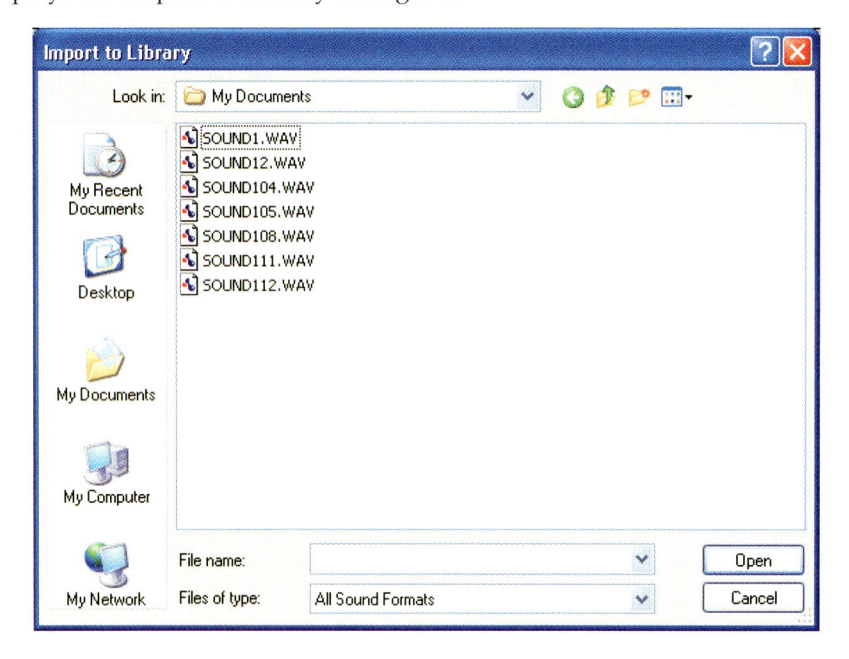

In the Files of type list, All Sound Formats should be selected and then the Look in list and the contents box below used to navigate to the file. Selecting the file name and then Open imports the file to the Library.

adding a sound layer

Sound files need to be on a separate layer in an animation. After adding a layer, it should be descriptively named, for example, classical music clip. Next, the start keyframe for the movie is selected and then the sound file dragged from the Library to the Stage. Finally, the end keyframe for the movie is created. A sound wave is displayed in the Timeline between the keyframes:

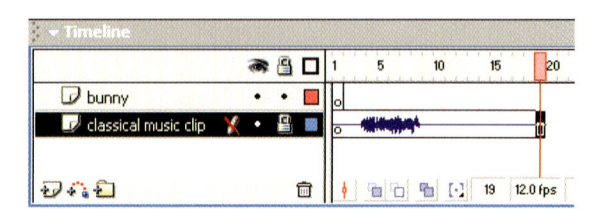

The steps for adding sound to an animation include:

1. Import the sound file to the Library.
2. Create a descriptively named layer.
3. Create the start keyframe in the sound layer.
4. Display the Library and drag the sound file to the Stage.
5. Create an end keyframe.
6. Preview the animation.
7. Export the document.

When the frames that contain sound are selected, the Property inspector displays their properties:

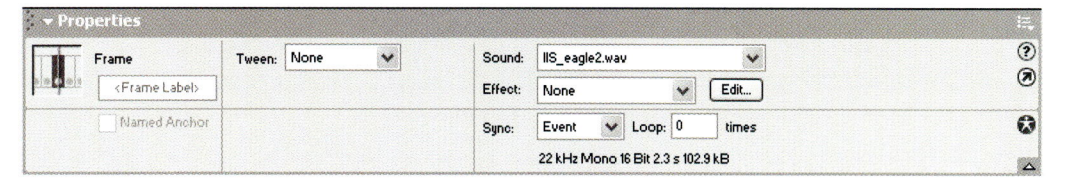

- Effect is the sound effect such as Fade In or Fade Out to increase and decrease the amplitude of the sound, respectively. A new effect can be selected from the list.
- Loop is the number of times the sound file will play. A new value can be typed.

Practice 9

In this practice you will add sound to an animation. Start Flash and open hola.fla if it is not already displayed. This practice assumes you have speakers or head phones and a sound card in your computer.

① ADD SOUND TO THE HOLA ANIMATION

a. Select File → Import to Library. A dialog box is displayed.
   1. Use the Look in list to navigate to the folder containing data files for this text.
   2. In the File of type list, select All Sound Formats.
   3. Select the HOLA.wav file.
   4. Select OK.
b. Select Window → Library. The Library window is displayed with the sound file.
c. Select the H layer and then select Insert → Layer. A new layer is added above layer H.
d. In the Layers list, double-click the new layer and rename it: greeting
e. In the Timeline, click the first frame in the music layer, which is an blank keyframe.
f. From the Library, drag the HOLA.wav file onto the Stage. A sound wave is displayed.
g. In the music layer, click frame 20 and select Insert → Keyframe. A keyframe is added.
h. Save the modified hola.

② PLAY THE ANIMATION

Introducing Flash   8 – 33

③ **CREATE A MOVIE**

a. Click anywhere in the workspace. Document properties are displayed in the Property inspector.
b. Click the button for the Size option. A dialog box is displayed. Change the dimensions for the Stage by clicking Contents and then selecting OK.
c. Save the modified hola.
d. Export the movie to the media folder in the SAMPLER Web site folder, naming it: hola.swf
e. Close hola.

④ **INSERT THE FLASH MOVIE IN DREAMWEAVER**

a. Switch to Dreamweaver.
b. Open the SAMPLER Web site for editing if it is not the working Web site.
c. In the Site panel, open the video_and_sound.htm Web page document.
d. In the Assets panel, display the Flash category and refresh the list.
e. Drag the hola.swf file from the Assets panel to the empty cell to the right of the text that reads "This example includes sound:"
f. In the Property inspector, deselect Loop. The sound file will play just once when the Web page is loaded.
g. Save the modified video_and_sound.htm.

⑤ **PREVIEW THE FLASH MOVIE**

a. Press F12. The Web page document is displayed in a browser with the hola animation. If you have speakers, you will also hear the sound as the movie plays.
b. Switch back to Dreamweaver.

8.20 Importing Video

Video can be imported to Flash and then exported as a Flash movie. Supported video file formats include AVI, DV, MPG, MPEG, and MOV, and depend on if QuickTime 4 or DirectX 7 is installed on your computer.

importing a video file   A new Flash document must be created to import a video. After creating a new document, selecting File → Import displays the Import Video Settings dialog box:

Video Compression

Flash imports and exports video using the Sorenson Spark codec, which is a compression/decompression algorithm.

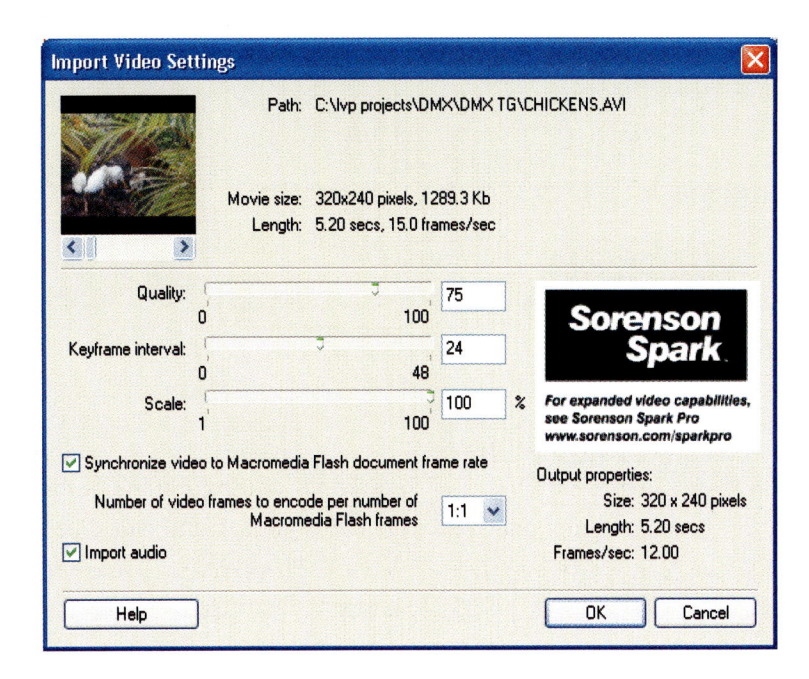

Options such as movie quality, size the movie should be scaled to, and whether the video audio should be included can be specified in this dialog box. Note that the dialog box displays the length of the movie in seconds. Selecting OK imports the video. If the Timeline does not contain enough frames to display the video, a dialog box will be displayed:

testing a video movie Selecting Yes inserts the required frames in the Timeline. Selecting Control → Test Movie plays the video and the accompanying audio in Flash.

To use a video in Dreamweaver, it must be exported in the SWF format, which can be played with the Flash Player plug-in. A video exported to the SWF format is considerably smaller than the native file format of the video. A movie is exported by selecting File → Export Movie.

The steps for creating a Flash movie from video include:

1. Import the video file to a new Flash document.
2. Save the Flash document.
3. Preview the movie.
4. Export the document.

Practice 10

In this practice you will create a Flash movie from a video file. Start Flash if it is not already displayed.

① CREATE A NEW FLASH DOCUMENT

a. Close any open Flash documents, saving if necessary.
b. Select File → New. A new document with a blank Stage is displayed.

② CREATE A MOVIE FROM VIDEO

a. Select File → Import. A dialog box is displayed.
   1. Use the Look in list to navigate to the folder containing data files for this text.
   2. In the File of type list, select All Video Formats.
   3. Select the CHICKENS.avi file.
   4. Select Open. A dialog box is displayed.
      a) Set Quality to 75.
      b) Select OK. The video is imported.
   5. A dialog box is displayed with video frame requirements. Select Yes. The first frame of the video is displayed.

③ TEST THE MOVIE

a. Save the document in a folder that is outside of any Web site folder, naming it: chickens.fla
b. Select Control → Test Movie. The movie is played in a separate window.
c. Close the preview window.

④ CREATE A MOVIE

a. Click anywhere in the workspace. Document properties are displayed in the Property inspector.
b. Click the button for the Size option. A dialog box is displayed. Change the dimensions for the Stage by clicking Contents and then selecting OK.
c. Save the modified chickens.fla.
d. Export the movie to the media folder in the SAMPLER Web site folder, naming it: chicks.swf
e. Close chickens.

⑤ INSERT THE FLASH MOVIE IN DREAMWEAVER

a. Switch to Dreamweaver.
b. Open the SAMPLER Web site for editing if it is not the working Web site.
c. In the Site panel, open the video_and_sound.htm Web page document, if it is not already open.
d. Scroll so that an empty cell is displayed.
e. In the Assets panel, display the Flash category and refresh the site list.
f. Add the chicks.swf file from the Assets panel to the empty cell to the right of the text that reads "This example is a movie from a video file:"
g. Save the modified video_and_sound.htm.

⑥ **PREVIEW THE FLASH MOVIE**
   a. Press F12. The Web page document is displayed in a browser with the movie.
   b. Close the browser window.
   c. Switch back to Dreamweaver.

⑦ **QUIT DREAMWEAVER AND FLASH**

Chapter Summary

Flash is the technology used to create a movie file for a Web site. A Flash movie file can be an animated button, animated text, or an entire Web application.

Dreamweaver includes predefined Flash buttons that can be added to a Web page. A Flash button is added to a saved Web page document by clicking the Flash Button button. Flash buttons added to a Web page document should be arranged in a nested table with each button in a separate cell. Flash text allows the use of fonts without worrying about whether the user's computer has the font installed. Flash text is added to a saved Web page document by clicking the Flash Text button. The Assets panel helps Web site development by listing Flash movies that are available in a Web site.

Animation is the result of many images shown quickly one after the other to create the effect of movement. A Flash movie animation can be broken into components. A Timeline correlates images to a particular moment in the movie. At any point in a movie, there is a frame that shows an image. The image in a frame can be several images that are layered.

The Flash MX application is used to create custom animations. A new Flash document is saved by selecting File → Save. Flash documents are automatically saved in FLA format. To use a Flash document in Dreamweaver it must be exported to the SWF format by selecting File → Export Movie.

The process of creating a Flash movie involves setting Flash document properties, creating images, using the Timeline to lay out the sequence of the images, previewing the animation, and exporting the document.

Frame-by-frame animation is a movie created from a set of specified images. To help position and edit images, two or more frames can be displayed at the same time using a technique called onion skinning. Common ways to modify an image for the next keyframe include scaling, rotating, and skewing objects.

A tweened animation is created by allowing Flash to generate the keyframes between the first frame and the last. One form of tweened animation is shape tweening, which is similar to morphing an image. Morphing is a technique that turns one shape into another.

Techniques for optimizing an animation for size include using symbols for images that appear more than once, using tweened animation, and using layers for objects that do not change from frame to frame.

Symbols are stored in a Flash Library and are used to create instances on the Stage. An instance is a reference to a symbol, rather than an copy of an image. Any image that is to be used more than once in a movie file should be converted to symbol. In motion tweening, a symbol is tweened to move from a start location to an end location.

Flash documents of any complexity should be divided into layers. Layers can be thought of as images drawn on transparent sheets of paper placed one on top of the other. Text can be broken apart into separate letters and then placed onto layers so that a word or phrase can be motion tweened.

Sound can be added to a Flash movie by importing a sound file and then adding the file to a layer by selecting File → Import to Library. Video can be imported to Flash and then exported as a Flash movie by selecting File → Import. Selecting Control → Test Movie plays the video and the accompanying audio in Flash.

Vocabulary

Animation The result of many images shown quickly one after the other to create the effect of movement.

Frame A Flash movie component that shows an image.

Instance A reference to a symbol.

Layering A technique used place separate images.

Layers A component of a Flash document that can be compared to images drawn on transparent sheets of paper placed one on top of the other.

Morphing A technique that turns one shape into another.

Motion Tweening A form of tweened animation where a symbol is tweened to move from a start location to an end location.

Onion skinning A technique used to help position and edit images.

Property inspector Area of the Flash window that contains options to modify object properties.

Shape Tweening A form of tweened animation which morphs an image.

Stage The area used to create a Flash movie.

Symbols Stored in a Flash Library and used to create instances on the Stage.

Timeline A Flash movie component which correlates images to a particular moment in the movie.

Tools panel Area of the Flash window that contains tools for drawing, painting, and selecting.

Tweened Animation An animation where Flash generates the keyframes between the first frame and the last frame.

Vector graphic A graphic that is composed of lines connected by points.

Workspace The gray area around the Stage, which is used as a temporary storage area while working.

Dreamweaver Commands and Buttons

▶ button Clicked to play the selected Flash movie. Found in the Assets panel.

■ button Clicked to stop the playing of the selected Flash movie. Found in the Assets panel.

Edit button Displays a dialog box used to edit a selected Flash button, Flash text, or a Flash movie. Found in the Property inspector.

Flash Button button Displays a dialog box used to add a Flash button to a saved Web page document. Found in the Media tab in the Insert bar.

Flash icon Displays a list of all the Flash files in the Web site. Found in the Assets panel.

Flash Text button Displays a dialog box used to add Flash text to a Web page document. Found in the Media tab in the Insert bar.

Insert button Inserts the selected movie at the insertion point. Found in the Assets panel.

Play button Previews a Flash button, Flash text, or a Flash movie. Found in the Property inspector.

Refresh Site List command Updates the list of movies in the Assets panel. Found in the Files panel group.

Stop button Stops a Flash button, Flash text, or Flash movie preview. Found in the Property inspector.

Flash Commands and Buttons

Arrow tool   Selects objects. Found in the Tools panel.

Break Apart command   Breaks text in a selected text block in separate letter objects. Found in the Modify menu.

Brush Mode changes what is painted. Found in the Tools panel.

Brush Shape changes the shape of the brush stroke.

Brush Size changes size of the brush stroke.

Brush tool   Paints with brush-like strokes. Found in the Tools panel.

Convert to Symbol command   Displays a dialog box used to convert a selected object to a symbol. Found in the Insert menu.

Delete Layer button   Deletes a selected layer. Found below the Layer list.

Distribute to Layers command   Automatically distributes separate letter objects to an individual layer and names the layer. Found in the Modify menu.

Eraser tool   Deletes parts of a shape. Found in the Tools panel.

Export Movie command   Displays a dialog box used to export a Flash movie in SWF format. Found in the File menu.

Fill Color changes the fill color of a selected tool. Found in the Tools panel.

Import command   Displays a dialog box used to import a video. Found in the File menu.

Import to Library command   Displays a dialog box used to import a sound file. Found in the File menu.

Keyframe command   Creates a new keyframe and adds the image from the previous keyframe to progress an animation. Found in the Insert menu.

Layer command   Adds a layer to a document. Found in the Insert menu.

Library command   Displays the Flash Library. Found in the Window menu.

Line tool   Draws a line. Found in the Tools panel.

Onion Skin button   Displays Onion Skin markers. Found in the Timeline.

Oval tool   Draws an oval shape. Found in the Tools panel.

Paintbucket tool   Fills enclosed areas with a selected color. Found in the Tools panel.

Pen tool   Draws straight or curved lines. Found in the Tools panel.

Pencil tool   Draws free-form lines and shapes. Found in the Tools panel.

Play command   Previews an animation. Found in the Control menu.

Rectangle tool   Draws a rectangular shape. Found in the Tools panel.

Rulers command   Displays rulers along the top and left side of the work area. Found in the View menu.

Save command   Displays a dialog box used to save a Flash document. Found in the File menu.

Show Grid command   Displays a set of gridlines on the Stage. Found in the Grid submenu in the View menu.

Subselection tool   Adjusts anchor points, which define sections of a line or shape. Found in the Tools panel.

Test Movie command   Previews a Flash movie in a separate Flash window. Found in the Control menu.

Text tool   Creates a text block. Found in the Tools panel.

Transform command   Displays a window used to scale, rotate, and skew an object. Found in the Window menu.

Stroke Color changes the outline color of the tool.

Zoom tool changes the magnification level of the Stage. Found in the Tools panel.

Introducing Flash

Review Questions

1. a) What is Flash?
   b) What can a Flash movie file be?

2. a) What application is used to create Flash buttons and Flash text?
   b) What application is used to create a Flash Web application?

3. List the steps required to add a Flash button to a saved Web page document.

4. Why should a nested table sized in pixels with cell widths also in pixels be used to arrange Flash buttons in a Web page document?

5. a) List the step required to display a list of the Flash movies available in a Web site.
   b) List the step required to update the list of Flash movies in the Assets panel.

6. a) List one advantage of using Flash text.
   b) List the steps required to add Flash text to a saved Web page document.
   c) What is the rollover color?

7. What is animation?

8. a) What function does a Timeline perform in an animation?
   b) What does a frame show in an animation?
   c) Why is layering used in an animation?

9. a) What is the Stage?
   b) What is the workspace?

10. a) Where should a Flash document be saved?
    b) What format is a Flash document saved in?
    c) What format must a Flash document be exported to in order to be used in a Web page document?

11. List the five steps involved in the process of creating a Flash movie.

12. What is the frame rate?

13. What are the tools in the Tools panel used for?

14. What are two features that can help with the precise placement of objects?

15. a) How does the file size of a vector-based graphic compare to the file size of a bitmap graphic?
    b) What is a vector graphic?

16. a) What is the Timeline used for?
    b) What does a keyframe contain?
    c) What does a static frame contain?
    d) What is the elapsed time?

17. What does previewing an image show and demonstrate?

18. a) What is frame-by-frame animation?
    b) How can the image for the first frame of a frame-by-frame animation be created?

19. a) List the steps required to add a keyframe.
    b) Why are static frames needed?

20. What should be done if an animation is moving too slowly?

21. What is onion skinning?

22. List three common ways to modify an image.

23. List the steps required to export a Flash document so that it can be used in Dreamweaver.

24. Where should Flash movies created in Flash MX for a Web site be stored?

25. What is displayed when a movie created in Flash is added to a Web page document?

26. a) What does Flash generate in a tweened animation?
    b) List one type of tweened animation.
    c) What is morphing?

27. What type of images can shape tweening be applied to?

28. Why should Flash movie files be a small file size?

29. a) Where are symbols stored?
    b) What is an instance?

30. List the steps required to convert a selected object to a symbol.

31. a) What is motion tweening?
    b) What can motion tweening be applied to?

32. List the steps required to create a motion tweened animation.

33. What path does motion tweening use?

34. a) What can layers be compared to?
    b) What advantage is there to working in layers?

35. Where do images on layer 1 appear?

36. List the step required to hide a layer.

37. List the steps required to animate text so that the individual letters of a word move onto the Stage from different directions.

38. Why are sound files imported to the document's Library?

39. List the steps required to add sound to an animation.

40. List three video file formats supported by Flash.

41. List the step required to test a movie that contains video.

Exercises

Exercise 1 ——————————————————————— CAT TOYS

Use Flash and Dreamweaver to modify the CAT TOYS Web site by completing the following steps:

a) In Dreamweaver, open the CAT TOYS Web site for editing, a Web site provided with the data files for this text.

b) Modify the copyright library item by replacing Student Name with your name. Allow Dreamweaver to update all occurrences of the library item.

c) Modify the index.htm Web page document as follows:

1. In the second row, insert a nested table with 1 row, 2 columns, a width of 400 pixels, no border, a cell padding of 4, and no cell spacing.
2. In the left cell of the nested table, insert a Flash button in a style of your choice, with the text Rolling Toys and linked to roll.htm. Save the Flash button using the name: bt_roll.swf
3. In the right cell of the nested table, insert a second Flash button using the bt_roll.swf button with the text Bouncing Toys and linked to bounce.htm. Save the Flash button using the name: bt_bounce.swf
4. Adjust the widths of the nested table and table cells appropriately by previewing the Web page document in a browser and setting the W property as necessary in Dreamweaver.

d) Modify the roll.htm Web page document as follows:

1. In the second row, insert a nested table with 1 row, 2 columns, a width of 400 pixels, no border, a cell padding of 4, and no cell spacing.
2. In the left cell of the nested table, insert a Flash button using the bt_roll.swf button with the text Home and linked to index.htm. Save the Flash button using the name: bt_home.swf
3. In the right cell of the nested table, insert the bt_bounce.swf Flash button.
4. Adjust the widths of the nested table and table cells appropriately by previewing the Web page document in a browser and setting the W property as necessary in Dreamweaver.

e) Modify the bounce.htm Web page document as follows:

1. In the second row, insert a nested table with 1 row, 2 columns, a width of 400 pixels, no border, a cell padding of 4, and no cell spacing.
2. In the left cell of the nested table, insert the bt_home.swf Flash button.
3. In the right cell of the nested table, insert the bt_roll.swf Flash button.
4. Adjust the widths of the nested table and table cells appropriately by previewing the Web page document in a browser and setting the W property as necessary in Dreamweaver.

f) Modify the index.htm Web page document as follows:

1. In the empty cell below the cat photo, add Flash text in a font of your choice, with a size of 24, a color and rollover color of your choice, using the text See the Rolling Toys! and linked to roll.htm. Save the Flash text using the name: text_roll.swf

2. In the empty cell below the Flash text just added, add Flash text in the same font, size, and colors as the text_roll.swf, using the text See the Bouncing Toys! and linked to bounce.htm. Save the Flash button using the name: text_bounce.swf

g) In the CAT TOYS root folder, create a folder named media.

h) In Flash, create animated text as follows:

1. Create animated text with letters that start in a pile (on top of each other) and move to the right to recreate the words Cat Toys Inc. in a font and color of your choice and a size of 60.
2. Save the Flash file naming it: cattoysinc.fla
3. Export the Flash movie to the CAT TOYS Web site media folder naming it: cattoysinc.swf

i) In Flash, create a motion-tweened animation as follows:

1. Draw a solid circle in a red color and convert it to a symbol named toy.
2. Create keyframes and apply motion tweening so that the circle moves in a straight line from the left to the right on the stage and back again.
3. Change the dimensions of the stage to just accommodate the objects.
4. Save the Flash file naming it: ani_roll.fla
5. Export the Flash movie to the CAT TOYS Web site media folder naming it: ani_roll.swf

j) In Flash, create a motion-tweened animation as follows:

1. Draw a solid circle in a red color and convert it to a symbol named toy.
2. Create keyframes and apply motion tweening so that the circle moves in a straight line from the top to the bottom on the stage and back again.
3. Change the dimensions of the stage to just accommodate the objects.
4. Save the Flash file naming it: ani_bounce.fla
5. Export the Flash movie to the CAT TOYS Web site media folder naming it: ani_bounce.swf

k) In Dreamweaver, modify the index.htm Web page document by inserting the cattoysinc.swf file in the top cell. With the Flash movie placeholder selected, clear the Loop check box in the Property inspector.

l) In Dreamweaver, modify the roll.htm Web page document as follows:

1. Insert the cattoysinc.swf file in the top row and, with the Flash movie placeholder selected, clear the Loop check box in the Property inspector.
2. Insert the and the ani_roll.swf file in the third row.

m) In Dreamweaver, modify the bounce.htm Web page document as follows:

1. Insert the cattoysinc.swf file in the top cell and, with the Flash movie placeholder selected, clear the Loop check box in the Property inspector.
2. Insert the ani_bounce.swf file in the tall empty cell to the left of the description and prices.

n) View each Web page document in a browser window and test the Flash buttons and Flash text.

o) Print a copy of each Web page document from the browser.

Exercise 2 ———————————————————— MEASUREMENTS

Use Flash and Dreamweaver to modify the MEASUREMENTS Web site by completing the following steps:

a) In Dreamweaver, open the MEASUREMENTS Web site for editing, a Web site provided with the data files for this text.

b) Modify the copyright library item by replacing Student Name with your name. Allow Dreamweaver to update all occurrences of the library item.

c) Modify the index.htm Web page document as follows:

1. In the top row, add Flash text in a font of your choice, with a size of 38, a color and rollover color of your choice, using the text Scientific Measurement and linked to index.htm. Save the Flash text using the name: logo.swf
2. In the second row, in the left cell of the nested table, insert a Flash button. The button should be in a style of your choice, with the text SI Prefixes and linked to prefix.htm. Save the Flash button using the name: bt_prefix.swf
3. In the right cell of the nested table, insert a second Flash button using the bt_prefix.swf button with the text SI Derived Units and linked to derive.htm. Save the Flash button using the name: bt_derive.swf
4. Adjust the widths of the nested table and table cells appropriately by previewing the Web page document in a browser and setting the W property as necessary in Dreamweaver.

d) Modify the prefix.htm Web page document as follows:

1. In the top row, add the Flash text logo.swf.
2. In the second row, in the left cell of the nested table, insert a Flash button using the bt_prefix.swf button with the text Home and linked to index.htm. Save the Flash button using the name: bt_home.swf
3. In the right cell of the nested table, insert the bt_derive.swf Flash button.
4. Adjust the widths of the nested table and table cells appropriately by previewing the Web page document in a browser and setting the W property as necessary in Dreamweaver.

e) Modify the derive.htm Web page document as follows:

1. In the top row, add the Flash text logo.swf.
2. In the second row, in the left cell of the nested table, insert the bt_home.swf Flash button.
3. In the right cell of the nested table, insert the bt_prefix.swf Flash button.
4. Adjust the widths of the nested table and table cells appropriately by previewing the Web page document in a browser and setting the W property as necessary in Dreamweaver.

f) View each Web page document in a browser window and test the Flash buttons and Flash text.

g) Print a copy of each Web page document from the browser.

Exercise 3 — Cooking Herbs

The Cooking Herbs Web site was created in Chapter 4, Exercise 1. Use Flash and Dreamweaver to further modify the Cooking Herbs Web site by completing the following steps:

a) In Dreamweaver, open the Cooking Herbs Web site for editing.

b) Modify the index.htm Web page document as follows:

1. Add a new row above the top row in the table.
2. In the top row, add Flash text in a font of your choice, with a size of 38, a color and rollover color of your choice, using the text Cooking Herbs and linked to index.htm. Save the Flash text using the name: logo.swf
3. In the second row, delete the text Cooking Herbs.
4. In the second row, insert a nested table with 1 row, 2 columns, a width of 400 pixels, no border, a cell padding of 4, and no cell spacing.
5. In the left cell of the nested table, insert a Flash button in a style of your choice, with the text Herbs and linked to popular_herbs.htm. Save the Flash button using the name: bt_popular.swf
6. In the right cell of the nested table, insert a second Flash button using the bt_popular.swf button with the text Recipes and linked to recipes.htm. Save the Flash button using the name: bt_recipes.swf
7. Adjust the widths of the nested table and table cells appropriately by previewing the Web page document in a browser and setting the W property as necessary in Dreamweaver.

c) Modify the popular_herbs.htm Web page document as follows:

1. Add two new rows above the top row in the table.
2. In the top row, add the Flash text logo.swf
3. In the second row, insert a nested table with 1 row, 2 columns, a width of 400 pixels, no border, a cell padding of 4, and no cell spacing.
4. In the left cell of the nested table, insert a Flash button using the bt_popular.swf button with the text Home and linked to index.htm. Save the Flash button using the name: bt_home.swf
5. In the right cell of the nested table, insert the bt_recipes.swf Flash button.
6. Adjust the widths of the nested table and table cells appropriately by previewing the Web page document in a browser and setting the W property as necessary in Dreamweaver.

d) Modify the recipes.htm Web page document as follows:

1. Add a new row above the top row in the table.
2. In the top row, add the Flash text logo.swf
3. In the second row, delete the text Recipes and merge the two cells in the second row into one cell.
4. In the second row, insert a nested table with 1 row, 2 columns, a width of 400 pixels, no border, a cell padding of 4, and no cell spacing.
5. In the left cell of the nested table, insert the bt_home.swf Flash button.
6. In the right cell of the nested table, insert the bt_popular.swf Flash button.
7. Adjust the widths of the nested table and table cells appropriately by previewing the Web page document in a browser and setting the W property as necessary in Dreamweaver.

e) View each Web page document in a browser window and test the Flash buttons and Flash text.

f) Print a copy of each Web page document from the browser.

Exercise 4 (advanced) — transformation

Create a Flash file that uses shape tweening to change a red oval into an orange rectangle and then into to a blue oval. Save the Flash file naming it transformation.fla.

Exercise 5 (advanced) — puzzle

Create a Flash file that uses frame-by-frame animation to assemble shapes into a large image. For example, a few squares of varying sizes could fit together to make a large square. Another example would be squares and circles that move into a square or round formation. Save the Flash file naming it puzzle.fla.

Exercise 6 (advanced) — Flash Logos

Develop a Web site that showcases your talent for creating logos in Flash. The Web site should contain:

- at least three Web page documents: a home page, a page with logos created in Flash MX, and a page with logos created using Flash text
- navigation bars that include using Flash buttons
- at least four logos that are created in Flash and exported to the Flash Logos Web site
- at least four logos created in Dreamweaver with Flash text

Preview the Web site in a browser. When satisfied with the Web site, print a copy of each Web page document from the browser.

Exercise 7 (advanced) — Flash Button Samples

Develop a Web site that contains many different Flash buttons. The Web site should contain at least:

- four Web page documents, each with a different navigation bar created using Flash buttons
- one animated text logo, created in Flash and exported to the Flash Button Samples Web site

Preview the Web site in a browser. When satisfied with the Web site, print a copy of each Web page document from the browser.

Exercise 8 (advanced) —————————————— gumball

Create a Flash file that is a gumball machine that has the gumballs roll out of it through a dispenser opening. You will need to use motion tweening and layers. Save the Flash file naming it gumball.fla. Your gumball machine could look similar to:

Introducing Flash

Chapter 9
Web Site Categories and Types

Chapter 9 Expectations

After completing this chapter you will be able to:

1. Explain the purpose and content of a personal Web site.
2. Discuss advantages of an electronic portfolio over a traditional portfolio.
3. Design an electronic portfolio.
4. Explain the purpose and content of an informational Web site.
5. Explain the purpose and content of a corporate presence Web site.
6. Display the Dreamweaver site map.
7. Create a FAQ page.
8. Create and modify external hyperlinks.
9. Display a linked Web page in a new window.
10. Import tabular data.
11. Create a site map Web page.
12. Distinguish between static and dynamic Web pages.
13. Include a form on a Web page.
14. Add form objects to a form.
15. Create a download hyperlink.

This chapter discusses different categories of Web sites. Site maps and forms are introduced. Creating electronic portfolios is also discussed.

9.1 Web Site Categories

Most Web sites are considered to be in one of the following general categories: personal, commercial, informational, media, or portal. There are many specific types of Web sites that are associated with each of these categories, for example electronic portfolios are a type of personal Web site. This chapter discusses personal, informational, and commercial Web sites, and also electronic portfolios.

9.2 Personal Web Sites

A personal Web site conveys the opinions, knowledge, or skills of an individual. A Web site that is considered personal may have a variety of content:

> **Personal Web Site Content**
>
> A personal Web site is not an appropriate sounding board for slanderous remarks. A Web site is a publication and a level of accountability should be maintained.

- a **focus** on one topic of the person's interest, such as sea shells, model airplanes, or competitive swimming. For example, the Web site above focuses on the person's interest in beaches.

Web Site Categories and Types 9 – 1

> **Internet Safety**
>
> A personal Web site should not contain any identifying information such as a home address, telephone number, or age.

- a **compilation** of the person's likes and dislikes, which would include a list of links to their favorite Web sites, an essay on why they like or dislike a topic, or an essay on their opinions.
- **personal information**, such as a description of their life and photos of their house, family, and pets. Posting this personal information on the Web is not recommended.

The purpose and target audience of a personal Web site vary depending on the focus of the content. The purpose of the personal Web site shown on the previous page is to present beach information gathered from vacations, and the target audience is anyone interested in beaches.

9.3 The Electronic Portfolio

A *portfolio* is a collection of work that clearly illustrates effort, progress, and achievement of knowledge and skills. Traditional portfolios typically take the form of a file folder or a three-ring binder. An *electronic portfolio* stores and presents portfolio content in a digital format such as a Web site. Electronic portfolios are preferred because they:

> **Electronic Portfolios**
>
> Other popular terms used to describe electronic portfolios include "e-portfolios" and "Web-based portfolios."

- are interactive
- can include sound, video, and digital images
- are easy to distribute and share
- take up less space than a binder or stack of work samples
- can be updated easily
- demonstrate your technical knowledge
- are accessible any hour of the day

> **Access to an Electronic Portfolio**
>
> An electronic portfolio Web site contains personal information and therefore should only be on a secure server with limited access or distributed on a CD.

Electronic portfolios may also be burned to a CD to distribute with a paper résumé, which gives the potential employer a nice package of both printed and electronic information. Some universities and colleges now require an electronic portfolio as part of their admissions process.

9.4 Electronic Portfolio Design Considerations

The content and design of electronic portfolios vary depending on the purpose and target audience. For example, an electronic portfolio for admission to college would have a design that reflects individuality and creativity and includes detailed academic information and samples of school projects. An electronic portfolio for a job search would have a professional appearance and include career objectives, résumé information, work samples, and links to related Web sites.

electronic portfolio structure

In general, an electronic portfolio Web site should include a home page that contains an introduction, links to Web pages in the site and in other sites, and contact information:

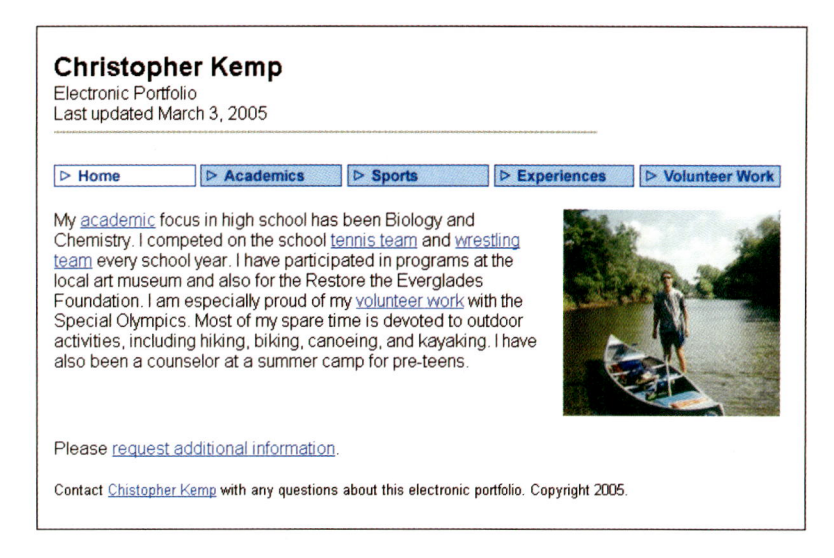

Christopher Kemp
Electronic Portfolio
Last updated March 3, 2005

| ▷ Home | ▷ Academics | ▷ Sports | ▷ Experiences | ▷ Volunteer Work |

My academic focus in high school has been Biology and Chemistry. I competed on the school tennis team and wrestling team every school year. I have participated in programs at the local art museum and also for the Restore the Everglades Foundation. I am especially proud of my volunteer work with the Special Olympics. Most of my spare time is devoted to outdoor activities, including hiking, biking, canoeing, and kayaking. I have also been a counselor at a summer camp for pre-teens.

Please request additional information.

Contact Chistopher Kemp with any questions about this electronic portfolio. Copyright 2005.

design considerations   Other Web pages that may be included in an electronic portfolio and design considerations are:

- **Résumé information** should be included, such as education, work history, and other experience. One possible design is to have a Web page with a list of educational accomplishments and the rest of the résumé information on another Web page. Another design is a Web page with a general list of education and jobs, where each list item is a link to another Web page with details for that item.

- An **e-mail link** to the person should be included at least on the home page and, if design permits, on other pages to allow users to send comments, questions, or request additional information.

- The **person's name** should be included in the page title of every Web page in the Web site, as well as on each Web page. A logo with the name in an appropriate design could be created in Fireworks, or the name could be typed in the top cell of the table on each Web page.

- **Samples** of work or creations should be included, or links to files that contain work.

> **Download Hyperlinks**
>
> A hyperlink that displays a dialog box for downloading a file is called a *download hyperlink*. Web sites sometimes contain links to files that may be of interest to the user, such as a price list from an e-commerce Web site.
>
> A download hyperlink is created by selecting the text or graphic for the link and then typing the entire FTP address of the file in the Link box in the Property inspector.

9.5 The Informational Web Site

The informational Web site are created for the purpose of displaying factual information about a particular topic and are often created by educational institutions, governments, and organizations. For example, organizations use informational Web sites to educate users about the organization's interests and goals. An informational Web site can have a wide variety of content:

- a **site map** for easier navigation
- a **search form** so that users can search the Web site for specific information
- a **list of links** to Web sites that contain related information
- tables of **tabular data**
- may also contain **banner ads** to help pay for site maintenance

The purpose of an informational Web site is to provide factual information, and therefore the site should be updated frequently to keep the content accurate. The target audience varies for informational Web sites, but all users of this type of Web site are looking for information that is easy to find.

> **Banner Ads**
>
> Banner ads are covered in Appendix B, Banner Ads and ActionScript.

9.6 The Corporate Presence Web Site

branding

A corporate presence Web site is created by a company or organization to present information about their products or services. The corporate presence Web site is a form of branding. *Branding* is the technique of raising awareness about a company by making a company logo visible in many places. Successful branding means the user will recognize the logo at a later time, such as when deciding which product to purchase at a store. The Bellur Web site includes a distinctive logo:

Depending on services and products offered, the corporate presence Web site often includes:

- a **company history**
- a **list of products** or services
- a **FAQ** page
- a **site map**
- **search** capabilities
- a description of **employment opportunities**
- a **feedback** page
- a **promotion** or contest to keep users returning to the site

The purpose of a corporate presence Web site is to make users aware of the products and services offered by a company. Corporate presence Web sites are different from e-commerce sites because online ordering is usually not offered. The target audience varies greatly for the corporate presence Web site, but users of this type of Web site may be looking for information about a particular product or service.

9.7 The Dreamweaver Site Map

In Dreamweaver, a navigational site map of the working site can be displayed. The site map resembles a sketch of the navigation structure. Clicking the Expand/Collapse button (▢) in the Site panel expands the Site panel to the size of the workspace. Clicking the Site Map button ( ) and selecting **Map and Files** displays the site map and files:

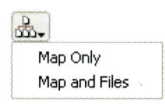

Web Site Categories and Types

Site Map button — *Expand/Collapse button*

icon — *files*

site map

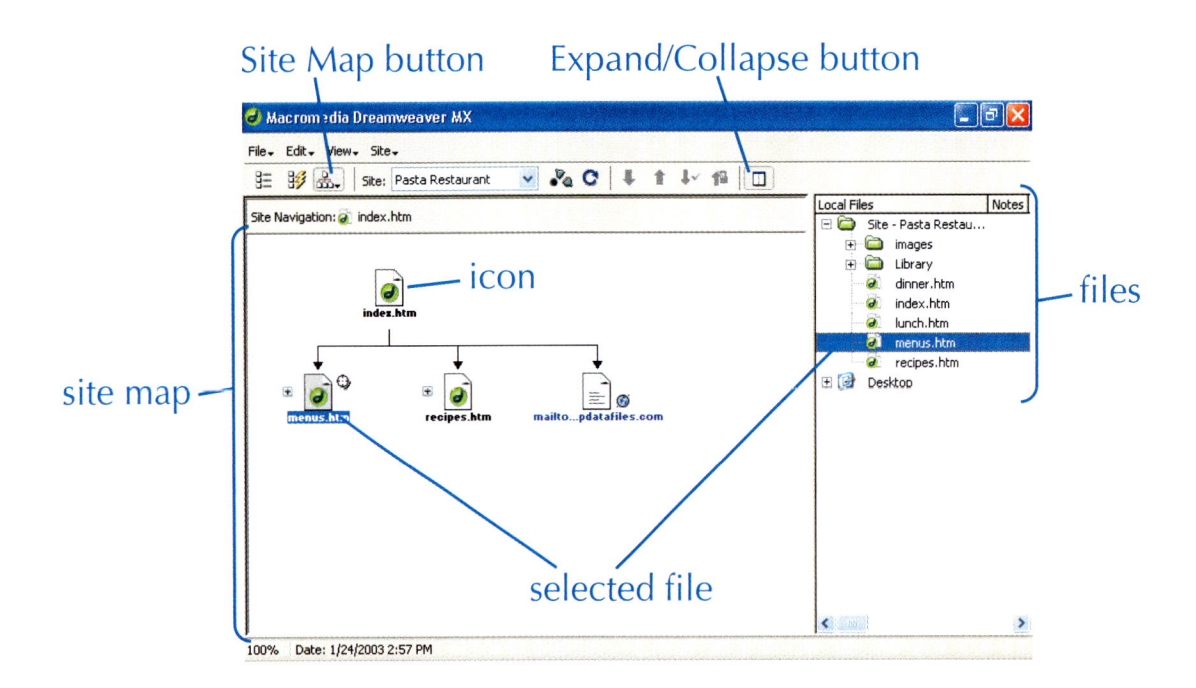

selected file

The Order of the Links

In the site map, the links are displayed in the order that they appear in the HTML.

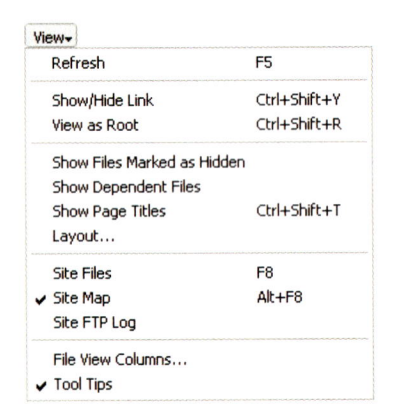

dependent files

Refresh the Site Map

After making changes, the site map may need to be refreshed by selecting View → Refresh.

In the expanded Site panel, the site files are listed on the right. The left side contains the site map which consists of icons representing Web page documents. Lines and arrows indicate links from one Web page document to another. Clicking ⊞ shows the destinations of the links for that Web page document. Clicking ⊟ hides them. Colors indicate status:

- red text indicates a broken link
- blue text with a 🌐 indicates an e-mail link or an external link

The way the site map is viewed can be changed using commands in the View menu in the expanded Site panel:

- In the example above, the menus.htm document is the focus of the site map. The focus can be changed to another Web page document by selecting the document in the site map or file and then selecting View → View as Root.
- Selecting View → Show Page Titles displays the page title below each icon instead of the file name. This is useful for reviewing the page titles and finding untitled documents.
- Selecting View → Show Dependent Files displays additional icons for dependent files. *Dependent files* are images, library items, or other non-HTML files that load with the Web page in a browser.

The site map is useful for viewing a Web site's navigational structure and can also be used to work with the Web page documents in the site:

- Selecting File → Save Site Map displays a dialog box, which is used to save the site map as a BMP file. This image can be used as a reference when developing and maintaining a Web site.
- Double-clicking a Web page document in the site map returns to the Dreamweaver workspace and opens the file.
- The page title of a Web page document can be modified by displaying the page titles (View → Show Page Titles) clicking a title and typing a new one.

9 – 6   *A Guide to Web Development Using Macromedia Dreamweaver MX*

Practice 1

In this practice you will display the site map for a Web site.

① OPEN THE BELLUR WEB SITE FOR EDITING

a. Start Dreamweaver.
b. In the Site panel, open the BELLUR Web site for editing, a Web site provided with the data files for this text.
c. In the Site panel, familiarize yourself with the files and folders for this Web site.
d. Open the index.htm Web page document and then view the page in a browser.
e. Click the links to explore the other Web pages of the Web site.
f. Close the browser window.

② DISPLAY THE SITE MAP

a. In the Site panel, click the Expand/Collapse button (▫). The Site panel expands to the size of the workspace.
b. Click the Site Map button ( ) and from the displayed menu select Map and Files. The site map and files are displayed. Use the scroll bars to view all of the icons.
c. Next to the sweeps.htm icon ( ), click the ⊞. The destinations of the links for that Web page document are displayed in a list below it.
d. Next to the sweeps.htm icon, click ⊟. The list is hidden.

③ CHANGE THE FOCUS

a. Note that index.htm is currently the icon at the top of the site map.
b. Click the sweeps.htm icon to select it.
c. Select View → View as Root. The sweeps.htm icon is now the focus, at the top of the site map.
d. Click the index.htm icon to select it.
e. Select View → View as Root. The index.htm icon is again at the top of the site map.

④ DISPLAY PAGE TITLES AND DEPENDENT FILES

a. Select View → Show Page Titles. The page title is now displayed below each icon instead of the file name.
b. Select View → Show Page Titles. The file name is again displayed below each icon.
c. Select View → Show Dependent Files. Note the additional icons that are displayed, including images and a library item.
d. Select View → Show Dependent Files. The dependent files are no longer displayed.

⑤ RETURN TO THE DREAMWEAVER WORKSPACE

a. Click the Expand/Collapse button (▫). The Dreamweaver workspace is again displayed.
b. In the Site panel, click the Expand/Collapse button (▫). The site map is displayed.
c. Double-click the sweeps.htm icon. The Dreamweaver workspace is displayed and the sweeps.htm Web page document is opened.
d. Close the sweeps.htm Web page document.
e. Close the index.htm Web page document.

9.8 Creating a FAQ Page

A *FAQ* (pronounced *fak*) page is a page that contains frequently asked questions and their answers. This conveniently provides answers to commonly asked questions without the user having to call or send an e-mail. The FAQ often lists questions about where to find a company's products, use of certain products, what makes a product or service special, and so on. Depending on the type of company, a FAQ may list technical support questions. The FAQ page below lists several questions and answers:

9.9 External Hyperlinks

A hyperlink that displays a Web page document that is from another Web site is called an *external hyperlink*, also called an *absolute hyperlink*. For example, personal Web sites may contain external hyperlinks to Web sites that the person recommends.

An external hyperlink is created by selecting the text or graphic for the link and then typing the entire URL of the Web page to be displayed in the Link box in the Property inspector.

Links should be tested in a browser window. Links are modified in Dreamweaver by selecting the link text and then selecting Modify → Change Link or Modify → Remove Link.

Entire URL

An external hyperlink requires the entire URL, including a protocol such as http://.

testing and modifying a hyperlink

9.10 Displaying a Linked Web Page in a New Window

External hyperlinks take the user away from the current Web site. In cases where the user should be able to easily get back to the original site, a new browser window should open when the link is clicked. Displaying a new window allows the user to browse the other Web site and then close the window to again display the original Web site.

A linked Web page is displayed in a new browser window by selecting the hyperlink and then selecting _blank in the Target list in the Property inspector.

testing and modifying a hyperlink

A link that displays a Web page in a new window should be tested in a browser window. A link can be changed back to displaying the Web page in the current window by selecting _self in the Target list in the Property inspector.

Practice 2

In this practice you will modify a FAQ page and make an external hyperlink that opens the linked Web page in a new window. Dreamweaver should be started and the BELLUR Web site should be the working site.

① MODIFY THE FAQ PAGE

a. Open the faq.htm Web page document.
b. At the bottom of the list of questions and answers, place the insertion point after the period in craftsmanship. and press Enter.
c. Type the following text, allowing the text to wrap:

   Q: What materials are used to make the very comfortable, long-lasting handles of the spoons and spatulas?

d. Insert a line break and then type the following text, allowing the text to wrap:

   A: We use a special compound called PlazTik, which was developed and is produced by the NowPont Chemical Company. The company has extensive information about PlazTik at their Web site.

e. Select all of the questions and answers in the list and apply the faqtext CSS style. The text is sized smaller.

② CREATE AN EXTERNAL HYPERLINK

a. At the bottom of the list of questions and answers, select the text: NowPont Chemical Company.
b. In the Property inspector, in the Link box type http://www.lpdatafiles.com/dmx/plaztik and press Enter.
c. Press F12. The Web page document is displayed in a browser window.
d. Click the NowPont Chemical Company link. The PlazTik Web page is displayed in the browser window.

③ OPEN THE LINKED WEB PAGE IN A NEW WINDOW

a. Switch back to Dreamweaver. The faq.htm Web page is displayed and the linked text should still be selected.

b. In the Property inspector, in the Target list select _blank.

c. Press F12 to switch back to the browser window. The faq.htm Web page document is displayed.

d. Print a copy of the Web page.

e. Click the NowPont Chemical Company link. A new browser window is opened and the PlazTik Web page is displayed in the new browser window.

f. Close the new browser window.

g. Switch back to Dreamweaver.

h. Save and close the modified faq.htm.

9.11 Using Tables to Display Tabular Data

tab-delimited

Tables are used extensively for Web page layout. Tables are also used for displaying tabular data. *Tabular data* is data that has been created in another application and is saved in a delimited text format, which can be a TXT file. *Tab-delimited* data indicates that each item in each row is separated by a tab character. For example, the page below uses a table with nine rows and three columns. A border of 1 has been used which includes lines that help the user read the data. The event, location, and time were separated by tabs in the imported data:

> **Importing Tab-Delimited Data**
>
> Tab-delimited data is usually in a TXT file, which may have been created from a word processor document or a spreadsheet. Saving a spreadsheet in TXT format adds a tab character between each cell's contents.

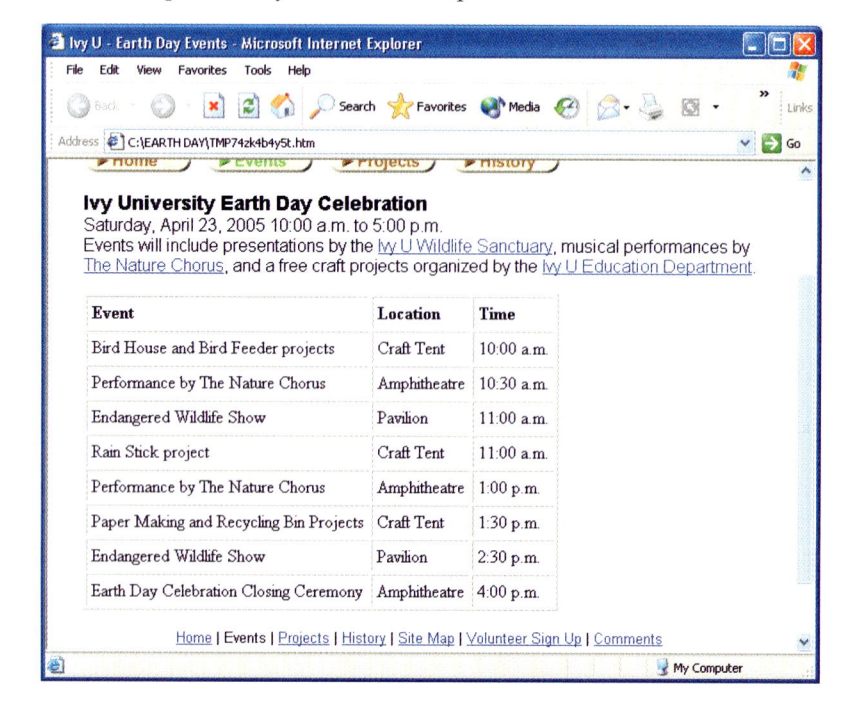

9 – 10   *A Guide to Web Development Using Macromedia Dreamweaver MX*

Tabular data can be imported from a file and a table created for it in one step. Clicking the Tabular Data button (📄) on the Common tab in the Insert bar displays a dialog box:

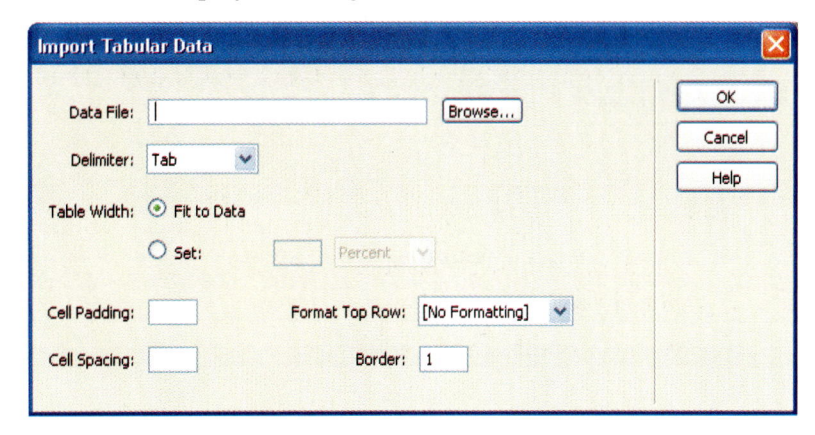

- The Browse button is used to navigate to the file that is to be imported and display the file name in Data File box.
- The Delimiter box should be Tab for tab-delimited data.
- The Fit to Data option sizes the table to fit all the imported data.
- The Cell Padding, Cell Spacing, and Border options all apply to the new table. It is recommended to include a border of at least 1 for a table of data to make the table more readable.
- The Format Top Row list is used to format the data in the top row of the table if the top row of the imported data contains column headings.

Selecting OK creates the table at the insertion point. Cell contents can be further formatted just like any cells in a table. The Insert → Table Objects → Import Tabular Data can also be used to import tabular data.

Practice 3

In this practice you will add a table of data to a Web page document. Dreamweaver should be started and the BELLUR Web site should be the working site.

① ADD A TABLE OF DATA

    a. Open the products.htm Web page document.

    b. In the empty cell below the text Price List, place the insertion point.

    c. On the Common tab in the Insert bar, click the Tabular Data button (📄). A dialog box is displayed.

        1. Click Browse. A dialog box is displayed.

            a) Navigate to the root folder of the Bellur site if it is not already displayed.

            b) Select the bellur_price_list.txt file.

            c) Select Open. The file is listed in the Data File box.

        2. In the Delimiter list, select Tab if it is not already selected.

        3. Select the Fit to Data option if it is not already selected.

        4. In the Cell Padding box, type: 4.

        5. In the Border box type 1 if it is not already set to 1.

6. In the Format Top Row list, select Bold.
7. Select OK. A new table is created and placed at the insertion point. The table contains data and text in the top row is bold.

d. Save the modified products.htm.

② VIEW THE TABLE IN A BROWSER

a. Press F12. The Web page document is displayed in a browser window. Scroll to the table and note how the border lines make the table more readable.
b. Print a copy of the Web page.
c. Switch back to Dreamweaver.
d. Close products.htm.

9.12   A Site Map Web Page

A *site map* is a Web page that contains links to information on other pages of the Web site. The links are usually arranged in alphabetical order or grouped by subject, as in the Earth Day site map:

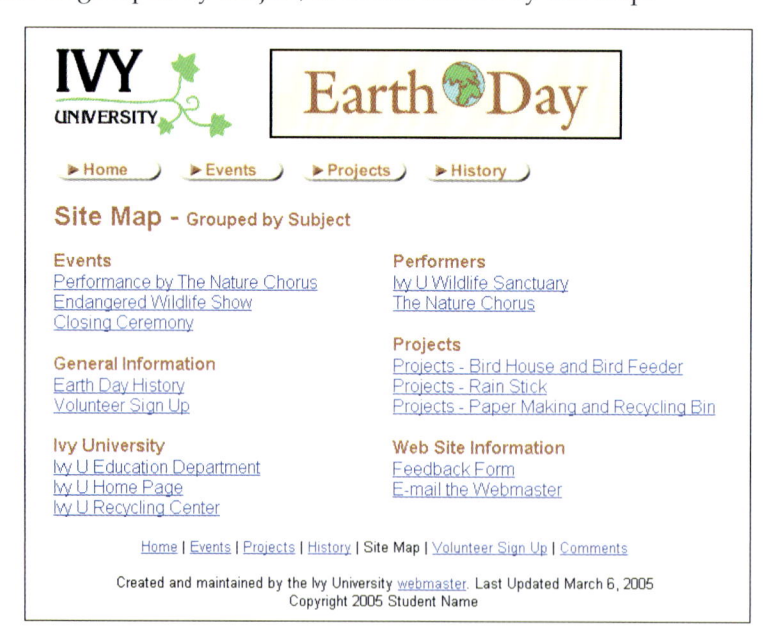

A site map helps users find the Web page they are looking for if they cannot find the Web page using the navigation bars. The links on a site map Web page also give an overview of the Web site's contents.

Practice 4

In this practice you will add links to a site map Web page document. Dreamweaver should be started and the BELLUR Web site should be the working site.

① ADD THE LINKS TO THE SITE MAP WEB PAGE DOCUMENT

a. Open the site_map.htm Web page document.
b. In the empty cell below the top global navigation bar, place the insertion point.

c. Type the following text, pressing Enter at the end of each line:

>Bellur Utensil Company Site Map
>
>Company History
>
>Employment Opportunites
>
>FAQ Page
>
>Feedback Form
>
>Products and Prices
>
>Sweepstakes

d. Select the text Bellur Utensil Company Site Map and tag the text with <h1> and </h1>. The text is formatted larger and bold.

e. Link text to Web page documents as follows:

Link the text	to the Web page document
Company History	history.htm
Employment Opportunites	employment.htm
FAQ Page	faq.htm
Feedback Form	feedback.htm
Products and Prices	products.htm
Sweepstakes	sweeps.htm

f. Save the modified site_map.htm.

② VIEW THE SITE MAP IN A BROWSER

a. Press F12. The Web page document is displayed in a browser window. Test the links in the site map.

b. Print a copy of the Web page.

c. Switch back to Dreamweaver.

d. Close site_map.htm.

9.13 The Jump Menu Form Object

A *jump menu* contains a set of text hyperlinks and can be used as a navigation tool:

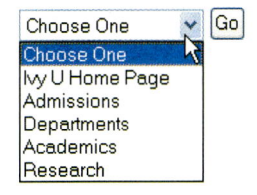

A Jump Menu form object is added to a Web page document at the insertion point by clicking the Jump Menu button ( ) on the Forms tab in the Insert bar, which displays a dialog box:

Web Site Categories and Types 9 – 13

[Screenshot of the Insert Jump Menu dialog box]

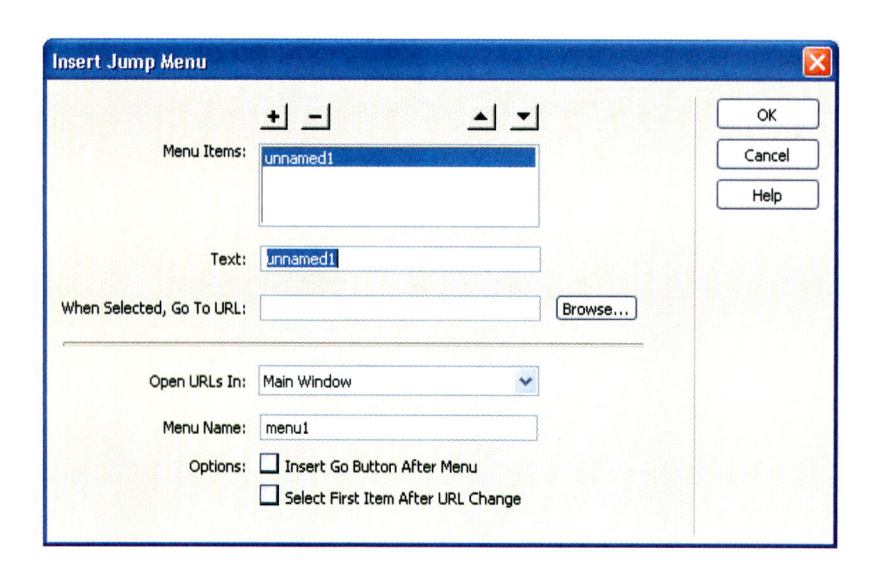

- Text and the target URL for the selected menu item are set in the Text box and the When Selected, Go To URL box.
- Menu Items are added or deleted by clicking ➕ or ➖.
- The ▲ and ▼ are used to move a selected item up or down.
- Selecting Insert Go Button After Menu adds a Go button ([Go]) next to the jump menu in the form.
- Selecting Select First Item After URL Change returns the list to the first item, which should be a prompt. A prompt is text in the first menu item that guides the user to select an item from the menu, for example Choose One or Select a Page.

Selecting OK displays another dialog box with a message about adding a form tag. Selecting OK creates the jump menu.

the GO button   It is a good idea to include either a Go button or a first item prompt. The first time a user chooses a jump menu item, the target is immediately displayed. After that, if the menu is not set to return to the first item, the user is required to click the Go button to choose the same item. It is not recommended to include both the Go button and a prompt.

editing a jump menu   Once created, a selected jump menu can be edited by double-clicking the Jump Menu action in the Behaviors panel. Just the items in the list can be edited by clicking [List Values...] in the Property inspector.

testing a jump menu   A jump menu can be tested in a browser window.

Practice 5

In this practice you will add a jump menu to a Web page document. Dreamweaver should be started and the BELLUR Web site should be the working site.

① ADD A JUMP MENU

a. Open the index.htm Web page document.
b. Place the insertion point to the left of the "10th Annual Bellur Utensil Sweepstakes" image.

c. On the Forms tab in the Insert bar, click the Jump Menu button ( ). A dialog box is displayed.

    1. Type: Employment

    2. Click Browse. A dialog box is displayed.

        a) Select employment.htm and then select OK. The Menu Items list contains Employment and the When Selected, Go To URL box displays employment.htm.

    3. Click ➕. Another menu item is added.

    4. In the Text box, replace the text with: FAQ

    5. Click Browse, select faq.htm and then select OK.

    6. Add the following menu items, selecting the appropriate URLs:

        Feedback
        Home
        History
        Products
        Site Map
        Sweepstakes

    7. In the Menu Items list, click the History menu item and then click ▲ to move History above Home.

    8. Select Insert Go Button After Menu.

    9. Select OK. If another dialog box is displayed, select OK. A form is added with a jump menu and a Go button.

    10. Save the modified index.htm.

② VIEW THE FORM IN A BROWSER

    a. Press F12. The Web page document is displayed in a browser window.

    b. Print a copy of the Web page.

    c. Test the Jump Menu links.

    d. Switch back to Dreamweaver.

    e. Close index.htm.

9.14 Dynamic Database-Driven Web Applications

A *static Web page* contains only text and images. A Web page that contains any animation or is interactive, for example a rollover behavior, is a *dynamic Web page*. Dynamic Web pages can also have *dynamic content*, which is content that changes based on input from the user. A Web site that includes dynamic content on any of the Web pages is a *dynamic Web site*, also called a *Web application*. A dynamic Web site employs a server technology such as ASP.NET or ColdFusion to process input from the user and then send a Web page with dynamic content to the user's browser. The information that is returned to the user is from a data source such as a database file.

A form allows the user to interact with the server. Dynamic form objects are practiced here in this chapter but will not work properly unless a server-side script or application has been defined.

> **What is a Database?**
>
> A database is a collection of related information organized into tables. Information can be easily retrieved from a database using criteria to perform queries. In a Web application, input from a form is used by the server to query a database.

9.15 What is a Form?

A *form* can contain dynamic objects that allow the user to interact with a Web server. Form objects are used to obtain information from the user, such as a guest book that allows users to submit their name and comments about a Web site. Form objects are also used to allow the user to submit information that returns data based on their submission, such as a search box at a search engine Web site.

A form should be as short as possible, simple to use, and easy to understand. The Web page below contains a form for a guest book:

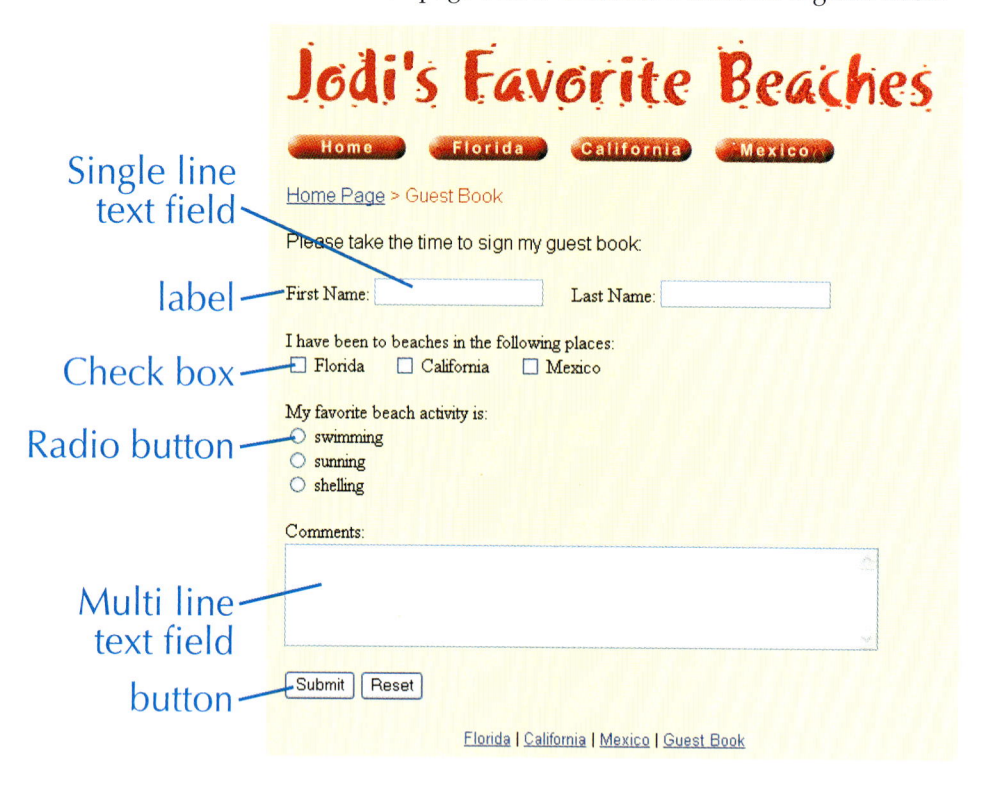

form object A *form object* is used to obtain information from the user. The form on the Jodi's Favorite Beaches Web page contains the form objects:

- **Single line text field** for the user to type a short amount of text.
- **Check boxes** and **Radio buttons** allow the user to select options. These form objects are discussed in Section 9.17.
- **Multi line text field** for the user to type one or more lines of text.
- **button** which includes a Submit button to send the form results to a file or to an e-mail address, and a Reset button that clears the form entries.

label A *label* is text that describes the purpose of a form object. For example, in the Jodi's Favorite Beaches form, "First Name" is the label for a Single line text field.

Formatting Labels

A label can be formatted in the same manner as any other text.

9.16 Creating a Form

A form and form objects are created using buttons on the Forms tab in the Insert bar:

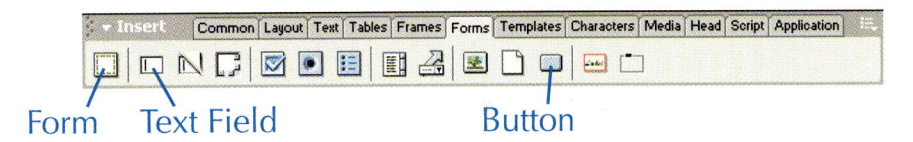

Form   *Text Field*   *Button*

A form should be created in a table cell to control the form layout. A form is created by first placing the insertion point in a table cell and then clicking the Form button ( ) in the Insert bar, which inserts a form indicated by a dashed red outline and places the insertion point in the form:

adding a label   A label is added by typing the text for the label. Objects are added at the insertion point by clicking a button on the Forms tab in the Insert bar. For example, in the form above, typing First Name:, clicking the Text Field button ( ), pressing Enter and then clicking the Button button ( ) creates the following:

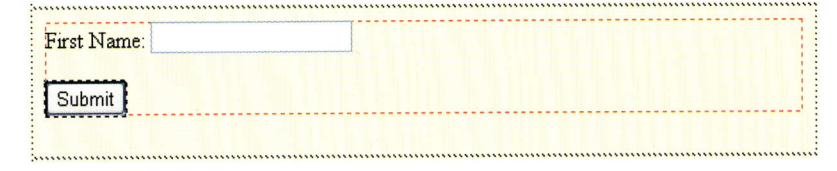

First Name:

Submit

text field   Form object properties are set in the Property inspector. For example, selecting a text field displays the following properties:

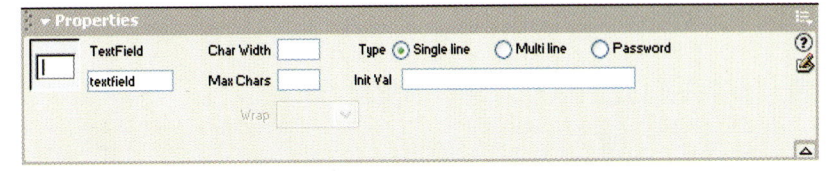

- TextField is the form object name. A new name can be typed. Each object in a form should have a descriptive name because the names are included in the file containing the form results. Object names cannot contain spaces.
- Multi line is selected to change the field to a multi-line text field.
- Char Width is the number of characters that can be displayed. This affects the width of the text field in the form. A value greater than 0 should be typed.
- Max Chars is the maximum number of characters that the field can accept. Note that this may be more or less than the number of characters that can be displayed.
- Init Val is text that should appear in the text field when the form loads. This property is often left empty. Text can be typed by the user to set the initial value.

Adding a Form

If no form exists when a form object is inserted, Dreamweaver displays a dialog box asking if a form tag should be added. Selecting Yes creates a form and the form object is added in the form.

Web Site Categories and Types   9 – 17

Button form object A Button form object has the following properties:

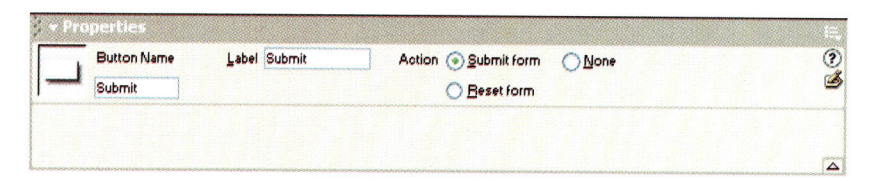

- Button Name is the form object name.
- Label is the text that appears on the button. The Button form object automatically resizes to accommodate the text.
- Action is used to determine what action is taken when the user clicks the button. Submit form sends the form contents to the server. Reset form clears the form fields and allows the user to start over again. None indicates no action.

Form objects may also be added at the insertion point by selecting commands in the Insert → Form Objects submenu.

Form objects can be tested in a browser window. However, the form will not interact with a server unless a server-side script or application has been defined.

Practice 6

In this practice you will add a form and form objects to a Web page document. Dreamweaver should be started and the BELLUR Web site should be the working site.

① ADD A FORM TO A WEB PAGE DOCUMENT

a. Open the sweeps.htm Web page document.
b. In the empty cell in the right half of the table, place the insertion point.
c. On the Forms tab in the Insert bar, click the Form button (▢). A form is inserted in the cell, indicated by a dashed red outline, and the insertion point is in the form.

② ADD A LABEL AND FORM OBJECTS

a. On the Text tab in the Insert bar, click the Paragraph button (¶) and then type First Name: followed by a space.
b. On the Forms tab in the Insert bar, click the Text field button (▢). A text field is inserted.
c. In the Property inspector, set Char Width to 15. The width of the text field is now smaller.
d. In the Property inspector, set TextField to: firstnamesweeps
e. Place the insertion point to the right of the text field and Press Enter.
f. Type Last Name: followed by a space.
g. On the Forms tab in the Insert bar, click the Text Field button (▢).
h. In the Property inspector, set Char Width to 15.
i. In the Property inspector, set TextField to: lastnamesweeps
j. Place the insertion point to the right of the text field and press Enter.
k. Type E-mail address: followed by a space.
l. On the Forms tab in the Insert bar, click the Text Field button (▢).
m. In the Property inspector, set Char Width to 40.
n. In the Property inspector, set TextField to: emailsweeps

9 – 18   *A Guide to Web Development Using Macromedia Dreamweaver MX*

Check—Your form should look similar to:

```
Enter the Bellur Utensil
       Sweepstakes!
   One entry per e-mail address.

First Name: [    ]
Last Name: [    ]
E-mail address:
[                    ]
```

③ ADD A BUTTON FORM OBJECT

a. Place the insertion point to the right of the last text field and press Enter.
b. On the Forms tab in the Insert bar, click the Button button (▢). A button is inserted in the form.
c. In the Property inspector, set **Label** to: Enter Sweepstakes
d. In the Property inspector, set **Button Name** to: submitsweeps
e. Save the modified sweeps.htm.

④ VIEW THE FORM IN A BROWSER

a. Press F12. The Web page document is displayed in a browser window.
b. Print a copy of the Web page.
c. Fill out the form and click **Enter Sweepstakes**. The form just resets because interaction with a server has not been defined.
d. Switch back to Dreamweaver.
e. Close sweeps.htm.

9.17 The Check Box and Radio Button Form Objects

The check box and radio button form objects are commonly included on a form for user input.

Check Box form object

A *Check Box form object* allows the user to select an option by clicking a check box. More than one check box can be selected at the same time.

Radio Group form object

The *Radio Group form object* allows the user to only select one radio button from each group.

creating a Check Box form object

A Check Box form object is added to a form at the insertion point by clicking the Checkbox button (☑) on the Forms tab in the Insert bar. A check box form object has the following properties:

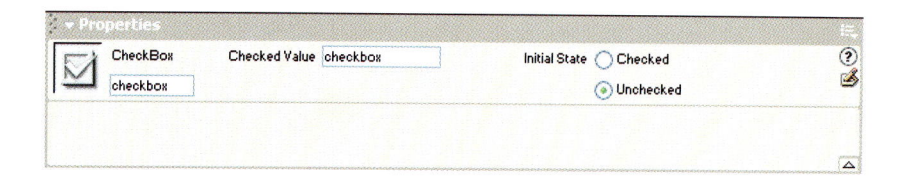

- **CheckBox** is the form object name.
- **Checked Value** indicates the value returned if the user selects the check box, which can be text or a numeric value.
- **Initial State** sets the check box to checked when the form loads. Note that the check box can be unchecked by the user.

creating a Radio Button Group form object

Radio button form objects should be added in groups, which is done by clicking the Radio Group button ( ) on the Forms tab in the Insert bar. A dialog box is displayed:

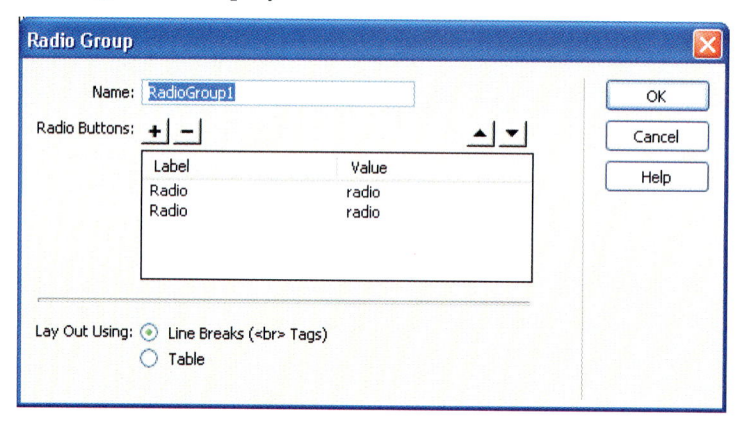

- The **Name** box is used to give the radio button group a name.
- The radio button group is created with at least two buttons, which are already listed in the **Radio Buttons** list and include labels Radio and the values radio. Selecting each one and typing a new label and value changes the radio buttons. More radio buttons can be added by clicking +. A selected radio button is deleted by clicking -.
- The **Lay Out Using** options indicate the way the radio buttons will be separated in the Web page document. Selecting Line Breaks (
 Tags) adds a line break after each radio button. The **Table** value creates a one-column table with each radio button in a separate cell.

Selecting OK creates the radio buttons in the form at the insertion point.

Form objects can be tested in a browser window. However, the form will not interact with a server unless a server-side script or application has been defined.

9.18 The List/Menu Form Object

Forms often include a scrolling list or a pop-up menu, which allow users to easily select from a list of predetermined choices rather than typing responses. With limited choices, a form is more likely to be completed by the user and the form results are easier to evaluate. A scrolling list and a pop-up menu are both List/Menu form objects and each is used in a slightly different manner:

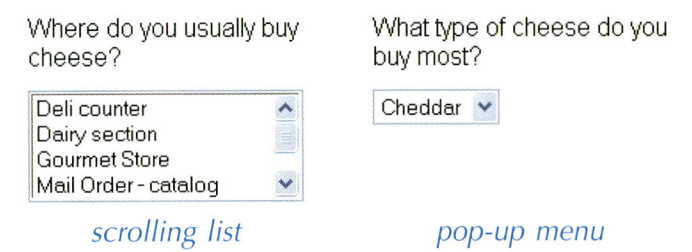

scrolling list   *pop-up menu*

- A *scrolling list* allows the user to select an option from a list of items by scrolling the list using a scroll bar.

- A *pop-up menu* allows the user to select an option from a list of items that appear when the user clicks the ⌄ next to the list.

creating a scrolling list

A List/Menu form object is added to a form at the insertion point by clicking the List/Menu button (▦) on the Forms tab in the Insert bar. A scrolling list is created by selecting List in the Property inspector. A name for the list should be typed in the List/Menu box. Clicking [List Values...] displays a dialog box:

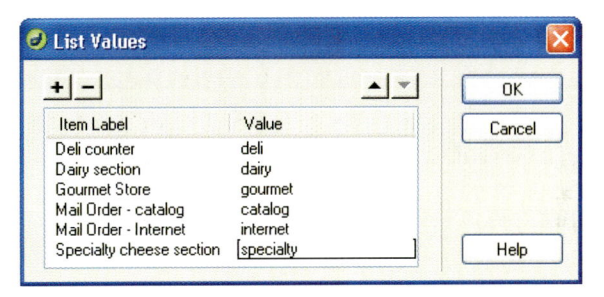

The list items are added in this dialog box. Each item should have an Item Label, which is the text that is displayed in the scrolling list, and a value, which is returned to the server. Clicking ➕ adds an item and clicking ➖ deletes the selected item. The ▲ and ▼ are used to move a selected item up or down in the list. Selecting OK adds the items to the form object.

In the Property inspector, the scrolling list can be further modified:

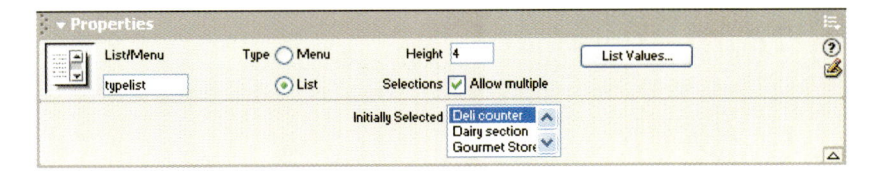

- Height is the number of items that should be displayed in the list. The rest of the items will be displayed when the list is scrolled.

Web Site Categories and Types   9 – 21

- Allow multiple is selected to enable the user to select more than one list item.
- Initially Selected is the list item that will appear selected in the form object when the Web page loads.

creating a pop-up menu

A pop-up menu is created by adding a List/Menu form object and selecting Menu in the Property inspector. A name for the menu should be typed in the List/Menu box. Clicking [List Values...] displays a dialog box:

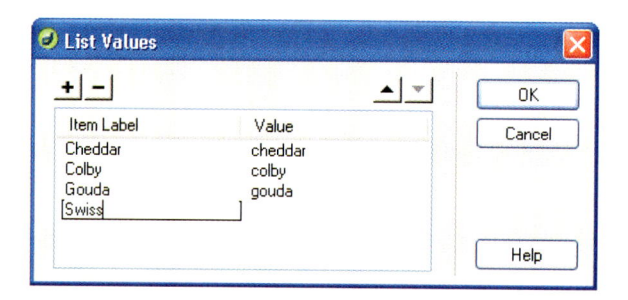

The menu items are added in this dialog box. Each item should have an Item Label, which is the text that is displayed in the menu, and a value, which is returned to the server. Clicking + adds an item, and clicking − deletes the selected item. The ▲ and ▼ are used to move a selected item up or down in the list. Selecting OK adds the items to the menu form object.

In the Property inspector, one menu item can be selected in the Initially Selected list, and that item will be selected in the form object when the Web page loads.

Form objects can be tested in a browser window. However, the form will not interact with a server unless a server-side script or application has been defined.

Practice 7

In this practice you will add a Check Box, Radio Button Group, and List/Menu form objects to a form in a Web page document. Dreamweaver should be started and the BELLUR Web site should be the working site.

① ADD CHECK BOX FORM OBJECTS

a. Open the feedback.htm Web page document.
b. A form, labels, and text fields have already been added to this Web page document. Place the insertion point to the right of the e-mail address text field and press Enter.
c. Type: What Bellur utensils do you own? (check all that apply)
d. Insert a line break.
e. On the Forms tab in the Insert bar, click the Checkbox button (☑). A Check Box form object is inserted in the form.
f. In the Property inspector, set CheckBox to: utility
g. In the Property inspector, set Checked Value to: utility spoon
h. Place the insertion point to the right of the check box, type Utility Spoon and insert a line break.

i. On the **Forms** tab in the Insert bar, click the Checkbox button (☑). A Check Box form object is inserted in the form.
j. In the Property inspector, set **CheckBox** to: perforated
k. In the Property inspector, set **Checked Value** to: perforated spoon
l. Place the insertion point to the right of the check box, type Perforated Spoon and insert a line break.
m. Insert a Check Box form object and in the Property inspector, set **CheckBox** to spatula and set **Checked Value** to: spatula
n. Place the insertion point to the right of the check box, type Spatula and insert a line break.
o. Insert a check box form object and in the Property inspector, set **CheckBox** to None and set **Checked Value** to: None
p. Place the insertion point to the right of the check box and type none and then press Enter.

② ADD A RADIO BUTTON GROUP FORM OBJECT

a. Type: How often do you cook?
b. Insert a line break.
c. On the **Forms** tab in the Insert bar, click the Radio Group button (▦). A dialog box is displayed.
   1. In the **Name** box, type: Cook
   2. Click the first Radio label in the list and type: Often
   3. Click the first radio value in the list and type: often
   4. Click the next Radio label in the list and type: Sometimes
   5. Click the next radio value in the list and type: sometimes
   6. Click ➕. Another radio button is added to the list.
   7. Click the new Radio label in the list and type: Rarely
   8. Click the new radio value in the list and type: rarely
   9. Select **OK**. The radio buttons and labels are added to the form.

Check—Your form should look similar to:

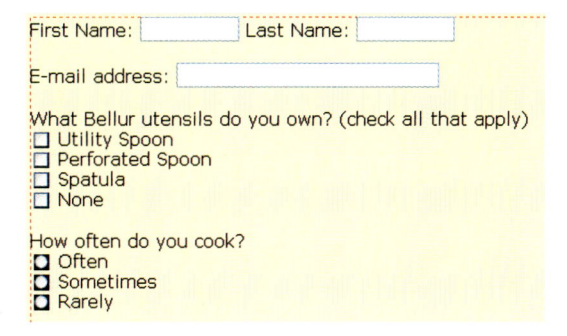

```
First Name: [    ]    Last Name: [    ]
E-mail address: [                ]

What Bellur utensils do you own? (check all that apply)
☐ Utility Spoon
☐ Perforated Spoon
☐ Spatula
☐ None

How often do you cook?
☐ Often
☐ Sometimes
☐ Rarely
```

③ ADD A SCROLLING LIST

a. The insertion point should be just below the radio button group. Press the Backspace key to delete the extra line break and then press Enter.
b. Type: Where do you purchase other cooking products?
c. Insert a line break.
d. On the **Forms** tab in the Insert bar, click the List/Menu button (▦). A List/Menu form object is added to the form.
e. In the Property inspector, select **List**.
f. In the Property inspector, set **List/Menu** to: where

Web Site Categories and Types 9 – 23

g. In the Property inspector, click [List Values...]. A dialog box is displayed.
   1. Click in the Item Label list and type: Grocery
   2. Click in the Value list and type: grocery
   3. Click +. Another item is added to the list.
   4. For the new item, type Catalog for the Item Label and catalog for the Value.
   5. Add another item and type Specialty Shop for the Item Label and shop for the Value.
   6. Add another item and type Internet for the Item Label and internet for the Value.
   7. Select OK. The dialog box is removed.
h. In the Property inspector, set Height to: 3
i. In the Property inspector, in the Initially Selected list select Grocery. The scrolling list now displays three items and Grocery is selected.

④ ADD A POP-UP MENU

a. Place the insertion point to the right of the scrolling list and press Enter.
b. Type: What new product would you most likely buy?
c. Insert a line break.
d. On the Forms tab in the Insert bar, click the List/Menu button ( ). A List/Menu form object is added to the form.
e. In the Property inspector, set List/Menu to: newprod
f. In the Property inspector, click [List Values...]. A dialog box is displayed.
   1. Click in the Item Label list and type: Whisk
   2. Click in the Value list and type: whisk
   3. Add another item and type Pasta Fork for the Item Label and pasta for the Value.
   4. Add another item and type Ladle for the Item Label and ladle for the Value.
   5. Select OK. The dialog box is removed.
g. In the Property inspector, in the Initially Selected list select Whisk. Whisk is selected in the pop-up menu.

⑤ ADD A MULTI LINE TEXT FIELD

a. Place the insertion point to the right of the pop-up menu and press Enter.
b. Type: Comments:
c. Insert a line break.
d. On the Forms tab in the Insert bar, click the Text Field button ( ).
e. In the Property inspector, select Multi line.
f. In the Property inspector, set TextField to: comments

⑥ ADD BUTTON FORM OBJECTS

a. Place the insertion point to the right of the Multi line text field and press Enter.
b. On the Forms tab in the Insert bar, click the Button button ( ). A button is inserted.
c. Place the insertion point to the right of the button.
d. On the Forms tab in the Insert bar, click the Button button ( ). A button is inserted.
e. In the Property inspector, select Reset form.
f. In the Property inspector, set Button Name to Clear.
g. In the Property inspector, set Label to: Clear Form
h. Save the modified feedback.htm.

⑦ VIEW THE FORM IN A BROWSER

   a. Press F12. The Web page document is displayed in a browser window.
   b. Print a copy of the Web page.
   c. Fill out the form and click Clear Form. The form just resets because interaction with a server has not been defined.
   d. Switch back to Dreamweaver.
   e. Close feedback.htm.

Chapter Summary

Most Web sites are considered to be in one of the following general categories: personal, commercial, informational, media, or portal. A personal Web site conveys the opinions, knowledge, or skills of an individual. An electronic portfolio stores and presents portfolio content in a digital format such as a Web site. A corporate presence Web site is created by a company or organization to present information about their products or services.

In Dreamweaver, a navigational site map that resembles a sketch of the navigation structure can be displayed. In the site map, lines and arrows indicate links from one Web page document to another. The page titles can be displayed below each icon instead of the file name in the site map. Dependent files can also be displayed.

A FAQ page is a page with frequently asked questions and their answers. A hyperlink that displays a Web page document that is from another Web site is called an external hyperlink, also called an absolute hyperlink. External hyperlinks take the user away from the current Web site. A new browser window can be opened when a link is clicked by selecting _blank in the Target list in the Property inspector.

Tables can be used for displaying tabular data, which is data that has been created in another application and is saved in a delimited text format. Tab-delimited data indicates that each item in each row is separated by a tab character. The Tabular Data button ( ) is used to import tab-delimited text and display it in a table.

A site map is a Web page that contains links to information on other pages of the Web site. A site map helps users find the Web page they are looking for if they cannot find the Web page using the navigation bars.

A jump menu contains a set of text hyperlinks and can be used as a navigation tool.

A static Web page contains only text and images. A Web page that contains any animation or is interactive is a dynamic Web page. A Web site that includes dynamic content on any of the Web pages is a dynamic Web site, also called a Web application.

Web Site Categories and Types

A form can contain dynamic objects that allow a user to interact with a Web server. Form objects are used to obtain information from the user. Form objects include text fields, check boxes, radio button groups, buttons, and List/Menu objects, and are all created using buttons on the Forms tab in the Insert bar. Form objects usually have a label, which is text that describes the purpose of a form object. Labels are created by typing text. Form objects can be tested in a browser window. However, the form will not interact with a server unless a server-side script or application has been defined.

Vocabulary

Absolute hyperlink See External hyperlink.

Branding The technique of raising awareness about a company by making a company logo visible in many places.

Check Box form object A form object that allows the user to select an option by clicking a check box.

Dependent files Images, library items, or other non-HTML files that load with the Web page in a browser.

Dynamic content Content that changes based on input from the user.

Dynamic Web page A Web page that contains any animation or is interactive.

Dynamic Web site A Web site that includes dynamic content on any of the Web pages.

Electronic portfolio Stores and presents portfolio content in a digital format such as a Web site.

External hyperlink A hyperlink that displays a Web page document that is from another Web site.

Form Allows the user to interact with a Web server.

Form object An object in a form that is used to obtain information from the user.

Jump menu A form object that contains a set of text hyperlinks.

Label Text that describes the purpose of a form object.

Pop-up menu A form object that allows the user to select an option from a list of items that appear when the user clicks the ˅ next to the list.

Portfolio A collection of work that clearly illustrates effort, progress, and achievement of knowledge and skills.

Radio Group form object A form object that allows the user to only select one radio button from each group.

Scrolling list A form object that allows the user to select an option from a list of items by scrolling the list using a scroll bar.

Site map A Web page that contains links to information on other pages of the Web site.

Static Web page A Web page that contains only text and images.

Tab-delimited data Data where each item in each row is separated by a tab character.

Tabular data Data that has been created in another application and is saved in a delimited text format.

Web application See Dynamic Web site.

Dreamweaver Commands and Buttons

Button button Inserts a button form object at the insertion point. Found on the Forms tab in the Insert bar.

Checkbox button Inserts a check box form object at the insertion point. Found on the Forms tab in the Insert bar.

Expand/Collapse button Expands the Site panel to the size of the workspace. Found in the Site panel.

Form button Inserts a form at the insertion point. Found on the Forms tab in the Insert bar.

Import Tabular Data **command** Displays a dialog box used to import tab-delimited data from a file into a table in a Web page document. Found in the Table Objects submenu in the Insert menu. The Tabular Data button on the Common tab in the Insert bar can be used instea of the command.

Jump Menu button Displays a dialog box used to insert a jump menu form object at the insertion point. Found on the Forms tab in the Insert bar.

List/Menu button Inserts a List/Menu form object at the insertion point. Found on the Forms tab in the Insert bar.

Radio Group button Displays a dialog box used to insert a radio button group form object at the insertion point. Found on the Forms tab in the Insert bar.

Save Site Map **command** Displays a dialog box which is used to save the site map as a BMP file. Found in the File menu in the expanded Site panel.

Show Dependent Files **command** Displays additional icons for dependent files in the site map. Found in the View menu in the expanded Site panel.

Show Page Titles **command** Displays the page title below each icon instead of the file name in the site map. Found in the View menu in the expanded Site panel.

Site Map button Displays the site map and files. Found in the expanded Site panel.

Text field button Inserts a text field form object at the insertion point. Found on the Forms tab in the Insert bar.

View as Root **command** Changes the focus in the site map to a selected Web page document. Found in the View menu in the expanded Site panel.

Review Questions

Sections 9.1 — 9.13

1. List the five general Web site categories.

2. What does a personal Web site convey?

3. a) What is a portfolio?
   b) What is an electronic portfolio?
   c) List three reasons why electronic portfolios are preferred.

4. List four elements that could be included in an electronic portfolio designed for admission to college.

5. a) What is the purpose of an informational Web site?
   b) List three elements or content often included on an informational Web site.

6. a) What is the purpose of a corporate presence Web site?
   b) What is branding?
   c) List three elements or content often included on a corporate presence Web site.

7. a) What does the Dreamweaver site map resemble?
   b) In the site map, what does red text indicate?

8. a) What does a FAQ page contain?
   b) What is the purpose of a FAQ page?

9. a) What is an external hyperlink?
   b) What is another name for an external hyperlink?
   c) List the steps required to create an external hyperlink.

10. List the steps required to display an existing hyperlink in a new browser window.

11. a) What is tabular data?
    b) What does tab-delimited data indicate?

12. What is a site map?

13. a) What is a jump menu?
    b) List the steps required to add a Jump Menu form object to a form.

Sections 9.14 — 9.18

14. a) What type of content does a static Web page contain?
    b) What is a dynamic Web page?
    c) What is a dynamic Web site?

15. What is a form?

16. a) What is a form object?
    b) List three examples of form objects.

17. What is a label?

18. List the steps required to create a form.

19. In a text field, what does the **Max Chars** property set?

20. When can a form be tested?

21. a) What is a Check Box form object?
    b) What is a Radio Group form object?

22. a) List two objects that allow users to select from a list of predetermined choices on a form.
    b) Why is it better to have limited choices on a form?

Exercises

Exercise 1 — CAKE DELIVERY

Modify the CAKE DELIVERY Web site by completing the following steps:

a) Open the CAKE DELIVERY Web site for editing, a Web site provided with the data files for this text.

b) Modify the copyright library item by replacing Student Name with your name. Allow Dreamweaver to update all occurrences of the library item.

c) Modify the faq.htm Web page document as follows:

1. At the bottom of the list of questions and answers, place the insertion point after the period in from us. and press Enter.
2. Type the following text:
   Q: How many calories are in each cake?
3. Insert a <br> and then type the following text:
   A: One entire cake has 8,867 calories.

d) Modify the win.htm Web page document as follows:

1. In empty cell below the text One entry per e-mail address. create a form with labels, text fields, and buttons as follows:

   ```
   One entry per e-mail address.
   First Name: [    ]
   Last Name: [    ]
   E-mail address: [        ]
   [Send] [Clear Form]
   ```

   For each text field, include an appropriate TextField name and set the Char Width to approximate the examples above. For each button, include an appropriate Button Name.

e) Modify the order.htm Web page document as follows:

1. Place the insertion point to the right of the bold text Order a Cake and press Enter.
2. Add a form at the insertion point.
3. In the form, insert a nested table with 8 rows, 2 columns, a width of 500 pixels, no border, a cell padding of 10, and no cell spacing.
4. In the cells of the nestaed table, add labels, text fields, a scrolling list, radio button groups, a pop-up menu, and buttons as shown on the next page, merging cells as necessary:

Order a Cake

Order placed by:

First Name: [   ]   Last Name: [   ]

Street address: [   ]

City: [   ]   State: [   ]   Zip: [   ]

Phone: [   ]

Place of delivery (if different):

First Name: [   ]   Last Name: [   ]

Street address: [   ]

City: [   ]   State: [   ]   Zip: [   ]

Phone: [   ]

Date of delivery: [   ]

Time:
```
before noon
between noon and 3 p
```

Select a cake flavor:
☐ chocolate
☐ white
☐ yellow
☐ red velvet
☐ lemon

Select a frosting type:
☐ buttercream
☐ chocolate

Select a frosting color (only available with buttercream frosting):
☐ red
☐ green
☐ blue
☐ pink
☐ purple
☐ yellow
☐ orange
☐ white

Select a greeting:
[Happy Birthday Name ▾]

If you would like a Name included in your greeting, enter it here:
[   ]

[Place Order] [Clear Form]

For each form object, include an appropriate name. Set the Char Width for each text field to approximate the examples above. Use the following list items for the scrolling menu and pop-up menu, adding appropriate values for each item:

Scrolling List Items	**Pop-Up Menu Items**
before noon	Happy Birthday Name
between noon and 3 pm	Happy Anniversary Name
between 3 pm and 6 pm	Congratulations Name

Web Site Categories and Types   9 – 31

f) Modify the feedback.htm Web page document as follows:

1. In empty cell below the text We'd love to hear from you! Send us your comments: create a form with labels and form objects as follows:

![Form screenshot showing: "We'd love to hear from you! Send us your comments:" with First Name and Last Name text fields, E-mail address field, "Please rate your last Carter Cake delivery:" with radio buttons for Excellent, Good, Not Quite Satisfactory, Terrible, I have never ordered. "How would you like us to improve our cakes? Please check all that apply." with checkboxes for More shapes, More sizes, More flavors. Comments and suggestions textarea. Send Feedback and Clear Form buttons.]

For each form object, include an appropriate name. Set the Char Width for each text field to approximate the examples above.

g) Modify the sitemap.htm Web page document as follows:

1. In the empty cell in the third row, place the insertion point and type the following text, pressing Enter at the end of each line:

SITE MAP
Cakes
FAQ
Feedback Form
Home
Order a Cake
Site Map
Win a Cake

2. Link text to Web page documents as follows:

Link the text	to the Web page document
Cakes	cakes.htm
FAQ	faq.htm
Feedback Form	feedback.htm
Home	index.htm
Order a Cake	order.htm
Site Map	sitemap.htm
Win a Cake	win.htm

h) Modify the cakes.htm Web page document as follows:

    1. Place the insertion point after the bold text Price List and press Enter.

    2. Insert tabular data, using the carterprices.txt tab-delimited file, a table width that fits the data, a cell padding of 8, no cell spacing, a border of 1, and format the top row of data as bold.

i) View each Web page document in a browser window.

j) Print a copy of each Web page document from the browser.

Exercise 2 — MEASUREMENTS

The MEASUREMENTS Web site was last modified in Chapter 8, Exercise 2. Modify the MEASUREMENTS Web site by completing the following steps:

a) In Dreamweaver, open the MEASUREMENTS Web site for editing.

b) Modify the index.htm Web page document as follows:

    1. In the empty cell in the right side of the third row, place the insertion point.

    2. Insert tabular data, using the si_base_units.txt tab-delimited file, a table width that fits the data, a cell padding of 6, no cell spacing, a border of 1, and format the top row of data as bold.

    3. Near the bottom of the Web page document, place the insertion point after the period in the text table at right. and press Enter.

    4. Type the following text, allowing the text to wrap:
For more information on the International System of Units, visit the Web site of the Bureau International des Poids et Mesures (BIPM), which is based in France.

    5. Link the text Bureau International des Poids et Mesures (BIPM) using an external hyperlink to the following URL:
http://www.bipm.fr/enus/welcome.html

c) Modify the prefix.htm Web page document as follows:

    1. Near the bottom of the Web page document, place the insertion point below the text SI Prefix Chart.

    2. Insert tabular data, using the si_prefixes.txt tab-delimited file, a table width that fits the data, a cell padding of 6, no cell spacing, a border of 1, and format the top row of data as bold.

d) Modify the derive.htm Web page document as follows:

    1. Near the bottom of the Web page document, place the insertion point below the text SI Derived Units Chart.

    2. Insert tabular data, using the si_derive.txt tab-delimited file, a table width that fits the data, a cell padding of 6, no cell spacing, a border of 1, and format the top row of data as bold.

e) View each Web page document in a browser window.

f) Print a copy of each Web page document from the browser.

Exercise 3 — CACTUS

The CACTUS Web site was last modified in Chapter 6, Exercise 2. Modify the CACTUS Web site by completing the following steps:

a) In Dreamweaver, open the CACTUS Web site for editing.

b) Modify the index.htm Web page document as follows:

1. Above the photos, add text after A Gallery of Cactus Photographs so that it appears similar to:

   A Gallery of Cactus Photographs Taken at the Desert Botanical Garden

2. Link the text Desert Botanical Garden using an external hyperlink to the following URL:

   http://www.dbg.org/

c) Modify the types.htm Web page document as follows:

1. Place the insertion point after the period in the text roots of larger cacti. and press Enter.
2. Create a form with labels, text fields, and buttons as follows:

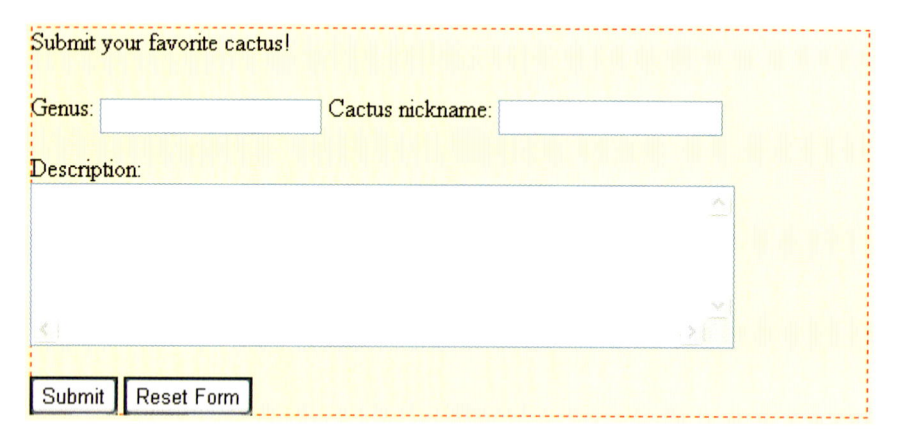

   ```
   Submit your favorite cactus!

   Genus: [        ]    Cactus nickname: [        ]

   Description:
   [                                              ]
   [                                              ]
   [                                              ]

   [Submit] [Reset Form]
   ```

   For each text field, include an appropriate **TextField** name. For the Multi line text field, set the **Char Width** to 70 and the **Num Lines** to 5. For the other text fields, set the **Char Width** to approximate the examples above. For each button, include an appropriate **Button Name**.

Exercise 4 — Cooking Herbs

The Cooking Herbs Web site was last modified in Chapter 8, Exercise 3. Modify the Cooking Herbs Web site by completing the following steps:

a) In Dreamweaver, open the Cooking Herbs Web site for editing.

b) Modify the recipes.htm Web page document as follows:

1. In the bottom row, merge the two cells.
2. Insert a row above the bottom row and place the insertion point in the new row.
3. Create a form with labels, text fields, and buttons as follows:

```
Submit your favorite recipe!

First Name: [    ]     Last Name: [    ]

E-mail address: [              ]

Recipe title: [            ]

Type the recipe here:
[                    ]
[                    ]
[                    ]

[Submit Recipe] [Reset]
```

For each text field, include an appropriate TextField name. For the Multi line text field, set the Char Width to 50 and the Num Lines to 6. For the other text fields, set the Char Width to approximate the examples above. For each button, include an appropriate Button Name.

4. In the cell below the top global navigation bar, place the insertion point before the text People have made and press Enter.
5. Move the insertion point to the blank paragraph just created above the text People have made.
6. Add a form at the insertion point.
7. In the form, add a jump menu that contains the following menu items:

Menu Item Text	Go To URL
Popular Herbs	popular_herbs.htm
Recipes	recipes.htm

Include a GO button next to the jump menu.

c) View each Web page document in a browser window and test the Flash buttons and Flash text.

d) Print a copy of the popular_herbs.htm and recipes.htm Web page documents from the browser.

Exercise 5 (advanced) ——————————— Name Portfolio

Develop an electronic portfolio Web site for yourself, naming it Name Portfolio, replacing Name with your name. The Web site should include:

- a home page with your name, contact information, a greeting, and a photo if possible
- a Web page document that contains your detailed academic history
- a Web page document that contains your detailed work history
- at least one other Web page document that presents information about your accomplishments

Web Site Categories and Types

- a Web page document that contains a writing sample
- at least one other Web page document that presents work samples or contains links to samples of your work on other Web sites

Preview the Web site in a browser. When satisfied with the Web site, print a copy of each Web page document from the browser.

Exercise 6 (advanced) — Photographer

The Photographer Web site was created in Chapter 6, Exercise 7 (advanced). Modify the Photographer Web site to include a feedback form at the bottom of one of the Web pages. Include at least the following form objects:

- two text fields
- one radio button group
- two check boxes
- one List/Menu form object
- one button

Preview the Web site in a browser. When satisfied with the Web site, print a copy of the modified Web page document from the browser.

Exercise 7 (advanced) — Flash Logos

The Photographer Web site was created in Chapter 8, Exercise 6 (advanced). Modify the Flash Logos Web site as follows:

a) Add another Web page document to the Web site naming it orderform.htm. Modify the new Web page document to include a table similar to the other Web page documents in the Web site and the same buttons, footer, and other elements. Include links to the home page and other pages.

b) On each Web page document except orderform.htm, add Flash text that reads Order Your Logo and links to orderform.htm.

c) Add a form to orderform.htm that can be used to order a logo. Include form objects that allow the user to select the color, font, and finished size of the logo.

Preview the Web site in a browser. When satisfied with the Web site, print a copy of each Web page document from the browser.

Exercise 8 (advanced) ——————————————— Local Club

The Local Club Web site was created in Chapter 5, Exercise 6 (advanced). Modify the Local Club Web site as follows:

a) Add another Web page document to the Web site naming it joinform.htm. Modify the new Web page document to include a table similar to the other Web page documents in the Web site and the same buttons, footer, and other elements. Include links to the home page and other pages.

b) On each Web page document except joinform.htm, add Flash text that reads Join Our Club! and links to joinform.htm.

c) Add a form to joinform.htm that can be used to join the club. Include form objects that allow the user to submit their name, e-mail, and appropriate information that pertains to the topic of the club.

Preview the Web site in a browser. When satisfied with the Web site, print a copy of each Web page document from the browser.

Chapter 10
Publishing and Promoting a Web Site

Chapter 10 Expectations

After completing this chapter you will be able to:

1. Outline the process of publishing a Web site.
2. Check the spelling and grammar on each Web page of a Web site.
3. Assess the download time of a Web page document.
4. Define target browser and determine which target browser should be used to test a site.
5. Preview a Web site in a target browser.
6. Test the HTML associated with a Web page for target browser compatibility.
7. Test a Web site for broken and missing links.
8. Check a Web site for HTML problems.
9. Explain what a Web host is and distinguish between virtual and non-virtual hosting.
10. Publish a Web site to a Web server and to a local/network server.
11. Update a published site.
12. Promote a published Web site.
13. Add meta tags.
14. Describe ways to measure the success of a Web site.

This chapter discusses publishing and promoting a Web site, and measuring its success. Maintaining a Web site is also discussed.

10.1 Publishing a Web Site

Publishing a Web site is the process of uploading a local site to a Web server so that the site can be accessed on the World Wide Web. The Web sites developed in this text are referred to as *local sites* because the sites have been saved and edited on a local disk. A *remote server* can be a Web server provided by an ISP, an intranet server, or a local/network server.

local sites
remote server

> **Web Server**
>
> A Web server responds to requests from clients, usually a Web browser, for HTML documents and any associated files or scripts. A Web server is also called an HTTP server.

Before a Web site is published, it should be checked and tested:

- each Web page document should be checked for misspellings and grammar errors
- the download time of each Web page document should be checked to ensure that they are not too long
- target browsers should be determined and then each Web page document should be previewed in each target browser
- the HTML should be tested for target browser compatibility
- the site should be checked for broken links and missing links
- the HTML should be checked for problems such as missing Alt text, empty tags, and untitled pages

After a Web site is published, it still needs attention:

- the Web site should be constantly maintained in order to keep the content updated
- the Web site may need to be promoted so that users are aware that the Web site is available
- some measure of success should be used to ensure that the Web site is serving its intended purpose

Notice that there is substantial preparation before publishing a Web site, and once it is published the Web site is still modified periodically.

10.2 Checking Spelling and Grammar

A Web site with spelling or grammar errors seems less credible. Before a site is published, all Web page documents in the site should be checked for spelling and grammar errors just before publishing because errors are often created from last minute changes.

Each Web page document in a site has to be checked for spelling errors by opening the Web page document and selecting Text → Check Spelling.

Grammar errors are found by proofreading each Web page document. The Web page documents should be printed from a browser because it is easier to proofread a hard copy than text on a screen. It is also a good idea to get another person to proofread the hard copy because it is often difficult to thoroughly proofread your own work.

10.3 Checking the Download Time

download time

weight of the page

Before a site is published, each Web page document should be opened and the download time checked. The *download time* is the time it takes the Web page document to load into a user's browser. The status bar at the bottom of a Document window displays the *weight of the page*, which is the Web page Document's file size and the estimated download time:

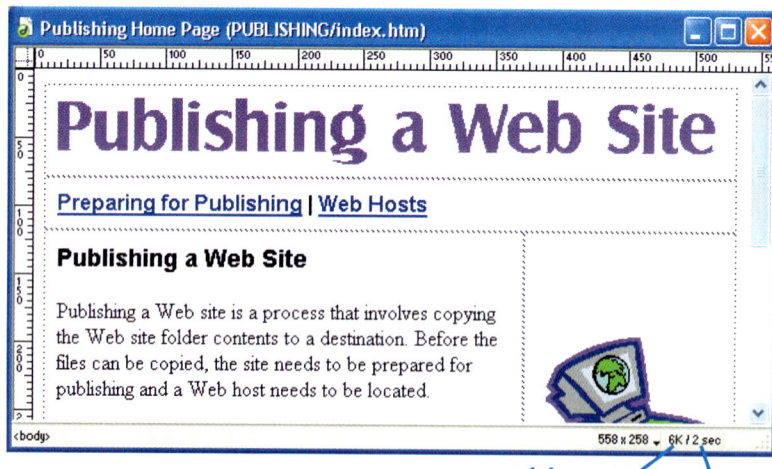

file size
estimated download time

Kilobytes and Megabytes

File size is usually expressed in kilobytes (K) or megabytes (M). A kilobytes is approximately 1,000 bytes and a megabyte is approximately 1,000,000 bytes.

In the example above, the file size is 6K (kilobytes) and is estimated to take 2 seconds to download the page.

Download time is calculated based on a connection speed. The default is 28.8 Kbps per second. The download time for a page is important because users will only wait about 12 seconds for a page to load before clicking a link or the Back button in their browser. A Web page document that is estimated to take a long time to load may need to be separated into two Web pages. Large image file sizes or many images in one document can also affect the download time.

Changing the Connection Speed

The connection speed used to calculate the download time is changed by selecting Edit → Preferences, selecting Status Bar in the Category list, and selecting a connection speed.

A Guide to Web Development Using Macromedia Dreamweaver MX

Practice 1

In this practice you will check a Web site for spelling errors and check the download times.

① OPEN THE PUBLISHING WEB SITE FOR EDITING

    a. Start Dreamweaver.

    b. In the Site panel, open the PUBLISHING Web site, a Web site provided with the data files for this text.

    c. In the Site panel, familiarize yourself with the files and folders for this Web site.

    d. Open the index.htm Web page document and then view it in a browser.

    e. Click the links to explore the two other Web pages of the Web site.

    f. Close the browser window.

② CHECK THE SPELLING

    a. Open the index.htm Web page document if it is not already displayed.

    b. Select Text → Check Spelling. A dialog box is displayed.

        1. In the Suggestions list, select Publishing.

        2. Select Change. The dialog box is removed and another dialog box is displayed.

            a. Select OK.

    c. Save the modified index.htm.

    d. Check the spelling in the other two Web page documents and save any changes.

③ CHECK THE DOWNLOAD TIMES

    a. Display index.htm and note the file size and download time.

    b. Note the file sizes and download times for the other two Web page documents.

10.4 Target Browsers

A Dreamweaver Web site may include elements that are not supported by all browsers, such as JavaScript. A *target browser* is a browser and version, such as Internet Explorer 6.0, in which the Web site is designed to display correctly. The Web sites developed in this text have been designed using Internet Explorer 6.0 as the target browser.

A Web site on the Web is going to be viewed with different browsers, monitor sizes, screen resolutions, and connection speeds. Therefore, the site should be viewed and tested in more than one target browser and resolution. It is recommended that at least a version of the two most widely used browsers, Internet Explorer and Netscape Navigator, be used to preview the site.

determining target browsers

One way to determine which browsers to target is to extend the definition of the target audience for the Web site by asking the following questions:

1. What platform will be used? Windows, Linux, or another?

2. What type of connection and speed will be used? Dial-up, DSL, cable?

> **Browsers**
>
> Netscape Navigator and Internet Explorer are the most widely used Web browsers. Another Web browser, Opera, is known for its strict adherence to W3C standards and small file size.

> **Linux**
>
> Linux is an operating system which is distributed free of charge. The source code for the Linux operating system is open source code, which means it can be modified by anyone.

3. What browser will be used? Internet Explorer, Netscape Navigator, or another?
4. What screen resolution will be used? Perhaps 800x600, or 1024x768?

A Web site that is going to be published to a controlled environment, such as a company intranet, need only be tested using the browser and resolution that the company employees use.

10.5 Previewing in a Target Browser

Once the target browsers have been determined, the Preview in Browser command can be used to preview the site in the target browsers. When previewing the site in a target browser, check for:

- fonts and colors displaying correctly
- tables and alignments displaying correctly and acting appropriately when the browser window is resized
- images displaying correctly

Selecting File → Preview in Browser displays a submenu with a list of browsers installed on the computer.

A browser is added to the Preview in Browser submenu by selecting File → Preview in Browser → Edit Browser List, which displays the Preferences dialog box. Selecting Preview in Browser in the Category list displays those options:

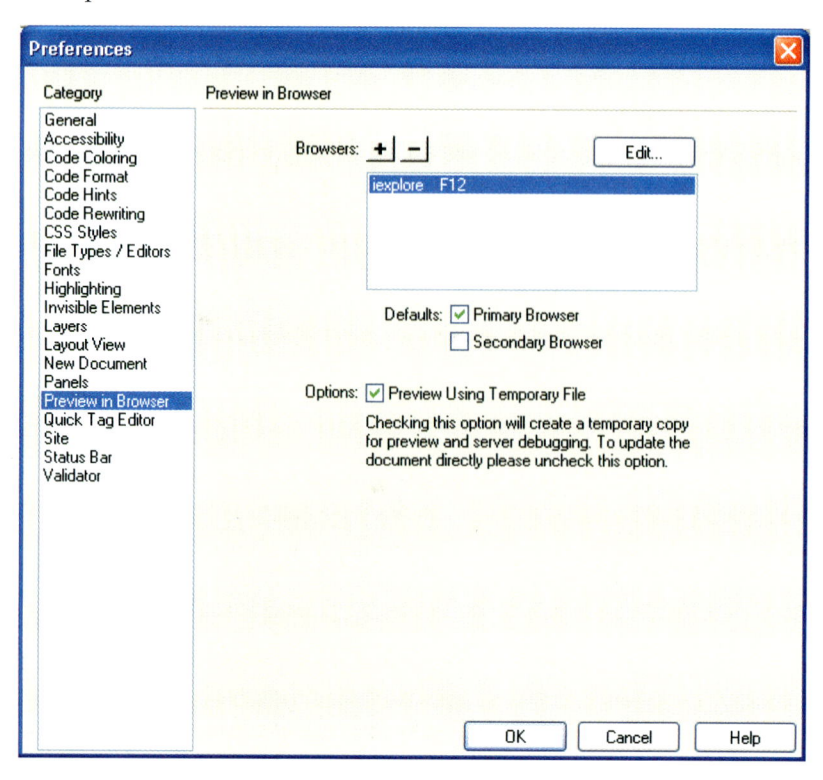

> **Screen Resolution**
>
> When previewing in a target browser, the screen resolution should be changed to view the site at different resolutions. The screen resolution can be changed by selecting Appearance and Themes in the Control Panel.

> **Downloading Browsers**
>
> In order to preview a Web site in a browser, the browser must be installed on the local computer. Browsers can be downloaded from the Web.

Clicking ➕ displays the Add Browser dialog box:

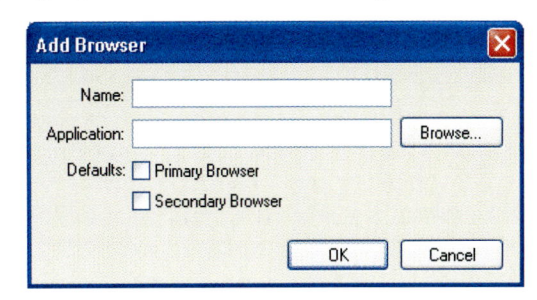

Add Browser
Name:
Application: [Browse...]
Defaults: ☐ Primary Browser
☐ Secondary Browser
[OK] [Cancel]

A name for the browser is typed in the Name box and Browse is clicked to navigate to the browser application file. Up to 20 browsers can be listed.

Practice 2

In this practice you will preview a Web page document in more than one target browser, if possible. Dreamweaver should be started and the PUBLISHING Web site should be the working site.

① PREVIEW THE WEB SITE IN THE DEFAULT BROWSER

a. Open the index.htm Web page document if it is not already displayed.

b. Select File → Preview in Browser and select the primary browser, which is the first browser listed in the submenu. The Web page document is displayed in the browser window. Note the way the fonts, colors, alignments, and images are displayed.

c. Size the browser window larger and smaller by dragging the bottom-right window corner. Note how the layout adjusts as the browser is sized.

d. Close the browser window.

② PREVIEW THE WEB SITE IN A DIFFERENT BROWSER

a. If an additional browser is installed on the computer, select File → Preview in Browser and select the second browser in the submenu. The Web page document is displayed in the browser window. Compare the way the fonts, colors, alignments, and images are displayed.

b. Size the browser window larger and smaller by dragging the bottom-right window corner. Note how the layout adjusts as the browser is sized.

c. Close the browser window.

10.6 Testing the HTML for Target Browser Compatibility

The Check Target Browsers command tests the HTML associated with a Web page to see if any tags or attributes are not supported by the selected target browsers. Unlike the Preview in Browser command, the Check Target Browsers command does not require the browser and version to be installed on the local computer. Selecting File → Check Page → Check Target Browsers displays the Check Target Browsers dialog box:

Saving a Report

Reports are temporary files, but can be saved by selecting the Save Report button (💾) in the Reports Group panel. The report is saved as an XML document.

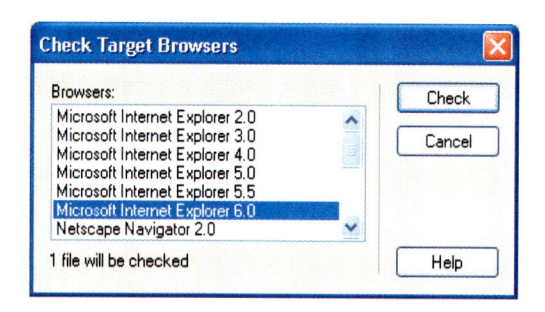

In the Browsers list, select the browsers to test. More than one browser can be selected by holding down the Ctrl key while selecting. Selecting Check displays a report in the Target Browser Check panel in the Results panel group:

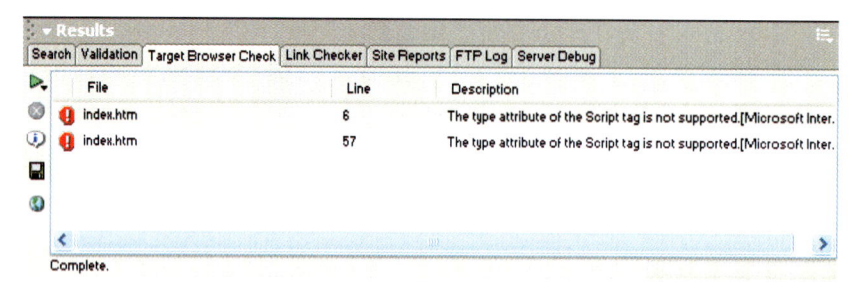

The report generates a list of tags and attributes that are not supported by a selected browser. Double-clicking an entry in the File column of the Link Checker panel opens the corresponding Web page document so that it can be edited. Note that each Web page document in a site must be tested individually.

A Web page should be designed to *fail gracefully*, which is a design technique used to ensure that a site displays appropriately when some elements are not supported. Using this technique, when a Web page contains elements that will not display in certain browsers, another Web page document is created containing elements that will display correctly.

Check Browser and Check Plugin Actions

The Check Browser action checks which browser the user has and displays the appropriate Web page document. This action is commonly used with the fail gracefully technique of creating more than one Web page with similar content.

The Check Plugin action is used in a similar manner, to check the version of Plugins that the user has installed.

10.7 Testing for Broken Links and Missing Links

Document-relative links in an entire Web site can be checked for broken and missing links by selecting Site → Check Links Sitewide in the Site panel, which displays a report in the Link Checker panel in the Results group panel:

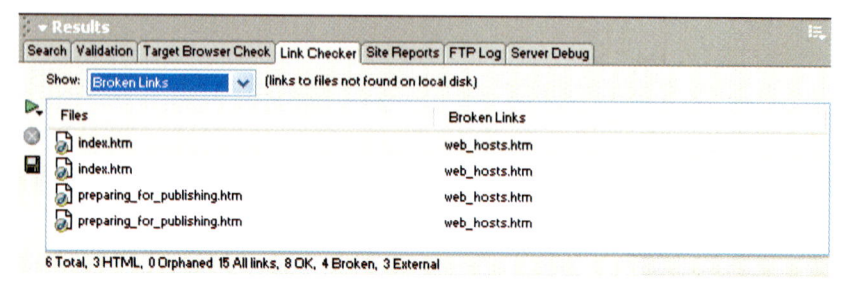

broken links   A Broken Links report is displayed by default. Any broken links need to be fixed before the site is published. Double-clicking a broken link entry in the Files column of the Link Checker panel opens the appropriate Web page document, selects the broken link, and selects the path and file name in the Property inspector. Correcting the link results in the entry being automatically removed from the list.

external links   A list of external or absolute links is displayed by selecting External Links in the Show list. Note that external links are just listed, not checked.

orphan files   An *orphan file* has no links to it in the entire site. Selecting Orphaned Files in the Show list displays a list of orphan files, which may indicate missing links.

10.8 Checking for HTML Problems

In Dreamweaver, a report can be generated that checks external links, accessibility, missing Alt text, and untitled documents of the entire Web site. Selecting Site → Reports displays the Reports dialog box:

> **Language References**
>
> If the code needs to be checked or edited before a site is published, the Reference panel in Code view can be used to access information about markup languages, JavaScript, and cascading style sheets.

Selecting Entire Current Local Site in the Report on list checks the entire site. Selecting the appropriate HTML Reports and then selecting Run creates a report and displays it in the Sites Reports panel in the Results panel group:

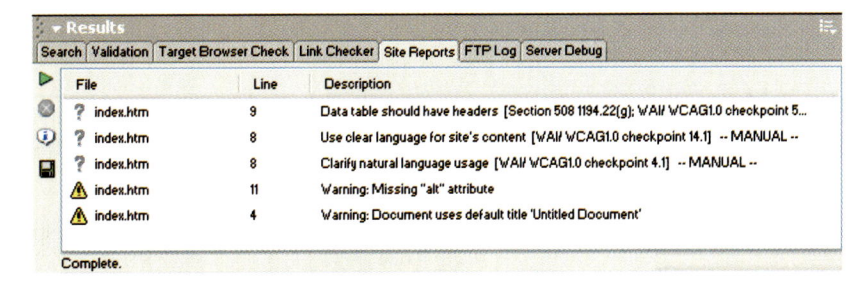

> **Accessibility**
>
> Section 508 of the Federal Rehabilitation Act stipulates that U.S. Federal agencies have to make their electronic and information technology accessible to individuals with disabilities. One requirement of this Act is that Alt (alternative) Text in the form of labels or descriptors be provided for all graphics.

Double-clicking a file name in the File column opens the Web page document so that it can be edited. Note that HTML errors listed in the report may be able to be corrected in the open Web page document by selecting Commands → Clean up HTML.

Publishing and Promoting a Web Site

Practice 3

In this practice you will test HTML for target browser compatibility, test for broken and missing links, and check for HTML problems. Dreamweaver should be started and the PUBLISHING Web site should be the working site.

① **TEST THE HTML FOR BROWSER COMPATIBILITY**

   a. Open the index.htm Web page document if it is not already displayed.
   b. Select File → Check Page → Check Target Browsers. A dialog box is displayed.
      1. Hold down the Ctrl key and, in the Browsers list, click Microsoft Internet Explorer 3.0, Microsoft Internet Explorer 5.0, and Netscape Navigator 4.0.
      2. Select Check. A report is displayed in the Target Browser Check panel in the Results panel group. Note that the report is empty, indicating all the elements are supported in the selected target browsers.

② **CHECK FOR BROKEN OR MISSING LINKS**

   a. In the Site panel, select Site → Check Links Sitewide. A report is displayed in the Link Checker panel in the Results panel group. Note that the report is empty, indicating that there are no problems with the links.

③ **GENERATE A SITE REPORT**

   a. Select Site → Reports. A dialog box is displayed.
      1. In the Report on list, select Entire Current Local Site.
      2. In the Selected Reports box, select Missing Alt Text and Untitled Documents.
      3. Select Run. A report is displayed in the Site Reports panel in the Results panel group. Note that the Site report lists two entries.
   b. Double-click the index.htm entry, which indicates an untitled document. The HTML associated with index.htm is displayed.
   c. On the Document toolbar, in the title box, replace the text Untitled Document with Publishing Home Page.
   d. Save the modified index.htm.
   e. Double-click the preparing_for_publishing.htm entry, which indicates an image on the page is missing the alt attribute. The HTML associated with preparing_for_publishing.htm is displayed.
   f. On the Document toolbar click the Show Design View button (). The Web page document is displayed in Design view. The image in the top cell of the table is selected because it is missing Alt text.
   g. In the Property inspector, set Alt to: Publishing a Web Site.
   h. Save the modified preparing_for_publishing.htm.

10.9 What is a Web Host?

TCP/IP software
HTTP software

A Web site on the Web has been published to a Web server. A Web server computer runs *TCP/IP software* (Transmission Control Protocol/Internet Protocol) in order to be connected to the Internet and *HTTP software* (Hypertext Transfer Protocol) in order to handle the hyperlinks between Web pages.

Web hosting companies
Web hosts

Web servers are often managed by *Web hosting companies*, also called *Web hosts*, which provide space on their server for a fee. Web hosts also provide services such as registering a domain name for a Web site. *Domain names* are used to identify a particular Web page and are made up of a sequence of parts, or subnames, separated by periods that may stand for the server, organization, or organization type. For example, www.lpdatafiles.com is a domain name.

domain names

domain name considerations

A consideration when choosing a domain name is that users should associate it with the Web site, such as the business name or major topic that the site is about. It is also good if the domain name is easy to remember, and is one that users can probably guess if they do not know it. Registering a domain name provides the exclusive right to use that name. A periodic renewal fee is required to keep the domain name.

virtual hosting

non-virtual hosting

There are two types of hosting options. *Virtual hosting* is the most common type and allows a Web site to be identified by a selected domain name, such as www.lpdatafiles.com. *Non-virtual hosting* requires a Web site to be identified by a subdirectory name, which is on the host's domain. For example, www.webhostname.com/sitename. While this option is free, the domain name is not as easy for a user to remember. Companies that offer free non-virtual hosting include GeoCities, Tripod, and Angelfire.

IP Address

An IP address (Internet Protocol address) is a 32-bit binary number that identifies a computer or device connected to the Internet. An IP address is four numbers separated by periods, such as 1.120.05.123. Typing an IP address in a Web browser accesses a Web site.

Since it is difficult to remember IP addresses, the Domain Name System (DNS) is used. When a domain name is entered, it is automatically translated into an IP address.

10.10 Publishing to a Web Server

Publishing a Web site requires obtaining a Web host, defining the remote site, and then uploading the site. *Uploading* means to post the files to a Web server. Select Site → Edit Site, which displays the Edit Site dialog box:

defining a remote site

Select a site and then Edit to display the Site Definition dialog box. Select the **Advanced** tab and then select the **Remote Info** category. In the **Access** list, select a method for connecting to the remote server:

FTP

FTP (File Transfer Protocol) is used to rapidly transfer (upload and download) files from one computer to another over the Internet.

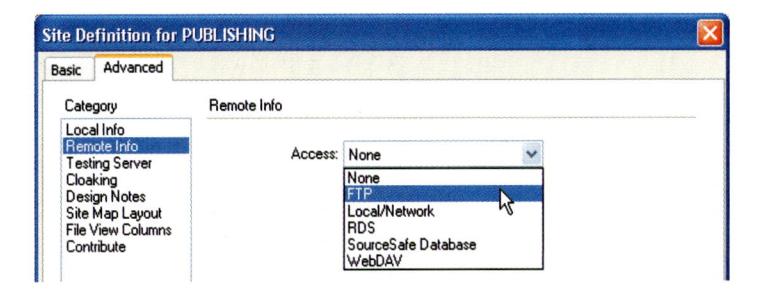

Publishing and Promoting a Web Site

FTP is a common method of publishing to a Web server. Select FTP to display additional options:

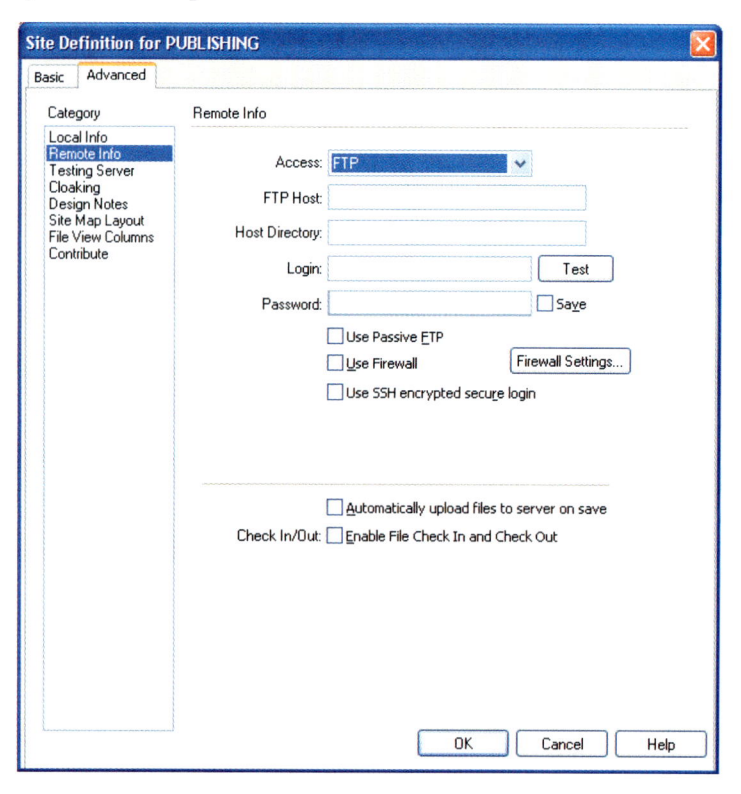

[Screenshot of Site Definition for PUBLISHING dialog, Advanced tab, Remote Info category, with Access set to FTP, showing FTP Host, Host Directory, Login, Password fields, Use Passive FTP, Use Firewall, Use SSH encrypted secure login options, and Check In/Out settings.]

- The FTP Host box is used to indicate the hostname of the server, which usually starts with ftp.
- Information for the Host Directory, Login, and Password boxes is provided by the Web host.

Select OK to finish setting up the remote site, and then select Done to remove the Edit Sites dialog box.

uploading the files

The Web site is uploaded to the remote site by selecting the site's root folder in the Site panel and then clicking the Put File(s) button (⬆). All of the site file's are uploaded to the remote server. The site should then viewed at the appropriate URL and tested.

> **The Put Command**
>
> In the Site panel, Site → Put can be used instead of the button.

10.11 Publishing to a Local/Network Server

A Web site can be published to a local or network server instead of a Web host's Web server. Intranets are on local servers. Publishing a Web site to a local or network server requires obtaining server space where a local/network site can be set up, setting up the local/network site, and then uploading the site. Select Site → Edit Site, which displays the Edit Site dialog box. Select a site and then select Edit to display the Site Definition dialog box. Select the Advanced tab and then select the Remote Info category. In the Access list, select Local/Network, which displays additional options:

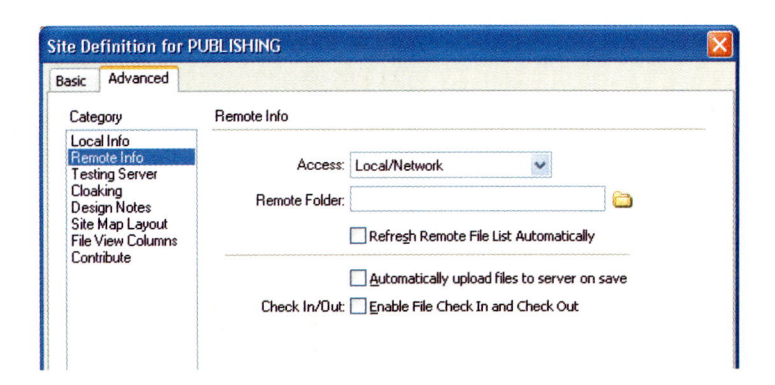

Click the folder icon (📁) to display the Choose Remote Root Folder dialog box:

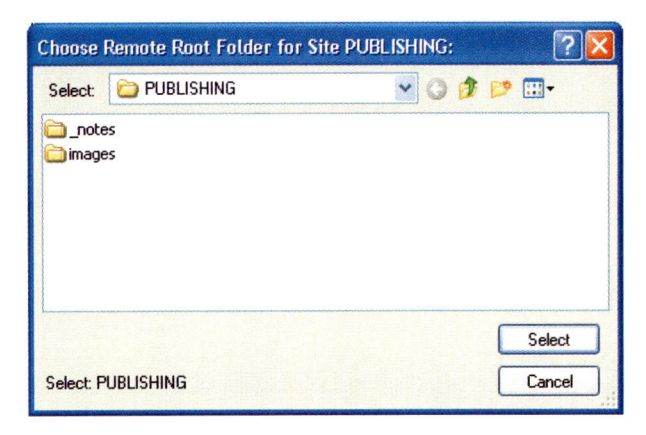

Navigate to the remote server folder location and click Select. The folder location is placed in the Remote folder box. Select OK to finish setting up the local/network site, and then select Done to remove the Edit Sites dialog box.

The Web site is uploaded to the remote site by selecting the site's root folder in the Site panel and then clicking the Put File(s) button (⬆). In the Site panel, Site → Put can be used instead of the button. All of the site file's are uploaded to the remote site. The site should then viewed at the appropriate URL and tested.

uploading the files The Web site is uploaded to the local/network server by selecting the site's local folder in the Site panel and then clicking the Put File(s) button (⬆), which displays a dialog box:

FTP Log

Dreamweaver keeps a record of all FTP activity. This activity can be viewed by selecting View → Site FTP Log in the Site Panel.

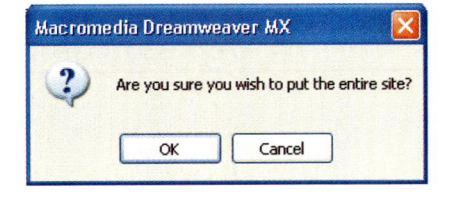

Selecting OK uploads the files to the server. The site should then be viewed and tested in a browser.

Publishing and Promoting a Web Site 10 – 11

10.12 Maintaining a Web Site

A Web site requires frequent updating in order to keep users coming back to the site. The parallel structure of the local site and the remote site makes maintaining a Web site simple. Both the local site and the remote site can be viewed and accessed from the Site panel.

The file structure of the remote site can be viewed by selecting the Connects to remote host button ( ) and then selecting Remote View in the Site panel:

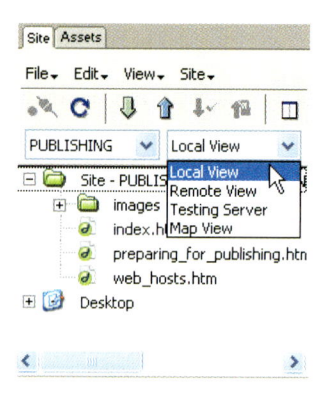

In Remote View, a file is downloaded from the remote site to the local site by selecting the file in the Site panel and then clicking the Get File(s) button ( ).

editing a file and uploading

In Local View, the local site folder is displayed in the Site panel. A Web page document can be edited in the local site and uploaded to the remote site. Clicking the Put File(s) button ( ) uploads a selected file to the remote site. Edited pages should be viewed and tested in a browser. Note that the Put File(s) button automatically connects to the remote site if a connection is not already established.

collaboration

A *collaboration* is when more than one person is working on the same Web site. This is accomplished by selecting the Enable File Check In and Check Out option when setting up the remote site. In a collaborative environment, people check out files from the remote site, modify the files, and check in the files when work is completed. This way, another person cannot work on the same file at the same time. Instead of using the Get File(s) and Put File(s) buttons, the Check Out File(s) button ( ) and the Check In button ( ) is used. In the Site panel, and Checked out file that you are working on has a green check mark next to it. A red check mark indicates a Checked out file someone else is working on:

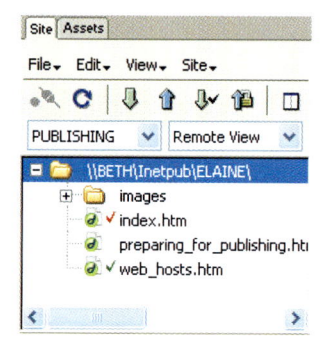

10.13 Promoting a Web Site

Once a Web site is published, there are various promotion techniques that can be used to help users find the site. One technique is to add additional meta tags to the home page of a Web site, to increase the probability that a Web site is found by a search engine.

meta tag

meta data

Meta tags apear in the HTML head section of a document. There are several different meta tags that are used to add meta data to a document. *Meta data* is information about the Web site contents, and can be added to a document using several different meta tags. Note that meta tags are not required, nor do they affect the layout of a Web page.

keywords

description

One type of meta data is *keywords*, which are words or phrases that describe the site's content. Many search engines use keywords to index Web sites, so the keywords should be ones that may be used as search criteria. Another type of meta data is a *description*, which search engines use to display in the search results:

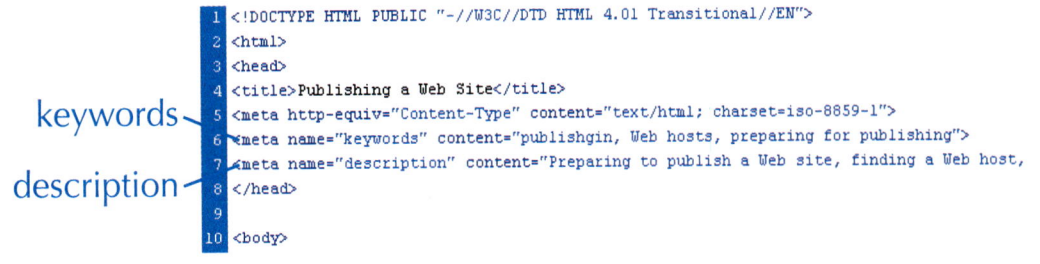

```
1  <!DOCTYPE HTML PUBLIC "-//W3C//DTD HTML 4.01 Transitional//EN">
2  <html>
3  <head>
4  <title>Publishing a Web Site</title>
5  <meta http-equiv="Content-Type" content="text/html; charset=iso-8859-1">
6  <meta name="keywords" content="publishgin, Web hosts, preparing for publishing">
7  <meta name="description" content="Preparing to publish a Web site, finding a Web host,
8  </head>
9
10 <body>
```
keywords → line 6
description → line 7

A document's Code view

The Content-Type meta tag shown above is automatically added by Dreamweaver. The keywords and description meta tags can be added to the displayed Web page document using buttons on the Head tab in the Insert bar:

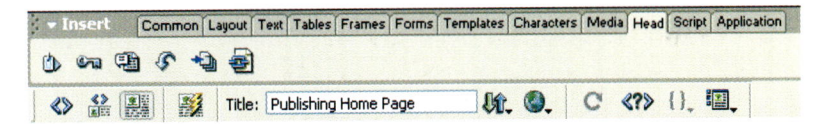

adding keyword meta data

Clicking the Keywords button ( ) displays the Keywords dialog box:

Keywords are typed in the Keywords box, separating each keyword or phrase with a comma. Selecting OK adds the meta tag. Note that the most important keywords should be listed first because some search engines limit the number of keywords that can be specified.

adding description meta data

Clicking the Description button ( ) displays the Description dialog box:

Publishing and Promoting a Web Site   10 – 13

A description of the Web site is typed in the Description box. Selecting OK adds the meta tag.

more promoting techniques

reciprocal links

Another technique for promoting a Web site is to list it with search engines and directories. Some search engines and directories charge a fee for this service. Another technique often used involves *reciprocal links*, where Web sites with complementary information post links to each other's sites. Another promotion technique is advertising by e-mail or in printed media. Including Web site addresses on company documents such as letterhead or business cards can also help to make more people aware of the Web site.

Practice 4

In this practice you will add a meta tags to a home page. Dreamweaver should be started and the PUBLISHING Web site should be the working site.

① ADD A META TAG WITH KEYWORDS

a. Open the index.htm Web page document if it is not already displayed.

b. On the Document toolbar click the Show Design View button ( ). The Web page document is displayed in Design view.

c. In the Insert bar, select the Head tab and then click the Keywords button ( ). A dialog box is displayed.

   1. In the Keywords box, type: publishing, Web hosts, preparing for publishing
   2. Select OK. A meta tag with keywords has been added to index.htm.

② ADD A META TAG WITH A DESCRIPTION

a. On the Head tab, in the Insert bar, click the Description button ( ). A dialog box is displayed.

   1. In the Description box, type: Preparing to publish a Web site, finding a Web host, and publishing a Web site
   2. Select OK. A meta tag with a description has been added to index.htm.

b. Save the modified page index.htm.

③ VIEW THE CODE

a. On the Document toolbar click the Show Code View button ( ). The code for the Web page document is displayed in the Document window. Note the newly added meta tags:

    <meta name="keywords" content="publishing, Web hosts, preparing for publishing">
    <meta name="description" content="Preparing to publish a Web site, finding a Web host, and publishing a Web site.">

④ QUIT DREAMWEAVER

10.14 Measuring Success

There are a several ways to measure the success of a Web site. One way is to have an online form and analyze the feedback from users to see if there are ways to improve the site.

Web tracking software

Information can also be obtained from the Web host if *Web tracking software* is installed on the server. This software produces a report that contains information about users, such as the IP address, the URL requested, the browser, and the time spent at the site.

Negative feedback or a low amount of user traffic may require additional promoting of the site, changing site content, or changing the design of the site.

Chapter Summary

Publishing a Web site is the process of uploading a local site to a remote server so that the site can be viewed in a Web browser. A remote server can be a Web server provided by an ISP, an intranet server, or a local/network server.

Before a site is published, all Web page documents should be checked for spelling and grammar errors.

The status bar at the bottom of a Document window displays the file size and estimated download time of the Web page document.

A target browser is a browser and version, such as Internet Explorer 6.0, in which a Web site is designed to display correctly. A site should be viewed and tested in more than one target browser. The Preview in Browser command can be used to preview the Web site in different browsers. A browser is added to the Preview in Browser submenu by selecting File → Preview in Browser → Edit Browser List.

The Check Target Browser command tests the HTML associated with a Web page for compatibility problems with target browsers. A Web page should be designed to fail gracefully, which is a design technique used to ensure that a site displays appropriately if some elements are not supported.

Document-relative links in an entire Web site can be checked for broken links by selecting Site → Check Links Sitewide. A report can also be generated that checks external links, accessibility, missing Alt text, and untitled documents by selecting Site → Reports. HTML errors listed in the report may be corrected by selecting Commands → Clean up HTML.

A Web server computer runs TCP/IP software in order to be connected to the Internet and HTTP software in order to handle the hyperlinks between Web pages. Web servers are often managed by Web hosting companies, also called Web hosts, which provide space on their server for a fee.

A Web site can be published to a Web server or to a Local/Network server. A Web site requires frequent updating in order to keep users coming back to the site. A Web page document can be edited from the local site and then uploaded to the remote site. In a collaborative environment, the Check Out File(s) button ( ) and the Check In button ( ) is used to check files out and back in to a remote site.

Once a Web site is published, there are various promotion techniques that can be used to help users find the site. To increase the probability that a Web site is found by a search engine, the Web site should contain meta tags that specify keywords and a description.

There are several ways to measure the success of a Web site. One way is to have an online form and analyze the feedback from users. Information can also be obtained from the Web host if Web tracking software is installed on the server.

Vocabulary

Collaboration When more than one person works on the same Web site.

Description A type of meta data which search engines use to display in the search results.

Domain name Used to identify a particular Web page and is made up of a sequence of parts separated by periods that may stand for the server, organization, or organization type.

Download time The time it takes the Web page document to load into a user's browser.

Fail gracefully A design technique used to ensure a site displays appropriately when some elements are not supported.

HTTP software Software that a Web server computer runs in order to handle the hyperlinks between Web pages.

Keyword A word or phrase that describes the site's content and may be used as search criteria to locate the site.

Local sites Sites that have been saved and edited on a local disk.

Meta data Information about the Web site contents.

Meta tags Tags that appear in the HTML head section of document used to add meta data to a document.

Non-virtual hosting A free hosting option that requires a Web site to be identified by a subdirectory name, which is on the host's domain.

Orphan file A file that has no links to it in the entire Web site.

Publishing a Web site The process of uploading a local site to a Web server so that the site can be accessed on the World Wide Web.

Reciprocal links A technique used to promote a Web site where Web sites with complementary information post links to each other's sites.

Remote server A Web server provided by an ISP, an intranet server, or a local/network server.

Target browser A browser and version, such as Internet Explorer 6.0, in which the Web site is designed to display correctly.

TCP/IP software Software that a Web server computer runs in order to be connected to the Internet.

Uploading Posting files to a Web server.

Virtual hosting The most common type of Web hosting offered by Web hosts. It allows a Web site to be identified by a selected domain name.

Web hosting company A company that manages a Web server and provides space on their server for a fee.

Web hosts *See* Web hosting company.

Web tracking software Software installed on a server that allows a report to be produced containing information about users to the site such as the IP address, the URL requested, the browser, and the time spent at the site.

Weight of the page A Web page document's file size and the estimated download time.

Dreamweaver Commands and Buttons

Check In button Uploads checked-out files to a remote server and removes the checked out mark(s). Found on the Site panel toolbar.

Check Links Sitewide command Checks the site for broken links and displays a report in the Link Checker Panel in the Results group panel. Found in the Site menu in the Site panel.

Check Out File(s) button Downloads file(s) from a remote server and marks them as checked out. Found on the Site panel toolbar.

Check Spelling **command** Finds misspelled words in a Web page document. Found in the Text menu.

Check Target Browsers **command** Displays a dialog box used to see if any tags or attributes are not supported by selected target browser. Found in the Check Page submenu in the File menu.

Clean up HTML command Displays a dialog box used to correct HTML errors. Found in the Commands menu.

Connects to remote host button Connects to the remote server. Found on the Site panel toolbar.

Description button Displays a dialog box used to type a description of the Web site for a meta tag. Found on the Head tab in the Insert bar.

Edit Browser List **command** Displays a dialog box used to add a browser at the Preview in Browser submenu. Found in the Preview in Browser submenu in the File menu.

Edit Site **command** Displays a dialog box used to edit an existing site. Found in the Site menu.

Folder icon Displays a dialog box used to select the remote root folder. Found in the Site Definition for Publishing dialog box.

Get File(s) button Downloads file(s) from a remote server to the local site. Found on the Site panel toolbar.

Keywords button Displays a dialog box used to type keywords for a meta tag. Found on the Head tab in the Insert bar.

Preview in Browser **command** Displays a submenu used to select a browser to preview the Web page document in. Found in the File menu.

Put File(s) button Uploads file(s) from the local site to a remote site. Found on the Site panel toolbar.

Reports **command** Displays a dialog box used to generate a report that checks external links, accessibility, missing Alt text, and untitled documents. Found in the Site menu.

Review Questions

Sections 10.1 — 10.8

1. a) What is publishing a Web site?
   b) Where are local sites saved and edited?

2. What should be checked and tested before a Web site is published?

3. Why should Web page documents be checked for spelling and grammar errors?

4. What does the "weight of the page" refer to?

5. How long will users typically wait for a page to load before clicking on a different link?

6. a) What is a target browser?
   b) Why should a Web site be viewed and tested in more than one target browser?

7. List four questions that could be asked about the target audience to help define which browsers to target when testing a Web site.

8. a) List the step required to add a browser to the Preview in Browser submenu.
   b) How many browsers can be listed in the Preview in Browser submenu?

9. a) What does the Check Target Browsers command test?
   b) List the steps required to select two browsers in the Check Target Browsers dialog box and then test the page.

10. What does "fail gracefully" mean?

11. List the step required to check the document-relative links in a Web site for broken links.

12. What does the Orphaned Files report display?

13. a) What can be checked in the report that is generated by selecting Site → Reports?
    b) List the steps required to correct HTML errors if any are listed in a report that has been generated in the Site Reports panel.

Sections 10.9 — 10.14

14. a) Why does a Web server run TCP/IP software?
    b) Why does a Web server run HTTP software?

15. What do Web hosting companies provide?

16. a) What are domain names used for?
    b) List one consideration when choosing a domain name.

17. a) Explain the difference between virtual hosting and non-virtual hosting options.
    b) List three companies that offer free non-virtual hosting.

18. a) What does publishing a Web site to a Web server require?
    b) What is uploading?

19. What does publishing a Web site to a local/network server require?

20. a) List the steps required to download files from the remote site to the local site.
    b) List the steps required to upload an edited file from the local site to the remote site.

21. What is collaboration?

22. a) What is a meta tag?
    b) What is meta data?
    c) Why should a meta tag be used?
    d) What are keywords?

23. a) Are meta tags required in a Web site?
    b) Does the meta tag affect the content of a Web site?
    c) List the steps required to add a meta tag with keywords.
    d) List the steps required to add a meta tag with a description.

24. What are reciprocal links?

25. List two ways to promote a Web site.

26. List two ways to measure the success of a Web site.

27. What is Web tracking software?

Exercises

Exercise 1

Publish a previously created Web site to a Local/Network site by completing the following steps:

a. Check the spelling of each of the Web page documents in the Web site.

b. Check the file size and download time of each of the Web page documents in the Web site.

c. Determine which target browsers the Web site should be tested in.

d. Preview the Web site in more than one browser, if possible.

e. Test the HTML in each Web page document for compatibility with at least three browsers.

f. Test the Web site for broken and missing links.

g. Check the Web site for Missing Alt Text and Untitled Documents.

h. Add keyword meta data with at least two appropriate keywords.

i. Add description meta data with an appropriate description of the Web site.

j. Publish the Web site to a Local folder.

Exercise 2 — Nonvirtual

Use the Internet to research the steps required to publish the Web site to a non-virtual host. Present the research in the form of an informational Web site.

Exercise 3 — Virtual

Use the Internet, newspapers, and local contacts and businesses to research the costs involved and steps required to publish the Web site to a virtual host. Present the research in the form of an informational Web site.

Appendix A
HTML

This appendix lists commonly used HTML tags and attributes.

Document Tags

<html> </html>
Indicates the start and end of an HTML document.

<head> </head>
Indicates the start and end of the HEAD section.

<title> </title>
Used to display a title in the title bar of the browser's window.

<body> </body>
Indicates the start and end of the BODY section. Attributes include:

> bgcolor="*value*"
> Sets the background color for the Web page where value is a name or hexadecimal value.
>
> text="*value*"
> Sets the text color for the Web page where value is a name or hexadecimal value.
>
> link="*value*"
> Sets the color of the link where value is a name or hexadecimal value.
>
> alink="*value*"
> Sets the hyperlink color of the active link where value is a name or hexadecimal value.
>
> vlink="*value*"
> Sets the hyperlink color of previously visited links where value is a name or hexadecimal value.

<link rel="stylesheet" href="*style.css*" type="text/css">
Links a style sheet to a Web page where *style.css* is the file name of the style sheet.

Script Tag

`<script> </script>`
Inserts a script into the HTML.

`<noscript> </noscript>`
Defines the start and end of instructions for browsers that do not support scripts.

Meta Tag

`<meta>`
Defines keywords used by search engines, expiration date, author, and page generation software.

Format Tags

`<!--comment-->`
Defines a comment.

`<p> </p>`
Defines the start and end of a paragraph. Attributes include:

> align="*value*"
> Sets the alignment of the paragraph where value is left, right, center, or justify.
>
> style
> Indicates inline styles.

`<br>`
Inserts a line break.

`<blockquote> </blockquote>`
Indents text on both sides of a paragraph.

`<ul> </ul>`
Defines the start and end of a bulleted (unordered) list.

`<ol> </ol>`
Defines the start and end of a numbered list.

`<li> </li>`
Defines an item in a bulleted or numbered list.

`<dl> </dl>`
Defines the start and end of a definition list.

`<dt>`
Defines a definition term in a definition list.

`<dd>`
Defines a definition in a definition list.

`<style> </style>`
Defines an internal style.

Text Tags

<h1> </h1> ...<h6> </h6>
Tag used to emphasize text. Heading 1 has the largest font size and is used to represent the most important information. Heading 6 has the smallest font size.

<strong> </strong>
Displays the text in bold.

<em> </em>
Emphasizes the text.

<u> </u>
Displays the text underlined.

<blink> </blink>
Displays blinking text.

<cite> </cite>
Defines the start and end of a citation.

<font size="*value*"> </font>
Specifies the size of the text where value is a number from 1 to 7, with 1 being the smallest.

<font color="*value*"> </font>
Specifies the color of the text where value is a name or hexadecimal number.

<pre> </pre>
Creates preformatted text in which all spaces and line endings are preserved.

<abbr title="*value*"> </abbr>
Displays the full version of an abbreviated word when the pointer rests on the word where value is the full version of the word.

<acronym title="*value*"> </acronym>
Displays the full version of an acronym when the pointer rests on the word where value is the full version of the word.

Table Tags

<table> </table>
Creates a table.

<th> </th>
Defines a table header, which is a normal cell with bold, centered text.

<tr> </tr>
Defines the start and end of a table row.

<td> </td>
Define the start and end of a table data cell.

<table> </table>
Specifies the table. Attributes include:

    border="*value*"
    Specifies the thickness of the cell border.

    cellpadding="*value*"
    Sets the amount of space between a cell's border and contents where value is a number.

    cellspacing="*value*"
    Specifies the amount of space between table cells where value is a number.

    width="*value*"
    Specifies the width of a table where value is a number in pixels or as a percentage of the document's width.

<tr align="*value*"> or <td align="*value*">
Specifies cell(s) horizontal alignment where value is left, center, or right.

<tr valign="*value*"> or <td valign="*value*">
Specifies cell(s) vertical alignment where value is top, middle, or bottom.

<td nowrap>
Prevents lines in a cell from wrapping.

<td colspan="*value*">
Specifies the number of columns a cell should span where value is a number.

<td rowspan="*value*">
Specifies the number of rows a cell should span where value is a number.

Links

<a href="*URL*"> </a>
Creates an external hyperlink where *URL* is the target URL.

<a href="mailto:*email_address*"> </a>
Creates an e-mail hyperlink where *email_address* is the target e-mail address.

<a name="*named_anchor*"> </a>
Creates a named anchor where *named_anchor* is the name of the location.

<a href="#*named_anchor*"> </a>
Creates a hyperlink to a named anchor where *named_anchor* is the target location.

<a href="*file name*"> </a>
Creates an internal hyperlink where *file name* is the file name of the target page.

Graphics

<img scr="*file name*">
Inserts an image where *file name* is the file name of the graphic.

<img scr="*file name*" align="*value*">
Specifies the alignment of an image where value is left, center, right, top, bottom, or middle.

<img scr="*file name*" border="*value*">
Specifies the size of border around the image where value is a number in pixels.

<img scr="*file name*" alt="*value*">
Specifies alternate text for the graphic where value is the alternative text.

<hr>
Inserts a horizontal rule (line). Attributes include:

> noshade
> Specifies a rule without a shadow.
>
> align="*value*"
> Specifies the alignment of a horizontal rule where value is left, center, right, top, bottom, or middle.
>
> width="*value*"
> Specifies the width of a horizontal rule where value is a number in pixels or as a percent of the window.
>
> size="*value*"
> Specifies the height of a horizontal rule where value is a number in pixels.

Image Maps

<map name="*value*"> </map>
Inserts an image map where *value* is the name of the image map.

<area href="*link*" shape="*shape*" coords="*w, x, y, z*">
Specifies an image map hotspot where *link* is a URL, *shape* is the hotspot shape, and *w*, *x*, *y*, and *z* are the coordinates of the hotspot.

Forms

<form> </form>
Inserts a form.

<input type="*button*">
Specifies an input field where *button* can be Reset, Submit, Checkbox, or Radio.

<select> </select>
Specifies the definition of a drop-down menu field.

<option> </option>
Specifies a menu option.

Appendix A – HTML   A – 5

Color Constants and Corresponding Hexadecimal Values

Black	(#000000)
Silver	(#C0C0C0)
Gray	(#808080)
White	(#FFFFFF)
Maroon	(#800000)
Red	(#FF0000)
Purple	(#800080)
Fuchsia	(#FF00FF)
Green	(#008000)
Lime	(#00FF00)
Olive	(#808000)
Yellow	(#FFFF00)
Navy	(#000080)
Blue	(#0000FF)
Teal	(#008080)
Aqua	(#00FFFF)

Appendix B
Banner Ads and ActionScript

This appendix discusses banner ads and introduces ActionScript.

B.1 Banner Ads

It is common to find advertisements, called banner ads, on Web sites. A *banner ad* is an image that promotes a product or service and is usually a link to the advertiser's site. Most Web sites host banner ads for a fee. Banner ads are usually placed at the top or bottom of a page. There are several standard banner ad sizes including 468x60, 120x240, and 125x125 pixels.

rich media

Rich media banner ads are a type of banner ad that are designed to capture the user's attention by containing animated or dynamic content. They are also interactive in that they are designed to entice a user to click it, which in turn displays the advertiser's page. For example, clicking the graphic link in the top right corner of the banner ad below takes the user to the company's Web site:

Rich media banner ad

> **Free Hosting Requirements**
>
> Non-virtual hosting companies, which offer free hosting, usually require that banner ads be on your Web site or pop up in a new window when your Web site is viewed. Non-virtual hosting companies are discussed in Chapter 10.

Many rich media banner ads on the Internet are created using the Flash MX application. Rich media banner ads can also be created using JavaScript or an animated GIF.

B.2 Ad Templates in Flash

Flash contains predefined templates that can be used set the dimensions for a standard sized ad. Selecting File → New From Template displays the New Document dialog box. Selecting Ads in the Category list displays a list of ad templates in the Category Items list:

Appendix B – Banner Ads and ActionScript

Banner Advertising Agencies

Banner advertising agencies create banner ads for a fee and find hosts for banner ads through its members, who are Web site publishers. Publishers hosting banner ads receive payment based on several factors:

Cost per action (CPA) The fee paid when a user clicks the ad and then completes a transaction with the advertiser.

Cost per click (CPC) The fee paid when a user clicks an ad.

Cost per thousand (CPM) The fee paid for every 1000 times an ad is viewed.

One measure of ad effectiveness is its click through rate (CTR), which is the percentage of users that click the ad. However, banner ads are often used to create product or logo awareness which cannot be measured by the CTR.

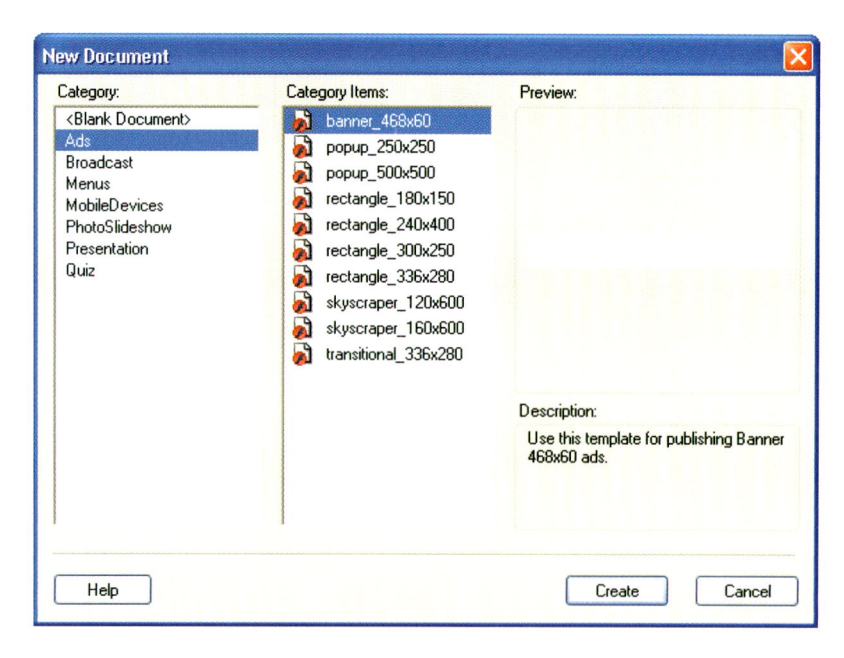

Clicking a template, such as banner_468x60, displays a preview of the template in the Preview window. Clicking Create displays template instructions on the Stage:

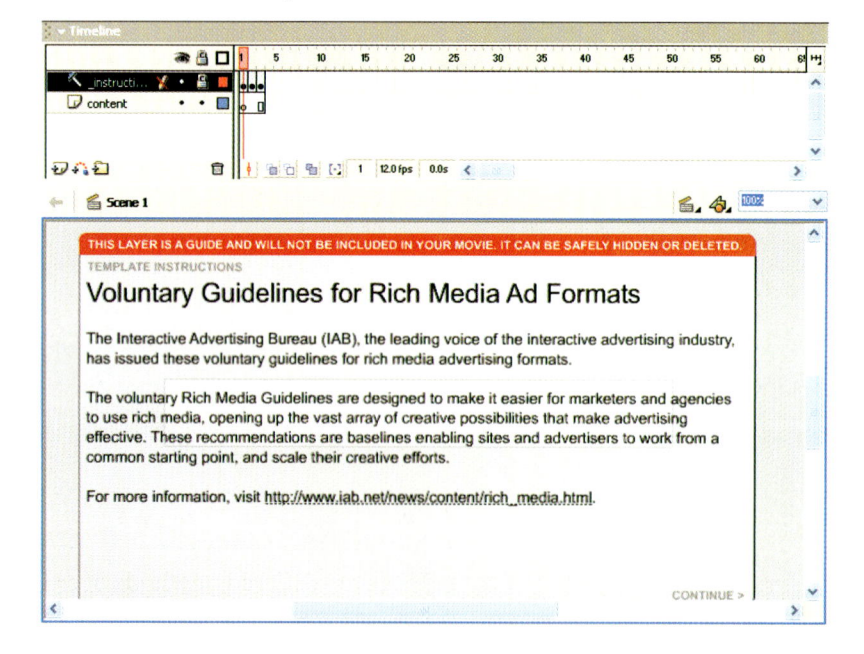

Note that template consists of two layers, an instructions layer and a content layer, with the instructions layer selected.

The Template Instructions screen explains that the IAB (Interactive Advertising Bureau) has created voluntary guidelines for rich-media advertising formats that they would like advertisers to follow. These guidelines include using standard dimensions and file sizes for banner ads. Clicking Continue displays specifications about the selected banner ad template:

IAB

The IAB is an organization that helps online companies increase their revenue. One aspect of the organization is to set standards and guidelines for rich media ad formats. Further information can be found at their Web site, www.iab.net.

Clicking Continue displays guidelines for testing the banner ad once it has been published.

Once the instructions have been reviewed, the instructions layer can be deleted by clicking instructions in the Layer list and then clicking the Delete Layer button (🗑) at the bottom of the Layers list, which displays the banner ad on the Stage:

A 468x60 Banner Ad

Now that the dimensions of the banner ad have been set using the template, the banner ad can be created.

B.3 Creating a Banner Ad

nested symbols

There are different methods of creating a banner ad. One method uses *nested symbols*, which places one symbol on top of another symbol. One symbol contains the banner ad content and is a frame-by-frame animation that has Movie Clip behavior, which allows the animation to play continuously like a banner ad. The other symbol is a button that covers the entire banner ad area and has Button behavior, which allows the banner ad to display another Web page when it is clicked.

B.4 Adding Banner Ad Content

The banner ad content is created by selecting Insert → New Symbol, which displays a dialog box where a descriptive name is typed for the symbol and Movie Clip is selected to create a movie clip symbol:

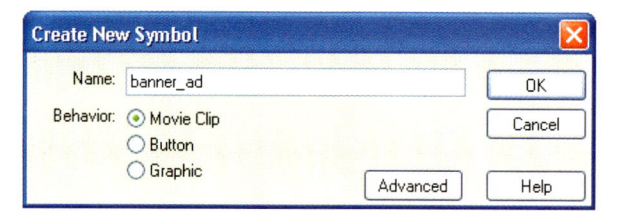

Clicking OK displays an empty Stage. Click the Rectangle tool (☐) and drag on the Stage to create a rectangle. In the Property inspector, set the width and height of the rectangle to the same dimensions as the banner ad. For example, to create a 468x60 banner ad, set W to 468 and set H to 60.

The image for the first frame of the banner ad can then be created by either drawing an image with the Tools panel or by importing an image:

Frame-by-frame animation is then used to create an animated banner ad from a set of specified images. Clicking a new frame on the Timeline and selecting Insert → Keyframe adds the image from the previous keyframe. The image in the new keyframe can then be modified to progress the animation. For example, the image in frame 15 could be modified to:

The process of inserting keyframes and modifying the image is repeated until the final frame of the animation. Note that since the banner ad has Movie Clip behavior, it will play continuously so static frames should be inserted after the final frame to create a pause before the banner ad loops back to the first frame. The banner ad content is now complete and is stored in the Library.

B.5 Creating a Button Symbol

Next, the button that will cover the entire area of the banner ad is created by selecting Insert → New Symbol, which displays a dialog box where a descriptive name is typed and Button is selected to create a button symbol. Clicking OK displays an empty Stage with the button states displayed on the Timeline:

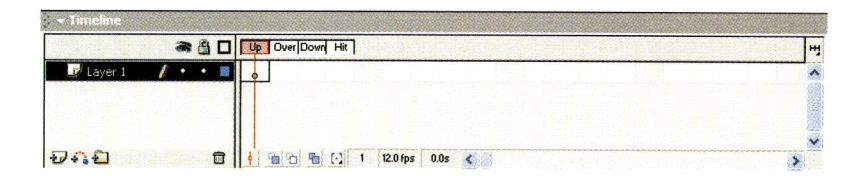

The banner ad should not change when the mouse is over or away from the banner ad so with the Playhead on the Up state, drag the banner ad from the Library panel onto the Stage. This creates an instance of the button over the entire area of the banner ad content. A button instance has to be named by typing a descriptive name, such as button_for_banner, in the **Instance Name** box in the Property inspector:

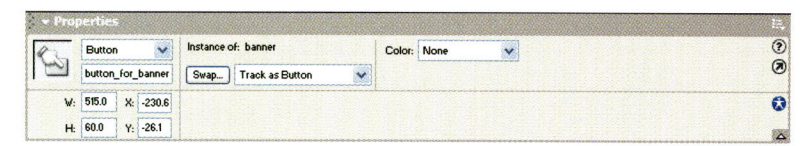

Note that an instance name cannot contain spaces.

B.6 Adding ActionScript

> **ActionScript**
>
> Scripts can be added to a Flash movie to make the movie interactive using a scripting language called *ActionScript*. A *script* is a list of commands that are automatically executed by a Web browser.

ActionScript can now be added to the instance of the button to create a link to another Web page when the banner ad is clicked. Right-clicking the button instance and selecting **Actions** from the menu displays the Actions panel below the Stage:

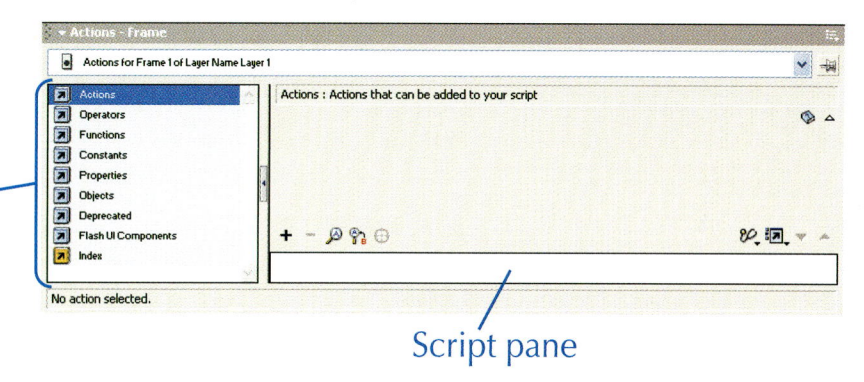

adding a mouse event

A *mouse event* is now added to control the button. The *onRelease* event is used since it occurs when the user releases the mouse button, or clicks on the banner ad in this case. In the Actions toolbox, click **Actions → Objects → Movie → Button → Events** to display the mouse events:

Double-clicking the onRelease event places a line of code in the Script pane. Note that a red <not yet set> is displayed indicating the instance name of the button has not been set yet:

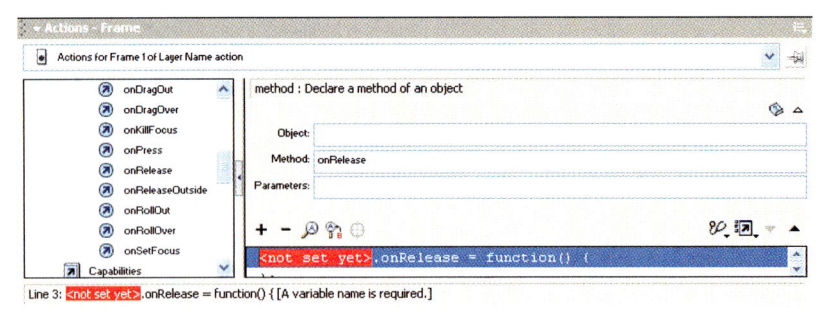

Clicking the Object box to place the insertion point and then clicking the Insert a target path button (⊕) in the Script pane displays the Insert Target Path dialog box:

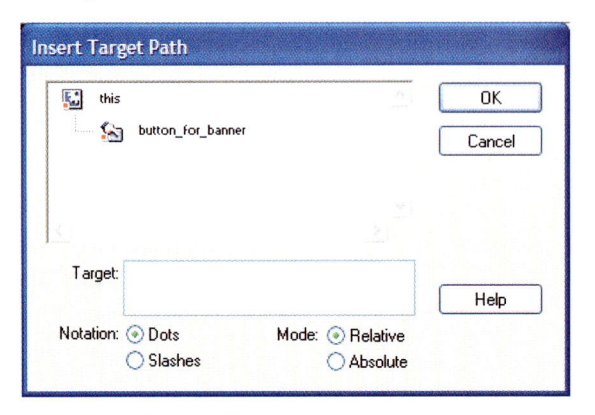

The Insert Target Path dialog box displays a list of the objects in the movie that could be the target of the ActionScript. Selecting button_for_banner and clicking OK adds the instance name to the line of code:

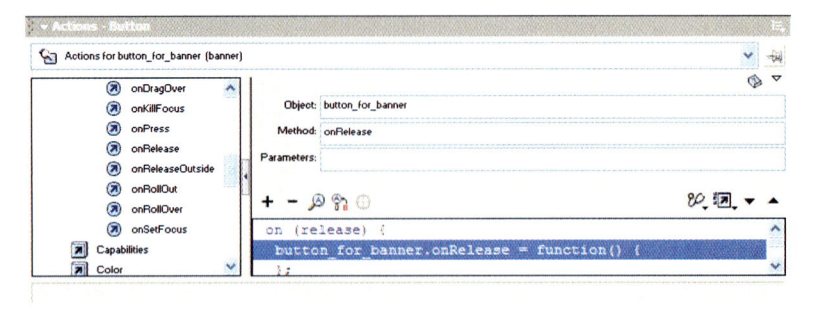

Now that the event has been defined, the URL to be displayed needs to be specified. In the Actions toolbox, click Actions → Browser/Network → GetURL, which displays ActionScript code in the Script pane:

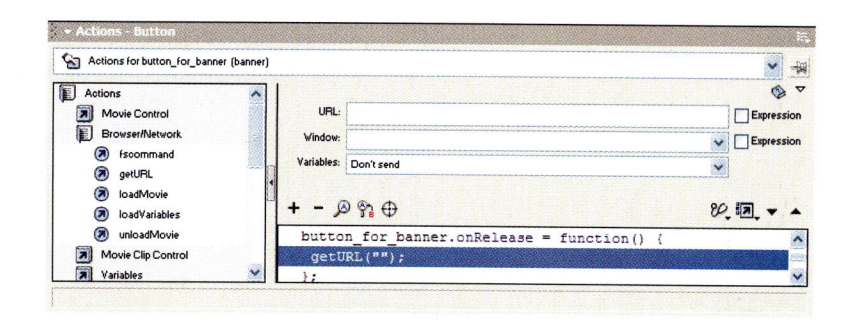

In the URL box, type the name of the Web page document, such as index.htm, or to link to an external Web site, type the complete URL, such as http://www.ad.lpdatafiles.com. The Window list can be used to specify how the linked page is displayed. For example, selecting _blank from the Window list displays the linked page in a separate browser window.

B.7 Completing and Testing the Banner Ad

To complete the banner ad, click Scene 1 at the top of the page to return to the original banner ad template. From the Library drag the button symbol onto the Stage. Test and view the banner ad by selecting Control → Test Movie. The banner ad can then be exported to be used in a Web page document.

B.8 Other Types of Web Ads

interstitial ads

Other types of Web ads include interstitial and SUPERSTITIAL™ ads. *Interstitial ads* appear in a separate browser window while a Web page loads. One type of interstitial ad plays in a smaller browser window. For example:

Interstitial ad

> **SUPERSTITIAL™**
>
> The SUPERSTITIAL™ ad format is a standard that was created by company called Unicast.

SUPERSTITIAL™ ads appear in a separate window, can be any size on the computer screen, and are considered "polite" ads since they only play when a user stops surfing. They also typically contain animation, sound, and graphics. For example:

SUPERSTITIAL™ ad

Appendix C
Digital Camera Files

Digital cameras are widely available and affordable. Even the least expensive digital cameras can produce images of acceptable quality for use on the Web. Digital cameras have settings that affect the image files produced by the camera. This appendix explains some aspects of digital camera image files and how to use Fireworks to change the image size and resolution for use in a Web page.

C.1 Digital Camera File Formats

When a digital camera takes a photograph, a chip in the camera collects light and converts it to data. Settings in the digital camera determine what the camera does with the data that is collected. Common file settings in digital cameras are JPEG, TIFF, and RAW. The JPEG setting processes the data into a JPG file and the TIFF setting processes the data into a TIF file, which can then be transferred to a computer or printer. The TIF format has better quality than a JPG, but the file size is usually larger and a TIF must be converted to a JPG for use in a Web page.

RAW   The RAW setting indicates that the data for a photograph is not processed in the camera. The photograph's data must be transferred to a computer that has software from the camera's manufacturer installed. The RAW file can then be manipulated using the software and saved in many image file formats. Manipulating a RAW file and saving the image in a different file format can be thought of as processing the digital film, because it allows adjustments to be made such as exposure and color balance. RAW files have different extensions depending on the camera, for example .mrw is a Minolta camera RAW file, .crw is a Canon camera RAW file, and .nef is a Nikon camera RAW file.

C.2 Maintaining Image Quality in JPG Files

Setting a digital camera to process the photograph data as JPEG is a fast, convenient way to produce image files for use in a Web page. However, every time a JPG image is saved it is compressed again and loses data, because the JPG format has lossy compression.

To retain excellent image quality, the camera should set to process the photograph data as TIFF, and then the TIF file can be modified in a computer as needed and saved in JPG format. This way, the image will

---

Images and Fireworks

Images, image file formats, and Fireworks are discussed in Chapter 6.

> **Megapixels and Resolution**
>
> One megapixel is one million pixels. The megapixel specification for a digital camera is dependent on the number of pixels on the chip in the camera that collect light and convert it to data. For example, a camera with a chip that is 1,600 pixels wide and 1,200 pixels tall has a total of 1,920,000 pixels and is considered to be a two megapixel camera with a resolution of 1,600 x 1,200.

have much better quality than if it was processed as JPG and then modified and saved a few times. The TIF can also be saved in Fireworks as a PNG and then exported many times using different JPG settings without loss of quality.

When using a high-resolution digital camera such as 3 megapixel camera or more, processing the photograph data as JPG is acceptable. Because the image is at such as high resolution, it can be modified in a computer, saved at a proper resolution for use on a Web page, and it will retain sufficient quality for an image on a Web page.

C.3 Digital Camera Image Resolution

Digital cameras have settings that affect the resolution of the saved images. These settings may be called "File Size" or "Quality" or something similar and have settings such as Large, Medium, and Small, which affect the resolution of the image file processed by the camera. For example, selecting Large may result in images that are 1600 x 1200 pixels, and Small may result in images that are 640 x 480 pixels. The file size (in kilobytes) of the Large image will be larger than the file size of the Small because it contains more data.

C.4 Changing Image Size and Resolution in Fireworks

Fireworks can be used to change the image size and resolution of an image file. Once an image file from a digital camera is saved in Fireworks as a PNG, there are two main considerations in preparing the image for use in a Web page. The image size (dimensions) in pixels, and the screen resolution in pixels per inch. Although the size of the file (in kilobytes) should be considered, if the image size and resolution are appropriate, the file size will be small.

The word "resolution" is used to describe the dimensions of an image in pixels and the pixels per inch of an image. Both uses are correct, but when referring to images from a digital camera, resolution is the dimensions of the image in pixels. In Fireworks, resolution refers to the pixels per inch of the image.

Most computer monitors display at a resolution of 72 pixels per inch. An image file used in a Web page should therefore have a resolution of 72 pixels per inch. Any larger number includes image data that will not be able to be displayed on a screen, and therefore just increases the file size.

In Fireworks, an image can be modified by clicking the [Image Size...] button in the Property inspector or selecting Modify → Canvas → Image Size, which displays a dialog box:

> **Smaller, not Larger**
>
> The dimensions of an images should never be changed to a larger size because the software extrapolates data information to fill in the additional pixels, which results in poor image quality. The resolution (dpi) of an image also cannot be increased without resulting in poor image quality.

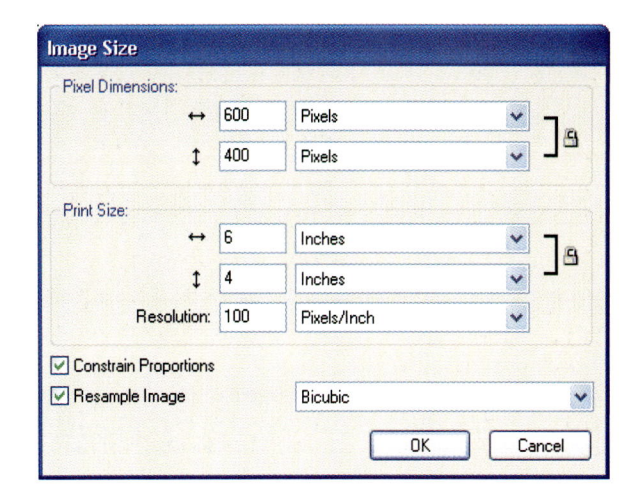

changing dimensions   To change the dimensions of an image, make sure the Constrain Proportions check box is selected and then change the Pixel Dimensions of the image. Note that the Resolution does not change as this modification is made. Selecting OK changes the image.

changing resolution   To change the resolution of an image, first clear the Resample Image check box, which disables the Pixel Dimensions so they cannot be changed. Changing the Resolution to 72 Pixels/Inch and selecting OK changes the resolution of the image.

If both the dimensions and resolution of an image need to be changed, first change the dimensions, select OK to apply the changes, and then click the [Image Size...] button again and change the resolution.

Appendix D
Templates

Collaboration in Web site development is achieved in many ways. One approach is through the use of templates.

D.1 Templates

Web site development tasks can be divided among different people. For example, a designer creates the page layout, a graphic artist creates images, and a writer writes text. The designer creates a template and the graphic artist and writer create content for designated regions of the template.

A *template* defines the structure, or layout, of a Web page document. A designer will use a template to create the basic layout for the Web pages of a specific site. The template "locks down" the design because Web page documents created from a template are linked to the template. Layout elements, such as tables, cannot be changed without breaking the link to the template. Several templates may be needed for a site depending on the number and variety of Web pages in the site.

editable region The areas of a template that should be modified to customize a page are marked by named editable regions. An *editable region* is a placeholder for content. The page below is a template with editable regions, which are marked as blue boxes:

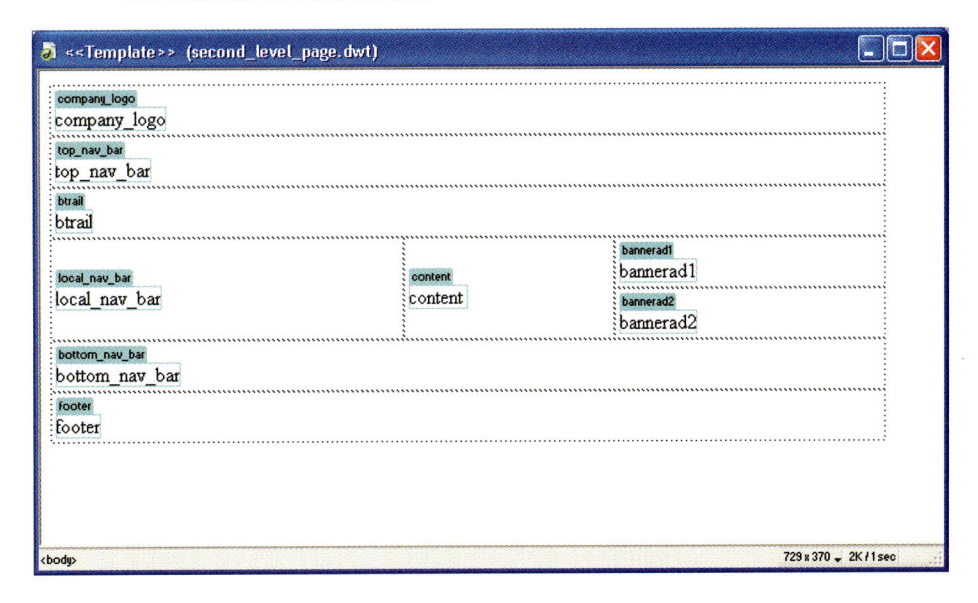

D.2 Using the Templates Category

Assets panel

The Assets panel can be used to create and apply templates. Clicking the Templates icon ( ) in the Assets panel displays template files:

> **DWT**
>
> A template is a DWT file. The extension .dwt is automatically added to the file name.

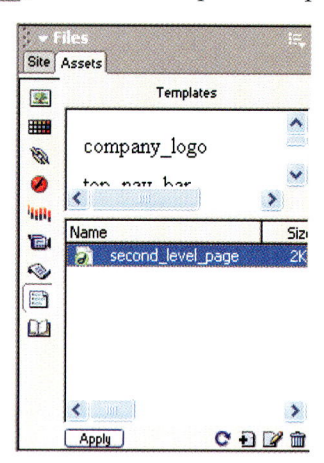

creating a template

Selecting → New Template creates a new template file. Clicking the Edit button ( ) at the bottom of the Assets panel opens a window with <<Template>> in the title bar. Tables and other "fixed" elements can then be added to the template. A template must also contain editable regions, discussed in the next section. After the completing the template, selecting File → Save saves the changes. Dreamweaver automatically adds a Templates folder to the Web site root folder when a template is created. A template may also be created from an existing Web page by selecting File → Save As Template.

deleting a template

A template is deleted by selecting it in the Assets panel and then pressing the Delete key.

D.3 Adding Editable Regions to a Template

Although the structure presented in a template should not change, areas within the structure must be editable so that content can be added. Editable regions are added using the Templates tab in the Insert bar:

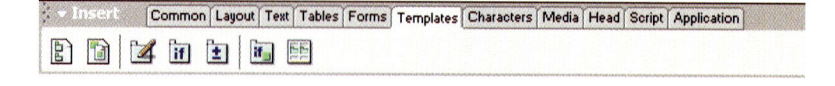

Clicking the Editable Region button ( ) displays a dialog box:

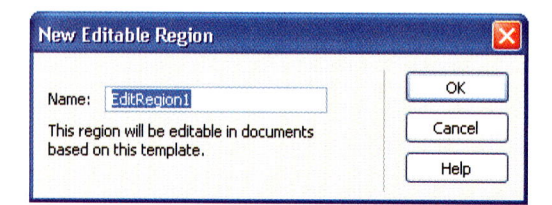

A descriptive name should be typed for a region

Typing a descriptive name and then selecting OK inserts the region into the template.

A Guide to Web Development Using Macromedia Dreamweaver MX

D.4 Applying a Template to a Web Page Document

applying a template

yellow background

A template is applied to an open Web page document by dragging it from the Assets panel into the Document window. Clicking [Apply] at the bottom of the Assets panel also applies the template to the current document. The template appears with a yellow background in the Web page document. The yellow background does not appear in a browser:

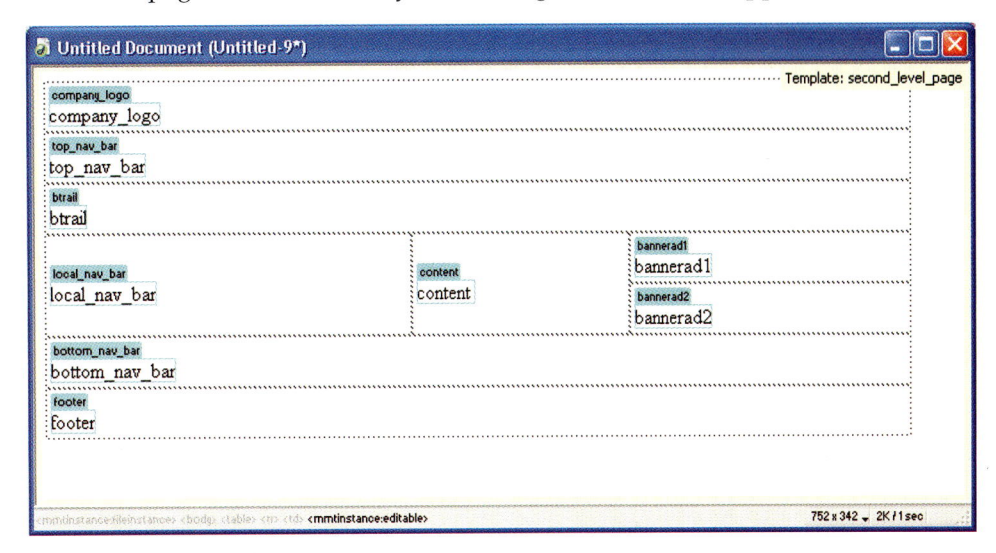

The editable regions can be modified to include content and the appropriate style sheet attached to format the Web page document. The Web page document is saved like any Web page.

Templates

Index

– (minus)   2-17
*   3-3
.crw   C-1
.css   7-5
.dwt   D-2
.fla   8-11
.gif   6-21
.htm   3-3, 4-5, 4-20, 6-31
.lbi   5-19
.mrw   C-1
.nef   C-1
.png   6-15
.swf   8-3
/   3-1
//   2-6
:   3-3
?   3-3
@   2-20
_   4-5
_blank   9-9, B-7
_self   9-9
| 5-6
+ plus sign   2-17
<!--comment-->   3-13, A-2
📁   6-3, 6-6, 7-21
✥   4-10
👁   8-29
✋   2-8, 6-3, 6-5, 8-7
🔖   8-29
✂   6-36
🔍   6-20
+   6-6
+   6-15
✒   6-20
🔎   6-20
↘   6-11, 6-37
🗑   8-29
<>   2-5, 3-1
<a>   3-14, A-4
<abbr>   A-3
<acronym>   A-3
<area>   A-5
<blink>   A-3

<blockquote>   A-2, 7-15
<body>   2-5, 3-1, 3-2, 6-32, A-1

   3-8, A-2
<cite>   A-3
<dd>   A-2
<dl>   A-2
<dt>   A-2
<em>   A-3, 7-11
<font>   A-3
<form>   A-5
<h1>   3-11, 7-12, A-3
<h2>   3-11, 7-12, A-3
<h3>   3-11, 7-12, A-3
<h4>   3-11, 7-12, A-3
<h5>   3-11, 7-12, A-3
<h6>   3-11, 7-12, A-3
<head>   3-1, 3-2, A-1
<hr>   3-12, A-5
<html>   3-1, 3-2, A-1
<img>   A-5
<input>   A-5
<li>   7-16, A-2
<link>   A-1
<map>   A-5
<meta>   A-2
<noscript>   A-2
<ol>   7-16, A-2
<option>   A-5
<p>   3-7, 7-7, 7-8, A-2
<pre>   A-3
<script>   A-2
<select>   A-5
<strong>   A-3, 7-11
<style>   A-2
<table>   4-10, A-4
<td>   5-16, A-3
<th>   A-3
<title>   2-5, 3-1, 3-2, A-1
<tr>   5-16
<u>   A-3
<ul>   A-2
>   5-6

Index   I – 1

A

About.com 2-14
above the fold 5-9
absolute hyperlink 9-8
academic information 9-2
Acceptable Use Policy 1-8
accessibility 6-3
Accessories command 3-3
account 1-4
Action property 9-18
Actions command B-5
Actions toolbox B-5
ActionScript B-1, B-5
Active Area tab 6-27
ADA 6-3
Add button 2-11
Address bar 2-7
Address button 2-22
admissions, college 9-2
ADSL 1-5
advertising 1-7
ads 2-5, 9-4, B-1
agent 2-14, 2-21
AI 8-15
align attribute 3-9, 3-12
Align Center button 6-11
Align command 6-18
Align Left button 6-11
Align property 4-11
Align Right button 6-11
alignment 3-9, 7-3
    buttons 6-17
All Programs command 2-6, 3-3
Allow Multiple property 9-22
Alpha transparency 6-21
Alt property 6-3, 6-26
Alt text *see* alternative text
AltaVista 2-14
alternative text 6-2, 6-3, 6-5, 10-7
Amazon.com 2-3
Americans with Disabilities Act 6-3
anchor tag 3-14
AND 2-17
Andreesen, Marc 2-5
animated GIF B-1
animation, defined 8-10
    exporting 8-13
    previewing 8-13
    rewinding 8-13
antivirus software 2-22
AOL 1-5
Apple Computer 1-4
AppleTalk 1-4

appropriateness of design 5-8
ARCnet 1-4
Arial 7-2
ARPA 1-4
ARPANET 1-4
Arrow tool 8-11, 8-15
Ask Jeeves 2-14
ASP 8-34
ASP .NET 9-15
Assets panel 5-15, 5-19, 6-25, 8-4, 8-18, D-2
Attach button 2-21
Attach Style Sheet button 7-5
attached file 2-22
attribute
    align 3-9, 3-12
    bgcolor 3-13
    CSS styles 7-4
    href 3-14
    size 3-12
    tag 3-1
    text 3-13
    width 3-12
AVI 8-34

B

Back button 2-7
backbone 1-2
background color
    cell 7-20
    page 3-13, 7-19
bandwidth 1-3
banner ads 2-5, 9-4, B-1
banner advertising agencies B-1
base-16 3-13
baseband 1-3
Basic Page 4-20
BBS 1-6
behavior, defined 6-26
    changing 6-32
Behaviors panel 6-32, 9-14
Berners-Lee, Tim 2-1
Bezos, Jeff 2-3
bgcolor attribute 3-1, 3-13
bit 1-3
bitmap graphic 6-1
bits per second 1-3
Block Quote button 7-15
blockquote 7-14
    tag 7-15
    removing 7-15
blog 2-3
blue text 9-6
BMP 8-15, 9-6

body tag 3-2
book 7-2
Boolean logic 2-17
borders 4-9
bottom global navigation bar 5-6, 7-3, 7-19
bps 1-3
breadcrumb trail 5-6, 5-10, 7-3, 7-19
Break Apart command 8-20, 8-29
break tag 3-8
breaking a library item link 5-20
broadband 1-3
broken link 9-6
Broken Links report 10-7
Browse for File icon 4-22, 6-3, 6-6
browser 3-5, 3-6, 3-16
    downloading 10-4
    printing from 4-16
    window 3-1
    window, resized 6-8
Brush Mode 8-12
Brush Shape 8-12
Brush Size 8-12
Brush tool 8-11
bullet 7-16
bulleted list 7-16
bulletin board service 1-6
bus 1-2
bus topology 1-2
button 6-24
    previewing 6-26, 6-27
    testing 6-26, 6-27
    Flash 8-2
        aligning 8-3
        editing 8-3
        previewing 8-3
Button behavior B-3
Button button 9-17
Button Editor window 6-26
Button form object 9-16
ButtonName property 9-18

C

ca 2-6
cable 10-3
cable modem 1-5
cable television 1-3
canvas 6-14, 6-15
    modifying 6-18
    resizing 6-36
Canvas Color command 6-18
Canvas Color property 6-14
Canvas command 6-18
Canvas Size command 6-18

capitalization 7-1
card 1-1
career objectives 9-2
careers, Web 2-23
cascading 7-4
cascading style sheets *see* CSS
Cc button 2-21
CD, distributing a portfolio 9-2
cell 4-8
    height 4-11
    padding 4-9
    properties 4-11
    spacing 4-9
    width 4-11
cells
    merging 5-15
    splitting 5-15
Center Horizontal command 6-18
Center Vertical command 6-18
CERN 2-1
certificate of copyright 5-21
Change command 6-3
Change Link command 4-22, 4-23, 9-8
Char Width property 9-17
Characters tab 4-13
chatting 1-6
Check box 9-16, 9-16
Check Box form object 9-19
Check Browser action 10-6
Check In button 10-12
Check Links Sitewide command 10-6
Check Out File(s) button 10-12
Check Plugin action 10-6
Check Spelling command 4-14, 10-2
Check Target Browsers command 10-5
Checkbox button 9-19
CheckBox property 9-20
Checked Value property 9-20
checking grammar 10-2
checking spelling 10-2
child page 5-3
Children's Online Privacy Protection Act of 1998 1-8
cipher text 1-8
citing online sources 2-19
citing Web page sources 2-19
class 7-4
    names 7-7
    adding a new 7-7
    applying 7-7
Clean up HTML command 10-7
clear a form 9-16
Clear command 4-14
click through rate B-2
client 1-2, 1-4
client/server 1-2

Index   I–3

Clone command 6-26
clones 6-30
Close button 2-9, 2-13, 4-2, 4-17, 6-15, 8-11
Close command 4-17
closing, Web page document 4-17
coaxial cable 1-3
Code and Design view 4-6, 7-8
codec 8-34
Code view 4-6
ColdFusion 9-15
collaborating 7-24
collaboration 10-12
college degrees 2-24
color 7-18
    analogous 7-18
    background 3-13, 7-18, 7-20
    complementary 7-18
    constants A-6
    cool 7-18
    list 6-20
    wheel 7-18
    text 7-18
    triads 7-18
    warm 7-18
com 2-6
comments
    about a Web site 9-16
    HTML 3-13
commercial Web site 2-2
company history 9-5
compression 6-2, 8-34, C-1
computer
    ethical implications 1-8
    social implications 1-8
    virus 2-22
connection speed, changing 10-2
Connects to remote host button 10-12
consistency 5-10
constraining lines 6-15
content 4-8, 5-4
    arranging 4-8
    editing 4-14
contest *see* promotion
conventional modem 1-5
Convert to Symbol command 6-25, 8-23
cookies 1-7
copy 7-24
Copy command 4-14, 5-13, 7-24
Copy Graphic button 6-27
Copy HTML command 6-32
copying Web site files 2-1
copyright 2-18, 3-17, 5-21
    notice 5-21
    symbol 4-13

corporate presence Web site 2-2, 9-4
cost per action B-2
cost per click B-2
cost per thousand B-2
Courier New 7-2
cracker 1-10
Create Image in Fireworks command 6-14
Create Mail button 2-20
Create New Folder button 8-18
creating a Web site 4-2, 5-1
criteria 9-15
Crop tool 6-36
cropped 6-36
CSS rule 7-6
CSS selector style 7-22
CSS style sheet 7-4, 7-5
CSS class 7-7
CSS Styles panel 7-5, 7-7, 7-10
CSS2 7-4
Ctrl key 5-13
currency symbols 4-13
Cut command 4-14

D

daemons 2-21
data source 9-15
data, importing 9-11
database 1-10, 2-14, 3-15, 9-15
Datapoint Corporation 1-4
Date button 5-20
Date command 5-20
declaration 7-4
degrees, college and university 2-24
Delete button 2-22
Delete Column command 4-11
Delete CSS Style button 7-11
Delete Layer button B-2
Delete Row command 4-11
deleting 4-14
delimited text format 9-10
demodulation 1-5
Department of Defense 1-4
description meta data, adding 10-13
design
    considerations 7-19, 7-22
    fluid 4-8
    liquid 4-8
Design panel group 6-32
Design view 4-6
Dial-up 10-3
digital camera C-1
    image resolution C-2
Digital Equipment Corporation 1-4

DirectX 7   8-32, 8-34
Distribute to Layers command   8-30
DNS   *see* Domain Name System
document
    creating   3-4
    HTML   3-1
    opening   3-4
    sizing window   4-5
    style   3-2
    tags   3-2
    template   D-2
Document toolbar   4-2
Document window   4-2
document-relative hyperlink   4-22
domain name   2-6, 2-19
domain name considerations   10-9
Domain Name System   10-9
Domain names   10-9
dot-com   2-2
dots per inch   6-1
Down state   6-26, 6-33
Down tab   6-27
download time   6-20, 10-2
downloading browsers   10-4
dpi   6-1
drawing
    circles   6-15
    from the center   6-16
    objects   6-15
    squares   6-15
Dreamweaver   2-23, 4-1
Dreamweaver style sheets   7-5
DSL   1-5, 10-3
duplicating   4-14
DV   8-34
DWT   D-2
dynamic
    content   9-15
    form objects   9-15
    pages   1-10
    Web page   9-15
    Web site   9-15

E

e-commerce Web site   2-2, 5-8, 9-5
editable region   D-2
Editable Region button   D-2
Edit Browser List command   10-4
Edit button   5-19, 5-20
Edit command   5-20
Edit Site command   10-9, 10-10
Edit Style Sheet button   7-11
editing content   4-14

editing graphics   6-2
edu   2-6
education   2-23
educational institutions   9-3
Effect property   8-33
elapsed time   8-13
Electronic Communications Privacy Act of 1986
    1-8, 1-10
Electronic Freedom of Information Act of 1996
    1-8
electronic mail   1-6, 2-19
electronic portfolio   2-25, 9-2
element   3-1
em dash   4-13
em tag   7-11
e-mail   1-6, 2-19, 2-22
    address   2-19
    attachments   2-22
    etiquette   2-22
    hyperlink   5-20
    link   9-6
    message window   5-20
EMF   8-15
Emphasize button   7-11
employer   9-2
employment opportunities   9-5
encryption   1-8
e-portfolios   9-2
EPS   8-15
Eraser tool   8-11
Ethernet   1-4
Ethernet, Fast   1-4
ethical implications, of computers   1-8
ethical responsibilities, of a Web developer   1-10
Eudora   2-20
euro symbol   4-13
European Laboratory for Particle Physics   2-1
Events command   B-5
Excite   2-14
Exit command   2-22, 3-4, 4-17
Expand/Collapse button   9-5
Export Movie command   8-17, 8-35
Export Wizard command   6-19, 6-31
exporting
    Fireworks document   6-18, 6-21, 6-24, 6-30, 6-32
    Flash document   8-11, 8-12, 8-17, 8-34
    HTML and Images   6-30
external hyperlink   9-6, 9-8, 9-9, 10-7
extranet   1-7
Eye column   8-29

Index   I – 5

F

F12 key 4-6
fail gracefully 10-6
Fair Credit Reporting Act of 1970 1-9
FALSE 2-17
FAQ page 9-5, 9-8
Fast Ethernet 1-4
FAST Search 2-14
Favorites button 2-7, 2-10
Favorites list 2-10
Federal Rehabilitation Act 10-7
feedback page 9-5
fiber optic cable 1-3
File Transfer Protocol *see* FTP
file
    adding to site 5-13
    attach to e-mail message 2-22
    copying 5-13
    dependent 9-6
    editing and uploading 10-12
    load 9-6
    name 3-3, 4-2
    uploading 10-10
    size 6-20, 10-2
Files panel group 4-2, 5-15
Fill Color 6-16, 6-17, 8-11
Filo, David 2-4
Financial Privacy Act of 1978 1-9
Find button 2-22
firewall 1-7
Fireworks
    application 6-13, 7-2
    document, saving 6-15
    image, editing 6-32, C-2
First page button 2-13
Fit Canvas command 6-18
fixed width 4-8, 5-7
FLA 8-11, 8-19
Flash
    application 7-2, 8-1, 8-10, B-1
    buttons 8-2
        aligning 8-3
        editing 8-3
        previewing 8-3
    document 8-12
        setting properties 8-12
    movie
        editing 8-18, 8-19
        inserting 8-18
        previewing 8-19
    text
        creating 8-7
        editing 8-9
        modifying 8-9
        previewing 8-9

Flash Library 8-23
Flash Player plug-in 8-17
fluid design 4-8
folder icon 4-18, 10-11
folders 2-11, 5-12
font family 7-4
Font list 6-17
fonts 6-17, 7-1
    choosing 7-2
footer 3-3, 5-7
form 9-15, 9-16
    adding 9-17
    clearing 9-16
    creating 9-17
    layout 9-17
    object 9-16
Form Objects command 9-18
Forms button 9-17
Forms tab 9-13, 9-17
Forward button 2-7, 2-22
frame 8-10, 8-13
    adding 8-14
    rate 8-12, 8-13
    removing 8-14
frame-by-frame animation 8-13
free-form document 3-2
frequently asked questions 9-8
FTP 1-7, 10-9, 10-10
FTP Host 10-10
FTP Log 10-11

G

Geneva 7-2
Georgia 7-2
Get File(s) button 10-12
GetURL B-6
GIF 6-1, 6-2, 6-13, 6-14, 6-21, 8-15
Go button 2-7, 9-14
Go Network 2-14
Google 2-14, 2-15
Gopher 1-7
gov 2-6
governments 9-3
grammar errors 10-2
graphic 6-1, *see also* image
    editing 6-2
graphic hyperlink
    button 6-24
    creating 6-3
    modifying 6-3
    testing 6-3
Graphics Interchange Format 6-1
greater than sign 5-6
guest book 9-16

H

H property   4-11, 6-11, 6-16, 6-36
hacker   1-10
HAN   1-1
Head tab   10-13
head tag   3-2
header   3-3, 5-7
Heading 1 button   7-12
Heading 2 button   7-12
heading tags   3-11, 7-12
headings   7-12
Height property   6-14, 9-21
hexadecimal values   3-13, A-6
hierarchy, Web pages   5-4
History button   2-7, 2-9
History command   4-14
History list   2-9
Home button   2-7
home page   2-2, 4-6, 5-3
   links   5-6
   setting in a browser   2-7
horizontal rule   3-12
host name   2-19
HotBot   2-14
Hotmail   2-20
hotspot   6-6
href attribute   3-14
HTML   2-5, 2-23, 3-1, 4-6, 6-30, 6-33, 7-6,
   see also tags listed on I-1
   document   3-1, 3-3
   viewing   4-10
   tag   3-2, 7-8, A-1
   testing for target browser compatibility   10-5
HTML and Images, exported   6-32
HTTP   1-7
http   2-6
HTTP server   *see* Web server
HTTP software   10-8
hub   1-2
hyperlink   2-2, 3-14, 4-22, 5-5, 6-3, 9-8
   blue   2-8
   colors, changing   7-22
   colors, nonstandard   7-22
   grouping   9-12
   in a jump menu   9-13
   label   3-15
   modifying   4-23, 7-22
   purple   2-8
   testing   4-23
   to named anchor   7-21
   to information on other pages   9-12
hyperstitial   2-5
hypertext   3-15
HyperText Markup Language   2-5, 3-1

I

IAB   B-2
IBM   1-4
Illustrator   2-23
image   5-8, 6-1, 6-11, 9-6
image, alignment   6-11
   changing background color   7-33
   creating   8-12
   editing in Fireworks from Dreamweaver   6-37
   files   5-12
   importing   8-15
   placeholders   6-14
   resetting size   6-11
   resize   6-11
   size, changing in Fireworks   C-2
   updating in Dreamweaver   6-37
image map
   creating   6-6
   defined   6-5
Image Placeholder button   6-14
Image Size command   C-2
Images icon   5-15
implementing a Web site   5-1 *see also* creating
Import command   8-15, 8-34
Import Tabular Data command   9-11
Import to Library command   8-32
importing
   data   9-11
   sound file   8-32
   video file   8-34
Inbox window   2-20
indent   7-15
   increasing   7-15
Indent command   7-16
Index transparency   6-21
index.htm   4-6
information
   age   1-8
   architect   2-23, 5-2
   technology   2-22
informational Web site   2-3, 9-3
infrared signals   1-3
Init Val   9-17
Initial State property   9-20
Initially Selected list   9-22
Initially Selected property   9-22
Insert a target path button   B-6
Insert bar   4-1, 4-10, 4-13, 7-8, 8-2, 8-8, 9-13, 9-17,
   10-13, D-2
Insert button   5-15, 5-19
Insert Column command   4-11
Insert Row command   4-11
Insert Table button   4-10
inserting special characters   4-13
insertion point, moving in a table   4-14

Index   I–7

instance   6-25, 6-26, 8-22
   adding to the Stage   8-23
   name   B-5
instructions area   6-27
Intel Corporation   1-4
interactive   1-4
interlaced   6-2
Internet   1-4, 1-5, 2-6
   browsing services   1-7
   growth   2-4
   history of   1-4
   safety   2-2, 9-2
Internet Explorer   2-5, 2-6, 10-3, 10-4
Internet Explorer   see browser
Internet Explorer command   2-6
Internet Explorer, quitting   2-7
Internet Explorer, starting   2-6
Internet Relay Chat   1-6
Internet Use Agreement   1-8
interstitial   2-5, B-7
intranet   1-7
   analyst   2-24
   server   10-1, 10-4
IP Address   10-9
IRC   1-6
ISDN   1-5
ISP   1-5, 2-24, 10-1
IT   2-22
   career, pursuing   2-24
   companies   2-24
   department   2-24

J

JavaScript   6-26, 10-3, 10-7, B-1
job search   9-2
Joint Photographic Experts Group   6-1
JPG   6-1, 6-2, 6-13, 6-14, 8-15, C-1
   maintaining image quality in   C-1
jump menu   9-13
Jump Menu button   9-13
Jump Menu form object   9-13

K

Kbps   1-5
keyframe   8-13
Keyframe command   8-13, B-4
keyword meta data, adding   10-13
keywords   2-14, 10-13
kilobytes   10-2

L

label form object   9-16
Label property   9-18
label, URL   2-6
LAN   1-1
   standards   1-4
Language References   10-7
Last page button   2-13
layer
   creating a new   8-28
   deleting   8-29
   hiding   8-29
   locking   8-29
   naming   8-28
   order   8-28
layering   8-10
layers   8-28
   distributing to   8-30
layout   4-8
   testing   5-10
Layout tab   4-10
Layout view   4-10
LBI   5-19
leading   7-2
   choosing   7-3
leased/dedicated lines   1-5
li tags   7-15, 7-16
library item   5-19, 9-6
   deleting   5-19
   editing   5-19, 5-20
   placing   5-19
Library folder   5-19
Library icon   5-19
Library panel   6-25, 6-26
line break   3-8, 4-13
Line Break button   4-13
line height   7-3
Line tool   6-15, 8-11
link   2-2, 3-14   *see also* hyperlink
   broken   9-6
   list of links   9-4
   testing   6-3
Link box   9-8
Link Checker panel   10-6
Link list   4-23
Link property   6-26
Linux   10-3, 10-4
liquid design   4-8
list item tags   7-16
List/Menu form objects   9-21
list style, creating   7-16
listserv   1-6
LISTSERV   1-6
local navigation bar   5-6, 7-3, 7-19
   links in   7-4

local sites 10-1
local/network server 10-1
Local-Area Network 1-1
Lock/Unlock All column 8-29
logical topology 1-3
logo 9-4
Looksmart 2-14
Loop property 8-19, 8-33
lossless compression 6-2
lossy compression 6-2, C-1
Lycos 2-14

M

Mac OS X 1-2
Macintosh computer 7-3
Macromedia Studio MX suite 6-13, 8-1
Mail button 2-20
mailing list 1-6
Make Link command 4-22
MAN 1-1
Map and Files command 9-5
Map property 6-6
match 2-15
Max Chars property 9-17
Maximize button 4-2, 4-5
Mbps 1-5
media folder 8-18
Media tab 8-2, 8-8
media Web site 2-4
megabytes 10-2
megapixel C-2
menu bar 2-7, 4-1
menu, on Web page 9-13
Merge cells button 5-15, 5-16
meta data 10-13
meta tag 10-13
Metcalfe, Bob 1-4
mil 2-6
Minimize button 4-2
MLA 2-19
modem 1-5
modulation 1-5
monitor size 4-8
morphing 8-20
Mosaic 2-5
motion path, modifying 8-25
motion tweened 8-28
motion tweening 8-24
mouse event B-5
mouse event, adding B-5
MOV 8-34
Movie Clip behavior B-3, B-4
movie, placing in a Web page document 8-6
moving 4-14

MP3 8-32
MPEG 8-34
MPG 8-34
Multi line property 9-17
Multi line text field 9-16
multitasking 3-6
My Computer 3-4

N

named anchor 7-21
Named Anchor button 7-21
native file format 6-15, 7-24
navigation
    bar 5-5, 5-6, 6-26
        creating 8-6
        formatting 7-4
    structure 5-3
    site map 9-5
Nelson, Ted 3-14
nested
    lists 7-15
    symbols B-3
    table, creating 8-3
net 2-6
netiquette 1-4
Netscape 3-6
Netscape Navigator 2-5, 10-3, 10-4
network 1-1
    administrator 2-24
    architecture 1-2
    interface card 1-1, 1-4
    news 1-6
New command 3-4, 4-19, 6-13, 7-5
New CSS Style button 7-6, 7-22
New File command 4-20
New Folder command 5-12
New From Template B-1
New Library Item command 5-19
New Message window 2-20
New Site command 4-2, 4-17
New Symbol command B-4
newsgroup 1-6
Next page button 2-13
No CSS Style button 7-11
node 1-2
non-virtual hosting 10-9, B-1
normal 7-2
Northern Light 2-14
NOT 2-17
Notepad 3-2, 3-3, 3-6, 7-24
    quitting 3-4
Notepad command 3-3
numbered list 7-16
numeric data, in a table 4-9

Index I-9

O

objects
    aligning   6-18
    drawing   6-15
    moving   6-16
    resizing   6-16
    selecting   6-18
ol tags   7-15
Onion Skin button   8-14
onion skinning   8-14
online
    information service   1-5
    newspaper   2-4
    ordering   9-5
    profiling   1-7
onRelease event   B-5
Open button   4-19
Open command   3-4, 3-5, 4-19
Open Source command   3-6
operating search engine   2-15
operating system   1-2
optimization techniques   8-22
optimizing, Fireworks image   6-11, 6-18
OR   2-17
Ordered list button   7-16
org   2-6
Organize button   2-11
organizing files   2-11
orphan files   10-7
Other Characters button   4-13
Outdent command   7-15
Outlook Express   2-20, 5-20
Oval Hotspot tool   6-6
Oval tool   8-11
Over state   6-26
Over tab   6-27
Over While Down state   6-26
Over While Down tab   6-27
Overture   2-14

P

p tag   7-6, 7-8
page   *see* Web page
page layout, checking   5-10
Page Properties command   4-6
Page Setup command   4-17
page title   4-2, 4-6, 9-6
    modifying   9-6
Paint Bucket tool   8-11
pane, closing   2-9
pane, sizing   2-9
Panel groups   4-2

paragraph
    alignment, choosing   7-6
    indent   7-14
    tag   3-7
Paragraph button   7-8
Paragraph Format command   7-12
parent page   5-3
password   1-4
Paste command   4-14, 5-13, 7-24
Paste HTML command   6-32
path   5-6
peer-to-peer network   1-2
Pen tool   8-11
Pencil tool   8-11
personal Web site   2-2, 9-1, 9-8
PhotoShop   2-23
phrases, searching   2-15
PIC   8-15
picture element   3-12
pipe symbol   5-6
piracy   1-9
pixel   3-12, 4-8, 6-1
placeholder   8-18
placement
    of the content   5-7
    of Web page elements   5-9
planning a Web site   5-1
Play command   8-13
Playhead   8-13
PNG   6-1, 6-2, 6-13, 6-15, 6-18, 8-15, C-2
PNG source file   6-32
Point to File icon   4-23, 6-3, 6-6
Pointer button   6-20
Pointer Hotspot tool   6-6
Pointer tool   6-16, 6-18, 6-26
points   7-2
Polly, Jean Armour   2-8
polygon   6-16
Polygon Hotspot tool   6-6
POP3   2-22
pop-up menu   9-21
Portable Network Graphic   6-1
portal Web site   2-4
portfolio   9-2
posting   2-1
pound currency symbol   4-13
Preview in Browser command   4-6, 10-4, 10-5
Preview tab   6-26, 6-27
preview windows   6-20
previewing a Web page   2-12
Previous page button   2-13
Print button   2-7, 2-13, 2-22, 4-16
Print Code command   4-17
Print command   2-13, 3-3, 4-16
print preview buttons   2-13

Print Preview command   2-12, 4-16
printer-friendly version   5-11
printing a Web page document   4-16
privacy   1-7
    invasion of   1-9
    laws   1-9
    policy   1-8
Privacy Act of 1974   1-9
progressive   6-2
promoting techniques   10-14
promotion   9-5
Property inspector   4-2
protocol   1-4, 1-7, 2-6, 2-22
public domain   5-21
published work   5-21
publishing
    a Web site   10-1
    to a local/network server   10-10
    to a Web server   10-9
purpose   5-2
Put command   10-10
Put File(s) button   10-10, 10-11, 10-12

Q

query a database   9-15
QuickTime 4   8-32, 8-34
QuickTime Player   8-32
quitting
    Dreamweaver   4-17
    Internet Explorer   2-7
    Notepad   3-4

R

Radio button   9-16, 9-19
Radio Group button   9-20
Radio Group form object   9-19
radio wave   1-3
raising awareness   9-4
RAW   C-1
real-time   1-6
real-time information   1-10
reciprocal links   10-14
Rectangle Roundness   6-16
Rectangle tool   8-11, B-4
Rectangular Hotspot tool   6-6
red
    outline   9-17
    text   9-6
Reference panel   10-7
Refresh button   2-7, 3-6
Refresh command   9-6
Refresh Site List command   5-15, 8-18

registered trademark symbol   4-13
regular   7-2
remote server   10-1
    options   4-2
Remove Link command   4-23, 6-3, 9-8
Remove Tag <a> command   4-22
Repeat command   4-14
Reply button   2-22
Reports command   10-7
resampling   6-11
Reset button   9-16
resetting image size   6-11
resize   6-11
    image, editing   6-11
    proportionately   6-11
resolution   6-1, C-2
Resolution property   6-14
resolution, changing in Fireworks   C-2
Restore button   4-5
Results panel group   10-6, 10-7
résumé   9-2
Rewind command   8-13
rich media   B-1
ring topology   1-3
rollover   6-26
    behavior   6-26, 6-30, 8-7, 9-15
    color   8-7
roman   7-2
root folder   5-12
Rotate command   8-15
router   1-4
rule   3-12, 7-4, 7-7
    applying   7-7
    creating   7-6
Rulers command   8-12

S

Safety and Freedom through Encryption Act of 1999   1-8
same-level pages   5-3
sans serif   7-1, 7-3
Save command   4-5, 5-19, 6-15, 8-11
Save Site Map command   9-6
saving   4-5
saving, a report   10-6
Scale tool   6-16
school projects   9-2
screen resolution   4-8, 5-10, 10-4
script   B-5
Script pane   B-5, B-6
script, server-side   9-15
scroll bar   2-7
scrolling list   9-21

Index   I–11

search   9-5
   criteria   2-15
      engine   2-14, 9-16
      form   9-4
Search button   2-7
Section 508   10-7
Select section   6-15, 6-16
selector   7-4
Send and Receive All button   2-21
Send button   2-21
serif   7-1, 7-3
server   1-2, 2-1, 3-1, 9-15, *see* Web server
   application   9-15
   remote   10-1
   secure   9-2
   technology   4-2
server-side script   9-15
Set magnification   6-20
shape tweening   8-20, 8-28
Shift+Enter   4-13
Shift+Tab   4-14
shopping cart   5-8
Show Dependent Files command   9-6
Show Grid command   8-12
Show Page Titles command   9-6
Single line text field   9-16
site   *see* Web site
Site FTP Log command   10-11
site maintenance   9-4
site map   9-4, 9-5, 9-12
Site Map button   9-5
Site panel   4-2, 4-17, 4-19, 5-12
Site Reports panel   10-7
size attribute   3-12
Size box   6-17
sizes, choosing   7-3
sketch   5-7
Skew command   8-15
slanderous remark   9-1
slicing   6-25
Snap.com   2-14
social implications, of computers   1-8
Sorenson Spark codec   8-34
sound layer, adding   8-32
sound wave   8-32
Source command   3-16
sources, citing   2-19
space in a Web page   5-10
spacer GIF   6-8
spaces in HTML document   3-2
special characters, inserting   4-13
spell checker   4-14
spelling errors   10-2
spider   2-14
Split cell button   5-15, 5-16

split view buttons   6-20
spreadsheet   9-10
Stage   8-11
Stage, resizing   8-12
Standard view   4-10
Stanford Research Institute   1-4
Stanford University   2-4
star
   shape   6-16
   topology   1-2
starting Internet Explorer   2-6
state tab   6-27
static
   frames   8-13, 8-14
   Web page   9-15
status bar   2-7
sticky notes   5-4
Stop button   2-7
stretch   6-11
Stroke Color   8-11
Stroke Color box   6-16
Strong button   7-11
strong tags   7-11
style
   applying   6-17
   choosing   7-3
   buttons   6-17
   deleting   7-11
   duplicating a   7-11
   editing a   7-11
   removing   6-17
   removing an applied style   7-11
   sheet   7-4
      cascading   7-4
      creating new   7-5
      linking to an existing style   7-5
Subject box   2-21
subject tree   2-15
Submit button   9-16
submit, from a Web page   9-16
subscriber   1-6
Subselection tool   8-11
SUPERSTITIAL™   2-5, B-8
surfing the net   2-8
SWF   4-13, 8-11, 8-17, 8-22
symbol   6-25, 8-15, 8-24
Symbol command   6-25
System agent   2-21

T

T-1   1-5
tab character   9-10
tab-delimited data   9-10

Tab key 4-14
table 4-8, 5-7, 9-10
    alignment 4-11
    cell 4-11
        determining width 8-3
    creating 4-10
    for a form 9-17
    for buttons 8-3
    modifying cells 5-15
    nested 8-3
    properties 4-9
    selecting 4-10
    width 4-8, 4-11
        determining 8-3
tables, database 9-15
Table command 4-10
tabular data 9-4, 9-10
Tabular Data button 9-11
Tag selector 4-2, 5-16
tags 3-1
    document 3-2
target
    audience 5-2
    browser 10-3
        determining 10-3
Target Browser Check panel 10-6
Target list 9-9
TCP/IP 1-4
TCP/IP software 10-8
telecommunications 1-5
telephone 1-3
Telnet 1-7
templates B-1, D1
Templates category D-2
Templates icon D-2
Test Movie command 8-35, B-7
text
    adding 6-16
    attribute 3-13
        choosing 7-6
    block 6-16, 6-17
        breaking apart 8-29
        creating 829
        fixed-width 6-17
        modifying text in 6-17
        moving 6-17
        resizing 6-17
    box 9-17
    color, changing 7-20
    copying 7-24
    document 3-3
    hyperlink 4-22, 6-6
    pasting 7-24

Text Field button 9-17
Text property 6-26
Text tab 7-8
Text tool 6-16, 6-17, 8-11
TextField property 9-17
TIF C-1, C-2
TIFF C-1
time stamp 5-20
Timeline 8-10, 8-11, 8-12, 8-13
Times New Roman 7-2
Tip size 6-16
title bar 2-7
Title box 4-6
title tag 3-1, 3-2
To box 2-21
To button 2-21
Token Ring network 1-4
Tomlinson, Ray 2-20
toolbar 2-7, 6-15
Tools panel 6-15, 6-16, 8-11
top global navigation bar 5-6, 7-3, 7-19
    links in 7-4
top-level domain 2-6, 2-19
top-level page 5-3
topology 1-2
trademark symbol 4-13
Transform command 8-15
Transform panel 8-15
transmission media 1-3
transparency 6-2
transparency button 6-20
Transparency list 6-21
transparent color 6-1, 6-2, 6-20
    adding 6-20
    removing 6-20
    selecting 6-20
Trim Canvas command 6-18
TRUE 2-17
Tween property 8-20, 8-24
tweened animation 8-20
twisted-pair wiring 1-3
TXT 7-24, 9-10
type size and styles 7-2
typeface 7-1
typography 7-1

U

uk   2-6
ul tag   7-16
under construction   5-9
underline style   7-3
underscore character   3-3
underscores   4-5
undo   4-14
Undo command   4-14
Undo Crop Document command   6-36
Unicast   2-5
United States Copyright Office   5-21
university degrees   2-24
University of California Los Angeles   1-4
Unordered list button   7-16
Unordered list tags   7-16
Up state   6-26
Up tab   6-27
uploading   10-9
URL   2-6, 2-7
URL, in footer   4-17
usability   5-10, 6-6, 7-18, 7-19
USENET   1-6
user name   2-19

V

vector graphic   6-15, 8-11
Vector section   6-15
Verdana   7-1, 7-2
video compression   8-34
video movie, testing   8-35
View as Root command   9-6
View button   2-9
virtual hosting   10-9
virus   1-10, 2-22
visual cue   5-10
visual noise   5-10
voice synthesizer   6-2

W

W property   4-11, 6-11, 6-16, 6-36
W3C   2-1, 6-3
WAI   6-3
WAN   1-1
WAV   8-32

Web   1-5, 3-15
   Web Accessibility Initiative   6-3
   ad   2-5
   application   9-15
   author   2-23
   browser   2-5, 3-5
   bugs   1-7
   careers   2-23
   designer   2-23
   developer   2-23
   developer, ethical responsibilities of   1-10
   directory   2-15
   hosting companies   2-1, 2-24, 10-9
   hosts   2-1, 2-24, 10-9
   page   1-6, 3-1
      adding to Favorites list   2-11
      browse   2-8
      cite   2-19
      design   5-8
      evaluating   2-18
      layout   4-8, 5-7
      level   5-3
      creating   4-19
      in a browser   4-6
      long   7-21
      opening   4-19
      printing   2-12, 4-16
      template   D-1
      viewing   4-6
   server   2-1, 4-6, 10-1
   site   1-6, 2-2
      active   4-17
      creating   4-2
      defining   4-18
      designing pages   5-4
      development   5-1
      editing   4-17
      evaluating   2-18
      opening   4-17
      root folder   6-15
Web tracking software   10-15
Web-based portfolios   9-2
WebCrawler   2-14
Weblog   2-3
Webmaster   2-23
weigh, bold text   7-2
weight of the page   10-2
white space   5-10
Wide-Area Network   1-1
width attribute   3-12
Width property   6-14
Window menu   4-19
Window Size button   5-10
window, resizing   4-5

Windows   1-2, 10-3
Windows taskbar   3-6
wireless network   1-3
WLAN   1-3
WMF   8-15, 8-34
word processor document   9-10
words, searching   2-15
work area   6-27
work samples   9-2
workspace   4-1
World Wide Web   1-5, 2-1
WWW   1-5

X

X property   6-16
Xerox Corporation   1-4

Y

Y property   6-16
Yahoo!   2-4, 2-14, 2-20
Yang, Jerry   2-4
yellow background   5-19, 5-20, D-13
yen currency symbol   4-13

Z

Zoom button   6-20
Zoom In button   2-13
Zoom Out button   2-13